THE INDIVIDUAL IN THE LAW AND PRACTICE OF THE INTERNATIONAL COURT OF JUSTICE

The cornerstone of the World Court's identity is its resolution of inter-state disputes. This insightful critique challenges the implication that individuals have little importance in such disputes as a result. Arguing for individuals' enhanced integration, it reveals their relevance in a myriad of disputes beyond those centred on violations of multilateral human rights treaties and unveils a multitude of procedural practices with unquenched potential. It also carefully unpacks and interrogates the Court's legal reasoning in various contexts such as territorial and maritime disputes, amongst others. Finally, it critically analyses and evaluates the legal and political underpinnings for the Court's approaches and state litigants' choices from a lens of social idealism. This pioneering study sheds light on the imbalance between individuals as key stakeholders in inter-state disputes and their treatment in law and practice.

YUSRA SUEDI is a lecturer in International Law at the University of Manchester. She has worked for the United Nations and in international courts and tribunals, including the International Court of Justice. She has also worked in cases before the International Court of Justice.

CAMBRIDGE STUDIES IN INTERNATIONAL AND COMPARATIVE LAW: 192

Established in 1946, this series produces high quality, reflective and innovative scholarship in the field of public international law. It publishes works on international law that are of a theoretical, historical, cross-disciplinary or doctrinal nature. The series also welcomes books providing insights from private international law, comparative law and transnational studies which inform international legal thought and practice more generally.

The series seeks to publish views from diverse legal traditions and perspectives, and of any geographical origin. In this respect it invites studies offering regional perspectives on core *problématiques* of international law, and in the same vein, it appreciates contrasts and debates between diverging approaches. Accordingly, books offering new or less orthodox perspectives are very much welcome. Works of a generalist character are greatly valued and the series is also open to studies on specific areas, institutions or problems. Translations of the most outstanding works published in other languages are also considered.

After seventy years, Cambridge Studies in International and Comparative Law sets the standard for international legal scholarship and will continue to define the discipline as it evolves in the years to come.

A list of books in the series can be found at the end of this volume.

THE INDIVIDUAL IN THE LAW AND PRACTICE OF THE INTERNATIONAL COURT OF JUSTICE

YUSRA SUEDI
University of Manchester

CAMBRIDGE
UNIVERSITY PRESS

CAMBRIDGE
UNIVERSITY PRESS

Shaftesbury Road, Cambridge CB2 8EA, United Kingdom

One Liberty Plaza, 20th Floor, New York, NY 10006, USA

477 Williamstown Road, Port Melbourne, VIC 3207, Australia

314–321, 3rd Floor, Plot 3, Splendor Forum, Jasola District Centre, New Delhi – 110025, India

103 Penang Road, #05-06/07, Visioncrest Commercial, Singapore 238467

Cambridge University Press is part of Cambridge University Press & Assessment, a department of the University of Cambridge.

We share the University's mission to contribute to society through the pursuit of education, learning and research at the highest international levels of excellence.

www.cambridge.org
Information on this title: www.cambridge.org/9781009394499

DOI: 10.1017/9781009394512

When citing this work, please include a reference to the DOI 10.1017/9781009394512

First published 2025

A catalogue record for this publication is available from the British Library.

Library of Congress Cataloging-in-Publication Data
Names: Suedi, Yusra, author.
Title: The individual in the law and practice of the International Court of Justice / Yusra Suedi, University of Manchester.
Description: Cambridge, United Kingdom ; New York, NY : Cambridge University Press, 2024. | Series: Cambridge studies in international and comparative law ; 192 | Includes bibliographical references and index.
Identifiers: LCCN 2024029152 (print) | LCCN 2024029153 (ebook) | ISBN 9781009394499 (hardback) | ISBN 9781009394536 (paperback) | ISBN 9781009394512 (epub)
Subjects: LCSH: International Court of Justice. | Jurisdiction (International law) | International courts.
Classification: LCC KZ6275 .S84 2024 (print) | LCC KZ6275 (ebook) | DDC 341.5/52–dc23/eng/20240709
LC record available at https://lccn.loc.gov/2024029152
LC ebook record available at https://lccn.loc.gov/2024029153

ISBN 978-1-009-39449-9 Hardback

CONTENTS

FOREWORD

The relationship between the individual and the International Court of Justice might, *prima facie*, appear to be a curious choice for academic appraisal. After all, the World Court is distinguished on the international plane by its jurisdictional mandate to resolve legal disputes between states. This function of the Court may give the impression that the activities and output of the principal judicial organ of the United Nations are not of much relevance to individuals or to the protection of their rights. Yet, Yusra Suedi's book, *The Individual in the Law and Practice of the International Court of Justice*, illustrates that this relationship is richer than one might expect. It commendably provides a thorough examination of several previously underexplored questions, whilst purposefully taking an original approach when it comes to questions that have already been explored in the existing literature.

As the position of the individual in international law has evolved over the past century, so has the significance and impact of the Court's work on the rights of individuals in the context of inter-state disputes. Thus, the fact that individuals do not have *locus standi* before the ICJ has never been an obstacle to the consideration and, where necessary, protection of the rights of individuals by the Court. The jurisprudence of the Court examined and assessed in Yusra Suedi's book amply illustrates this point. It testifies to the fact that the Court, despite its state-centred function, has never been oblivious to and cannot afford to ignore or neglect the famous maxim '*hominum causa omne jus constitutum est*', that is, all law is created for the benefit of human beings.

The author could have easily demonstrated the relevance of the Court's work to the rights of individuals through an analysis of its contribution to the development of human and people's rights in international law, as has been done by many others. However, she chose to venture down an untrodden path. Indeed, this book offers significant new insights with respect to cases brought before the Court where the relevance of the rights of individuals might not be immediately obvious but where the Court has clearly and considerably addressed them as part of its function of interpreting and applying the law. These cases include inter-state disputes in diverse areas such as the delimitation of territorial or maritime boundaries, the protection of the environment, the interpretation of treaties, or the identification of customary international law. This innovative approach to the relevance of the Court's work to individuals is what makes Yusra Suedi's book particularly interesting.

This is a work of mapping and locating the scope and effect of the rules of international law. But the law is not and cannot be like a geographical location. It has to be more; it has to evolve and address the changing needs of society. This is also the case of contemporary international law. With the adoption of the UN Charter and the Universal Declaration of Human Rights, the international legal system has slowly shifted from a Westphalian state-centred model to one that recognises and serves to protect the rights of individuals. The interplay between the individual and the system of international justice has similarly evolved. Thus, in interpreting and applying the rules of international law, the effect of those rules on individuals cannot be ignored by the principal judicial organ of the United Nations, even though those rules may have originally been devised for different circumstances, such as maritime delimitation. Today's judge must pay attention to the impact of such rules on the rights of, for example, local fisherfolk or on their traditional way of life. There is no need any more for a state to exercise diplomatic protection for such fisherfolk's rights to be taken into consideration and thus to perpetuate the old and outdated fiction that it is the state's rights that might have been breached and not the individual's.

As a judge at the Court, I often have to deal with the intricate interplay between the rights of individuals and the mechanisms of international justice. I have, at times, considered that this relationship could be strengthened through the progressive development of the law by the Court. In *Jurisdictional Immunities*, for example, I dissented that the Court, in its consideration of the merits, limited its examination almost entirely to the general applicability of immunity to the acts committed by a state as a sovereign. In my view, this was too abstract and formalistic as compared to the real-life situation of the victims of Nazi atrocities who, for the lack of any alternative means of redress, had to submit their claims for reparation to Italian courts.

Similarly in *DRC v. Uganda (Reparations)*, I expressed the view that

> one of the inadequacies of the reparation awarded by the Court in this case flows from the overly narrow approach to reparations adopted in the

> Judgment and the lack of consideration of the communities, collectivities and individuals who have directly suffered as a result of the wrongful acts of Uganda through loss of life, personal injuries, destruction of private properties, conscription of child soldiers and the displacement of population. These individuals and communities have not yet recovered from the impact of the violent conflict on their lives. Their plight, therefore, deserved to be taken into account by adopting different forms of reparation that would fit their different circumstances and by clearly indicating that they were the direct addressees of these reparations.

Thus, despite the inter-state nature of the proceedings, it was possible, in my view, to envisage different forms of reparation that took into account the different categories of injury suffered by individuals and communities and to direct the reparations to them, and not to the state, in order to redress the harm caused.

This book serves as a most valuable guidepost, inviting a continued introspection into the intersectionality of two topics that have sustained great interest in international legal scholarship: the position of the individual in international law, on one hand, and the International Court of Justice, on the other. Yusra Suedi's comprehensive legal inquiry, which invites us to contemplate this interface, could not be more timely, given the nature of many issues coming before the Court through contentious and advisory channels. Her work, through its thorough research and compelling legal analysis, pushes the frontiers of international law in the right direction. It should be warmly welcomed by academics and practitioners alike.

Judge Abdulqawi Ahmed Yusuf
International Court of Justice
The Hague

ACKNOWLEDGEMENTS

It takes a village.

I am thankful to my village of people, without whom this book would not exist.

It would be an injustice to start any other way than by thanking my supervisor, Professor Makane Moïse Mbengue. He saw my potential to carry out this project before I even saw it in myself. He has inspired me through both his friendship and example, and continues to do so.

I was supported, advised and assisted in my years at the University of Geneva by Dina Khan, Guive Khan Mohammad, León Castellanos Jankiewicz, Djemila Carron, Olivia Le Fort, Bérénice Schramm, Stephanie de Mooerloose, Rukia Baruti, Luis Espinosa-Salas, Gleider Hernandez, Christian Walter, Jean d'Aspremont, Robert McCorquodale, Marco Sassoli, Antonella Angellini, Alvaro Lopez, Besnik Ibrahimi, Dimitri Donzé, Verra Gowlland-Debbas, Kari de Pryck, Vittorio Mainetti, Claire Poppelwell-Scevak, Ilyas Sobol, Angus Wallace, Yuliya Kaspiarovich, Flore Venackère, Tanya Pettay, Diana Cucos, Momchil Milanov, Fatoumata P. Doumbouya, Justine Bendel, Fransisco J. Pascual Vives, Jana Ruwayha and Laurence Boisson de Chazournes. I am so thankful for the ways they facilitated my journey.

A series of exchanges during my various professional experiences at the United Nations kept me going in the early stages of research: thanks to Professors Dire Tladi, Mathias Forteau, Chris Peter Maina, Concepción Escobar Hernandez, Charles Jalloh, Dražen Petrović and George Politakis.

Much of this book was written during my time in the Peace Palace. Thank you to the wonderful community there who provided assistance and inspiration: Vladyslav Lanovoy, Mamadou Hébié, Asier Garrido Munoz, Callum Musto, Julia Sherman, Rosine, Rosalind Elphick, Nawi Ukabiala, Solène Guggisberg, Rina Kuusipaalo, Cyril Emery, Avo Sevag Garabet, Nathalie Wiles, Judge Ivana Hrdličková, Cristina Hoss, Kirsten

Calhoun, Désiré Ahanhanzo, Moussa Sow, Judges Robinson, Bennouna, Cançado Trindade and *ad hoc* Dugard.

Thanks to Jean-Pelé Fomété and Professor Maya Hertig for carefully reviewing my book for my viva, and to other kind souls for their meticulous feedback and helpful advice: Massimo Lando, Brian McGarry, Mona Paulsen, Susan Kimani, Philippe Sands, Iain Scobbie, Gail Lythgoe and Emmanuel Voyiakis. I am grateful to the community of brilliant and kind academics at the London School of Economics – especially David Kershaw, Niki Lacey, Susan Marks, Devika Hovell and Gerry Simpson – who not only challenged me intellectually but pushed me to finalise this project. I could not have done so without the diligent assistance of Anna Kokla, Sarah Lok, Myrto Stavridi and Grete Labunski.

Special thanks go to my dear family and friends who celebrated my wins and patiently listened to my woes throughout the years. I am indebted to my mother, who was always there to listen, to encourage, and to provide the stability that I needed while completing this project. I am also grateful to Faheem for his unwavering support and patience during the long days and nights of finalising this book.

Finally, I would like to thank The One for giving me this opportunity, providing me with the ease within the hardship and seeing me through one of the most rewarding experiences of my life.

TABLE OF CASES

International Court of Justice

Accordance with International Law of the Unilateral Declaration of Independence in Respect of Kosovo (Advisory Opinion) [2010] ICJ Rep 403

Written contribution of the authors of the unilateral declaration of independence (7 April 2009)

Written statement of Serbia (17 April 2009)

Accordance with International Law of the Unilateral Declaration of Independence in Respect of Kosovo (Order) [2008] ICJ Rep 409

Admissibility of Hearings of Petitioners by the Committee on South West Africa (Advisory Opinion) [1956] ICJ Rep 23

Aegean Sea Continental Shelf (Greece v. Turkey) (Judgment) [1978] ICJ Rep 3

Aerial Herbicide Spraying (Ecuador v. Colombia) (Order of 13 September 2013) [2013] ICJ Rep 278

Application instituting proceedings (31 March 2008)

Memorial of Ecuador (28 April 2009)

Aerial Incident (Israel v. Bulgaria) (Preliminary Objections) (Judgment) [1959] ICJ Rep 127

Ahmadou Sadio Diallo (Republic of Guinea v. Democratic Republic of the Congo) (Preliminary Objections) (Judgment) [2007] ICJ Rep 582

Ahmadou Sadio Diallo (Republic of Guinea v. Democratic Republic of the Congo) (Merits) (Judgment) [2010] ICJ Rep 639

Reply of the Republic of Guinea (19 November 2008)

Ahmadou Sadio Diallo (Republic of Guinea v. Democratic Republic of the Congo) (Compensation) (Judgment) [2012] ICJ Rep 324

Alleged Violations of Sovereign Rights and Maritime Spaces in the Caribbean Sea (Nicaragua v. Colombia)

Application instituting proceedings (26 November 2013)

(Counter-Claims) (Order of 15 November 2017) [2017] ICJ Rep 289

(Judgment) [2022] ICJ Rep 266

Alleged Violations of the 1955 Treaty of Amity, Economic Relations, and Consular Rights (Islamic Republic of Iran v. United States of America) (Press Release) [2018]

Ambatielos Case (Greece v. United Kingdom) (Merits) (Judgment) [1953] ICJ Rep 10

Memorial submitted on behalf of the Hellenic Government (30 August 1951)

Anglo-Iranian Oil Co. (United Kingdom v. Iran) (Preliminary Objections) (Judgment) [1952] ICJ Rep 93

Application for Review of Judgment No. 158 of the United Nations Administrative Tribunal (Advisory Opinion) [1973] ICJ Rep 166

Application for Review of Judgment No. 273 of the United Nations Administrative Tribunal (Advisory Opinion) [1982] ICJ Rep 325

Written statements (30 November 1981)

Application for Review of Judgment No. 333 of the United Nations Administrative Tribunal (Advisory Opinion) [1987] ICJ Rep 18

Application of the Convention on the Prevention and Punishment of the Crime of Genocide (Bosnia and Herzegovina v. Serbia and Montenegro)

(Counter-claims) (Order of 1997) [1997] ICJ Rep 243

(Judgment) [2007] ICJ Rep 43

Application of the Convention on the Prevention and Punishment of the Crime of Genocide (Croatia v. Serbia) (Judgment) [2015] ICJ Rep 3

Application of the Convention on the Prevention and Punishment of the Crime of Genocide (The Gambia v. Myanmar) (Preliminary Objections) (Judgment) [2022] ICJ Rep 477

Verbatim record 2019/18

Armed Activities on the Territory of the Congo (Democratic Republic of the Congo v. Uganda) (Judgment) [2005] ICJ Rep 168

Response of the Democratic Republic of the Congo to the questions put by the Court (26 October 2018)

Armed Activities on the Territory of the Congo (New Application: 2002) (Democratic Republic of the Congo v. Rwanda) (Order of 10 July 2002) [2002] ICJ Rep 219

Armed Activities on the Territory of the Congo (New Application: 2002) (Democratic Republic of the Congo v. Rwanda) (Request for the Indication of Provisional Measures) [2002] ICJ Rep 219, 241

Arrest Warrant of 11 August 2000 (Judgment) [2002] ICJ Rep 3

Asylum (Colombia v. Peru) (Judgment) [1950] ICJ Rep 266

Memorial submitted by the Government of the Republic of Colombia (10 January 1950)

Correspondence (8 October 1949)

Avena and Other Mexican Nationals (Mexico v. United States of America) (Judgment) [2004] ICJ Rep 12

Memorial of Mexico (20 June 2003)

Barcelona Traction Light and Power Company Ltd. (Belgium v. Spain) (Preliminary Objections) (Judgment) [1964] ICJ Rep 6

Barcelona Traction Light and Power Company Ltd. (Belgium v. Spain) (Second Phase) (Preliminary Objections) (Judgment) [1970] ICJ Rep 3

Case concerning the Application of the Convention of 1902 Governing the Guardianship of Infants (Netherlands v. Sweden) (Judgment) [1958] ICJ Rep 55

Case concerning Sovereignty over Certain Frontier Land (Belgium/Netherlands) (Judgment) [1959] ICJ Rep 209

Case concerning the Temple of Preah Vihear (Cambodia v. Thailand) (Merits) (Judgment) [1962] ICJ Rep 6

Certain Activities Carried Out by Nicaragua in the Border Area (Costa Rica v. Nicaragua) and *Construction of a Road in Costa Rica along the San Juan River (Nicaragua v. Costa Rica)* (Judgment) [2015] ICJ Rep 665

Certain Activities Carried Out by Nicaragua in the Border Area (Costa Rica v. Nicaragua) (Application instituting proceedings) (18 November 2010)

Construction of a Road in Costa Rica along the San Juan River (Nicaragua v. Costa Rica) (Joinder of proceedings) (Order of 17 April 2013) [2013] ICJ Rep 184

Memorial of Costa Rica (5 December 2011)

Memorial of Nicaragua (19 December 2012)

Certain Expenses of the United Nations (Article 17, paragraph 2, of the Charter) (Advisory Opinion) [1962] ICJ Rep 151

Certain Norwegian Loans (France v. Norway) (Preliminary Objections) (Judgment) [1957] ICJ Rep 9

Certain Phosphate Lands in Nauru (Nauru v. Australia)

(Application instituting proceedings) (19 May 1989)

Memorial of the Republic of Nauru (20 March 1990)

(Order of 13 September 1993) [1993] ICJ Rep 322

(Preliminary Objections) (Judgment) [1992] ICJ Rep 240

Certain Property (Liechtenstein v. Germany) (Preliminary Objections) (Judgment) [2005] ICJ Rep 6

Constitution of the Maritime Safety Committee of the Inter-Governmental Maritime Consultative Organisation (Advisory Opinion) [1960] ICJ Rep 150

Continental Shelf (Libyan Arab Jamahiriya/Malta) (Judgment) [1985] ICJ Rep 13

Continental Shelf (Tunisia/Libyan Arab Jamahiriya) (Judgment) [1982] ICJ Rep 18

Corfu Channel (United Kingdom v. Albania) (Merits) (Judgment) [1949] ICJ Rep 15

Corfu Channel (United Kingdom v. Albania) (Preliminary Objection) (Judgment) [1948] ICJ Rep 15

Delimitation of the Maritime Boundary in the Gulf of Maine Area (Canada/United States of America) (Judgment) [1984] ICJ Rep 246

Memorial of the United States of America (27 September 1982)

Difference Relating to Immunity from Legal Process of a Special Rapporteur of the Commission on Human Rights (Advisory Opinion) [1999] ICJ Rep 62

Dispute regarding Navigational and Related Rights (Costa Rica v. Nicaragua) (Judgment) [2009] ICJ Rep 213

Memorial of Costa Rica (29 August 2006)

Reply of Costa Rica (15 January 2008)

Verbatim record 2009/6

Verbatim record 2009/7

East Timor (Portugal v. Australia) (Judgment) [1995] ICJ Rep 90

Effect of Awards of Compensation Made by the U.N. Administrative Tribunal (Advisory Opinion) [1954] ICJ Rep 47

Written proceedings (15 February 1954)

Correspondence (16 December 1953)

Elettronica Sicula S.p.A. (ELSI) (United States of America v. Italy) (Judgment) [1989] ICJ Rep 15

Federal Republic of Germany/Netherlands (Judgment) [1969] ICJ Rep 3

Fisheries Case (United Kingdom v. Norway) (Judgment) [1951] ICJ Rep 116

Fisheries Jurisdiction (Federal Republic of Germany v. Iceland) (Merits) (Judgment) [1974] ICJ Rep 175

Fisheries Jurisdiction (United Kingdom v. Iceland) (Merits) (Judgment) [1974] ICJ Rep 3

Frontier Dispute (Benin/Niger) (Judgment) [2005] ICJ Rep 90

Memorial of the Republic of Benin (27 August 2003)

Reply of the Republic of Benin (17 December 2004)

Verbatim record 2005/1

Frontier Dispute (Burkina Faso/Niger) (Judgment) [2013] ICJ Rep 44

Memorial of Niger (20 April 2011)

Replies of Burkina Faso and Niger to the questions put by Judge Cançado Trindade at the end of the public sitting held on 17 October 2012 (translation) (16 November 2012)

Verbatim record 2012/26

Frontier Dispute (Burkina Faso/Republic of Mali) (Judgment) [1986] ICJ Rep 554

Gabčíkovo-Nagymaros Project (Hungary/Slovakia) (Judgment) [1997] ICJ Rep 7

Verbatim record 1997/2

Interhandel (Switzerland v. United States of America) (Preliminary Objections) (Judgment) [1959] ICJ Rep 6

International Status of South West Africa (Advisory Opinion) [1950] ICJ Rep 128

Interpretation and Application of the International Convention on the Elimination of All Forms of Racial Discrimination (Republic of Azerbaijan v. Republic of Armenia) (Request for the Indication of Provisional Measures of Protection) [2021]

Interpretation of Peace Treaties with Bulgaria, Hungary and Romania (Advisory Opinion) [1950] ICJ Rep 65

Jadhav (India v. Pakistan) (Judgment) [2019] ICJ Rep 418

Jadhav (India v. Pakistan) (Provisional Measures) (Order of 18 May 2017) [2017] ICJ Rep 231

Verbatim record 2017/6

Judgment No. 2867 *of the Administrative Tribunal of the International Labour Organisation upon a Complaint Filed against the International Fund for Agricultural Development* (Advisory Opinion) [2012] ICJ Rep 10

Judgments of the Administrative Tribunal of the ILO upon Complaints Made against UNESCO (Advisory Opinion) [1956] ICJ Rep 7

Written statements (1 April 1956)

Jurisdictional Immunities of the State (Germany v. Italy: Greece intervening) (Judgment) [2012] ICJ Rep 99

Kasikili/Sedudu Island (Botswana/Namibia) (Judgment) [1999] ICJ Rep 1045

LaGrand (Germany v. United States of America) (Merits) (Judgment) [2001] ICJ Rep 466
Memorial of the Federal Republic of Germany (6 September 1999)

Land and Maritime Boundary between Cameroon and Nigeria (Cameroon v. Nigeria: Equatorial Guinea intervening) (Judgment) [2002] ICJ Rep 303

Land, Island and Maritime Frontier Dispute (El Salvador/Honduras: Nicaragua intervening)
(Application to Intervene) (Judgment) [1990] ICJ Rep 92
(Judgment) [1992] ICJ Rep 350
Memorial of the Republic of El Salvador (1 June 1988)
Memorial of the Government of the Republic of Honduras (1 June 1988)

Legal Consequences arising from the Policies and Practices of Israel in the Occupied Palestinian Territory, including East Jerusalem (Request for Advisory Opinion) [2023]

Legal Consequences of the Construction of a Wall in the Occupied Palestinian Territory
(Advisory Opinion) [2004] ICJ Rep 136
(Order) [2003] ICJ Rep 428

Legal Consequences for States of the Continued Presence of South Africa in Namibia (South West Africa) notwithstanding Security Council Resolution 276 (1970) (Advisory Opinion) [1971] ICJ Rep 16
Correspondence (29 July 1970)

Legal Consequences of the Separation of the Chagos Archipelago from Mauritius in 1965
(Advisory Opinion) [2019] ICJ Rep 95
Written comments of Mauritius (15 May 2018)
Verbatim record 2018/20

Legality of the Threat or Use of Nuclear Weapons (Advisory Opinion) [1996] ICJ Rep 226
Verbatim record 1995/32

Legality of the Use by a State of Nuclear Weapons in Armed Conflict (Advisory Opinion) [1996] ICJ Rep 66
Verbatim record 1995/32
Verbatim record 1995/33

Legality of Use of Force (Serbia and Montenegro v. Belgium) (Provisional Measures) (Order of 2 June 1999) [1999] ICJ Rep 124

Legality of Use of Force (Serbia and Montenegro v. Italy) (Preliminary Objections) (Judgment) [2004] ICJ Rep 865

Maritime Delimitation and Territorial Questions between Qatar and Bahrain (Qatar v. Bahrain)
(Jurisdiction and Admissibility) (Judgment) [1994] ICJ Rep 112
(Jurisdiction and Admissibility II) (Judgment) [1995] ICJ Rep 6

Maritime Delimitation in the Area between Greenland and Jan Mayen (Denmark v. Norway) (Judgment) [1993] ICJ Rep 38
Maritime Delimitation in the Black Sea (Romania v. Ukraine) (Judgment) [2009] ICJ Rep 61
Counter-memorial of Ukraine (19 May 2006)
Maritime Delimitation in the Indian Ocean (Somalia v. Kenya) (Judgment) [2021] ICJ Rep 206
Maritime Dispute (Peru v. Chile) (Judgment) [2014] ICJ Rep 3
Military and Paramilitary Activities in and against Nicaragua (Nicaragua v United States of America) (Jurisdiction of the Court and Admissibility of the Application) [1984] ICJ Rep 392
Military and Paramilitary Activities in and against Nicaragua (Nicaragua v. United States of America) (Merits) (Judgment) [1986] ICJ Rep 14
Minquiers and Ecrehos (France/United Kingdom) (Judgment) [1953] ICJ Rep 47
North Sea Continental Shelf (Federal Republic of Germany/Denmark; Federal Republic of Germany/Netherlands) (Judgment) [1969] ICJ Rep 3
Nottebohm (Liechtenstein v. Guatemala) (Second Phase) (Judgment) [1955] ICJ Rep 4
Nuclear Tests (Australia v. France) (Judgment) [1974] ICJ Rep 253
Application instituting proceedings (9 May 1973)
Verbatim record 1973
Nuclear Tests (New Zealand v. France) (Application instituting proceedings) (9 May 1973)
Obligations of States in respect of Climate Change (Request for Advisory Opinion) [2023]
Oil Platforms (Islamic Republic of Iran v. United States of America) (Merits) (Judgment) [2003] ICJ Rep 161
Pulp Mills on the River Uruguay (Argentina v. Uruguay) (Judgment) [2010] ICJ Rep 14
Application instituting proceedings (4 May 2006)
Counter-memorial of Uruguay (20 July 2007)
Memorial of Argentina (15 January 2007)
(Provisional measures) (Order of 13 July 2006) [2006] ICJ Rep 113
Rejoinder of Uruguay (29 July 2008)
Verbatim record 2006/46
Questions Relating to the Obligation to Prosecute or Extradite (Belgium v. Senegal) (Judgment) [2012] ICJ Rep 422
Reparation for Injuries Suffered in the Service of the United Nations (Advisory Opinion) [1949] ICJ Rep 174
Request for an Examination of the Situation in Accordance with Paragraph 63 of the Court's Judgment of 20 December 1974 in the Nuclear Tests (New Zealand v. France) [1995] ICJ Rep 288
Request for Interpretation of the Judgment of 20 November 1950 in the Asylum Case (Colombia v. Peru) (Judgment) [1950] ICJ Rep 395

Reservations to the Convention on Genocide (Advisory Opinion) [1951] ICJ Rep 15
Right to Strike under ILO Convention No. 87 (Request for Advisory Opinion) (10 November 2023)
South West Africa (Liberia v. South Africa; Ethiopia v. South Africa) (Preliminary Objections) (Judgment) [1962] ICJ Rep 319
(Second Phase) (Judgment) [1966] ICJ Rep 6
Sovereignty over Pedra Branca/Pulau Batu Puteh, Middle Rocks and South Ledge (Malaysia/Singapore) (Judgment) [2008] ICJ Rep 12
Sovereignty over Pulau Ligitan and Pulau Sipadan (Indonesia/Malaysia) (Judgment) [2002] ICJ Rep 683
Territorial Dispute (Libyan Arab Jamahiriya/Chad) (Judgment) [1994] ICJ Rep 6
Memorial written by the Great Socialist People's Libyan Arab Jamahiriya (26 August 1991)
Territorial and Maritime Dispute between Nicaragua and Honduras in the Caribbean Sea (Nicaragua v. Honduras) (Judgment) [2007] ICJ Rep 659
Territorial and Maritime Dispute (Nicaragua v. Colombia) (Judgment) [2012] ICJ Rep 624
Application for permission to intervene by the government of Costa Rica (25 February 2010)
Application for permission to intervene by the government of Honduras (10 June 2010)
Memorial of Peru (20 March 2009)
United States Diplomatic and Consular Staff in Tehran (United States of America v. Iran) (Judgment) [1980] ICJ Rep 3
Memorial of the Government of the United States of America (12 January 1980)
Vienna Convention on Consular Relations (Paraguay v. United States of America) (Order of 10 November 1998) [1998] ICJ Rep 426
Memorial of the Republic of Paraguay (9 October 1998)
Conditional request of Paraguay for an order conclusively established facts (9 October 1998)
Western Sahara (Advisory Opinion) [1975] ICJ Rep 12
Whaling in the Antarctic (Australia v. Japan: New Zealand intervening) (Judgment) [2014] ICJ Rep 226

Permanent Court of International Justice

Acquisition of Polish Nationality (Advisory Opinion) [1923] PCIJ Series B
Appeal from a Judgment of the Hungaro-Czechoslovak Mixed Arbitral Tribunal (The Peter Pazmany University) (Judgment) [1933] PCIJ Series A/B
Brazilian Loans (Judgment) [1929] PCIJ Series A
Case of Free Zones of Upper Savoy and the district of Gex (Order) [1930] PCIJ Series A
Case Relating to the Territorial Jurisdiction of the International Commission of the River Oder (Judgment) [1929] PCIJ Series A

The Case of the S.S. Lotus (Judgment) [1927] PCIJ Series A
Certain German Interests in Polish Upper Silesia (Merits) (Judgment) [1926] PCIJ Series A
Consistency of Certain Danzig Legislative Decrees with the Constitution of the Free City (Advisory Opinion) [1935] PCIJ Series A/B
Designation of the Workers' Delegate for the Netherlands at the Third Session of the International Labor Conference (Judgment) [1922] PCIJ Series B.
Eastern Carelia (Advisory Opinion) [1923] PCIJ Series B
Electricity Company of Sofia and Bulgaria (Judgment) [1939] PCIJ Series A/B
Factory at Chorzów (Jurisdiction) (Judgment) [1927] PCIJ Series A
Factory at Chorzów (Merits) (Judgment) [1928] PCIJ Series A
German Settlers in Poland (Advisory Opinion) [1923] PCIJ Series B
Interpretation of the Convention of 1919 concerning Employment of Women during the Night (Advisory Opinion) [1932] PCIJ Series A/B.
Jurisdiction of the Courts of Danzig (Pecuniary Claims of Danzig Railway Officials who have passed into the Polish Service, against the Polish Railways Administration) (Advisory Opinion) [1928] PCIJ Series B
'Jurisdiction of Danzig Courts in Actions Brought by Railway Officials against the Railway Administration', Decision of the High Commissioner (8 April 1927), English translation reproduced
Jurisdiction of the European Commission of the Danube between Galatz and Braila (Advisory Opinion) [1927] PCIJ Series B
Legal Status of Eastern Greenland (Judgment) [1933] PCIJ Series A/B
Lighthouses Case between France and Greece (Judgment) [1934] PCIJ Series A/B
Lighthouses in Crete and Samos (Judgment) [1937] PCIJ Series A/B
Mavrommatis Palestine Concessions (Judgment) [1924] PCIJ Series A
Oscar Chinn (Judgment) [1934] PCIJ Series A/B
Pajzs, Csáky and Esterházy (Judgment) [1936] PCIJ Series A/B
Panevezys-Saldutiskis Railway (Judgment) [1939] PCIJ Series A/B
Phosphates in Morocco (Judgment) [1938] PCIJ Series A/B
Right of Passage over Indian Territory (Portugal v. India) (Merits) (Judgment) [1960] ICJ Rep 6
Rights of Minorities in Upper Silesia (Minority Schools) (Judgment) [1928] PCIJ Series A
Serbian Loans (Judgment) [1929] PCIJ Series A
Société Commerciale de Belgique (Judgment) [1939] PCIJ Series A/B
S.S. 'Wimbledon' (Judgment) [1923] PCIJ Series A

Case-Law from Other Judicial and Quasi-judicial Bodies

Arbitration

Affaire Junghans (deuxième partie) (Allemagne/Roumanie) (1940) (Award) III RIAA 1883
Arbitration regarding the Delimitation of the Abyei Area between the Government of Sudan and the Sudan People's Movement/Army (2009) (Award) XXX RIAA 145

Arbitration regarding the Delimitation of the Maritime Boundary between Guyana and Suriname (2007) (Award) XXX RIAA 1
Barbados v. Trinidad and Tobago (2006) (Award) XXVII RIAA 147
Bay of Bengal Maritime Boundary Arbitration between Bangladesh and India (Bangladesh v. India) (2014) (Award) XXXII RIAA 1
Grant-Smith Case (the Gin and Angostura) (United Kingdom/Italy) (1952) (Award) XIV RIAA 13
The Grisbådarna case (Norway/Sweden) (1909) (Award) PCA XI RIAA 147
Island of Palmas (or Miangas) (The Netherlands/The United States of America) (1928) (Award) II RIAA 829
Mixed Claims Commission (United States/Germany) (1 November 1923–30 October 1939) (1923) (Award) (Administrative Decision II) VII RIAA 1
North American Dredging Company of Texas (USA) v. United Mexican States (1926) (Award) IV RIAA 26
Second Stage of the Proceedings between Eritrea and Yemen (Maritime Delimitation) (Eritrea/Yemen) (1999) XXII RIAA 335
South China Sea Arbitration (Philippines v. China) (2016) (Award) XXXIII RIAA 153
Territorial Sovereignty and Scope of the Dispute (Eritrea and Yemen) (1998) (Award) XXII RIAA 209
William A. Parker (USA) v. United Mexican States (1926) (Award) IV RIAA 35

World Trade Organisation

Canada – Certain Measures Affecting the Renewable Energy Generation Sector (2012) WT/DS412/R
European Communities – Anti-Dumping Measure on Farmed Salmon from Norway (2007) WT/DS337/R
United States – Certain Country of Origin Labelling (COOL) Requirements (2011) WT/DS384/R

International Tribunal for the Law of the Sea (ITLOS)

The 'Arctic Sunrise' Case (Kingdom of the Netherlands v. Russian Federation) (Order of 22 November 2013) [2013] ITLOS
Delimitation of the Maritime Boundary in the Bay of Bengal (Bangladesh/Myanmar) (Judgment) [2012] ITLOS
Responsibilities and Obligations of States Sponsoring Persons and Entities with Respect to Activities in the Area (Advisory Opinion) [2011] ITLOS

Human Rights Courts and Bodies

Hatton and Others v United Kingdom App no 36022/97 (ECHR, 8 July 2003)
The Environment and Human Rights (Advisory Opinion) [2017] IACtHR, OC-23/17

Firstov v Russia App no 42119/04 (ECHR, 20 February 2014)

Gbemre v Shell Petroleum Development Company of Nigeria Ltd et al. (Judgment) [2005] ACtHPR, FHC/B/CS/53/05

Gridin v Russia App no 4171/04 (ECHR, 1 June 2006)

Human Rights Committee, *General Comment No. 32 – Article 14: Right to Equality before Courts and Tribunals and to a Fair Trial*, CCPR/GC/32 (23 August 2007)

Lautsi v Italy App no 30814/06 (ECHR, 18 March 2011)

Lopez Ostra v Spain App no 16798/90 (ECHR, 9 December 1994)

Marangopoulos Foundation for Human Rights (MFHR) v Greece (Decision on the Merits) [2007] ECSR, Complaint No. 30/2005

Michelot Yogogombaye v Senegal (Judgment) [2009] ACtHPR, App no 1/2008

Peck v United Kingdom App no 44647/98 (ECHR, 28 January 2013)

Other

Decision on Request for leave to file amicus curiae brief (Judgment) [2014] ECCC Trial Chamber

Judgment No. 3003 [2011] ILOAT

Introduction

The law can never be oblivious to the changes in life, circumstance and community standards in which it functions.

—Philip Jessup, 1966[1]

The International Court of Justice (ICJ, the Court) is the principal judicial organ of the United Nations.[2] Based in The Hague, its subject matter jurisdiction extends across all areas of international law. The ICJ was modelled on its predecessor, the Permanent Court of International Justice (PCIJ), which was the first international judicial body empowered to settle legal disputes between states during the era of the League of Nations.[3] With a temporal advantage over the more recent judicial constructions as the 'only survivor of the League's institutional framework',[4] it was therefore the archetype for all judicial bodies that came after it in the twentieth century. Because of this, not only is the ICJ the *primus inter pares* in the system of international judicial fora, but it is the stronghold of state sovereignty, most prominent during the era of its predecessor. This is indicated by its personal jurisdiction ('*ratione personae*'): it only accepts disputes between states.[5]

The Court's personal jurisdiction is a key feature that has become one of the cornerstones of its identity. However, it has led to misconceptions about its judicial function. Many would purport that, as the ICJ deals

[1] *South West Africa (Liberia v. South Africa; Ethiopia v. South Africa)* (Second Phase) (Judgment) [1966] ICJ Rep 6, 439 (Dissenting opinion of Judge Jessup).

[2] Charter of the United Nations, 1 UNTS XVI (24 October 1945), Article 92 [hereafter, UN Charter].

[3] Karin Oellers-Frahm, 'Chapter XIV: The International Court of Justice, Article 92' in Bruno Simma et al (eds), *The Charter of the United Nations: A Commentary* (3rd edn, OUP 2012) 1902.

[4] Gleider Hernández, *The International Court of Justice and the Judicial Function* (OUP 2014) 4.

[5] Statute of the International Court of Justice, Article 34(1) [hereafter, ICJ Statute].

with disputes between states, individuals are irrelevant in such cases and have no reason to be considered in its decisions or involved procedurally.

This book challenges such an assertion. Academic literature has successfully documented and commented on the Court's jurisprudence in contentious disputes whose essence is the violation of international human rights treaties.[6] Such analyses offer understandings of how the Court has handled human rights issues in its case law, such as genocide, racial discrimination, or reparations for human rights violations.[7] Yet the focus of this book lies elsewhere.

This book takes a twofold interest in the relationship between the World Court and the individual. First, it takes an interest in comprehensively exploring the individual's procedural participation in contentious and advisory proceedings before the Court where such individuals are in focus. Such is the case for injured individuals in diplomatic proceedings, United Nations (UN) staff members wronged by their employers, or a community whose fate, health, or well-being is under discussion.

Second, it takes an interest in analysing the consideration for individuals in the Court's legal reasoning in contentious disputes beyond the violation of multilateral human rights treaties where they are nonetheless impacted. In territorial boundary disputes, for instance, individuals may have to change their nationality, their identity, their home, lose family ties, or lose property as a result of a decision to alter a boundary or to attribute a piece of land to another state. Similarly, in maritime delimitation disputes, individuals may lose access to waters and fishing rights that are necessary for their livelihood, as the result of the alteration of a maritime boundary. In environmental disputes, individuals may have to suffer the consequences of environmental degradation in their surround-

[6] Selected examples include: Rosalyn Higgins, 'Human Rights in the International Court of Justice' (2007) 20(4) *Leiden Journal of International Law* 745; Sandesh Sivakumaran, 'The International Court of Justice and Human Rights' in Sarah Joseph and Adam McBeth (eds), *Research Handbook on International Human Rights Law* (Elgar 2010) 299; Bruno Simma, 'Human Rights before the International Court of Justice: Community Interest Coming to Life?' in Christian J. Tams and James Sloan (eds), *The Development of International Law by the International Court of Justice* (OUP 2013) 300–25.

[7] E.g., *Interpretation and Application of the International Convention on the Elimination of All Forms of Racial Discrimination (Republic of Azerbaijan v. Republic of Armenia)* (Request for the Indication of Provisional Measures of Protection) [2021]; *Application of the Convention on the Prevention and Punishment of the Crime of Genocide (Croatia v. Serbia)* (Judgment) [2015] ICJ Rep 3.

ings without having been sufficiently consulted when the damaging government conducted environmental impact assessments. In other contexts, individuals may be affected due to the ruling of a certain practice as custom – they may be denied or granted rights to navigate a certain river for tourism or financial purposes. They may also be affected by the conferral or non-conferral of certain direct rights in international treaties – such as having the right to consular assistance. In such disputes, certain human dimensions may potentially be overlooked as they are not the principal focus of the dispute.

The objective of this study is therefore to assess the degree to which individuals are integrated in the procedural law of the Court, on the one hand, and considered in decisions of the Court, on the other hand. On the basis of these findings, the study also aims to analyse the reasons for state litigants' and the Court's choices. It argues that individuals impacted by the repercussions of inter-state disputes dealt with by the Court should and can be further integrated into its procedure and considered in its legal reasoning.

I.1 The 'Why'

Some of the most authoritative chroniclers on the World Court – such as Hersch Lauterpacht, Shabtai Rosenne, and Rosalyn Higgins – have expressed concern that its law and practice is not adapted enough to modern-day realities regarding individuals in the international legal order.[8] Members of the Court have expressed similar concerns regarding the limited involvement of, or consideration for, individuals in certain instances.[9]

[8] Hersch Lauterpacht, 'The Revision of the Statute of the International Court of Justice' (2002) 1(1) *The Law & Practice of International Courts and Tribunals* 55; Rosalyn Higgins, 'Conceptual Thinking about the Individual in International Law' (1978) 1(1) *British Journal of International Studies* 1; Shabtai Rosenne, 'Reflections on the Position of the Individual in Inter-State Litigation in the International Court of Justice' in Pieter Sanders (ed), *International Arbitration Liber Amicorum for Martin Domke* (Springer 1967) 240.

[9] Selected examples include: *Jurisdictional Immunities of the State (Germany v. Italy: Greece intervening)* (Judgment) [2012] ICJ Rep 99, 291–308 (Dissenting opinion of Judge Yusuf); *Frontier Dispute (Burkina Faso/Niger)* (Judgment) [2013] ICJ Rep 45, 95 (Declaration of Judge Bennouna); *Judgment No.2867 of the Administrative Tribunal of the International Labour Organization upon a Complaint Filed against the International Fund for Agricultural Development* (Advisory Opinion) [2012] ICJ Rep 10, 51–93 (Separate opinion of Judge Cançado Trindade).

The arguments of this book are underpinned by social idealism, a unique theoretical lens developed by Professor Philip Allott that calls for a change in the world's social organisation.[10] Social idealism retains faith in state sovereignty and in the inter-state system – yet disagrees with Vattelian positivism, which created the foundations of 'international unsociety': a world tailored exclusively to the interests of states as opposed to humanity.[11] Rather, it invites a shift of focus from an international community dominated by states and their interests to one centred 'on the claims, aspirations, and expectations of individual human beings, whose goals and values should matter more than the interests of states'.[12]

Social idealism therefore considers that the international community, while still organised on the basis of states, should 'discharge its community functions increasingly through international and regional institutions, and conferring rights and obligations on individuals'.[13] This is because individuals are not perceived as 'subjects of international law in the traditional positivist sense, but rather as members of an international society in which they are *the* subjects of all law'.[14] This reconceptualisation reflects an international society of all-humanity,[15] which prioritises the unity of mankind.[16]

Adopting the perspective of social idealism, I argue that the Court is compromising its effectiveness and legitimacy due to its reluctant approach towards including and considering relevant individuals in proceedings and disputes, respectively.

10 Philip Allott, *Eunomia: New Order for a New World* (OUP 1990); Philip Allott, *The Health of Nations: Society and Law beyond the State* (CUP 2002); Iain Scobbie, 'The Holiness of the Heart's Affection: Philip Allott's Theory of Social Idealism' in Alexander Orakhelashvili (ed), *Research Handbook on the Theory and History of International Law* (Edward Elgar Publishing 2011) 168.

11 Allott, *The Health of Nations* (n. 10) 56–58; Iain Scobbie, 'Slouching towards the Holy City: Some Weeds for Philip Allott' (2005) 16(2) *European Journal of International Law* 299, 301.

12 Andrea Bianchi, *International Law Theories: An Inquiry into Different Ways of Thinking* (OUP 2016) 246.

13 Clarence Wilfred Jenks, *The Common Law of Mankind* (Praeger 1958) 7.

14 Bianchi (n. 12) 247. See also Hersch Lauterpacht, 'The Subjects of International Law' in Elihu Luaterpacht (ed), *International Law: Being the Collected Papers of Hersch Lauterpacht* vol I (CUP 1970), 136, 149.

15 Allott, *Eunomia* (n. 10) xxvi–xxvii (quotation at xxvi), and also Allott, *The Health of Nations* (n. 10) 152–53, 5.60–5.61.

16 Clarence Wilfred Jenks, *A New World of Law?* (Longmans, Green and Company 1969) 292–98.

I.1.1 *Effectiveness*

The first reason to strengthen the relationship between the individual and the Court is to enhance the effectiveness of the Court. The assessment of effectiveness is the measurement of the degree to which a court accomplishes its specific objective aim.[17] Several aims can be advanced, which may lead to different conclusions about its effectiveness.[18] Beyond the aim to encourage the respect for international law, three aims are identified and discussed here:

First, the Court aims to peacefully resolve inter-state disputes. This is inferred by the UN Charter's aim to, *inter alia*, settle international disputes 'which might lead to a breach of the peace'.[19] However, it is submitted here that the dispute must be resolved in a way that ensures peace not only between states but also with respect to their populations. For instance, the Court's judgment rendered in 2002 ordering a transfer of sovereignty of the Bakassi peninsula from Nigeria to Cameroon may have curbed inter-state conflict but had nonetheless resulted in physical and structural violence on the ground.[20] Peace, in the words of one author, is 'a process or an institution that is not alien to the environment it is serving'.[21] It stems beyond the physical security that a boundary offers and encompasses human security, namely, 'respect for the fundamental human rights of the persons concerned and their protection, including by international justice', as Judge Bennouna has aptly stated.[22] The Court's effectiveness therefore hinges on its ability to adopt an all-encompassing approach to resolving disputes to ensure lasting peace.

[17] Yuval Shany, 'Assessing the Effectiveness of International Courts: A Goal-Based Approach' (2012) 106(2) *The American Journal of International Law* 225, 230.

[18] Joan E. Donoghue, 'The Effectiveness of the International Court of Justice' (2014) 108*The Effectiveness of International Law* 114, 117.

[19] UN Charter, Article 1(1). See also UN Charter, Article 2(3); ICJ Statute, Article 36(3). See also *Armed Activities on the Territory of the Congo (New Application: 2002) (Democratic Republic of the Congo v. Rwanda)* (Request for the Indication of Provisional Measures) [2002] ICJ Rep 219, 241; *Military and Paramilitary Activities in and against Nicaragua (Nicaragua v. United States of America)* (Jurisdiction of the Court and Admissibility of the Application) [1984] ICJ Rep 392, 434.

[20] Ndubuisi N. Nwokolo, 'Peace-Building or Structural Violence? Deconstructing the Aftermath of Nigeria/Cameroon Boundary Demarcation' (2020) 29(1) *African Security Review* 41.

[21] Ibid 49.

[22] *Frontier Dispute (Burkina Faso/Niger)* (Judgment) [2013] ICJ Rep 44, 95 (Declaration of Judge Bennouna).

A second aim of the Court is to contribute to the operation of the UN thereby supporting this regime.[23] Given its status as the principal judicial organ of the UN, the Court's goals have a 'high degree of proximity' to those of the UN.[24] These broadly include maintaining international peace and security – which, as explained before, should be interpreted to include human security – and encouraging respect for human rights. The Charter's preamble also indicates that individuals are at the forefront of the UN's mandate. Its opening sentence reads, 'We *The Peoples* of the United Nations',[25] referring to the populations of the UN Member States.[26] This reference is what divides the preamble into two parts. Only the second part refers to governments to address the Charter's contractual element.[27] The first part, however, declares that people – as opposed to governments – have established the Charter's object and purpose.[28] This interpretation of the UN's objectives should therefore be reflected in the Court's own mandate. Its ability to meet this aim, and therefore ensure its own effectiveness, hinges on its ability to adopt the UN's own preoccupation with people as reflected in its Charter's preamble.

The Court most clearly fulfils its aim of supporting the UN regime through its advisory function.[29] Advisory opinions have been recognised as means to respond to community interests[30] in the socially ideal sense: they have presented opportunities for the Court to respond to questions not only of interest to a collective of states but to a wider public of individuals.[31] Examples include the series of questions relating to the

[23] UN Charter, Article 96 and ICJ Statute, Articles 65–68.

[24] Yuval Shany and Rotem Giladi, 'International Court of Justice' in Yuval Shany (ed), *Assessing the Effectiveness of International Courts* (OUP 2014) 166.

[25] UN Charter, preamble (emphasis added).

[26] André Salomon, *Le préambule de la Charte: base idéologique de l'ONU* (des Trois Collines 1947) 72.

[27] The second part starts at "Accordingly, our respective Governments…"). See further Bruno Simma et al (eds), *The Charter of the United Nations: A Commentary* (3rd edn, OUP 2012) 102.

[28] The Court has relied on the preambular provisions of a treaty to interpret its object and purpose. See *Reservations to the Convention on Genocide* (Advisory Opinion) [1951] ICJ Rep 15, 23.

[29] UN Charter, Article 96 and ICJ Statute, Articles 65–68.

[30] James Crawford, *State Responsibility: The General Part* (CUP 2013) 374–75; Patricia W. Birnie, Alan E. Boyle and Catherine Redgwell, *International Law and the Environment* (4th edn, OUP 2021) 266–67.

[31] Yusra Suedi and Justine Bendel, 'Public Interest Litigation: A Pipe Dream or the Future of International Litigation?' in Justine Bendel and Yusra Suedi (eds), *Public Interest Litigation in International Law* (Routledge 2023) 43.

self-determination of specific populations[32] or the abstract legal questions about the well-being of individuals.[33] The Court's advisory function, through which it offers support to the UN regime, has indicated the degree to which its mandate serves and impacts individuals. In this sense, meeting this aim to ensure its effectiveness hinges on this consciousness.

A third aim of the Court is, more broadly, to confer legitimacy to the UN regime by positioning itself as a custodian of international law and justice.[34] This legitimacy does not stem from the sole fact of being a judicial body. Rather, the Court must be *perceived* as legitimate, in order to confer legitimacy to the UN.[35] I argue here that the Court's reticent approach to individuals may compromise its legitimacy.

I.1.2 Legitimacy

Legitimacy may broadly be understood as a 'right to rule'[36] or an 'authority (…) perceived as justified'.[37] This can be based on many competing standards, such as justice, fairness, democracy, or technocratic

[32] *Accordance with International Law of the Unilateral Declaration of Independence in Respect of Kosovo* (Advisory Opinion) [2010] ICJ Rep 403; *Legal Consequences of the Construction of a Wall in the Occupied Palestinian Territory* (Advisory Opinion) [2004] ICJ Rep 136; *Legal Consequences arising from the Policies and Practices of Israel in the Occupied Palestinian Territory, including East Jerusalem* (Request for Advisory Opinion) [2023] ICJ Rep 2024; *Legal Consequences of the Separation of the Chagos Archipelago from Mauritius in 1965* (Advisory Opinion) [2019] ICJ Rep 95; *Western Sahara* (Advisory Opinion) [1975] ICJ Rep 12.

[33] *Legality of the Threat or Use of Nuclear Weapons* (Advisory Opinion) [1996] ICJ Rep 226; *Legality of the Use by a State of Nuclear Weapons in Armed Conflict* (Advisory Opinion) [1996] ICJ Rep 66; *Obligations of States in respect of Climate Change* (Request for Advisory Opinion) [2023].

[34] Shany and Giladi (n. 24) 167.

[35] Yuval Shany, *Assessing the Effectiveness of International Courts* (OUP 2014) 137.

[36] Allen Buchanan, 'The Legitimacy of International Law' in S. Besson and J. Tasioulas (eds), *The Philosophy of International Law* (OUP 2010) 79; Daniel Bodansky, 'Legitimacy in International Law and International Relations' in J. L. Dunoff and M. A. Pollack (eds), *Interdisciplinary Perspectives on International Law and International Relations: The State of the Art* (CUP 2013) 321, 324; Daniel Bodansky, 'The Concept of Legitimacy in International Law' in R. Wolfrum and V. Röben (eds), *Legitimacy in International Law* (Springer-Verlag 2008) 309, 313; Harlan Grant Cohen, Andreas Follesdal, Nienke Grossman and Geir Ulfstein, 'Legitimacy and International Courts – A Framework' in Harlan Grant Cohen, Andreas Follesdal, Nienke Grossman and Geir Ulfstein (eds), *Legitimacy and International Courts* (CUP 2018) 1, 3.

[37] Daniel Bodansky, 'The Legitimacy of International Governance: A Coming Challenge for International Environmental Law?' (1999) 93(3) *American Journal of International Law*

expertise.[38] Assessing both the process and the outcome of a decision of the Court against these standards, this book illustrates how the Court's legitimacy may be compromised.

The process at the Court is legitimate insofar as it has been generated 'by way of a proper legal procedure'.[39] This is typically assessed by standards of fairness: whether the Court has met standards of procedural justice, such as the principle of the equality of parties. In contexts such as advisory proceedings reviewing decisions of certain administrative tribunals, this book demonstrates how the Court's legitimacy is compromised through its struggle to uphold this principle.[40] Procedural legitimacy can also be assessed by standards of democracy, concerned with giving voice to as many constituencies of international courts as possible.[41] Inter-state courts and tribunals have been observed to include non-state actors in their procedure to uphold democratic standards and therefore preserve their legitimacy.[42] The chapters in Part I demonstrate that the absence of individuals in proceedings where they are directly impacted may have repercussions on the Court's legitimacy in this sense. Finally, the Court's process can also be flawed when technocratic expertise is measured. This is derived from the judges' competence, knowledge, skills and reputation. When the judicial process does not incorporate the necessary procedural tools at disposal to incorporate individuals, such as oral witness testimony, this might impact the judges' ability to reach well-informed decisions. Indeed, enhanced participation may allow for more evidence that could facilitate the successful resolution of the dispute. Chapter 2 (in Part I) demonstrates instances in which greater participation of individuals may have led to more evidence being provided and therefore more satisfactory outcomes for the Court.[43] Such situations suggest that inadequate procedural tools might ultimately

596, 600; Nienke Grossman, 'Legitimacy and International Adjudicative Bodies' (2009) 41 (1) *George Washington International Law Review* 107, 115.

[38] See further Cohen et al (n. 36). 'Moral legitimacy' has also been separately identified in Grossman (n. 37) 115.

[39] Shany (n. 35) 141.

[40] Thomas M. Franck, *Fairness in International Law and Institutions* (Clarendon Press 1998) 26, 27.

[41] Brian McGarry and Yusra Suedi, 'Judicial Reasoning and Non-state Participation before Inter-State Courts and Tribunals' (2022) 21(1) *The Law & Practice of International Courts and Tribunals* 123, 142.

[42] Ibid 144–47.

[43] Conditional request of Paraguay for an order conclusively established facts (9 October 1998) [1], [6]; *Ahmadou Sadio Diallo (Republic of Guinea v. Democratic Republic of the Congo)* (Compensation) (Judgment) [2012] ICJ Rep 324, 332–33 [19].

undermine the judges' technocratic expertise, and therefore, the Court's legitimacy.

While legitimacy stems from the Court's process, it also comes from its decisions, which may give rise to challenge when the outcome 'sharply conflicts with the basic notions of justice'.[44] Justice is therefore a typical yardstick by which to assess judicial outcomes. A complex notion, justice can denote 'restoration of a "proper balance", fit[ting] with the idea of the "golden mean", the desirable middle between two extremes'.[45] In Part II of this book, many scenarios are examined that can be characterised as unjust from the perspective of social idealism, which aspires for more balance between states and individuals. Certain outcomes in territorial or maritime disputes, for instance, may cause disruption to peoples' lives, and in environmental disputes may exclude significant human factors.

Therefore, the absence of individuals in the Court's process – compromising technocratic expertise, fairness, and/or democracy – may impact the Court's legitimacy. Similarly, the lack of consideration for individuals in the Court's judgments may be characterised as unjust and therefore compromise the Court's legitimacy.

One further point should be raised with respect to legitimacy. Generally, the Court strives to maintain its legitimacy by ensuring that it meets the expectations of states. However, it may unknowingly be compromising its long-term legitimacy as a key player in the wider context of the international legal order, characterised by two relevant factors. First, the order is increasingly characterised by its variety of actors. Indeed, the capacity of individuals in international law has impressively evolved over the course of the twentieth century, and participation of a variety of actors is now a basic feature of modern international relations.[46] The Court's limitations *ratione personae* are therefore considered to be 'disconnected' from such developments.[47] This is not helped by the perception that it is 'isolated physically, symbolically, and systematically from the rest of international legal and social reality'.[48] The second characterisation impacting the Court's

[44] Shany (n. 35) 144.

[45] Patrick Keyzer, Vesselin Popovski and Charles Sampford, 'What Is "Access to International Justice" and What Does It Require?' in Patrick Keyzer, Vesselin Popovski and Charles Sampford (eds), *Access to International Justice* (Routledge 2015).

[46] Robert McCorquodale, 'An Inclusive International Legal System' (2004) 17(3) *Leiden Journal of International Law* 477.

[47] Pierre-Marie Dupuy and Cristina Hoss, 'Article 34' in Andreas Zimmermann et al (eds), *The Statute of the International Court of Justice: A Commentary* (3rd edn, OUP 2019) 666.

[48] Allott, *Eunomia* (n. 10) 240.

legitimacy is its application of international law, which has the purpose, *inter alia*, of 'giving a voice to those who have been excluded from powerful positions and are regularly treated as the objects of other peoples' policies'.[49] The Court often finds itself at the receiving end of such an objective: many cases examined in this book involve a community, population, or individual striving to overcome imposition by a more powerful force and vindicate their rights. A failure to engage with this to some degree reflects a failure to acknowledge the reality in which international law operates: that is, not in an intellectual vacuum.[50]

In sum, this book proposes a strengthening of the relationship between the Court and individuals for the Court's effectiveness and legitimacy. Both, from the perspective of social idealism, require greater acknowledgement of the relevant stakeholders.

The choice to focus on the Court is explained by my interests in the tensions between the nature of cases to come before its docket – many of which yield stakes for individuals – and the Court's often conservative or formal approach, deferential to state sovereignty.[51] This choice is also grounded in its prominence in the international legal order, historical longevity, and general subject matter jurisdiction, which results in the 'cast[ing of] a tremendous shadow on the development of international law'.[52]

I.2 Method

The method adopted in this book is, as indicated in its title, the analysis of the law and practice of the Court. 'Law' refers to the procedural law of the Court, which is determined by three key sources. The first is the Statute of the Court, which expounds the broad principles related to it featured in Articles 92–96 of the UN Charter, to which the Statute is annexed. The second is the Rules of the Court, which supplement the broad provisions of the Statute on technical procedure and practical details. The third is the Practice Directions, which supplement the Rules of the Court by specifying the Court's preferred practice in certain

[49] Martti Koskenniemi, 'What Is International Law For?' in Malcolm Evans (ed), *International Law* (5th edn, OUP 2018) 28.

[50] Iain Scobbie, 'A View of Delft: Some Thoughts about Thinking about International Law' in Malcolm Evans (ed), *International Law* (5th edn, OUP 2018) 51.

[51] Shany and Giladi (n. 24) 177.

[52] Hernández (n. 4) 4.

procedural matters. These three sources carve out the procedural infrastructure of the Court.[53] 'Practice', on the other hand, refers to over 100 years of case law, in the form of judgments on contentious cases and advisory opinions, emitted by the Court and its predecessor, across an array of disciplines in international law.

This book therefore adopts a doctrinal methodology, which is best suited to meet its objectives. It presents its findings *de lege lata* (the law which is presently in force or the law as it is). In advancing its argument that affected individuals should and can be further integrated into the Court's procedure and considered in its legal reasoning, it naturally incorporates reflections *de lege ferenda* (the law sought to be established, the law to be proposed, or the law as it 'ought' to be).

I.3 Scope and Structure

For the purpose of this book, an individual may be defined as a natural human person.[54] This study is not limited to cases involving a singular individual. While such scenarios are examined, it also explores contexts involving organised groups of individuals. Such collective structures include peoples: groups with a common destiny and a shared identity (racial, ethnic, linguistic, or other) as a result of a common heritage to which they are bound.[55] They also include local populations who only share a common land on which they live. They may also include a public: a collective of natural human persons who are not necessarily located in the same geographical space but connected in a 'relationship of mutuality' vis-à-vis a common concern.[56]

What the individuals identified in this book all share is their interest in the decision and the decision-making process of the ICJ as they are affected or likely to be affected by it. This book identifies both directly

[53] See further Hugh Thirlway, 'Article 30' in Andreas Zimmermann et al (eds), *The Statute of the International Court of Justice: A Commentary* (3rd edn, OUP 2019); Sergey M. Punzhin, 'Procedural Normative System of the International Court of Justice' (2017) 30 (3) *Leiden Journal of International Law* 661.

[54] Kate Parlett, *The Individual in the International Legal System: Continuity and Change in International Law* (CUP 2011) 3.

[55] *Accordance with International Law of the Unilateral Declaration of Independence in Respect of Kosovo* (Advisory Opinion) [2010] ICJ Rep 403, 228 (Separate opinion of Judge Cançado Trindade).

[56] Benedict Kingsbury and Nahuel Maisley, 'Infrastructures and Laws: Publics and Publicness' (2021) 17(1) *Annual Review of Law and Social Science* 353.

and indirectly affected individuals in Parts I and II, respectively. This dichotomy can be loosely inferred by the Court's practice. On this basis, this study is divided into two principal sections.

Part I focuses on the Court's integration of individuals in its procedure, examining to what degree the Court's procedural mechanisms are inclusive of such individuals. It first tackles the often-asked question of *locus standi* of individuals before the Court (Chapter 1). Next, it turns to situations equipped with their own procedural intricacies: the practice of diplomatic protection (Chapter 2), the involvement of individuals in advisory proceedings (Chapter 3), and the involvement of individuals in advisory proceedings regarding the review of the decisions of administrative tribunals (Chapter 4). Part I is concluded with an assessment of the degree to which individuals are integrated in the procedural law of the Court and reflections on the reasons (Chapter 5).

Part I therefore frames directly affected individuals as those around whom the dispute revolves – in other words, the crux of the matter before the Court pertains directly to the individual's rights. Diplomatic protection proceedings are instigated by an injured individual and concern the violation of the latter's rights. Many advisory requests are made in the interest of a population or wider public of individuals beyond states. Advisory requests made by certain UN administrative tribunals concerned the rights of UN staff members whose labour rights were violated. The fundamental questions for the Court to respond to are directly linked to peoples' experiences, and such people would directly open a contentious dispute if they had legal standing.

Part II analyses the Court's consideration of individuals in its jurisprudence, assessing to what degree individuals who are affected by the outcome of an inter-state litigation are factored into the Court's legal reasoning. It examines various areas of international law: maritime delimitation disputes (Chapter 6), territorial disputes (Chapter 7), environmental disputes (Chapter 8), and disputes involving the interpretation of international treaties and the identification of customary international law (Chapter 9). Part II offers summative reflections on the underlying reasons for its findings (Chapter 10). It focuses on indirectly affected individuals: the crux of the matter brought before the Court does not pertain directly to the individuals' rights but to other matters. Yet, the decisions made on such matters will still affect the individuals – for instance, their well-being, freedoms, identity, nationality, or livelihoods. The individuals identified in Part II therefore have an interest in the decision and the decision-making process. Chapter 11 concludes the book.

PART I

The Individual in the Law of the International Court of Justice

1

Standing

> Hardly a day passes without the Registry receiving applications from private individuals. However distressing the facts in such applications may be, the ICJ is unable to entertain them, and a standard reply is always sent: 'Under Article 34 of the Statute, only States may be parties in cases before the Court.'[1]

Over the last century, the individual's participation in the international legal system has considerably expanded. Indeed, they now participate as a party with legal standing (also referred to as *locus standi* or *jus standi*) in international adjudication before human rights courts, international criminal tribunals, and investment and mixed claims tribunals. Standing is a one's entitlement to be a part of judicial proceedings. However, Article 34 (1) of the Statute of the International Court of Justice (ICJ) reads that '[o]nly States may be parties in cases before the Court.'[2]

Article 34(1) is one of the essential pillars of the Court's jurisdiction insofar as it is one of the oldest rules, unaltered since the days of its predecessor. This clause illustrates the jurisdictional component of having access to the ICJ – in other words, the right to appear before the Court as a party to proceedings.[3] Article 34(1) has been described as the 'entrance door' to the settlement of its disputes[4] and by the Permanent Court of International Justice (PCIJ, Permanent Court) as 'one of the essential conditions of procedure before the Court'.[5] Indeed, Article 34 under the PCIJ Statute stipulated almost the same words that

[1] *The International Court of Justice: Handbook* (6th edn, ICJ, 2018) 33 [hereafter ICJ Handbook].

[2] Statute of the International Court of Justice, Article 34.

[3] Juan José Quintana Aranguren, *Litigation at the International Court of Justice: Practice and Procedure* (Brill/Nijhoff 2015) 3.

[4] Pierre-Marie Dupuy and Cristina Hoss, 'Article 34' in Andreas Zimmermann et al (eds), *The Statute of the International Court of Justice: A Commentary* (3rd edn, OUP 2019) 674.

[5] *Serbian Loans* (Judgment) [1929] PCIJ Series A, 17.

we find today in Article 34 of the ICJ Statute: 'Only States or Members of the League of Nations can be parties in cases before the Court.'[6]

Article 34(1) has been criticised for being '... if not definitely outdated, at least somewhat disconnected from the contemporary developments characterising the international community at a time when actual participation of active members of the "international civil society" in international cooperation for international law-making and monitoring has become one of the basic features of modern international relations'.[7] Similarly, former ICJ Judge Robert Jennings observed in 1995 that the 'change in effect and perspectives of Article 34(1)' had changed in a 'quiet and gradual (...) generally unremarked' way due to 'a very considerable part of international law directly affects individuals, corporations and legal entities other than States'.[8]

The Court itself has described the implications of Article 34(1) as follows:

> The Court has no jurisdiction to deal with applications from individuals, non-governmental organizations, corporations or any other private entity. It cannot provide them with legal counselling or help them in their dealings with the authorities of any State whatever. However, a State may take up the case of one of its nationals and invoke against another State the wrongs which its national claims to have suffered at the hands of the latter; the dispute then becomes one between States.[9]

Despite its clear wording, the Court often receives requests from individuals, as encapsulated in the quote that opens this chapter. A proposition of amending Article 34(1) to allow individuals to be parties has been contemplated by the likes of Hersch Lauterpacht, Shabtai Rosenne, and Rosalyn Higgins.[10] Indeed, many have penned their concerns about this clause, arguing that efforts should be made to open the

6 Statute of the Permanent Court of International Justice, Article 34.

7 Dupuy and Hoss (n. 4) 666.

8 Robert Jennings, 'The International Court of Justice after Fifty Years' (1995) 89(3) *The American Journal of International Law* 493, 504.

9 International Court of Justice, 'Frequently Asked Questions' www.icj-cij.org/en/frequently-asked-questions.

10 Hersch Lauterpacht, 'The Revision of the Statute of the International Court of Justice' (2002) 1(1) *The Law & Practice of International Courts and Tribunals* 109; Shabtai Rosenne, 'Reflections on the Position of the Individual in Inter-state Litigation in the International Court of Justice' in Pieter Sanders (ed), *International Arbitration Liber Amicorum for Martin Domke* (Springer 1967) 240–51; Rosalyn Higgins, *Themes and Theories: Selected Essays, Speeches, and Writings in International Law* (OUP 2009) 908. See also Mark Janis, 'Individuals and the International Court' in David Raic Muller and

Court's jurisdiction to entities other than states. W. Paul Gormley has even stated that '[t]he greatest single innovation required in international law is the liberalization of Article 34(1) of the Court's Statute in order that private parties may appear before the Hague Tribunal'.[11]

Yet, such propositions are often justified by theoretical observations of individuals' budding roles in the international legal system, falling short of examining the stakes, issues and procedural technicalities involved. In this chapter, I argue that despite the role of individuals in the international legal order justifying their legal standing at the Court, the practicalities of this endeavour make it an undesirable proposition. I first present how Article 34(1) was drafted, explaining that the principal reason for not granting the individual *locus standi* was largely due to the primacy of states, characteristic of the traditional positivist doctrine in the nineteenth and the early twentieth centuries (Section 1.1). Second, I speculate on the necessary adjustments to be made for this proposition to go forward – with respect to Statute amendments, workload, jurisdiction, and legal interest – to illustrate its practical infeasibility (Section 1.2). I then conclude (Section 1.3).

1.1 To Be or Not to Be a Party? Discussions within the Advisory Committee of Jurists

Article 34(1) was drafted by the Advisory Committee of Jurists, a group of ten jurists established on 12–13 February 1920 by the Council of the League of Nations, pursuant to Article 14 of the Covenant of the League of Nations.[12] To facilitate the debates within the Advisory Committee, several projects from governments and other entities were submitted regarding the broad question of *locus standi* at the PCIJ. They also submitted separate projects addressing a specific question: whether the Permanent Court may take cognisance of conflicts in which one or two of the parties are private persons.

Regarding the broad question of *locus standi* at the Court, most projects argued whether Members of the League (contracting parties)

J. M. Thuránszky (eds), *The International Court of Justice: Its Future Role after Fifty Years* (Brill 1996) 205–18.

[11] W. Paul Gormley, *The Procedural Status of the Individual before International and Supranational Tribunals* (Springer 1966) 62.

[12] Gleider Hernández, *The International Court of Justice and the Judicial Function* (OUP 2014) 20–22.

should be the only states with *locus standi*, or if other states that are not Members of the League should as well. Despite the restriction of this topic to the types of *states* to be granted *locus standi*, two propositions were made in relation to states' nationals: the Dutch project stated that '[t]he Court is open only to states Members of the League of Nations, *and to nationals of such states*',[13] while the Swedish project upheld the principle of diplomatic protection (the focus of Chapter 2): 'The Court is only to deal with disputes between states. A state can institute proceedings before the Court to establish a claim *on behalf of one of its nationals* against another.'[14]

Regarding the specific question of whether the Court may take cognisance of conflicts in which one or two of the parties are private persons, the responses were varied. The International Law Union, Denmark, Norway, Sweden, Switzerland, and Austria all stated in their projects that disputes should only be inter-state.[15] On the other hand, the Interparliamentary Union (an international organisation of national parliaments), the Netherlands, and Germany supported that private parties should have direct access to the Permanent Court.[16] Both the Five Neutral Powers' project[17] (proposed by Norway, Denmark, the Netherlands, Sweden, and Switzerland) and the Root–Phillimore plan[18] (proposed by former US Secretary of State Elihu Root and Lord Walter Phillimore of the UK) supported the concept of diplomatic protection that the state can bring a claim on behalf of one of its citizens.

Following this discussion, the next session of the Advisory Committee's meetings centred on the following question: 'Shall the Court constitute essentially a jurisdiction between states, or shall its competence extend to litigation concerning individuals? Under what conditions can the latter eventually occur?'[19] This question was raised in the first place mainly because Article 4(2) of the International Prize Court had recently established an international precedent of assuming jurisdiction over claims made by individuals.[20] Although this was the only precedent explicitly

[13] PCIJ Advisory Committee of Jurists, *Procès-verbaux of the Proceedings of the Committee* (16 June–24 July 1920) 79 (emphasis added).
[14] Ibid 79.
[15] Ibid 79–81.
[16] Ibid.
[17] Ibid 79.
[18] Ibid 523.
[19] Ibid 218.
[20] Ibid 205.

mentioned in the Advisory Committee's discussions, it is pertinent to note other then-existing international precedents, such as the Central American Court of Justice and the various Post-World War One Mixed Arbitral Tribunals.[21]

Two of the ten members of the Advisory Committee argued in favour of granting individuals access to an eventual Permanent Court: Dr. Bernard Loder, former Dutch Supreme Court judge and first president of the PCIJ, and Albert de Lapradelle, French Law Professor at the University of Sorbonne.[22] The other eight members were in favour of a strictly inter-state court. Despite the evident majority, the proposal was still debated, with several arguments being raised for and against it. I argue that the principal motive underpinning arguments against *locus standi* of the individual was the predominant positivist perception of the individual as no more than an 'object' of international law in the nineteenth and the early twentieth centuries.

There were three main arguments raised in favour of granting the individual *locus standi* at the Court: denial of justice, double nationality, and commercial relations. The first argument was the denial of justice. Early in the discussion, Albert de Lapradelle stated his concern about cases in which private individuals were faced with a denial of justice from their state. 'It sometimes happens that a private individual who has made a contract with a State, finds it impossible to obtain justice against it on account of a species of privileged right of sovereignty recognized by the legislation and jurisprudence of some countries, such as France,' he said.[23] Under these circumstances, individual access to the Court would be a worthy exception to make, giving the Court 'supplementary jurisdiction' as it was called, 'provided that the case was not of a political nature'.[24] It is interesting to note that this argument appears to prioritise the individual's needs over state sovereignty, placing a limit on what a state can or cannot do to its citizens and adopting consequences, should it surpass its moral obligation to uphold justice.

However, the argument of the denial of justice was refuted by the Committee; it was argued by British lawyer and judge Lord Walter

[21] Edward Hambro and Edgar Turlington, 'Individuals before International Tribunals' (1941) 35 *Proceedings of the American Society of International Law* 22, 24.

[22] Astrid Kjeldgaard-Pedersen, 'The Influence of the Concept of International Legal Personality in the Drafting of the Statute of the Permanent Court of International Justice' (2014) 16(1) *Journal of the History of International Law* 9, 7.

[23] *Procès-verbaux* (n. 13) 205.

[24] Ibid.

Phillimore that the PCIJ would not be able to do anything about a denial of justice on a national level, as it was not a Court of Appeal over national courts.[25] Furthermore, if an individual was not authorised to sue the government in a certain nation, 'the individual [will have] entered into the contract with the State, in full knowledge of this fact'.[26]

In relation to this argument, the question was raised whether the principle of subsidiarity – that an individual must have exhausted domestic judicial avenues and been denied justice from them, in order to seize an international judicial body – should be applicable if individuals were to have access to the Court. The President of the Committee had suggested the 'possibility of including a special clause demanding that, before a State take up the defense of its subject, national jurisdiction should have been exhausted'.[27] However, it was argued by former Brazilian delegate to the 1919 Versailles Peace Conference Raoul Fernandes that it would be a difficult principle to sustain in this context, as certain national jurisdictions of the world do not permit individuals to appeal against the government or allow it but not through judicial means *stricto sensu*, but rather through administrative procedure. This connects to a comment earlier made by Lord Phillimore that 'municipal law, according to the country, either gives or does not give to individuals the right to sue the State at law. If this right did not exist it was not admissible that it should be introduced by a roundabout method of international jurisdiction'.[28] Mr. Fernandes thus further considered that adding a clause about the denial of justice may be interpreted in 'too narrow a sense', as 'it might be concluded from this that no suit could be brought when it was not allowed to sue the State at law before the national Courts and, consequently, there would be no degrees of internal jurisdiction to be exhausted'.[29]

The second argument in favour of granting the individual *locus standi* at the Court was double nationality. In other words, as explained by Albert de Lapradelle,

> if each of two States claimed the same person as a subject, there would be no means of settling the dispute, except by a higher jurisdiction. Since there is a conflict of constitutional laws, it is extremely improbable that

[25] Ibid 214.
[26] Ibid.
[27] Ibid 215.
[28] Ibid 206.
[29] Ibid 216.

> the States would resort to arbitration; the individual in order to define his position must therefore have the power of bringing suit against the two States.[30]

In response, former Norwegian prime minister Francis Hagerup argued that 'cases of double nationality could not be taken before a Court, without a previous Convention between the two States concerned'.[31] Another more supported response was by Lord Phillimore who claimed that the individual who was the subject of such a dispute was not considered as a *civis mundi*, but rather the subject of one or two particular states. Thus, it was not for the Court to decide on the matter, but rather for the national legislations of the respective countries to feature a clause dealing with this situation.[32]

The third argument in favour of granting the individual *locus standi* at the Court was that commercial relations between an individual and other governments would create a certain equality between them, despite the doctrine of state sovereignty. In this case, it would be difficult for the individual to find justice on a national level because of the independence of that state. It would therefore be more logical for him to directly appeal to international justice.[33] In response, the President considered whether these cases could not be dealt with by national jurisdictions, also citing the principal obstacle of state consent (to be discussed in Section 1.2.1).[34] It was finally decided that with regard to the two special cases of double nationality and commercial relations, 'These problems may be interesting, but at the moment they are premature, because they tend to affect the sovereignty, independence and even existence of States.'[35] This sentence alone perfectly epitomises the influence of the traditional positivist doctrine prevalent at the time.

This influence is further reflected in the three main arguments raised against granting the individual *locus standi* before the PCIJ: the limits of Article 14 of the League Covenant, the issue of international legal personality, and the issue of state consent. The first argument raised against granting the individual *locus standi* before the PCIJ was anchored in a

[30] Ibid 210.
[31] Ibid 212.
[32] Ibid 214.
[33] Ibid 210.
[34] Ibid 212.
[35] Ibid 723.

restrictive interpretation of Article 14 of the Covenant of the League of Nations. This provision read as follows:

> The Council shall formulate and submit to the Members of the League for adoption plans for the establishment of a Permanent Court of International Justice. The Court shall be competent to hear and determine any dispute of an international character which the parties thereto submit to it. The Court may also give an advisory opinion upon any dispute or question referred to it by the Council or by the Assembly.[36]

Much reference was made to Article 14 during discussions, the Committee members seeming to have taken the text as indicative of certain restrictions or permissions regarding the Court's competence. For instance, Dr. Loder stated that the word 'parties' was written with a small 'p', which showed that 'the persons who drew up the Covenant had no intention of limiting only to States the right to be a party to a case before the Court'.[37] However, in the Committee's final decision, it was stated that 'parties' cannot be private individuals. The reasoning of the Committee was based on precedent: 'This answer, which was given in 1899 and 1907, and which was evidently intended to apply not only to the Court of Arbitration, but also to the Court of Arbitral Justice, was expressly laid down in the Five-Power Plan: "The Court shall take cognisance only of inter-state litigation."'[38]

The interpretation of the word 'international' in Article 14 was also a point of discussion. Elihu Root believed that this term indicated that 'the Court could deal with private individual interests, but only if the Government of the country of which the individual was the subject made them international by adopting them as its own'.[39] Lord Phillimore stated that 'the word "international" must be interpreted as having regard exclusively to relations between States' and 'based this interpretation on Articles 18 and 19 of the Covenant, which dealt with engagements between States and relations among States'.[40]

There is no clear answer as to whether Article 14 intended to carve the limits of the Court's competence.[41] Renowned PCIJ chronicler Manley O'Hudson interpreted that 'the terminology in Article 14 intended

[36] League of Nations, Covenant of the League of Nations.

[37] *Procès-verbaux* (n. 13) 206.

[38] Ibid 208.

[39] Ibid.

[40] Ibid.

[41] Hernández (n. 12) 21.

merely for the Council to give effect to the competence of a court as set forth by the Members of the League; nothing was to preclude them from later establishing a court "of lesser or greater competence"'.[42] However, the types of argument invoked reflect the positivist sentiment of the nineteenth and the early twentieth centuries that the individual does not have a place in the international legal system, reserved exclusively for states. Mr. Root's comment particularly reflects the doctrine of dualism, a characteristic of positivism at the time: international law was reserved for governments, while municipal law was reserved for individuals. The latter could only acquire international rights if they derived from municipal laws.[43]

The second argument against the individual's access to the PCIJ was centred on the concept of international legal personality. International legal personality is a concept that serves to distinguish between entities that are relevant to the international legal system and those excluded from it.[44] In and of itself a neutral theoretical concept, the inclusion and exclusion of entities is subject to many interpretations depending on one's perspective of international law.[45] While it is undisputed that states have international legal personality, the role of other entities has historically 'given rise to controversy'.[46] The exclusivity of international legal personality to states was long advocated by the traditional positivist doctrine. Indeed, they held that states are the sole 'subjects' of international law and, consequently, individuals are 'objects' of international law. Certain arguments invoked by Committee members were centred on this premise – for instance, 'States alone constituted legal persons in international matters',[47] 'the State should always be the *dominus litis*',[48] or 'in international affairs the State as always considered as a whole, and in the fullness of its attributes of sovereignty'.[49]

42 Ibid.
43 Lassa Francis Lawrence Oppenheim, *International Law: A Treatise* (3rd edn, Longmans, Green and Company 1920) 17–18 [13].
44 Roland Portmann, *Legal Personality in International Law* (CUP 2010) 1.
45 Astrid Kjeldgaard-Pedersen, *The International Legal Personality of the Individual* (OUP 2018) 1–13.
46 *Reparation for Injuries Suffered in the Service of the United Nations* (Advisory Opinion) [1949] ICJ Rep 174, 178.
47 *Procès-verbaux* (n. 13) 215.
48 Ibid 214.
49 Ibid.

Mr. de Lapradelle opined, 'One must not remain too much in the realm of theories; wrongs done to individuals resulting from the chaotic conditions of international relations must be taken into account.'[50] However, he clearly stood as a minority against the likes of Arturo Ricci-Busatti, legal advisor to the Italian Ministry of Foreign Affairs, who very plainly stated that 'it is impossible to put States and private individuals on the same footing; private individuals are not subjects of international law and it is entirely within the realm of that law that the Court is called upon to act'.[51] Senator, Belgian Minister of State, and President of the Advisory Committee Baron Edouard Descamps also commented that

> [t]he real object of the law of nations, of *jus inter gentes*, is the relation of State to State considered as sovereign groups, and, as such, Members of the League of Nations. The conditions of subjects of each State in another country, the co-ordination of public and private law of each State with that of the other nations, these are the concerns of nations in their mutual relations, but these questions enter only indirectly into the realm of the law of nations.[52]

The third argument raised against granting the individual *locus standi* before the PCIJ was in relation to state consent. In the discussions of the Advisory Committee, consent was the principal argument against the proposal for individuals to have access to the Court. Indeed, jurisdiction of the Court in contentious cases is always dependent on state consent. Therefore, not only does a state have to fulfil the conditions laid down in Articles 34 and 35 to be eligible, but it must also, as a preliminary condition, *accept* the jurisdiction of the Court. It is the combination of the eligibility of access and state consent, which will give the Court jurisdiction to entertain a certain dispute.

The principle of consent was already envisaged during the drafting of the PCIJ Statute. It was repeated that due to 'the principle of sovereignty of States, no State could be summoned before the Court without its previous consent'.[53] Mr. Root 'did not think that a private individual would gain any advantage by taking before the International Court a case which his Government did not consider justified'.[54] He also 'doubted

[50] Ibid 211.
[51] Ibid 208.
[52] Ibid 209.
[53] Ibid 207.
[54] Ibid.

whether the claim of a private individual which was not supported by his Government would carry enough weight before an international Court'.[55] Lord Phillimore went even further in claiming that '[a] State would never permit itself to be sued before a Court by a private individual'.[56]

To conclude, the issue of *locus standi* of the individual before the Permanent Court of International Justice was considered and examined from a number of angles. While there were arguments in favour and against granting the individual *locus standi* before the PCIJ, the majority of the Advisory Committee of Jurists opposed the proposition.

What can also be concluded after examining these exchanges is that no particular circumstance at the time dictated that the Court had to be inter-state in its nature, but for the sovereign sentiment at the time. The idea of creating a Permanent Court of International Justice first appeared in a British Draft Convention presented at the Paris Peace Conference after the First World War.[57] The Commission of the League of Nations, established in January 1919,[58] had before it several similar proposals.[59] Article 14 of the League Covenant ended up making no explicit statement about the competence of the Court. Certain members of the Advisory Committee had their interpretations, but a literary interpretation provided no decisive indication. While Article 13 of the League Covenant read that '[t]he *Members of the League* agree that whenever any dispute shall arise *between them* (...) they will submit the whole subject-matter to (...) judicial settlement',[60] the phrasing of Article 14 did not exclude an individual from being part of proceedings before the Permanent Court as well, provided that the individual is a party to a dispute of an international character. The fact that the issue was even debated was testimony that the answer was not clear-cut. Indeed, during that period, various other forms of judicial settlement involving individuals existed in practice. As well as the examples mentioned earlier, the Treaty of Versailles gave nationals of the Allied Powers the right to put forward claims for compensation, in their own name, against Germany.[61] From a

55 Ibid 208.

56 Ibid 207.

57 David Hunter Miller, *The Drafting of the Covenant* (W.S. Hein 2002) 106.

58 Manley O. Hudson, *The Permanent Court of International Justice, 1920–1942: A Treatise* (The Macmillan Company 1943) 96.

59 Ibid 96.

60 Covenant of the League of Nations, Article 13.

61 Treaty of Versailles, UKTS 4, Articles 297 and 304(b)(2).

legal standpoint, there was every possibility for such a Court to be one that was open to individuals as well as states.

However, it appears that the reasons for opposition were anchored in the need to preserve state sovereignty. The aforementioned arguments reflect this common theme: favourable arguments about double nationality and commercial relations were refuted as they would affect the sovereignty of states. Arguments against the proposition were explicitly about the international legal personality of individuals and the absence of state consent. Even the interpretation of Article 14 of the League Covenant was informed by positivist perceptions about states being the principal litigators on the international plane.

Astrid Kjeldgaard-Pedersen argues that the specific concept of international legal personality did not influence the outcome of Article 34(1) as much as would be expected, given the positivist sentiment at the time. In her view, the concept mostly held no more than academic value.[62] This might be true – but the understanding of international legal personality through the state-dominant lens and in the wider context of other state-dominant arguments indicate that the need to preserve state sovereignty was the overriding factor barring individuals from *locus standi* before the Permanent Court. Indeed, the overarching traditional positivist doctrine, wherein international legal personality dwells as a defining feature, was a driving force behind the deliberations, underpinning their outcome and largely explaining Article 34 still embedded in the ICJ Statute today.

Following this decision made by the Advisory Committee of Jurists, the PCIJ was closed off to litigating individuals, despite issuing a host of decisions stemming from conflicts between states and minority groups. Indeed, due to the remapping of borders, birth of new states, and movement of self-determination after the First World War, certain groups found themselves as minorities of a state with significant ethnic, linguistic, or cultural differences than their own.[63] Woodrow Wilson, founder of the League of Nations, had originally intended to incorporate minority rights into the League Covenant, but this was rejected by the

[62] Kjeldgaard-Pedersen (n. 22) 16, 20.

[63] See Catherine Brölmann, 'The PCIJ and International Rights of Groups and Individuals' in Christian Tams and Malgosia Fitzmaurice (eds), *Legacies of the Permanent Court of International Justice* (Martinus Nijhoff Publishers 2013) 124.

Council of the League.[64] Therefore, the issue was left to be implemented in a piecemeal fashion, through numerous bilateral treaties. These treaties were the legal basis upon which the League of Nations could get involved in establishing a minorities' petition system, as the League Council could be seized if any obligation therein was breached. These treaties also provided that any conflict of opinion regarding them would be submitted to the PCIJ.[65] The PCIJ therefore dealt with a number of cases in which it was requested to interpret bilateral treaty clauses related to minority rights.

Minority groups would submit their petitions to the League Secretariat, and a lengthy procedural process would ensue until the petitions arrived at the Permanent Court's docket. However, this was different than an individual party seizing an international court or tribunal, as minority groups were not granted *locus standi*. It was in fact the Council of the League requesting the Permanent Court to give an advisory opinion, and not the minority group itself making this request. The possibility for minority groups to have any formal international legal standing had been strongly refuted.[66] The League Council itself affirmed that 'the minorities treaties did not create organisations possessing the right to speak and act on behalf of the "minorities", but placed their protection in the hands of the members of the Council'.[67] The minorities were not considered to be organised entities with international legal personality. Furthermore, the petition itself had no legal value. As stipulated in a report detailing the League's connection with minorities entitled the Tittoni Report:[68] 'this act [of minorities seizing the League Secretariat] must retain the nature of a petition (. . .) pure and simple; it cannot have the legal effect of putting the matter before the Council and calling upon it to intervene'.[69] Furthermore, the Members of the Council had no obligation to use the information sent to them in the form of a petition from a minority group; they could ignore

64 Mary Gardiner Jones, 'National Minorities: A Case Study in International Protection' (1949) 14 *Law and Contemporary Problems* 599, 605.

65 Ibid 608.

66 Nathaniel Berman, '"But the Alternative Is Despair": European Nationalism and the Modernist Renewal of International Law' (1993) 106(8) *Harvard Law Review* 1792, 1860.

67 League of Nations Official Journal (July 1923) 717–18. See also Julius Stone, 'The Legal Nature of Minorities Petition' (1931) 12 *British Yearbook of International Law* 76, 81.

68 League of Nations Official Journal, vol 7 (November–December 1920); Giuseppe Motta, *Less than Nations: Central-Eastern European Minorities after WWI* (Cambridge Scholars Publishing 2013) 260.

69 League of Nations Official Journal, vol 1 (February 1920) 8.

it or use it, as they pleased.[70] Still, this was the closest that private persons came to having *locus standi* before the Court's predecessor.

1.2 Practical Considerations when Contemplating *Locus Standi* of the Individual before the Court

As the necessity to preserve state sovereignty appeared to be the main reason in refusing *locus standi* to individuals under Article 34(1), it is no surprise that relatively recent scholarship has argued for Article 34(1)'s amendment. Indeed, arguments that the Court's jurisdiction should be open to entities other than states are based on the rationale that non-state actors have played an increasingly important role during the course of the twentieth century. While I agree with the latter claim, a closer examination of the practical considerations indicates that such a proposal lacks in feasibility. Four issues will be considered in turn: consent and jurisdiction, legal interest, treaty amendment and implications for the Court's workload.

1.2.1 Consent to Jurisdiction

Granting the individual *locus standi* would radically alter the jurisdiction of the Court as we know it, which is 'very likely the most important aspect of the work of the ICJ'.[71] As it stands, there are many different avenues that states may use to seize the Court's jurisdiction, contemplated in Article 36 of its Statute. Article 36(1) provides for both consensual and treaty-based jurisdiction. The Court has *consensual jurisdiction* when states in a dispute on a particular matter spontaneously submit a special agreement, an arrangement concluded by the two parties particularly for the purpose of the subject under dispute. The Court will have *treaty-based jurisdiction* when the states in dispute rely on an already-existing treaty providing (in a compromissory clause) that in case a dispute arises, they may refer it to the Court. Another form of jurisdiction is *compulsory jurisdiction*, provided in Article 36(2). This is when a state submits a unilateral declaration recognising the jurisdiction of the Court as binding, with respect to any other state that also accepts it as binding, for any dispute in the future.

70 Stone (n. 67) 79.
71 Quintana Aranguren (n. 3) 40.

The lynchpin of all of these types of jurisdiction is the principle of consent. This cardinal principle of international adjudication means that the Court can only hear a dispute if it is requested to do so by the states in question. Its Statute does not allow the Court to take up a matter of international law and rule on it *proprio motu*. Without state consent, the Court has no jurisdiction. All of the types of jurisdiction examined here are expressions of consent by states.

The principle of consent has been recalled in various PCIJ and ICJ judgments. In the *Mavrommatis* judgment, the Court's predecessor commented that jurisdiction is 'invariably based on the consent of the respondent and only exists insofar as this consent has been given'.[72] The Court has also recalled the principle in a number of its judgments,[73] describing it as a 'well-established principle of international law'[74] and 'one of the fundamental principles of its Statute'.[75]

Indeed, the principle of consent is a natural component in the practice of the peaceful settlement of disputes. In Article 33 of the UN Charter alone, we find a panoply of choices at states' disposal for peacefully resolving their issues, judicial settlement being but one of them. States are not compelled to resort to any of these forms of dispute settlement, but rather they choose to do so. This quintessential premise is also featured in the 1970 Declaration on Principles of International Law Concerning Friendly Relations and Cooperation among states in accordance with the Charter of the United Nations, another important international legal source describing the peaceful settlement of disputes.[76] It derives from this that the principle of consent is also an expression

[72] *Mavrommatis Palestine Concessions* (Judgment) [1924] PCIJ Series A, 16. Other PCIJ judgments mentioning the principle of consent are: *Rights of Minorities in Upper Silesia (Minority Schools)* (Judgment) [1928] PCIJ Series A, 22; *Eastern Carelia* (Advisory Opinion) [1923] PCIJ Series B.

[73] *Corfu Channel (United Kingdom v. Albania)* (Preliminary Objection) (Judgment) [1948] ICJ Rep 15, 24; *Anglo-Iranian Oil Co. (United Kingdom v. Iran)* (Preliminary Objections) (Judgment) [1952] ICJ Rep 93, 102–3; *Maritime Delimitation and Territorial Questions between Qatar and Bahrain (Qatar v. Bahrain)* (Jurisdiction and Admissibility II) (Judgment) [1995] ICJ Rep 6, 23–24 [43]; *Oil Platforms (Islamic Republic of Iran v. United States of America)* (Merits) (Judgment) [2003] ICJ Rep 161, 182–83 [42].

[74] *Aerial Incident (Israel v. Bulgaria)* (Preliminary Objections) (Judgment) [1959] ICJ Rep 127, 142.

[75] *Armed Activities on the Territory of the Congo (New Application: 2002) (Democratic Republic of the Congo v. Rwanda)* (Order of 10 July 2002) [2002] ICJ Rep 219, 241 [57].

[76] A/RES/2625 (XXV).

of the principle of sovereign equality of states, which is the cornerstone of international law.

Considering this, the Court's jurisdiction would significantly change if individuals had *locus standi* before it. Notably, both consensual jurisdiction (by special agreement) and treaty-based jurisdiction require the existence of a treaty, defined by Article 2(1)(a) of the 1969 Vienna Convention on the Law of Treaties (VCLT) as an international agreement concluded between states in written form and governed by international law.[77] Such treaties must reflect commitments to which the parties consented and thus create international legal rights and obligations.[78]

An agreement between an individual and the state of their nationality would not meet these specific requirements to qualify as a treaty. Accordingly, consensual jurisdiction and treaty-based jurisdiction could not work in the context of a dispute between an individual and a state. Even if these two types of jurisdiction could work from an international legal perspective, accepting *locus standi* of individuals would require an amendment of these jurisdictional provisions in Article 36(1) of the ICJ Statute, where 'treaties and conventions in force' are explicitly mentioned. A phrase providing for 'agreements between individuals and States' would have to be added. As for consensual jurisdiction, the admittedly more imprecise phrase '[t]he jurisdiction of the Court comprises all cases which the *parties* refer to' still could not apply to individuals as the latter are not parties to the Court's Statute (pursuant to Article 34). This, too, would therefore require an amendment permitting individuals to also refer cases to the Court. This raises many multifarious questions as to which individuals could qualify to refer to such cases and under what grounds. Such issues preemptively erode the system of jurisdiction established by the Statute and manifestly alter the entire character of the Court.

It appears that if Article 34(1) were to ever be amended, then the only type of jurisdictional avenue available to such private persons would be compulsory jurisdiction, which appears to be somewhat different. Here, what can be imagined is that states are given the option to confer general compulsory jurisdiction to cases in which the claim is from an individual. An example of this can be found in the African Court on Human and

77 Vienna Convention on the Law of Treaties, 1155 UNTS 331.

78 *Maritime Delimitation and Territorial Questions between Qatar and Bahrain (Qatar v. Bahrain)* (Jurisdiction and Admissibility) (Judgment) [1994] ICJ Rep 112, 121 [25].

Peoples' Rights (ACtHPR), which accepts applications from states and individuals, provided that the defendant state has accepted the jurisdiction of this court to receive individual cases. Thus, the first case of the ACtHPR, *Michelot Yogogombaye v. Republic of Senegal* (15 December 2009), was deemed inadmissible as Senegal had not accepted jurisdiction over cases initiated by individuals.[79] In theory, this type of jurisdiction could still be exercised at the World Court.

Yet, the issue is the question of willingness; would states ever accept this option? The idea of an 'International Court of Human Rights' was proposed by Australia in 1948.[80] It was based 'to a large extent' on the Statute of the International Court of Justice, although both 'individuals' and 'groups of individuals' were to be given standing.[81] However, this was rejected by states, and subsequent initiatives to carry the idea forward were no more successful.[82] Even at the ACtHPR where it is possible for individuals to sue states, only eight out of thirty states Parties to the Protocol to the African Charter on Human and Peoples' Rights on the Establishment of the ACtHPR have consented to this.[83] Therefore, most African states appear to be opposed to it. If states have adopted this approach in face of a human rights court with the very purpose of upholding individuals' rights, what hope is there for them to accept it for a court that was established as a bastion of their own sovereignty?

The issue of compulsory jurisdiction was already historically controversial. While the Statute was drafted under the illusion that the PCIJ would enjoy compulsory jurisdiction, this did not come to fruition as the idea of one state bringing another state before the Court and condemning it without its acquiescence made most states uncomfortable.[84] The concept as featured in the Statute was therefore the compromise, enabling states to be seized at the Court on matters to which they had consented. Indeed, states may place reservations on the Court's jurisdiction, and many have done so in order to exclude matters that are essentially within

79 *Michelot Yogogombaye v. Senegal* (Judgment) [2009] ACtHPR, Appl. No. 1/2008, [37].
80 E/CN.4/AC.1/27.
81 E/CN.4/AC.1/27, Article 17.
82 Philip Alston, 'Against a World Court for Human Rights' 28(2) (2014) *Ethics & International Affairs* 197–212.
83 African Court on Human and Peoples' Rights, 'Basic Information' www.african-court.org/wpafc/basic-information.
84 Hernández (n. 12) 25.

the domestic jurisdiction of the state.[85] Individuals' claims against states towards the Court most certainly could be subject to such reservations, greatly limiting the number of states that would subject themselves to the ICJ's jurisdiction.[86]

Hersch Lauterpacht asked, '[I]s there a good reason, other than the persistence of certain traditional modes of thinking, why the Court should not be able to adjudicate upon a dispute which involves a question of international law and in which one party to the dispute is a state - provided that that state agrees in the specific case to the exercise of jurisdiction by the Court?'[87] The answer to this question would essentially be negative. The general reluctance of states to recognise individuals as subjects of international law,[88] which largely influenced the debates around Article 34 in the Advisory Committee of Jurists, arguably prevails to this very day.[89] As UN expert Paul Szasz aptly summarised,

> The development of international law is an objective that states tend to praise rather than seriously pursue. In particular, governments generally prefer to keep all law-creating and even law-defining processes firmly within their control, even at the cost of significantly retarding this work. Therefore, while political theorists and unengaged international lawyers might welcome increased activity by the World Court, just because the judgments and opinions of the Court will contribute to the still scant body of international law, the enthusiasm of states for even modest judicial legislation has always been most limited. That is one reason why access to the Court has jealously been restricted to states, whether acting individuals as parties to contentious proceedings or collectively through the organs of worldwide intergovernmental organizations authorized to request opinions. Thus the prospect that increased activity by the Court will help find interstices in the international legal fabric or even expand its bund, is likely to constitute, among diplomats, a negative rather than a positive argument for the proposals here under examination.[90]

[85] See International Court of Justice, 'Declarations Recognizing the Jurisdiction of the Court as Compulsory' www.icj-cij.org/en/declarations.

[86] Hersch Lauterpacht, 'The Subjects of the Law of Nations' (1947) 63(4) *Law Quarterly Review* 438, 456.

[87] Institut de Droit International, *Annuaire de l'Institut de Droit International* (Session d'Aix-en-Provence, 1954, vol 45(i)) 535.

[88] Gormley (n. 11) 64.

[89] Ibid.

[90] Paul C. Szasz, 'Enhancing the Advisory Competence of the World Court' in Leo Gross (ed), *The Future of the International Court of Justice*, vol 2 (Oceana Publications 1976) 511.

Ultimately, in connection to the unavoidable matter of consent and sovereignty, recourse to the World Court will take place if politically appropriate for the state in question. This can be seen as early as the minority system under the PCIJ, which was a political, rather than a humanitarian, novelty, designed to ensure international political peace and state security.[91] Rather than the Court's predecessor being a "champion of minorities", as some doctrine claims, it is perhaps more suitable and modest to describe it as a simple interlocutor, assisting sovereign governments to tackle their own domestic issues.[92] The Permanent Court was also significantly crippled by the lack of cooperation from the victors of the First World War, who were not interested in taking part,[93] despite their own issues and violations of minority rights,[94] making the system arbitrarily confined to a handful of Eastern and Central European nations 'obliged to participate as a result of wartime defeat or as a condition for receiving additions of territory or recognition of independence'.[95] There were repeated proposals to extend the system to be applicable to all states, but this was strongly refuted. This resulted in a strong feeling of resentment from the involved nations, leading to certain among them, such as Poland, eventually opting out of the system altogether.[96]

The PCIJ's experience with minority groups – coupled with contemporary examples such as the ACtHR mentioned earlier – demonstrates that states are generally reluctant to engage in international litigation against individuals. Therefore, although compulsory jurisdiction may be a possible avenue of consent for disputes between states and individuals, the attitude of states makes it difficult to envisage the individual being granted *locus standi* before the ICJ.

1.2.2 Legal Interest

A second complex issue is that of legal interest, which forms a part of standing. In establishing its standing to institute proceedings, a state may

[91] Tennent Harrington Bagley, *General Principles and Problems in the International Protection of Minorities: A Political Study* (Georg 1950) 42; Mark Mazower, 'Minorities and the League of Nations in Interwar Europe' (1997) 126(2) *Daedalus* 47, 51.

[92] Ibid (Mazower) 51.

[93] Jones (n. 64) 604–6. See also Peter Hilpold, 'The League of Nations and the Protection of Minorities – Rediscovering a Great Experiment' (2013) 17 *Max Planck Yearbook of United Nations Law* 87, 96.

[94] Ibid (Hilpold) 94.

[95] Alfred de Zayas, 'The International Judicial Protection of Peoples and Minorities' in Catherine Brölmann, René Lefeber and Marjoleine Zieck (eds), *Peoples and Minorities in International Law* (Nijhoff 1993) 258.

[96] See, generally: Hilpold (n. 93).

be required to demonstrate that it has a specific legal interest in the matter under consideration.[97] The legal interest of the state applicant has not been defined in the law nor practice of the Court. It has, however, been described in the context of third-party intervention governed by Articles 62 and 63 of its Statute. A necessary requirement for this practice is defined here as an 'interest of a legal nature which may be affected by the decision in the case'.[98] This must be of a legal nature, meaning 'a real and concrete claim (. . .) based on law',[99] and the state must demonstrate that its interest 'may be affected by the decision of the Court' in that case.[100] Although such conditions have only been elaborated in the context of third-party intervention, and not for the main applicant, it may logically be assumed that such conditions are also required for the main parties in the case.[101]

Therefore, were an individual wishing to seize the Court, they would not be exempt from the requirement of legal interest. Human rights, for instance, are undisputedly owed to individuals, putting them in a position to seize international tribunals over the violation of human rights treaties. In such instances, such individuals have a clear legal interest if they are victims of the alleged violation. Higgins explains that maritime or territorial disputes, for example, have traditionally been qualified as states' interests,[102] meaning that individuals would not be considered to have legal interests in such contexts. However, I argue in Part II of this monograph that individuals do in fact have such interests due to the repercussions of such disputes on their lives. Nonetheless, this will not

[97] Quintana Aranguren (n. 3) 15.
[98] Statute of the International Court of Justice, Article 62(1).
[99] *Territorial and Maritime Dispute (Nicaragua v. Colombia)* (Application for Permission to Intervene by the Government of Honduras) [2010], [37]. The Court made the same distinction in the decision concerning Application by Costa Rica, *Territorial and Maritime Dispute (Nicaragua v. Colombia)* (Application for Permission to Intervene by the Government of Costa Rica) [2010] [26].
[100] Ibid (Application by Honduras) [37]; Ibid (Application by Costa Rica) [26].
[101] *South West Africa (Liberia v. South Africa; Ethiopia v. South Africa)* (Preliminary Objections) (Judgment) [1962] ICJ Rep 319, 455–56 (Dissenting opinion of Judge Winiarski). For opposing views, see Malcolm Shaw, *Rosenne's Law and Practice of the International Court: 1920–2015*, vol 3 (5th edn, Brill/Nijhoff 2016) 1212; see also generally, Brian McGarry, 'Obligations *Erga Omnes* (*Partes*) and the Participation of Third States in Inter-State Litigation' (2023) 22(2) *The Law & Practice of International Courts and Tribunals* 273.
[102] Rosalyn Higgins, 'Remedies and the International Court of Justice' in Rosalyn Higgins (ed), *Themes and Theories: Selected Essays, Speeches, and Writings in International Law* (OUP 2009) 893.

automatically translate into the fulfilment of a jurisdictional requirement. Indeed, proving their legal interest may be difficult as it hinges on how the threshold were to be assessed, which is unclear in the Court's practice.

1.2.3 Amending the ICJ Statute

As the Court itself has stated, 'Like any other court, the ICJ can only operate within the constitutional limits that have been laid down for it'.[103] These constitutional limits are carved out in the Court's Statute. Thus, any change regarding *locus standi* would require the Statute's amendment.

According to Article 69 of the ICJ Statute, 'Amendments shall be effected by the same procedure as is provided by the Charter of the United Nations for amendments to that Charter (. . .)'.[104] Article 108 of the Charter provides that it may only be amended if there is a two-thirds majority of the United Nations General Assembly and if the clause in question has been ratified by two-thirds of Member States, including all permanent members of the Security Council.[105] Therefore, the amendment process is much heavier than for other international courts and tribunals. European states, for instance, have adopted protocols that make fundamental changes to the procedure of the European Court of Human Rights (ECtHR).[106] The ICJ Statute was not constituted to be easily amended. This holds particularly true as all Members of the United Nations are *ipso facto* parties to the Statute of the ICJ,[107] meaning that 193 Member States are bound to it. It is one of the multilateral treaties with the most ratifications in the world. It is difficult to amend a treaty with such a wide membership, and only two attempts to do so have been recorded in its history.[108]

Furthermore, it is very unlikely that this procedure could be successful for a change that poses no serious political problem for states.[109] Considering that so many other issues have also been raised and pushed

[103] ICJ Handbook (n. 1) 33.

[104] Statute of the International Court of Justice, Article 69.

[105] Charter of the United Nations, 1 UNTS XVI, Article 108 [hereafter UN Charter].

[106] For example, Protocol No. 14 to the Convention for the Protection of Human Rights and Fundamental Freedoms, Amending the Control System of the Convention, CETS 194.

[107] See UN Charter, Article 93,

[108] Wolfram Karl, 'Article 69' in Andreas Zimmermann et al (eds), *The Statute of the International Court of Justice: A Commentary* (3rd edn, OUP 2019) 1873.

[109] Szasz (n. 90) 509.

for amendment, such as doing away with the permanent members of the Security Council and their veto, amending one provision would be 'opening Pandora's Box' to amend several provisions that have been subject to complaint in the past. Many – if not most – Member States would be opposed to any extension of the activities of the Court. Judges would also most likely not accept to fundamentally change the essence of the Court's activity.

Thus, any proposals made to animate the Court's functions could only be implemented if they did not implicate any substantial changes in its constitution, the Statute.[110] The Court cannot appropriate powers that the international community did not vest in it.[111] Changes seem complicated and at a high cost.

This is particularly true if we recall that Article 34(1) is one of three pillars of the ICJ's jurisdiction, along with the principle of consent and its broad jurisdiction *ratione materiae*.[112] Being a pillar of the ICJ Statute, Article 34 has precast the parameters of the Court and has determined a number of other articles in the Statute (such as Articles 4(3), 5(1), 35, 36 or 40(3)) that were drafted upon its underlying logic. The very structure and function of the Court are largely based upon the assumption that only states can be parties in cases before it.[113] Revisiting and possibly reviewing one of these pillars would therefore possibly require a revision of many other articles as well, which would alter its entire judicial structure as we know it.[114]

1.2.4 Implications for the Court's Workload

Another key concern in response to the proposition of the individual's *locus standi* before the Court is the 'opening of the floodgates' to a Court that is not short of activity.[115] Individuals may not exercise the same

110 Ibid.

111 Kaiyan Homi Kaikobad, *The International Court of Justice and Judicial Review: A Study of the Court's Powers with Respect to Judgments of the ILO and UN Administrative Tribunals* (Kluwer Law International 2000) 302.

112 Christian Tams and Malgosia Fitzmaurice (eds), *Legacies of the Permanent Court of International Justice* (Martinus Nijhoff Publishers 2013) 13.

113 Gleider Hernández, 'Non-state Actors from the Perspective of the International Court of Justice' in Jean d'Aspremont (ed), *Participants in the International Legal System: Multiple Perspectives on Non-state Actors in International Law* (Routledge 2011) 154.

114 Ibid. See also Lauterpacht (n. 10) 55.

115 See, e.g., Judge Joan E. Donoghue, 'Speech by H.E. Judge Joan E. Donoghue, President of the International Court of Justice, on the Occasion of the Seventy-Seventh Session of the

degree of restraint that states have when it comes to international adjudication. A pertinent example is the ECtHR, whose policy of accepting individual petitions alleging human rights violations has resulted in tens of thousands of applications spanning all European countries.[116]

The lack of hesitance of individuals may, in part, have to do with their political motives to attract international attention on an issue of concern, to gain notoriety, or even to cause embarrassment to the state.[117] Indeed, during the era of the Court's predecessor, the Council of the League of Nations was completely overwhelmed by the petitions it received from minority groups, many of which – especially those from the German minorities – were used for political purposes, namely, to embarrass the Polish government.[118] A consequential fear is that "a constant agenda of trivial cases would lower the prestige of the organ."[119]

Lauterpacht has suggested that 'the heavy cost of international litigation would act as an effective deterrent against rash or malicious recourse to the machinery put at the disposal of private persons'.[120] It is also a possibility for the Court to open its doors yet choose to only hear a fraction of cases brought before it, as does the ECtHR.[121]

Filtering mechanisms could also be instituted, as seen under the League's minority petition system. A minority petition would pass through the Minorities Section[122] of the League Secretariat, followed by the 'Minorities Committee' (consisting of three members of the League Council) and finally, if negotiations between the state and the minority group could not settle the problem,[123] the League Council would ask the Permanent Court for a decision.[124] This dense procedural process meant

United Nations General Assembly' (77th Session of the United Nations General Assembly, New York City, 27 October 2022) 1 www.icj-cij.org/sites/default/files/press-releases/0/000-20221027-STA-01-00-EN.pdf.

116 See, e.g., European Court of Human Rights, *Annual Report 2022* (Council of Europe, 2023) 141.

117 See also Lauterpacht (n. 86) 458.

118 Gormley (n. 11) 42.

119 Szasz (n. 90) 510.

120 Lauterpacht (n. 86) 458. Leo Gross also reflects on the use of 'sensible safeguards' as deterrents to individuals. Leo Gross, *The Future of the International Court of Justice*, vol II (Oceana Publications 1976) 510.

121 E.g., 77.8 per cent of cases were declared inadmissible in 2022. European Court of Human Rights, *Analysis of Statistics 2022* (Council of Europe, January 2023) 3.

122 Jones (n. 64) 611. See also Carole Fink, 'The League of Nations and the Minorities Question' (1995) 157(4) *World Affairs* 197.

123 de Zayas (n. 95) 255.

124 A/2909, 7–12 [9]–[25]; 43–44 [21].

that very few petitions would actually arrive at the Permanent Court's docket.

It is difficult to provide accurate statistics from the first ten years of the PCIJ's lifespan. However, between 1920 and 1929, an estimated 345 petitions were submitted to the League, 143 of which were deemed admissible by the Minorities Section, and 18 of those were approved by the Minorities Committee (Committee of Three) and forwarded to the Council for consideration (as no reconciliation was reached between the state and the minority group).[125] In 1929, the League Council decided, through the Madrid Resolution (Council Resolution of 13 June 1929) that the minorities' petitions system should become transparent with annually published statistics.[126] Thus, between 1929 and 1939, statistics show that 950 petitions were filed, of which 758 were declared admissible by the Minorities Section, with 16 finally reaching the agenda of the Council to seize the PCIJ for an Advisory Opinion.[127] This is 1.68 per cent of the deposited petitions. Therefore, the heavy procedural channels significantly hampered the practice of minorities' petitions at the PCIJ and impeded the PCIJ from drowning from this floodgate effect. As was summarised by Professor Mark Mazower: 'It was difficult to bring cases to the League's attention, and even more difficult to push them through the Geneva machine and have them taken up by the Council'.[128]

In the case of the Inter-American Court of Human Rights, individuals must first file their petitions with the Inter-American *Commission* on Human Rights, an autonomous organ of the Organization of American States that receives and investigates such individual petitions alleging violations of provisions in the American Convention on Human Rights. The African human rights system follows this model, with its own African Commission on Human and Peoples' Rights considering individual petitions before they reach the African Court. A similar filtering mechanism could be established for the ICJ, safeguarded by the UN. However, this would not be free from its own bureaucratic and budgetary difficulties. It would imply a financial investment from the UN, undergoing financial strain at the time of writing. Furthermore, such a procedure would be more complicated as there would not be one

[125] Malcolm Evans, *Religious Liberty and International Law in Europe* (CUP 1997) 157–58.
[126] Ibid 154–55. League of Nations Official Journal, vol X (1929) 1005–6.
[127] Brölmann (n. 63) 130 n. 32.
[128] Mazower (n. 91) 51.

specific convention nor substantive regime to govern, due to the ICJ's jurisdiction *ratione materiae*.[129] Unlike the World Trade Organization Dispute Settlement Body, the Court of Justice of the European Union, or regional human rights courts, the ICJ is not the guardian over one specific legal corpus. In this sense, its scope is unlimited, which poses challenges for a hypothetical mechanism in terms of volume and diversity of applications to manage.

Another possible way to filter and manage the presumably increased number of cases from individuals could be an increased use of the Court's Chambers. According to Article 26(2) of the Statute, the Court has the power to form a special *ad hoc* chamber for the hearing of particular cases. Thus, a smaller number of judges from the 15 may be selected by the parties to deal with a particular matter. Article 26(1) provides that the Court could also form a chamber on a more permanent basis to deal with a particular category of cases; the Statute provides the examples of 'labour cases and cases relating to transit and communications'.[130] An example of this practice elsewhere may be found in the International Tribunal for the Law of the Sea (ITLOS), which has chambers for fisheries disputes, marine environment disputes, and maritime delimitation disputes. The Court has exercised this facility once, establishing a permanent chamber for environmental matters in 1993, but despite the growing number of environmental disputes in international law,[131] this chamber has never been used.[132] Another possibility is the use of the Chamber of Summary Procedure. Composed of five judges, it is established annually by the Court 'with a view to the speedy dispatch of business'.[133] Governed by Article 29 of the Court's Statute, the Chamber of Summary Procedure's objective is to provide parties with the option to have their case treated expeditiously, if desired.

The idea behind this ability to form chambers is to give the parties more flexible, efficient, and cost-effective ways of resolving their disputes. It also allows for the bench to be catered to the technical or regional expertise required for a particular matter. It could be a useful tool to resolve disputes between a state and an individual as it would be much

[129] Tams and Fitzmaurice (n. 112) 16.
[130] International Court of Justice Statute, Article 26.
[131] See Chapter 8.
[132] International Court of Justice, 'Chambers and Committees' www.icj-cij.org/en/chambers-and-committees.
[133] Ibid.

faster, also combining 'the advantage of the authoritative decision and the preservation of the continuity of the law with the requirements of expeditious disposal of claims'.[134] Despite these advantages, chambers have only been exercised six times in the Court's history.[135] A reason that could explain why this is not a popular choice for state litigants is their desire to be able to plead in front of *all* of the judges as opposed to some of them, and thus receive a judgment buttressed by the full Court. If individuals would be seeking international attention or notoriety, then they, too, would prefer the pre-eminence of the full bench. In sum, while filtering mechanisms are theoretically possible in response to a potentially higher workload, they appear to be financially and politically unfeasible in practice.

1.3 Conclusions

To conclude, the legal standing of individuals before the World Court's predecessor – and, consequently, the Court itself – was motivated by concerns about state sovereignty informed by dominant positivist legal thought. Today, Higgins has opined that were the individual to have access to the gates of the Peace Palace, the international legal system would conceptually survive.[136] This explains literature from abovementioned eminent scholars seeing no reason why the Court could not accommodate individuals as parties, at par with states, in proceedings.

There are many sound reasons to plead for this. Nonetheless, having discussed and explored the possibility of individuals acquiring *locus standi* at the Court, it has been noted that many difficulties would arise with regards to treaty law and, more specifically, amendments to be made to the Court's Statute. The hypotheses regarding treaty-based and consensual jurisdiction are also fraught with problems. As for compulsory jurisdiction, states would likely not be willing to bind themselves to claims brought by individuals. Beyond additional problems raised by the requirement of legal interest, one must consider the inevitable floodgates that the Court would open if individuals had *locus standi*. While

[134] Lauterpacht (n. 86) 458.

[135] International Court of Justice, 'Chambers and Committees' www.icj-cij.org/en/chambers-and-committees.

[136] Rosalyn Higgins, 'Conceptual Thinking about the Individual in International Law' in Rosalyn Higgins (ed), *Themes and Theories: Selected Essays, Speeches, and Writings in International Law* (OUP 2009) 76.

there have been scholarly suggestions to establish filtering mechanisms, this would entail a high bureaucratic and financial investment from the UN and most certainly increase the Court's workload, already high at the time of writing.

The somewhat audacious proposal of *locus standi* of the individual before the ICJ is one that suggests the carnage of the roots that ground the Court. Certain proposals here would imply an overhaul of the budget, financing and staffing of the Court. The fundamental structure of the Court would have to be dismantled, to accommodate the changes necessary for the individual's *locus standi* to come to fruition. While this would still be feasible, it is a jurisdictional amendment that would reflect a deeper shift in the Court's character and role in the international legal system as the unique venue for inter-state disputes. This would therefore transmute the World Court into, in essence, another tribunal altogether.[137]

Inasmuch as this proposal remains implausible, the Court is a master of its own procedure with all of the freedom to create and amend its own rules and reinterpret its powers through the Rules of the Court and the Practice Directions, so long as they do not contradict the Statute. Thus, the remainder of Part I explores how the Court may adjust its procedural mechanisms in a variety of contexts to circumvent its Article 34(1) and allow for the integration of concerned individuals in its proceedings to the best of its ability, where necessary or desirable.

[137] Kaikobad (n. 111) 302.

2

Diplomatic Protection

> When a State invokes a right of a national it is obliged, in one way or another, to involve the national at the level of procedure and of any transaction that takes place.[1]

As early as 1920, when the Permanent Court of International Justice (PCIJ, Permanent Court) was being created by the Advisory Committee of Jurists, Mr. Albert de Lapradelle from France questioned the extent to which the state should protect its citizens, from a procedural standpoint. 'Should the State leave to the individual the task of pleading his own case before the Court to which he has gained access by the aid of his Government, or should the State, having taken up the case for its subject, conduct the case alone before the Court?'[2] By quoting examples, he advocated that individuals wished to take part themselves in the proceedings.[3] Later in discussions, Mr. Francis Hagerup from Norway claimed that the individual could plead before the future Permanent Court, since arbitration accepts this practice.[4]

When contemplating the role of the individual in inter-state cases before the International Court of Justice (ICJ), diplomatic protection is perhaps the first example that comes to mind. Scholarship has focused considerably on the 'humanisation' of the practice of diplomatic protection in the Court's jurisprudence, which has made great strides over the last two decades.[5] In contrast, scholarship has overlooked how the

[1] A/CN.4/484 [51].

[2] PCIJ Advisory Committee of Jurists, *Procès-Verbaux of the Proceedings of the Committee* (16 June–24 July 1920) 211.

[3] Ibid.

[4] Ibid 213.

[5] See, for example: Sebastian tho Pesch, 'The Influence of Human Rights on Diplomatic Protection: Reviving an Old Instrument of Public International Law' in Norman Weiss and Jean-MarcThouvenin (eds), *The Influence of Human Rights on International Law* (Springer 2015) 55–67; Annemarieke Vermeer-Künzli, *The Protection of Individuals by Means of Diplomatic Protection: Diplomatic Protection as a Human Rights Instrument*

individual has been *procedurally* involved in diplomatic protection proceedings. Through exploring the nature and jurisprudential evolution of diplomatic protection, I argue in this chapter that while great strides have been made to humanise the law of diplomatic protection, its practice in the courtroom is not in alignment with this as the relevant individual does not participate in proceedings. This non-alignment impacts the procedural legitimacy of the Court in two ways: democratic standards are not upheld due to the absence of injured individuals in proceedings, and technocratic expertise is harmed where their non-participation results in the absence of significant evidence.

Diplomatic protection is an avenue of redress made available to a natural or legal person who has been injured by a foreign state, carried out by that individual's state of nationality, on his or her behalf. The International Law Commission's 2006 Draft Articles on Diplomatic Protection define it as 'The invocation by a State, through diplomatic action or other means of peaceful settlement, of the responsibility of another State for an injury caused by an internationally wrongful act of that State to a natural or legal person that is a national of the former State with a view to the implementation of such responsibility'.[6] The ICJ specified in its very first advisory opinion that an international organisation may also claim reparations from a government that injured one of the organisation's agents.[7] However, this chapter will focus on inter-state diplomatic protection cases involving individuals who are not agents of international organisations.

While this chapter focuses on diplomatic protection in the context of judicial settlement at the ICJ, diplomatic protection may be exercised by the state using any means of pacific settlement of disputes stipulated in Article 33 of the United Nations Charter: 'negotiation, enquiry, mediation, conciliation, arbitration, judicial settlement, resort to regional agencies or arrangements, or other peaceful means of their

(Leiden University 2007); Vasileios Pergantis, 'Towards a "Humanisation" of Diplomatic Protection?' (2006) 66(2) *Zeitschrift Für Ausländisches Öffentliches Recht Und Völkerrecht* 351; Enrico Milano, 'Diplomatic Protection and Human Rights before the International Court of Justice: Re-fashioning Tradition?' (2005) 35(1) *Netherlands Yearbook of International Law* 85; Flor de María Palaco Caballero, *La Cour Internationale de justice et la protection de l'individu* (Schulthess 2015).

[6] Draft Articles on Diplomatic Protection with Commentaries [2006] *Yearbook of the ILC*, vol II, Part Two.

[7] *Reparation for Injuries Suffered in the Service of the United Nations* (Advisory Opinion) [1949] ICJ Rep 174.

own choice'.[8] Given the jurisdictional hurdles before the ICJ, diplomatic protection is largely non-contentious in state practice.[9]

The practice of diplomatic protection existed years before its development by the World Court and its predecessor – in fact, "ever since the existence of international relations between [states]."[10] Although the concept of governments protecting their nationals can be traced back to much earlier,[11] diplomatic protection in the modern sense of the term finds its origins in the eighteenth century through the practice of letters of reprisal.[12] It was also seen in practice through many arbitral awards, such as the 1794 Jay Treaty (United States of America vs. United Kingdom), the 1795 Spanish–United States of America (US) Commission, and a number of arbitrations.[13] However, "the basic premise of diplomatic protection is traced to Vattel",[14] who wrote in 1797:

> Whoever uses a citizen ill, indirectly offends the state, which is bound to protect this citizen; and the sovereign of the latter should avenge his wrongs, punish the aggressor and, if possible, oblige him to make full reparation; since otherwise the citizen would not obtain the great end of the civil association, which is safety.[15]

Diplomatic protection was also practised in certain mixed claims commissions following the First World War.[16] It is therefore no surprise that this practice was consequently concretised in the judgments of the PCIJ; it was already anticipated by the Advisory Committee when it decided to reject the *locus standi* of individuals, as examined in Chapter 1.[17] Thus, in

[8] Charter of the United Nations, 1 UNTS XVI, Article 33.

[9] Dinh Nguyen Quoc, Patrick Daillier, and Alain Pellet, *Droit international public* (6th edn, L.G.D.J 1999) 909.

[10] Vermeer-Künzli (n. 5) 1.

[11] Carmen Tiburcio, *The Human Rights of Aliens under International and Comparative Law* (Brill/Nijhoff 2001) 35.

[12] Kate Parlett, *The Individual in the International Legal System: Continuity and Change in International Law* (CUP 2011) 48, fn. 2; Antonio Cançado Trindade, 'Origin and Historical Development of the Rule of Exhaustion of Local Remedies in International Law' (1976) 12 *Revue Belge de Droit International*499.

[13] Ibid (Parlett) 50–52, 124–33.

[14] Ibid 49.

[15] Emmerich de Vattel, *The Law of Nations: Or, Principles of the Law of Nature, Applied to the Conduct and Affairs of Nations and Sovereigns* (CUP 2011) 38. See also Ole Spiermann, *International Legal Argument in the Permanent Court of International Justice: The Rise of the International Judiciary* (CUP 2005) 82.

[16] See, for example: *Mixed Claims Commission (United States/Germany) (1 November 1923 – 30 October 1939)* (1923) (Award) (Administrative Decision II) VII RIAA 1, 26.

[17] *Procès-verbaux* (n. 2) 204–9, 211, 213, 215–16, 723. See also Spiermann (n. 15) 192.

its lifetime of seventeen years, the PCIJ produced numerous judgments on contentious cases which were related to the diplomatic protection of individuals.[18] Others were exercised in favour of corporations (legal persons).[19] Diplomatic protection was also indirectly invoked in other judgments.[20] In comparison, the ICJ has dealt with fewer diplomatic protection cases.[21] Although this chapter focuses on diplomatic protection of the individual, certain examples of cases involving corporations will be mentioned where pertinent.

There is a manifest reason why the practice of diplomatic protection seemingly occupies more of a residual role as opposed to its principal one of the past.[22] During the Permanent Court's lifetime, the practice of diplomatic protection filled somewhat of a void in the international legal

18 *Mavrommatis Palestine Concessions* (Judgment) [1924] PCIJ Series A, 12; *Certain German Interests in Polish Upper Silesia* (Merits) (Judgment) [1926] PCIJ Series A; *The Case of the S.S. Lotus* (Judgment) [1927] PCIJ Series A; *Serbian Loans* (Judgment) [1929] PCIJ Series A; *Brazilian Loans* (Judgment) [1929] PCIJ Series A; *Oscar Chinn* (Judgment) [1934] PCIJ Series A/B; *Pajzs, Csáky and Esterházy* (Judgment) [1936] PCIJ Series A/B; *Panevezys-Saldutiskis Railway* (Judgment) [1939] PCIJ Series A/B.

19 *Factory at Chorzów* (Merits) (Judgment) [1928] PCIJ Series A; *Lighthouses case between France and Greece* (Judgment) [1934] PCIJ Series A/B; *Lighthouses in Crete and Samos* (Judgment) [1937] PCIJ Series A/B; *Phosphates in Morocco* (Judgment) [1938] PCIJ Series A/B; *Electricity Company of Sofia and Bulgaria* (Judgment) [1939] PCIJ Series A/B; *Société Commerciale de Belgique* (Judgment) [1939] PCIJ Series A/B.

20 For example: *Appeal from a Judgment of the Hungaro-Czechoslovak Mixed Arbitral Tribunal (The Peter Pazmany University)* (Judgment) [1933] PCIJ Series A/B, 216, 221.

21 *Anglo-Iranian Oil Co. (United Kingdom v. Iran)* (Preliminary Objections) (Judgment) [1952] ICJ Rep 93; *Ambatielos case (Greece v. United Kingdom)* (Merits) (Judgment) [1953] ICJ Rep 10; *Nottebohm (Liechtenstein v. Guatemala)* (Second Phase) (Judgment) [1955] ICJ Rep 4; *Certain Norwegian Loans (France v. Norway)* (Preliminary Objections) (Judgment) [1957] ICJ Rep 9; *Interhandel (Switzerland v. United States of America)* (Preliminary Objections) (Judgment) [1959] ICJ Rep 6; *United States Diplomatic and Consular Staff in Tehran (United States of America v. Iran)* (Judgment) [1980] ICJ Rep 3; *Vienna Convention on Consular Relations (Paraguay v. United States of America)* (Order of 10 November 1998) [1998] ICJ Rep 426; *Elettronica Sicula S.p.A. (ELSI) (United States of America v. Italy)* (Judgment) [1989] ICJ Rep 15; *LaGrand (Germany v. United States of America)* (Merits) (Judgment) [2001] ICJ Rep 466; *Avena and Other Mexican Nationals (Mexico v. United States of America)* (Judgment) [2004] ICJ Rep 12; *Ahmadou Sadio Diallo (Republic of Guinea v. Democratic Republic of the Congo)* (Judgment) [2010] ICJ Rep 639; *Jadhav (India v. Pakistan)* (Judgment) [2019] ICJ Rep 418. Cases not brought under a diplomatic protection heading include *Arrest Warrant of 11 August 2000* (Judgment) [2002] ICJ Rep 3, [37]–[40]; *Certain Property (Liechtenstein v. Germany)* (Preliminary Objections) (Judgment) [2005] ICJ Rep 6. Cases not recognised by the Court as diplomatic protection cases include *Avena* [40].

22 Francisco Orrego Vicuña, 'Individuals and Non-state Entities before International Courts and Tribunals' (2001) 5(1) *Max Planck Yearbook of United Nations Law Online* 59.

system by allowing individuals to participate in it. Indeed, the practice implied, in its very essence, that the individual did not possess a legal personality of his or her own,[23] and was an object of international law or a good on which the state had a right (*jus in rem*).[24] Today, however, there are many different avenues of judicial redress for individuals directly on the international plane. Before the World Court, state litigants increasingly evade the formal channels of diplomatic protection but do claim to be acting as *parens patriae*: on behalf of their people to assert their putative private rights.[25]

This evolution may cause some to question the relevance or added value of diplomatic protection, which has arguably become gradually unbefitting with the rise of the individual as a bearer of obligations and rights under international law.[26] Despite this decline in popularity within the context of international adjudication, diplomatic protection remains one of many avenues for the individual. Further, given its rich history within the practice of the World Court, any study of this kind would be incomplete without it.

An undeniable dichotomy exists between the legal framework of diplomatic protection, unpacked in the first part of this chapter (Section 2.1), and its procedural enactment, explained in the second part (Section 2.2). To effectively describe the legal framework of diplomatic protection, I first dismantle the famous *Mavrommatis* fiction's claim that the state is the sole injured party (Section 2.1.1). I then argue that other conditions for diplomatic protection (such as nationality and the exhaustion of local remedies) and its features (such as state discretion and state responsibility), have been increasingly humanised to place emphasis on the individual. Nonetheless, the second part of this chapter points to the

[23] David Leys, 'Diplomatic Protection and Individual Rights: A Complementary Approach' (2016) 54 *Harvard International Law Journal* 2.

[24] Ibid fn. 21.

[25] For example: Colombia in *Alleged Violations of Sovereign Rights and Maritime Spaces in the Caribbean Sea (Nicaragua v. Colombia)* (Counter-Claims) (Order of 15 November 2017) [2017] ICJ Rep 289, 303 [43]; Iran in *Alleged Violations of the 1955 Treaty of Amity, Economic Relations, and Consular Rights (Islamic Republic of Iran v. United States of America)* (Press Release) [2018] 2; Azerbaijan in *Interpretation and Application of the International Convention on the Elimination of All Forms of Racial Discrimination (Republic of Azerbaijan v. Republic of Armenia)* (Request for the Indication of Provisional Measures of Protection) [2021] 26; Croatia in *Application of the Convention on the Prevention and Punishment of the Crime of Genocide (Croatia v. Serbia)* (Press Release) [2012] 1.

[26] Chittaranjan Felix Amerasinghe, *Diplomatic Protection* (OUP 2008) 74.

dichotomy: this directly injured individual does not participate in proceedings at the Peace Palace and does no more than occasionally provide written testimony in the government's pleadings. The third and final part of this chapter will therefore provide suggestions to advocate for stronger procedural participation for the injured individual in cases of diplomatic protection at the ICJ (Section 2.3). Section 2.4 concludes.

2.1 The *Mavrommatis* Fiction: Fabrication and Humanisation

The practice of diplomatic protection at the Court hinges upon the fulfilment of three conditions: the individual must be a national of the protecting state, the individual must have exhausted domestic remedies, and an international legal norm must have been violated. This aside, diplomatic protection is governed by three features: first, diplomatic protection is the discretionary right of the state; second, it can lead to reparations under the law of state responsibility, and third (and most importantly), there is a legal fiction upon which diplomatic protection rests. Collectively, these comprise the legal framework of diplomatic protection, at the heart of which lies the *Mavrommatis* fiction.

The concept of legal fiction was born with the very idea of diplomatic protection. The *Mavrommatis Palestine Concessions (Greece v. Britain)* PCIJ judgment of 30 August 1924 was the first judgment to not only consolidate the Vattelian premise (mentioned earlier) and the concept of the legal fiction but also to lay the groundwork for the development of the doctrine of diplomatic protection.[27] This judgment was centred on a dispute between a Greek national, Euripide Mavrommatis, and the British government. Before the First World War, when Palestine was part of the Ottoman Empire, the Ottoman authorities concluded certain contracts with Mr. Mavrommatis, which granted him concessions for certain public works to be constructed in Palestine. Some years later, after the collapse of the Ottoman Empire with its defeat in 1918, the British government, acting as the Mandatory for Palestine under a Mandate negotiated with the League, granted various concessions to a third party (the Rotenberg concessions), partly overlapping those of Mr. Mavrommatis. Mr. Mavrommatis believed that the British Government and Palestine did not recognise the full extent of his rights; they had

[27] Milano (n. 5) 110.

violated certain international legal obligations, namely, Protocol XII of the Lausanne Peace Treaty between Turkey and the Allied Powers. Eventually, the Greek government intervened and submitted the case to the PCIJ under Article 26 of the Mandate for Palestine.[28]

As Article 34 of the PCIJ Statute limited disputes before it to states alone, or members of the League, the Permanent Court explained that

> It is true that the dispute was at first between a private person and a State – i.e. between M. Mavrommatis and Great Britain. Subsequently the Greek Government took up the case. The dispute then entered upon a new phase; it entered the domain of international law, and became a dispute between two States. Henceforward therefore it is a dispute which may or may not fall under the jurisdiction of the Permanent Court of International Justice.[29]

It then wrote the following cardinal passage:

> It is an elementary principle of international law that a State is entitled to protect its subjects, when injured by acts contrary to international law committed by another State, from whom they have been unable to obtain satisfaction through the ordinary channels. By taking up the case of one of its subjects and by resorting to diplomatic action or international judicial proceedings on his behalf, a State is in reality asserting its own rights – its rights to ensure, in the person of its subjects, respect for the rules of international law. The question, therefore, whether the present dispute originates in an injury to a private interest, which in point of fact is the case in many international disputes, is irrelevant from this standpoint. Once a State has taken up a case on behalf of one of its subjects before an international tribunal, in the eyes of the latter the State is the sole claimant.[30]

This cemented the concept in diplomatic protection today known as a legal fiction – which is also referred to as the *Mavrommatis* fiction (both terms are used interchangeably in this chapter). This fiction stipulates that the injury to the individual as a national is an injury to the state itself, and thus, the state of nationality is seizing the Court on its *own* behalf.[31] The *Mavrommatis* fiction was affirmed by the PCIJ in other cases; for example, the *Chorzów Factory* case and the *Serbian Loans* case.[32] The consequence of this *Mavrommatis* fiction is that the

[28] *Mavrommatis Palestine Concessions* (n. 18) 7.
[29] Ibid 8.
[30] Ibid 12.
[31] Amerasinghe (n. 26) 23.
[32] *Factory at Chorzów* (n. 19); *Serbian Loans* (n. 18).

concerned private party is completely invisible to the Court. For instance, the Permanent Court stated in *Société Commerciale de Belgique* that it was not entitled to oblige the Belgian government to enter into negotiations with the Greek government 'and still less the company which is not before it'.[33] In brief, the *Mavrommatis* fiction tells us two crucial things: first, the state is defending its own right, and not the individual's right. Second, the state is the injured party in the eyes of the Court.[34]

This section argues that the legal fiction upon which the practice of diplomatic protection rests is at odds with the reality in which the individual is at the centre of the practice. It first argues that the fiction itself inaccurately portrays whose right is being invoked and whose injury is at the root of the dispute (Section 2.1.1). It then argues that the two individual-focused conditions of diplomatic protection – nationality of the individual and their exhaustion of local remedies – indicate that the individual is at the centre of the practice (Section 2.1.2). Furthermore, the more state-centred features of diplomatic protection – reparations to the state under the law of state responsibility, and state discretion – have both been recently challenged by human rights perspectives (Section 2.1.3). Both the conditions and features of diplomatic protection therefore serve to further weaken the *Mavrommatis* fiction.

2.1.1 *The* Mavrommatis *Fiction of Diplomatic Protection: Fabrication versus Reality*

A legal fiction may be defined as a claim accepted as true for legal purposes but that is, in reality, fallacious.[35] In the context of diplomatic protection, a legal fiction is applied when assessing whose right is being protected. In reality, a right of the individual has been violated. This, in turn, has left the individual injured. However, for the purposes of this practice, the state claims that it is defending its *own* right, as a result of its *own* fictive injury. This is because, during the Vattelian era in which diplomatic protection materialised, the traditional positivist doctrine was dominant, and individuals had very little to no means of accessing international justice (Section 1.1). Thus, in an era whereby individuals

[33] *Société Commerciale de Belgique* (n. 19) 177.

[34] Alain Pellet, 'The Second Death of Euripide Mavrommatis? Notes on the International Law Commission's Draft Articles on Diplomatic Protection' (2008) 7(1) *The Law & Practice of International Courts and Tribunals* 33, 35 [3].

[35] Vermeer-Künzli (n. 5) 35–29.

did not exist in the international legal system, their protection was guaranteed through this legal fiction.[36] With considerations of justice in mind, it arose out of the need to remedy the lack of *locus standi* of the individual on the international plane.[37] One may question to what extent this famous *Mavrommatis* maxim is still entirely valid today. The very notion may be called into question for two reasons: whose right is being invoked and whose injury is at the root of the dispute.

First, the veil has progressively been lifted to reveal that the right being invoked is predominantly the individual's as opposed to the state's. Historically, the legal fiction assumed that the state was 'in reality' exercising its own right – to demand that international law be respected towards its nationals and to act in order to enforce this right[38] – as opposed to the right of the individual.

Today, the International Law Commission (ILC), following a heated debate on this question,[39] settled for a formulation of Draft Article 2 on Diplomatic Protection that 'leave[s] open the question whether the state exercising diplomatic protection does so in its own right or that of its national – or both'.[40] Thus, the ILC's definition of diplomatic protection makes no reference to the right of the individual nor that of the state.[41] This definition was borrowed by the Court in the preliminary objections phase of the *Ahmadou Sadio Diallo* case *(Republic of Guinea v. Democratic Republic of the Congo)*, proving that the Court, too, considered this dual possibility.[42] Yet, in other instances, the Court has recognised individuals' rights in the context of diplomatic protection proceedings.[43] The premise that the real right being protected is the state's is inaccurate. In reality, the real right being protected is that of

36 Ibid 31.

37 Pergantis (n. 5) 371, fn. 84.

38 Leys (n. 23) 4.

39 A/CN.4/484 [51]; Draft Articles on Diplomatic Protection with Commentaries (n. 6) 25, commentary to Article 1; Vermeer-Künzli (n. 5) 55–57.

40 Draft Articles on Diplomatic Protection with Commentaries (n. 6) 26, commentary to Article 1.

41 Draft Articles on Diplomatic Protection, *Official Records of the General Assembly (2006)*, Sixty-first Session, Supplement No. 10 (A/61/10), Article 1.

42 *Ahmadou Sadio Diallo (Republic of Guinea v. Democratic Republic of the Congo)* (Preliminary Objections) (Judgment) [2007] ICJ Rep 582, 599 [39]. See also Luigi Condorelli, 'Protection diplomatique réussie et réparation due: une glose' in Pierre-Marie Dupuy et al (eds), *Unité et diversité du droit international: ecrits en l'honneur du Professeur Pierre-Marie Dupuy* (Nijhoff 2014) 483.

43 *LaGrand* (n. 21) 482–83 [42], 494 [77]; *Avena* (n. 21) 35–36 [40]. See further Chapter 9.

the individual, but, for the purposes of the fiction, the state's right is said to have been violated as well.

This is further emphasised by the condition of diplomatic protection that the minimum standard of the treatment of aliens or international human rights law must have been violated in order for the individual to request that his or her government seize the Court.[44] As the ICJ acknowledged in 2007 in the preliminary objections phase of *Diallo*, 'Owing to the substantive development of international law over recent decades in respect of the rights it accords to individuals, the scope *ratione materiae* of diplomatic protection, originally limited to alleged violations of the minimum standard of treatment of aliens, has subsequently widened to include, *inter alia*, internationally guaranteed human rights'.[45] As international human rights are individuals' rights, this serves to highlight the flaw in claiming that the state is 'in reality' exercising its own right.

The second reason why the concept of the legal fiction may be called into question pertains to its underlying assumption that in the eyes of the Court, the state is the sole injured party. The injury of the individual as the starting point is 'irrelevant', according to this maxim. However, the Court itself has slightly distanced itself from this idea in two ways. First, the Court has acknowledged an injury from the state *and* the individual in a number of cases. Indeed, a distinction has developed in the Court's jurisprudence of three types of claims: direct, indirect, or mixed. A direct claim is one in which the state has been directly injured and, therefore, has a reason distinct from the reason of its national to bring an international claim.[46] For instance, it may have suffered a moral damage (then the breach consists in conduct discriminating against individuals having its nationality) or a material damage (when the breach affects an economic interest of the state).[47] An indirect claim is one in which the individual has been principally injured, and the state only *indirectly* injured, through its national. Finally, a mixed claim is one in which the

[44] Nobuyuki Kato, 'The Role of Diplomatic Protection in the Implementation Process of Public Interests' in Teruo Komori and Karel Wellens (eds), *Public Interest Rules of International Law: Towards Effective Implementation* (Ashgate 2009) 189–205.

[45] *Diallo* (n. 42) 599 [39].

[46] Chittharanjan Felix Amerasinghe, *Local Remedies in International Law* (2nd edn, CUP 2004) 145–68.

[47] Giorgio Gaja, 'The Approach of the International Court of Justice to Injuries Suffered by Individuals' (2017) 103(125–30) *Boletim da Sociedade Brasileira de Direito Internacional* 571, 574.

injury of the individual and of the state are at par.[48] In each case, the Court will determine which injury – the individual's or the state's – is preponderant and, therefore, which type of claim applies. It is important to emphasise that the test based on preponderance is an admission in itself that all claims do in fact include an injury to an individual at their core. Thus, the direct claim does not advocate that the state's injury is the exclusive one but merely that the state's injury may be greater than the existing individual's injury. In an indirect claim, the state's injury could be entirely fictitious for purposes of the practice of diplomatic protection. However, the individual's injury cannot ever be fictitious; without a *true* injury, 'in reality', a diplomatic case will not be initiated.[49]

Second, despite this practice, the Court has gone even further by admitting the sole existence of the injury of the individual and not the state in *Diallo*. In the preliminary objections phase, it relied upon the ILC's definition of diplomatic protection in its 2006 Draft Articles, which only mentions the injury of the individual and makes no reference to the injury of the state.[50] In the merits phase, it referred to 'reparation due to Guinea for the *injury suffered by Mr. Diallo*',[51] and in the compensation phase, it clarified that its 'inquiry [would] be limited to the injury resulting from the breach of Mr. Diallo's rights as an individual'.[52] No mention was made of an injury suffered by Guinea.[53]

To summarise, the *Mavrommatis* fiction is, in itself, contradictory for two principal reasons. First, it claims that a state is 'in reality' exercising its own right, while it is 'in reality' exercising the right of the individual. Second, it claims that the state is the sole injured party, while, in fact, the true required injury for a diplomatic protection case to be opened is that of the individual, while the state's is a fictitious requirement. This problem with the very concept of legal fiction already exposes that the individual is, in fact, at the forefront of diplomatic protection, contrary to

48 Draft Articles on Diplomatic Protection with Commentaries (n. 6) 45 [10], commentary to Article 14; *Tehran Hostages* (n. 21); *Interhandel* (n. 21); *Avena* (n. 21).

49 Giorgio Gaja, 'Quel préjudice pour un État qui exerce la protection diplomatique?' in Denis Alland et al (eds), *Unité et diversité du droit international: Écrits en l'honneur du Professeur Pierre-Marie Dupuy* (Brill/Nijhoff 2014) 487–93.

50 *Diallo* (n. 42) 599 [39].

51 *Diallo* (n. 21) 691 [161].

52 *Ahmadou Sadio Diallo (Republic of Guinea v. Democratic Republic of the Congo)* (Compensation) (Judgment) [2012] ICJ Rep 324, 332–33 [17].

53 Gaja (n. 47) 573.

what was originally desired. This is further reinforced by the two conditions of diplomatic protection, which will be examined here.

2.1.2 *The Two Conditions of Diplomatic Protection: Nationality and the Exhaustion of Local Remedies*

An examination into the conditions required in the practice of diplomatic protection demonstrates that the individual is in fact the key actor in the process, serving to further weaken the *Mavrommatis* premise. The two conditions are as follows: first, the individual being protected must be a national of the protecting state; second, an individual wishing to seize an international jurisdiction through its government must have exhausted local remedies.

The first condition contradicting the *Mavrommatis* premise is that of nationality. This condition requires that the injured individual be a national of the state that will take up its claim at the ICJ. It was traditionally perceived as not only the link in the form of rights and obligations between an individual and his or her state but also the key for individuals to benefit from rights on the then state-exclusive international plane.[54] Article 3 of the ILC Draft Articles on Diplomatic Protection reads, 'The State entitled to exercise diplomatic protection is the state of nationality'.[55] The PCIJ defined the bond of nationality between the injured individual and the government as a prerequisite to the exercise of diplomatic protection in the *Panevezys-Saldutiskis Railway* case.[56]

The condition of nationality for the exercise of diplomatic protection stands in clear contradiction to the *Mavrommatis* fiction. If the practice of diplomatic protection is about the state's right 'in reality' and its injury, then why does it hinge upon the requirement of the individual's nationality? This requirement is linked to the identity of the individual who has seized the state, placing the the latter centre stage and thus weakening the fiction. The fact that the individual must be a national of that state continuously from the date of injury to the date of the official presentation of the claim is further evidence of this.[57] Without this

[54] Malcolm N. Shaw, *International Law* (9th edn, CUP 2021) Chapter 5 (Individuals); Jean Colette, *Les principes de droit des gens dans la jurisprudence de la Cour Permanente de Justice Internationale* (Berger-Levrault 1932) 43–47.

[55] Draft Articles on Diplomatic Protection (n. 41) Article 3.

[56] *Panevezys-Saldutiskis Railway* (n. 18) 16.

[57] Draft Articles on Diplomatic Protection (n. 41) Article 5(1).

requirement, the diplomatic protection case cannot be pursued in international adjudication.

The second condition of diplomatic protection contradicting the *Mavrommatis* doctrine is the exhaustion of local remedies. This cardinal condition requires, in the words of the ICJ, that 'the State where the violation occurred should have an opportunity to redress it by its own means, within the framework of its own domestic system'.[58] In other words, the individual should have sought to resolve the issue on the domestic plane before taking it to an international court. As well as being featured in international conventions[59] and codified by the ILC in both its Articles on State Responsibility[60] and on Diplomatic Protection,[61] the exhaustion of local remedies criterion has been consistently characterised as customary practice by the PCIJ and the ICJ.[62] The condition of the exhaustion of local remedies is one of the most evident examples of inconsistency with the *Mavrommatis* fiction that the state is asserting its own right. If this were so, then it is unclear why the individual must have exhausted local remedies first, in order for the state's claim to be admissible.[63] This condition underlines the central position of the individual in diplomatic protection.[64]

2.1.3 The Two Features of Diplomatic Protection: State Discretion and State Responsibility

The contradictions of the *Mavrommatis* fiction (Section 2.1.1), and the conditions of diplomatic protection (Section 2.1.2) point towards the key role of the individual in this context. This is further evidenced by two further features of diplomatic protection: the discretionary right of the

[58] *Interhandel* (n. 21) 27.

[59] For example: European Convention on Human Rights, 213 UNTS 221, Article 46; American Convention on Human Rights, 1144 UNTS 123, Article 35; Optional Protocol I, International Covenant on Civil and Political Rights, 999 UNTS 171, Article 5.

[60] Draft Articles on Responsibility of States for Internationally Wrongful Acts with commentaries [2001] *Yearbook of the ILC*, vol II, Part Two, Article 44.

[61] Draft Articles on Diplomatic Protection (n. 41) Article 14.

[62] *Panevezys-Saldutiskis Railway* (n. 18) 18–21; *Interhandel* (n. 21) 27; *United States of America v. Italy* (n. 21) 42; *United Kingdom v. Iran* (n. 21) 101 [10]; *Ambatielos case* (n. 21) 13–14 [4]–[6]; *Diallo* (n. 21) 654–59 [32]–[49].

[63] Pergantis (n. 5) 375.

[64] Antônio Cançado Trindade, *The Application of the Rule of Exhaustion of Local Remedies in International Law: Its Rationale in the International Protection of Individual Right* (CUP 1983).

state to take up the individual's matter and the due reparations under state responsibility. Both features have been challenged by an increasing human rights discourse, which serves to place more emphasis on the individual's key role in the practice of diplomatic protection. They will be examined in turn.

The first feature is state discretion. The state has the discretion to decide whether to take up the individual's case, as confirmed by the PCIJ when it stated, 'It is an elementary principle of international law that a state is entitled to protect its subjects, when injured by acts contrary to international law committed by another State'.[65] Indeed, governments have the right to protect their citizens but are not obliged to under international law. In other words, as confirmed by the Court in *Barcelona Traction*, *LaGrand* and the ILC in its Draft Articles on Diplomatic Protection, individuals are not entitled to diplomatic protection as a matter of right.[66]

This discretionary right has been perceived to stand starkly in contrast with a state's international treaty obligations to defend its nationals' human rights. It has been claimed that diplomatic protection is a legal or moral duty of the state.[67] Indeed, the Sixth Committee of the United Nations General Assembly had noted that some states enshrined in their domestic legislation that the state does indeed have an *obligation* to protect its nationals abroad: some phrased their legislation to state that the individual has a *right* to receive diplomatic protection or *is entitled* to this protection, and others *guaranteed* this protection or established that the government has a *duty*.[68] It has also been argued that a discretionary decision of the government may be reviewed by the national judiciary, which puts significant pressure on governments to respect human rights when confronted with a request for diplomatic protection.[69] It was even

65 *Mavrommatis Palestine Concessions* (n. 18) 12.

66 *Barcelona Traction Light and Power Company Ltd. (Belgium v. Spain)* (Second Phase) (Preliminary Objections) (Judgment) [1970] ICJ Rep 3, 44 [78]–[79]; *LaGrand* (n. 21) 492 [74]; Draft Articles on Diplomatic Protection with Commentaries (n. 6) 29, commentary to Article 2.

67 Edwin Montefiore Borchard, *The Diplomatic Protection of Citizens Abroad or the Law of International Claims* (The Banks Law Publishing Co. 1915) 29. See also A/CN.4/484 [48].

68 A/CN.4/506, 224.

69 Vermeer-Künzli (n. 5) 182; Francisco Orrego Vicuña, 'Changing Approaches to the Nationality of Claims in the Context of Diplomatic Protection and International Dispute Settlement' (2000) 15(2) *ICSID Review – Foreign Investment Law Journal* 340, 346.

proposed by former ILC Special Rapporteur John Dugard that the state's discretionary right in diplomatic protection should be limited where *jus cogens* norms have been violated.[70]

Although rejected by the ICJ in *Barcelona Traction*[71] and by the ILC,[72] the latter's Draft Article 19 reads that states should give due consideration to the possibility of exercising diplomatic protection when *a significant injury* has occurred.[73] The commentary further specifics that 'the protection of human beings by means of international law is today one of the principal goals of the international legal order',[74] and the commentary to Article 2 specifies that 'the discretionary right of a State to exercise diplomatic protection should therefore be read with Draft Article 19 which recommends to states that they should exercise that right in appropriate cases'.[75] Overall, there is a marked tension with respect to state discretion, which has been challenged by human rights claims.

The second feature of diplomatic protection that has been subject to attempts of humanisation is the practice of reparations in the context of state responsibility. Under the laws of state responsibility, the state in breach of an international legal obligation is required to make reparation.[76] The regime of state responsibility rests on traditional inter-state interactions, with the PCIJ describing it as established 'immediately as between the two States'.[77] The relationship between diplomatic protection and state responsibility reinforced the idea that the injury to the individual (as a national) is an injury to the state itself, and thus, the state of nationality is seizing the Court on its *own* behalf.

However, two elements of reparations have been challenged in the diplomatic protection context: the calculation of damages and the question of the recipient of compensation. Regarding the calculation of damages, there is now an accepted practice in the Court's jurisprudence and in customary international law of calculating damages on the basis of the injury suffered

70 A/CN.4/506 and Add. 1, Article 4.
71 *Barcelona Traction* (n. 66) 44 [78].
72 A/55/10, 157–58.
73 Draft Articles on Diplomatic Protection (n. 41) Article 19 (emphasis added).
74 Draft Articles on Diplomatic Protection with Commentaries (n. 6) 95 [2], commentary to Article 19.
75 Ibid 30 [3], commentary to Article 2.
76 *Factory at Chorzów* (Jurisdiction) (Judgment) [1927] PCIJ Series A, 21.
77 *Phosphates in Morocco* (n. 19) 28. See also *S.S. "Wimbledon"* (Judgment) [1923] PCIJ Series A, 30; *Factory at Chorzów* (n. 76) 21; *Factory at Chorzów* (n. 19) 29.

by the individual.[78] This again emphasises the central role of the individual in diplomatic protection, contrary to the *Mavrommatis* fiction.

The second development in favour of the individual in state responsibility is the question of the recipient of the compensation. The traditional rule confirmed by the ICJ in *Diallo* and the ILC is that the state itself will receive the compensation.[79] This supports the *Mavrommatis* fiction. This, however, has been challenged by Article 19(c) of the Draft Articles on Diplomatic Protection, which recommends that states 'transfer to the injured person any compensation obtained for the injury from the responsible state subject to any reasonable deductions'.[80] While the ILC admitted that it does not constitute a settled practice, 'public policy, equity and respect for human rights support the curtailment of the state's discretion in the disbursement of compensation'.[81] The heated debates within the ILC during the drafting of the 2006 Draft Articles on Diplomatic Protection, reflecting antagonism between traditional and modern approaches, serves as evidence of the evolving nature of this practice and the erosion of the fiction that held it together.[82]

Compensation to the individual has also been challenged by the Court, who stated in *Diallo* that 'the sum awarded to Guinea in the exercise of diplomatic protection of Mr. Diallo is intended to provide reparation for the latter's injury'.[83] Judge Abdulqawi Yusuf has questioned whether this statement was enough, contemplating that the Court could have gone further and explicitly stated that reparations accrue to individuals in case of injury to their rights.[84] This challenged premise supports once again the natural movement away from the *Mavrommatis* fiction and the emergent position of the individual in the practice of diplomatic protection.

78 *Factory at Chorzów* (n. 19) 28; *Barcelona Traction* (n. 66) 222–23 [3] (Separate opinion of Judge Morelli); *Diallo* (n. 52) 331 [11].

79 *Diallo* (n. 21) 691 [161]; Draft Articles on Diplomatic Protection with Commentaries (n. 6) 97.

80 Draft Articles on Diplomatic Protection with Commentaries (n. 6) commentary to Article 19(c). See also Article 33(2) of the ILC Draft Articles on State Responsibility.

81 Ibid (Draft Articles on Diplomatic Protection) [8], commentary to Article 19.

82 Vermeer-Künzli (n. 5) 55–57.

83 *Diallo* (n. 21) 691 [161]; *Diallo* (n. 52) 344 [57] (emphasis added).

84 Judge Abdulqawi Yusuf, 'Keynote Address' ("70 Years of the International Law Commission: Drawing a Balance for the Future" Conference, Geneva, 5 July 2018) 9 [36]. Statement available at: http://legal.un.org/ilc/sessions/70/pdfs/english/key_note_address_5july2018.pdf. See also Giorgio Gaja, 'The Position of Individuals in International Law: An ILC Perspective' (2010) 21(1) *European Journal of International Law* 11, 12–14.

2.2 Procedural *status quo* of Individual Participation

The traditional concept of the *Mavrommatis* fiction examined here concretely manifests itself in the Peace Palace whenever a case of diplomatic protection comes before the Court. Indeed, the state has taken up the case for its subject and thus conducts the case alone before it, as the 'sole claimant'. There is therefore a clear answer to Mr. Lapradelle's question from 1920 evoked in the opening of this chapter: the state does not authorise the individual to plead his or her own case at the ICJ. This would contradict the very essence of the *Mavrommatis* formula: that only the state may be seen. In the words of one commentator, 'I]l semble que ce soit par son absence, plutôt que par sa présence, que l'individu se distingue'.[85]

Yet, in light of the above analysis (Section 2.1), the procedural role of the state before a court could benefit from re-evaluation. The state is, in reality, mainly acting as an agent or representative for the individual's case, in response to the latter's injury and in defence of the latter's rights.[86] As one author has put it, '[L]'état ne ferait qu'exercer un droit procédural ou dit secondaire, compte tenu du fait qu'aucune violation de ses droits substantiels n'a eu lieu'.[87] The idea of the state as the individual's representative in diplomatic protection cases is not new. It has been confirmed in a number of past arbitral awards,[88] such as *William A. Parker (US) v. Mexico* (1926),[89] *Affaire Junghans* (1939),[90] and the *Grant-Smith Case (the Gin and Angostura)* (1952). In the latter case, the

[85] Bérénice Kafui Schramm, *La fiction juridique et le juge: Contribution à une autre herméneutique de la Cour internationale de justice* (Bruylant 2018) 152. Author's translation: It seems that it is by their absence, rather than their presence, that the individual distinguishes themselves.

[86] Alain Pellet, 'La seconde mort d'Euripide Mavrommatis? Notes sur le projet de la C.D.I sur la protection diplomatique' in Nicolas Angelet (ed), *Droit du pouvoir, pouvoir du droit: Mélanges offerts à Jean Salmon* (Bruylant 2007); August Von der Heydte, 'L'individu et les tribunaux internationaux' in *Collected Courses of the Hague Academy of International Law*, vol 107 (Brill 1962) 325–26.

[87] Schramm (n. 85) 159. Author's translation: The state would only be exercising a procedural or so-called secondary right, given that no violation of its substantive rights has occurred.

[88] Carlo Santulli, 'Entre protection diplomatique et action directe: La représentation (Éléments épars du statut international des sujets internes)' in *Le sujet en droit international* (Pedone 2005) 90–93.

[89] *William A. Parker (USA) v. United Mexican States* (1926) (Award) IV RIAA 35, 37 [2]. See also *North American Dredging Company of Texas (USA) v. United Mexican States* (1926) (Award) IV RIAA 26, 32 [19].

[90] *Affaire Junghans (deuxième partie) (Allemagne/Roumanie)* (1940) (Award) III RIAA 1883, 1888.

arbitral tribunal described the defending government of the injured national as 'only taking a part in the international dispute as the representative *ad litem* of its national'.[91] This seems to best describe what occurs at the Peace Palace in diplomatic protection proceedings. A clear acknowledgement of this would be an evolution from the practice that *Mavrommatis* sought to establish, where states act in substitution of individuals, the latter seen as mere commodities.[92]

As it stands, however, the procedural participation of the individual has been limited to providing documentary evidence or written testimony in the form of affidavits in the state's written pleadings. There is therefore an undeniable dichotomy between the legal nature of diplomatic protection and its procedural implications for the state, on the one hand (Section 2.1), and the procedural practice of diplomatic protection, on the other hand.

First, the individual has often collaborated with the protecting state to provide documentary evidence,[93] such as annexes to one of the written pleadings,[94] additional documents (produced after the delivery of a pleading but prior to the closure of the written stage of proceedings), supplemental documents (filed at any moment under authorisation of the Court), or new documents (produced after the closure of the written stage, under the special procedure governed by Article 56 of the Rules and Practice Direction IX).

For example, under the PCIJ, Oscar Chinn provided the UK government with instrumental documents to make its case in a dispute named after him.[95] Before the ICJ, Greek shipowner Nicolas Ambatielos provided the state of Greece with documents in *Ambatielos (Greece v. United Kingdom).*[96] The *Diallo* case indicated that an absence of such documentation by the individual could be detrimental to the outcome of the case. In that case, Guinea was representing Guinean businessman Ahmadou Sadio Diallo against the Democratic Republic of Congo (DRC), accusing the DRC of violating Diallo's human rights. Yet, Guinea was only compensated with a sum of 95,000 US dollars; 85,000 US dollars for non-material

91 *Grant-Smith Case (the Gin and Angostura) (United Kingdom/Italy)* (1952) (Award) XIV RIAA 13, 17 [3].
92 Schramm (n. 85) 157.
93 International Court of Justice, Rules of Court, Article 50.
94 Statute of the International Court of Justice, Article 43(1).
95 *Oscar Chinn* (n. 18) 151–52.
96 Memorial submitted on behalf of the Hellenic Government (30 August 1951) Annex A, 26; Annex B, 28; Annex C, 31; Annex D, 31; Annex F, 33; Annex H, 42; Annex J, 45.

injury and 10,000 US dollars for material injury, in staggering contrast to the astronomical amount that Guinea had originally claimed: over 35 billion US dollars (reduced to 12 million dollars in the compensation phase) and 15 billion ZRZ (Zairean zaire).[97] The main reason for this is that Guinea was unable to provide any evidence for its claims in the compensation phase, with the Court noting this stood in 'stark contrast' to evidence brought by Guinea at an earlier stage of the case.[98] While many reasons could explain this – such as the change of legal representation in the compensation phase or a lack of resources to collect the necessary evidence – it is possible that Mr. Diallo did not cooperate in providing the necessary documentary evidence beyond what the Court already had. While unsatisfactory as a form of participation, such cooperation is significant and may have led to higher compensation to the Guinean government. This example demonstrates how the individual's participation can contribute to the Court's technocratic expertise, thereby upholding its procedural legitimacy (Section I.1.2).

The second form of procedural participation of the individual in diplomatic protection proceedings is providing affidavits as valuable annexes in the protecting state's memorial (written pleadings). This was seen in the *Avena (Mexico v. United States of America)* case where Mexico had the burden of proof to prove that individuals were Mexican and not American. It met this, *inter alia*,[99] by providing forty-two declarations – in the form of affidavits – confirming that they had not acquired US nationality.[100] Some of these individuals were still claimed by the US to be US citizens – the Court therefore asked the United States to provide evidence for its claim, but it could not.[101] The Court stated that the United States could have obtained this information from Mexico, but in the absence of this, it had failed to meet its own burden of proof.[102] The Court had also been provided with declarations from a number of the Mexican nationals concerned who attested to their never having been informed of their rights under Article 36(1)(b) of the VCCR.[103] *Avena*

[97] *Diallo* (n. 52) 344–46 [61].
[98] Ibid 340 [41].
[99] *Avena* (n. 21) [55].
[100] Ibid.
[101] Ibid [56].
[102] Ibid [57].
[103] Ibid [76]. Mexico referred to these statements from its nationals countless times in its memorial. See Memorial of Mexico (20 June 2003) fns 9, 11, 17, 21, 23, 26, 35–37, 39, 45, 47–48, 51, 54, 57, 65, 67–68, 73, 75, 80, 82, 86, 88, 90–92, 95, 97, 100–3, 107, 110, 112, 115, 118–19, 121, 150, 154, 158, 160, 162, 166–67.

provides us with an example in which the individual played a strong indirect role in the litigation. To borrow from one commentator, 'As reflected in Mexico's inclusion in its submissions to the Court in the *Avena* case of information collected from the affected individuals, there are concrete possibilities to involve the individual rights-holders in the proceedings of the Court'.[104]

To conclude this section, the aforementioned cases illustrate the modest procedural prerogatives of injured individuals in the practice of diplomatic protection cases: they do no more than to provide documentary evidence or affidavits where required. This must be considered against the backdrop of the development of diplomatic protection in the Court's jurisprudence. There appears to be a disproportionate contrast between diplomatic protection in theory and in practice. Diplomatic protection in theory (Section 2.1), placing the individual at the centre of the practice, and diplomatic protection in practice (Section 2.2), where the individual is virtually excluded from a case that is essentially his or her own. Is it possible to bridge the gap?

2.3 'Bridging the Gap': Means to Procedurally Integrate the Injured Individual in Diplomatic Protection Proceedings

The final section of this chapter is dedicated to a discussion on how the individual may be further procedurally integrated in diplomatic protection cases at the Court. When Mr. de Lapradelle advocated that individuals wished to take part themselves in the proceedings,[105] which form could he have envisaged this participation taking?

The existence of an individual's substantive right has not always equated to a procedural prerogative to defend that right as a party in the international legal system.[106] It was also established in Chapter 1 that *locus standi* of the individual before the Court was not a reasonable option. Nonetheless, two conceivable solutions within the constraints of the Statute and the Rules of the Court come to mind.

The first is the government protecting the concerned individual to allow him or her to make a statement as part of the government's

[104] Martin Scheinin, 'The ICJ and the Individual' (2007) 9(2) *International Community Law Review* 123, 137.

[105] *Procès-verbaux* (n. 2) 211.

[106] Schramm (n. 85) 158; Maximilian Koessler, 'Government Espousal of Private Claims before International Tribunals' (1946) 13(2) *University of Chicago Law Review* 180, 189.

delegation during its speaking time in oral proceedings. This was excellently executed in the *Legal Consequences of the Separation of the Chagos Archipelago from Mauritius in 1965* advisory proceedings of September 2018. While these were advisory proceedings (see Chapter 3), this measure may also be carried out in contentious proceedings, including (but not limited to) diplomatic protection cases. The Chagossians, whose rights to self-determination were at the heart of the *Chagos* advisory opinion, not only contributed to the written pleadings of the government of Mauritius[107] but were also physically present at the Peace Palace and participated in the oral pleadings within the speaking time of the delegation of Mauritius. According to Mauritius, 'We think it is appropriate that the Court should hear the voice of the Chagossians directly'.[108] A group of Chagossians thus attended the oral hearings as representatives of the Chagossian community.[109] One of them, Ms. Marie Liseby Elysé, made a statement during the speaking time of the government of Mauritius via video.[110] One of the counsels specified that '[t]he words of Madame Elysé, who sits in this Courtroom, are not offered as testimonial evidence, but simply as a member of the delegation of Mauritius – if you like – a statement of impact, what the continuation of colonialism really means for real people'.[111] The same practice was exercised in the reparation phase of *Armed Activities on the Territory of the Congo (Democratic Republic of the Congo v. Uganda)*, where a video testimony from numerous victims of atrocities committed by the Ugandan army was displayed.[112]

Another solution within the constraints of the Statute and the Rules of the Court is the participation of the injured individual in oral proceedings as a witness. The *Diallo* case indicated that hearing directly from the witness may be valuable to the case – a report of Mr. Diallo's private hearing in October 2008 in the presence of Mr. Boubacar Télimélé Sylla and Mr. Aboubacar Camara was annexed to the Reply of the Republic of

[107] Written Comments of Mauritius (15 May 2018), [4.114].
[108] Verbatim record 2018/20, 71–72 [4] (Philippe Sands).
[109] Ibid 6 (Ms. Marie Suzelle Baptiste, Mr. Roger Alexis, Ms. Marie Nella Gaspard, Ms. Marie Mimose Furcy, Ms. Marie Janine Sadrien, Ms. Rosemonde Berthin, Marie Liseby Elysé).
[110] Ibid 72 [4] (Philippe Sands).
[111] Ibid.
[112] Response of the Democratic Republic of the Congo to the questions put by the Court (26 October 2018) [1.12]; Annex 1.11.

Guinea of 19 November 2008.[113] The report of his hearing was referred to in Guinea's 2008 Reply 12 times.[114] In its compensation judgment, the Court references a statement made by Mr. Diallo during this hearing.[115]

In certain diplomatic protection cases, the individual's participation would be impossible due to death (seen, for example, in *Vienna Convention on Consular Relations* and *LaGrand*), or challenging due to the individual's status on death row (seen in *Avena*)[116] or detention (seen in *Tehran Hostages*[117] or *Jadhav*[118]). While playing a video in oral hearings might circumvent the latter challenges, the ICJ denied permission to Pakistan to play a confessional video of Kulbhushan Sudhir Jadhav during the oral hearings in the provisional measures phase of *Jadhav (India v. Pakistan)*.[119] However, there may still be added value to an individual's oral testimony in terms of democratic participation and/or technocratic expertise.

A key example of such added value can be seen in *Application of the Convention of 1902 Governing the Guardianship of Infants (Netherlands v. Sweden)*. Although not formally brought to the Court under the header of diplomatic protection, the Netherlands sued Sweden for allegedly violating the 1902 Convention on the guardianship of infants by placing a Dutch child living in Sweden under a Swedish regime of protecting upbringing. Despite the Court's warning that it would not address "the proper appreciation of the grounds on which the challenged decisions are based",[120] the child's testimony could have provided insight into whether her treatment violated the Convention. Leading ICJ scholar Shabtai Rosenne opines that nothing in the pleadings indicated that the child was incapable of participating and stressed the importance of her preferences and welfare being considered in such

[113] Reply of the Republic of Guinea (19 November 2008) Annex 2.

[114] Ibid 8, 12, 13, 16, 17, 18, 44, 47, 54, 61, 63, 65, 66.

[115] *Diallo* (n. 52) 337 [31].

[116] Memorial of Mexico (20 June 2003) 1 [2].

[117] The USA explains in its Memorial that it was not even certain how many hostages there were; see Memorial of the Government of the United States of America (12 January 1980) 24, Part I, Letter C, and 133, Part II, Letter E.

[118] *Jadhav (India v. Pakistan)* (Provisional Measures) (Order of 18 May 2017) [2017] ICJ Rep 231.

[119] Verbatim record 2017/6, 10 [13] (Mohammad Faisal).

[120] *Case Concerning the Application of the Convention of 1902 Governing the Guardianship of Infants (Netherlands v. Sweden)* (Judgment) [1958] ICJ Rep 55, 63.

a case.[121] In other words, standards of democracy demanded that the child partake in proceedings.

Other similar examples formally brought to the Court under the header of diplomatic protection can also be identified: *Nottebohm (Liechtenstein v. Guatemala)*, *Vienna Convention on Consular Relations (Paraguay v. United States of America)*, and *Ahmadou Sadio Diallo (Republic of Guinea v. Democratic Republic of the Congo)*.

The first diplomatic protection case in which the participation of the injured individual as a witness would have been valuable was the *Nottebohm* case. Friedrich Nottebohm, a German national, was born in Germany in 1881 and moved to Guatemala in 1905, at the age of 24, where he resided and set up a business. In 1939, at the age of 58, he applied for naturalisation in Liechtenstein, where he had gone a few times to visit his brother who resided there. After having received Liechtenstein nationality in 1940, he went back to Guatemala to continue business until he was expelled as a result of war measures in 1943, at the age of 62. In 1946, he moved to Liechtenstein, and in 1951, he filed a claim at the ICJ against Guatemala through the government of Liechtenstein. One of Guatemala's two preliminary objections related to Friedrich Nottebohm's nationality: could it be relied upon to justify diplomatic protection before the Court? The Court defined nationality as 'a legal bond having as its basis a social fact of attachment, a genuine connection of existence, interests and sentiments, together with the existence of reciprocal rights and duties. (. . .) The individual upon whom nationality is conferred is in fact more closely connected with the population of the state conferring nationality than with that of any other state'.[122] It ultimately concluded that this was not the case between Mr. Nottebohm and Liechtenstein and therefore judged Liechtenstein's claim as inadmissible.[123]

The difficulty comes with the assumptions made about the motives behind Mr. Nottebohm's decision to acquire Liechtensteinian nationality. The legal reasoning in this judgment is based on psychological motives that the Court did not objectively prove in at least two instances. First, the Court stated that 'there is nothing to indicate that the application for

[121] Shabtai Rosenne, 'Reflections on the Position of the Individual in Inter-state Litigation in the International Court of Justice' in Pieter Sanders (ed), *International Arbitration Liber Amicorum for Martin Domke* (Springer 1967) 240–51, 114.

[122] *Liechtenstein v. Guatemala* (n. 21) 23.

[123] Ibid 26.

naturalisation then made by Nottebohm was motivated by any desire to dissociate himself from the Government of his country [Germany]'.[124] Judge John Read in his dissenting opinion disagrees, 'I am unable to agree that there is nothing to indicate that Mr. Nottebohm's naturalisation was motivated by a desire to break his ties with Germany. There are three facts which prove that he was determined to break his ties with Germany. The first is the fact of his application for naturalisation, the second is the taking of his oath of allegiance to Liechtenstein, and the third is his obtaining a certificate of naturalisation and a Liechtenstein passport'.[125] This is a motive that is difficult to assert without further inquiry to Mr. Nottebohm himself.

A second instance where Mr. Nottebohm's psychological motives were not objectively proven is where the Court assumed that he had no intention of residing in Liechtenstein. This was based on the fact that he moved back to Guatemala after having been naturalised in Liechtenstein and only left Guatemala because he was expelled. Although at face value, one may rapidly conclude that he had no intention to live in Liechtenstein, this is difficult to assert with confidence without inquiring the person in question. In line with this reasoning, Judge Read states, 'To begin with, Mr. Nottebohm was 58 years of age at the time-or within two years of the normal retirement age in the type of business activity in which he was engaged. The evidence shows that he was actually contemplating retirement. In October 1939 he was largely occupied with plans to save the business, but I find it hard to believe that he was not also thinking in terms of retirement and that Vaduz was in his mind'.[126] Judge Read also provides another reason as to why Mr. Nottebohm might have moved back to Guatemala: to clear his name and confront the multiple lawsuits open against him.[127] Again, these assumptions are difficult to sustain without interrogating Mr. Nottebohm.

I find myself in agreement with the dissenting opinions arguing that the Court should have stuck to an objective approach laid down by international law, as the subjective elements are difficult to prove without questioning the individual in focus. Judge *ad hoc* Paul Guggenheim, for instance, dissented that, 'In order to judge as to the bond between the State and its national, that is to say, in order to ascertain whether this bond is

[124] Ibid 25.
[125] Ibid 43 (Dissenting opinion of Judge Read).
[126] Ibid 45 (Dissenting opinion of Judge Read).
[127] Ibid.

real and effective and not merely fictitious, international law only has regard to the external elements of legal facts to which it attaches certain consequences, without concerning itself with the mental attitude of the legal person responsible for a juridical act such as the act of naturalisation, and without considering the motives (which it is very difficult to determine), which have led the individual to apply for naturalisation'.[128] Judge Read made the same comment in his dissenting opinion.[129] Judge *ad hoc* Guggenheim added that it was sought to substitute legal considerations with 'subjective considerations such as the "genuineness of the application", "loyalty to the new State", "creation of a centre of economic interests in the new State", "the intention to become integrated in the national community"; or, again, rules (. . .) which are in no way in accordance with present international practice, or vague principles (. . .) which would open the door to arbitrary decisions'.[130]

Ideally, however, Mr. Nottebohm's motives could have been more credibly clarified with his participation in oral proceedings in the form of a witness, questioned by the judges and counsel. This would have demonstrated the Court's technocratic expertise – its specialised understanding of the complex facts at hand and its efforts to address them carefully. The impact would have enhanced the Court's procedural legitimacy in this instance. Rosenne supported this view, arguing that '[t]his case required some – indeed considerable – investigation not merely of the actions of the individual concerned, but more significantly of his motives, that is of psychological factors to necessarily present in the record. . .'[131] There are indications that this may have indeed occured: although this is not evidenced by archives, the Court mentioned that 'other members of his family have asserted Nottebohm's desire to spend his old age in Guatemala',[132] and Rosenne observed that 'the ICJ accurately evaluated those actions and motives so that no practical injustice issues from the fact that in this case the individual was not able to present himself before the Court'.[133]

The second case in which the participation of the relevant individual as a witness would have been valuable is *Vienna Convention on Consular*

[128] Ibid 52–53 (Dissenting opinion of Judge *ad hoc* Guggenheim).
[129] Ibid 42 (Dissenting opinion of Judge Read).
[130] Ibid 55–56 (Dissenting opinion of Judge *ad hoc* Guggenheim).
[131] Rosenne (n. 122) 113–14.
[132] *Liechtenstein v. Guatemala* (n. 21) 26.
[133] Rosenne (n. 122) 114.

Relations (Paraguay v. United States of America). In a separate document that Paraguay filed along with its Memorial on the merits, entitled 'Conditional request of Paraguay for an order Conclusively established facts' (9 October 1998), Paraguay argued that the United States's disregard for the Court's provisional measures order cost Paraguay its 'principal source of evidence (. . .) Mr. Breard himself', causing it to suffer 'evidentiary prejudice'.[134] This was reiterated in Paraguay's Memorial as well.[135] Through this 'Conditional request', Paraguay appealed to the Court to declare that any disputed issues of fact that are material to Paraguay's claims as to which Mr. Breard's testimony would have been relevant, be established in Paraguay's favour.[136] More significantly, Paraguay claimed reparation from the United States, requesting the Court to issue an order protecting Paraguay from evidentiary prejudice suffered from the absence of Mr. Breard's testimony.[137] As the proceedings were discontinued, the Court was not able to act on this request. However, it demonstrates the importance of the injured individual's participation and testimony in cases that directly concern him or her. Beard's participation would have allowed Paraguay to provide more accurate information to better address the legal matters under consideration and thereby evidence the Court's legitimacy through its technocratic expertise.

The third diplomatic protection case whereby the injured individual's participation in proceedings as a witness would have been desirable is the *Ahmadou Sadio Diallo (Republic of Guinea v. Democratic Republic of the Congo)* case. As aforementioned (Section 2.1.3), very little compensation was received in the compensation phase due to a lack of evidence concerning the material injury incurred by the victim. Although the Republic of Guinea advocated that 'Mr. Diallo suffered moral and mental harm, including emotional pain, suffering and shock, as well as the loss of his position in society and injury to his reputation as a result of his arrests, detentions and expulsion by the DRC',[138] the Court noted that no evidence for this had been provided by the Applicant.[139] It therefore resorted to 'equitable considerations' to make its decision on Mr. Diallo's

[134] Conditional request of Paraguay for an order conclusively established facts (9 October 1998) [1] and [6].
[135] Memorial of the Republic of Paraguay (9 October 1998) [4.29].
[136] Conditional request of Paraguay (n. 134) [3].
[137] Ibid [6] and [14].
[138] *Diallo* (n. 52) 333 [18].
[139] Ibid [19].

non-material injury, without the need for proof. Many human rights courts take this approach (as many forms of non-pecuniary damage are, by their nature, not amenable to proof).[140] Therefore, Mr. Diallo's testimony would not have impacted the Court's determination of his non-material injury. However, in the merits phase, testimony from Mr. Diallo under the procedural guise of a witness may have been useful in the ascertainment of certain facts with regard to the violations of his human rights. Greater accuracy would have underscored the Court's technocratic expertise in this respect and, therefore, the procedural legitimacy in this dispute. While Rosenne suggested that in some instances, the presence of a concerned individual may be redundant,[141] an appearance in person would have allowed him to clarify certain potentially abstruse elements in the written pleadings, allowed him to provide his version of events, allowed counsel to cross-examine him for truthfulness, and allowed for judges to ask him questions. Furthermore, the idea of a case surrounding an individual to be decided in his or her absence is somewhat disquieting, harming democratic standards of procedural legitimacy supported by social idealism.

2.4 Conclusion

Professor Rosenne has accurately written as follows:

> In [a diplomatic protection case] the individual concerned, whatever may have been his actions, his conceptions, his expectations, or his intentions in regard to the transaction under discussion apparently is not granted any opportunity to make known to the Court, in his own way, his own views on the questions of fact and the questions of law involved. In all of these respects, it is entirely a matter for the government which has espoused his claim to decide whether or not, or to what extent, it will include its own presentation of its own case (which may or may not be the same as that of the individual) argument presented to it by the individual. The government is the *dominus litis*, and in most cases in fact also.[142]

Diplomatic protection cases are *prima facie* inter-state cases like any other at the World Court. But a closer look demonstrates that they are,

[140] See, for example, from the European Court of Human Rights: *Peck v. United Kingdom* App no 44647/98 (ECHR, 28 January 2013) [118]; *Gridin v. Russia* App no 4171/04 (ECHR, 1 June 2006) [20]; *Firstov v. Russia* App no 42119/04 (ECHR, 20 February 2014) [49].

[141] Rosenne (n. 122) 115.

[142] Ibid 112.

in fact, disguised disputes between an individual and a foreign state. Indeed, the individual is no longer invisible on the international plane – they have recognised rights and injuries and must fulfil certain conditions in order for the Court to take up the case, through the façade of their government. This reality is coupled with an increasing humanisation of the practice of diplomatic protection in state practice and doctrine and at the Court itself. Scholarship has gone as far as saying that the *Mavrommatis* fiction has not only been undermined as a result of these developments but has also ceased to exist all together.[143] However, this state of affairs strongly contrasts with the absence of procedural prerogatives granted to the injured individual, who solely cooperates with the state to provide documentary evidence or, at the most, a written testimony in the form of an affidavit, attached to the government's written pleadings.

This contrast compromises the Court's procedural legitimacy in at least two ways. First, standards of democracy used to measure legitimacy are not met where injured individuals are absent in proceedings where they are directly impacted. Second, technocratic expertise is compromised where the individual's enhanced participation may have allowed for more evidence that could have facilitated the Court's tasks.

This dichotomic gap could be bridged by state litigants making space for injured individuals to make statements in their delegation or as witnesses, where feasible and relevant. Indeed, governments should consider the importance of inclusion in an increasingly interconnected international legal order with a number of actors beyond the state.

[143] Schramm (n. 85) 167; Pellet (n. 86) 1359; Pellet (n. 34).

3

Advisory Proceedings

> I believe that attenuation of participation is unwise as a political strategy and ill-considered as a technique for increasing the rationality of judicial decision.[1]

Conforming to its role as the principal judicial organ of the United Nations,[2] the International Court of Justice (ICJ, the Court) is competent not only to resolve conflicts between states but also to provide its opinion on any legal questions from authorised United Nations (UN) organs and specialised agencies – not from states and much less from individuals.

In this chapter, I observe that individuals are no more procedurally integrated in advisory proceedings than they are in the contentious cases examined in other chapters of this book. One would imagine that in advisory proceedings where the dichotomy of 'parties versus non-parties' is absent and everybody – governments and non-state actors alike – is technically a 'non-party', that individuals may play a more prominent role. I observe in this chapter that this is not the case.

The Court's *ratione personae* jurisdiction in the advisory realm excludes states, although it has been subject to debate in the past. The rationale for excluding both states and individuals remains the same. Under the League of Nations, Article 14 of the League Covenant authorised the Permanent Court of International Justice (PCIJ, Permanent Court) to 'give an advisory opinion upon any dispute or question referred to it by the Council or the Assembly'.[3] Following the Second World War, however, the Informal Inter-Allied Committee wished to expand this to 'all international associations of an inter-State or inter-

[1] Michael Reisman, 'Accelerating Advisory Opinions: Critique and Proposal' (1974) 68(4) *The American Journal of International Law* 648, 668–69, fn. 89.

[2] Charter of the United Nations, 1 UNTS XVI, Article 92 [hereafter United Nations Charter].

[3] Juan José Quintana Aranguren, *Litigation at the International Court of Justice: Practice and Procedure* (Brill/Nijhoff 2015) 1227.

governmental character possessing the necessary status',[4] and even to 'any two or more States acting in concert' upon certain conditions.[5] The 1944 Dumbarton Oaks Conference, on the other hand, adopted proposals to restrict the capacity to request advisory opinions to the Security Council alone.[6] Later, the Washington Committee of Jurists struck a balance between these two extremes, by extending jurisdiction to the UN General Assembly[7] and specialised agencies within the context of the General Assembly's powers.[8] As for the proposal to allow states to request advisory opinions, this was rejected to avoid the Court becoming 'overloaded with individual applications, thus detracting from the Court's more important duties'.[9] The same concern holds true for the inclusion of individuals.

Despite this, advisory opinions have often and increasingly been requested for matters directly related to individuals. Requests in the form of abstract legal questions have been filed for matters of public interest related to the wellbeing of individuals – such as the legality of nuclear weapons or climate change obligations of states.[10] Such questions have also concerned human rights obligations of direct application to individuals, as seen in the *Reservations to the Genocide Convention* (1951) advisory opinion.[11] The Court has also been asked legal questions 'actually pending between two or more States', according to Rules 102(3) and 106 of the Rules of the Court. Such requests have often related to the rights of identified communities (for instance, the Kosovars, Palestinians,

4 United Nations, 'Report of the Informal Inter-Allied Committee on the Future of the Permanent Court of International Justice' (1945) 39(1) Supplement: Official Documents *The American Journal of International Law* 1, 40 [143].

5 Ibid 21–22 [68].

6 United States, Department of State, 'Dumbarton Oaks Proposals for a General International Organisation: To Be the Subject of the United Nations Conference at San Francisco' (1945) 66 *Conference Series*, Chapter VIII, Section A [6] http://cdm16614.contentdm.oclc.org/cdm/ref/collection/isl3/id/9851.

7 Michla Pomerance, *The Advisory Function of the International Court in the League and U.N. Eras* (Johns Hopkins University Press 1973) 27.

8 Ibid 30.

9 Ibid 28.

10 *Legality of the Threat or Use of Nuclear Weapons* (Advisory Opinion) [1996] ICJ Rep 226, 241–42 [29]; A/RES/77/276.

11 *International Status of South West Africa* (Advisory Opinion) [1950] ICJ Rep 128; *Legal Consequences for States of the Continued Presence of South Africa in Namibia (South West Africa) notwithstanding Security Council Resolution 276 (1970)* (Advisory Opinion) [1971] ICJ Rep 16.

Namibians, Western Saharans or Chagossians).[12] Certain rights of UN staff members have also been the subject of other requests.[13] Individuals have therefore been at the heart of most advisory requests. Thus, their participation in advisory proceedings is not an absurd proposition.

In this chapter, I argue that the Court's procedural rules enable individuals' participation in advisory proceedings despite its reluctance to facilitate this. In the advisory context, procedural flexibility is encouraged to meet standards of democracy, a yardstick by which to measure legitimacy of the judicial process (Section I.1.2). Their participation is also relevant for the Court's effectiveness, given one of its aims to support the UN regime and its protection of human beings through its advisory function.

I first dispel the myth that witnesses are limited to the confines of contentious proceedings (Section 3.1). I then discuss the Court's sparse engagement with *amici curiae* in the advisory context (Section 3.2). Finally, I explore the potential of the analogous extension of Article 66(2) of the Court's Statute, authorising the furnishing of information by entities beyond states and international organisations (Section 3.3). Section 3.4 concludes.

3.1 Witnesses in Advisory Proceedings?

There are two main ways for individuals to have their voices heard in relevant advisory proceedings. The first is by the government participating in oral proceedings and allowing an affected individual to make a statement as part of the government's delegation during its speaking time, as discussed in Chapter 2. Such authorisation was first granted to Professor Rotblat as part of the delegation of the Solomon Islands in the

[12] *Accordance with international law of the unilateral declaration of independence in respect of Kosovo* (Advisory Opinion) [2010] ICJ Rep 403; *Legal Consequences of the Construction of a Wall in the Occupied Palestinian Territory* (Advisory Opinion) [2004] ICJ Rep 136; Ibid (*Namibia*); *Western Sahara* (Advisory Opinion) [1975] ICJ Rep 12; *Legal Consequences of the Separation of the Chagos Archipelago from Mauritius in 1965* (Advisory Opinion) [2019] ICJ Rep 95; *Legal Consequences arising from the Policies and Practices of Israel in the Occupied Palestinian Territory, including East Jerusalem* (Request for Advisory Opinion) [2023].

[13] *Reparation for Injuries Suffered in the Service of the United Nations* (Advisory Opinion) [1949] ICJ Rep 174; *Difference Relating to Immunity from Legal Process of a Special Rapporteur of the Commissionon Human Rights* (Advisory Opinion) [1999] ICJ Rep 62.

Nuclear Weapons advisory proceedings,[14] though he was an expert as opposed to an affected individual. The *Chagos* advisory opinion stands as the only example in practice at the time of writing whereby an affected individual made a statement to shed light on the human dimensions of the (Section 2.3).[15] This option is procedurally straightforward and relies entirely on the initiative of the government concerned, which must either recognize the value of the individual's oral contribution in terms of democratic standards for measuring legitimacy or view it as advantageous to its litigation strategy.

The alternative option, which will be the focus of this section, is for the individual to provide oral witness testimony. The participation of concerned witnesses can generally assist the Court in the elucidation of facts necessary to resolve the matter, while also giving a platform to individuals to contribute to a case that will bear consequences for them. However, the Court has not been receptive to individuals' requests to give oral testimony. One of the reasons for this is that it does not wish to deal with fact-finding in advisory proceedings, believing that its Statute and Rules do not equip it with fact-finding capacity in the advisory context.

The role of evidence varies between contentious and advisory proceedings, influencing the degree of involvement an individual may have. The term 'evidence' is not even employed in the context of advisory proceedings, but rather the terms 'information'[16] or 'written statements'[17] are used. Evidence, *stricto sensu*, is a more appropriate term for contentious proceedings where alleged facts are established or disproved. Conversely, Article 65 limits the competence of the Court to give advisory opinions on legal questions only, and the Court has specified that '[i]f a question is not a legal one, the Court has no discretion in the matter; it must decline to give the opinion requested'.[18] The Court therefore does not wish to deal with fact-finding in advisory proceedings.

However, it is quite commonplace to be presented with an advisory request on a matter that, while legal in its nature, does require some

[14] Verbatim record 1995/32, 32 [14].

[15] Verbatim record 2018/20, 71–72 [4] (Philippe Sands).

[16] Statute of the International Court of Justice, Article 66 (2).

[17] International Court of Justice, Rules of Court, Article 105.

[18] *Certain Expenses of the United Nations (Article 17, paragraph 2, of the Charter)* (Advisory Opinion) [1962] ICJ Rep 151, 155.

probe into facts. According to the Court, the inclusion of factual enquiries does not obliterate the question's legal quality. Indeed, in its advisory opinion on the *Legal consequences for States of the continued presence of South Africa in Namibia (South West Africa) notwithstanding Security Council Resolution 276* (1971), it stated, '[T]he contingency that there may be factual issues underlying the question posed does not alter its character as a "legal question" as envisaged in Article 96 of the Charter. The reference in this provision to legal questions cannot be interpreted as opposing legal to factual issues'.[19] It is therefore possible for the Court to receive a request for an advisory opinion on a legal question in which facts play a role.

Should this be the case, it can be envisaged to call witnesses to speak on such facts. This can be presumed as the Court refused a request for oral witness testimony in a case where it considered that no factual component existed. In the 1950 advisory opinion on the *International Status of South West Africa*, the then-Registrar received a request from Mr. R.H. Swale, chief of the Zulus in South Africa, offering his services as a witness in the case. Mr. Swale justified this request to represent the native population of South West Africa by asserting that he is highly competent, given his unique experience and qualifications that relate to the facts of the case.[20] The proposal was refuted by the Court's President at the time, on the basis that the advisory opinion 'involves only legal questions. It is therefore believed that it will not be necessary to call witnesses during the hearings.'[21]

One can imagine that witnesses would be particularly valuable if the facts of the case were controversial and needed elucidation. However, in such instances, the Court takes the more firm approach of declining to give the advisory opinion altogether. This approach was established by the Court's predecessor. The Informal Inter-Allied Committee on the future of the PCIJ insisted that an advisory question 'must be based on an agreed and stated set of facts'[22] and that advisory questions with diverging facts should be refused.[23] Furthermore, the PCIJ had once declined giving an advisory opinion because the particular question 'raised a

[19] *Legal Consequences for States of the Continued Presence of South Africa in Namibia* (n. 11).

[20] *International Status of South West Africa* (n. 11) 340–41.

[21] Ibid 342.

[22] 'Report of the Informal Inter-Allied Committee on the Future of the Permanent Court of International Justice' (n. 4) 22 [69].

[23] Ibid 23 [73].

question of fact which could not be elucidated without hearing both parties'.[24] Indeed, it stated in *Eastern Carelia* that 'there is [not] an absolute rule that the request for an advisory opinion may not involve some enquiry as to the facts, but, under ordinary circumstances, it is certainly expedient that the facts upon which the opinion of the Court is desired should not be in controversy, and it should not be left to the Court itself to ascertain what they are'.[25] It then deemed itself 'unable to pursue the investigation' due to a lack of consent from the Russian government, as well as 'other considerations already averted to in this opinion, which point to the same conclusion'.[26]

Over half a century later, in the *Western Sahara* advisory opinion, the Court reflected on the PCIJ's *Eastern Carelia* judgment and concluded that while the refusal of a state to take part in the proceedings certainly played a role, it was in fact the 'actual lack of "materials sufficient to enable it to arrive at any judicial conclusion upon the question of fact"'[27] that prevented the PCIJ from rendering an advisory opinion.[28] Indeed, the Court deems itself toothless when it comes to establishing evidence in advisory proceedings. This is because while Articles 48–52 of the ICJ Statute cover matters pertaining to evidence on contentious cases, no similar provisions were drafted in the context of advisory proceedings. The Court believes that it must depend on the underlying facts of the advisory request being sufficient and uncontested.

For this reason, the government of Spain was against the Court pronouncing an advisory opinion on the question of Western Sahara in 1974, as it considered the Court unequipped to 'fulfil the requirements of good administration of justice as regards the determination of the facts'.[29] Judge Federico de Castro agreed, pronouncing in a separate opinion that 'Today, it would seem certain that, when the fact on the existence of which an advisory opinion is requested is disputed or in controversy, the Court has no competence to decide upon its existence'.[30] He discussed that this would require the Court to adopt a more active

[24] *Interpretation of Peace Treaties with Bulgaria, Hungary and Romania* (Advisory Opinion) [1950] ICJ Rep 65, 72; *Eastern Carelia* (Advisory Opinion) [1923] PCIJ Series B, 28.

[25] Ibid (Eastern Carelia) 28–29.

[26] Ibid 29.

[27] Ibid 28.

[28] *Western Sahara* (n. 12) 28–29 [45]–[46].

[29] Ibid 28 [44].

[30] Ibid 138–39 (Separate opinion of Judge de Castro).

fact-finding role in order to establish the disputed facts but that its Statute and Rules do not equip the Court with the powers to do so.[31] However, the Court considered that it had sufficient evidence before it to provide an advisory opinion in this affair[32] and came to the same conclusion in the *Wall* advisory opinion.[33] Therefore, the Court has made clear that it does not wish to deal with fact-finding in advisory proceedings, only accepting advisory questions with a factual component only when uncontroversial.

Practice has demonstrated that the Court does not believe the Statute and the Rules provide it with the procedural tools needed to clarify potentially contentious facts. In the advisory opinion on the *Legality of the Threat or Use of Nuclear Weapons*, the mayors of Hiroshima and Nagasaki wished to give witness oral testimony about the devastating damage caused in their respective cities, even though they had originally requested the Court to be experts. Given that neither the practice of inviting witnesses nor that of inviting experts was commonplace in the Court's advisory context, it suggested that – similarly to the Chagossians in the Mauritian delegation in the *Chagos* advisory proceedings – the mayors be included within the delegation of Japan, even though they were not pleading any point of law.[34] According to former ICJ President Rosalyn Higgins, 'not only was this sensible in the particular circumstances of these mayors; but it also for the time being put to one side [a] complex issue: can the usual procedures regarding witnesses applicable in contentious cases be applied also in advisory proceedings?'[35]

I believe that the Court has every right to analogously apply Articles 48–52 of its Statute where it considers it necessary to acquire relevant information from relevant private persons. This would enhance the Court's technocratic expertise and therefore the procedural legitimacy attached to the opinion. This is possible through Article 68 of the ICJ Statute, which reads that 'In the exercise of its advisory functions the Court shall further be guided by the provisions of the present Statute which apply in contentious cases to the extent to which it recognises

[31] Ibid.

[32] Ibid 29 [47].

[33] *Wall* (n. 12) 162 [58].

[34] Rosalyn Higgins, 'The Judicial Determination of Relevant Facts, Speech to the Sixth Committee of the General Assembly, 2 November 2007' in Rosalyn Higgins (ed), *Themes and Theories: Selected Essays, Speeches, and Writings in International Law* (OUP 2009) 1369.

[35] Ibid.

them to be applicable'.[36] Article 68 is an umbrella provision and a residual rule that allows the entire body of rules regarding contentious cases to be applied by analogy in advisory proceedings.[37] It is therefore an appropriate path to apply the rules of evidence to advisory proceedings. It is reinforced by Rule 102(2) of the Court's Rules: 'The Court shall also be guided by the provisions of the Statute and of these Rules which apply in contentious cases to the extent to which it recognises them to be applicable. For this purpose, it shall above all consider whether the request for the advisory opinion relates to a legal question actually pending between two or more states'.[38]

The term 'to the extent to which it recognises them to be applicable' in Article 68 must be emphasised. It indicates that the Court has the power and the discretion to determine if certain articles of the Statute pertaining to contentious cases may be applicable to the advisory context.[39] This has been confirmed on two occasions. The first was in the 1950 *Advisory Opinion Concerning the Interpretation of Peace Treaties with Bulgaria, Hungary and Romania*, in which the Court explained that '[i]t is (...) clear that [Article 68's] application depends on the particular circumstances of each case and that the Court possesses a large amount of discretion in the matter'.[40] In another instance, in the *Reservations to the Convention on the Prevention and Punishment of the Crime of Genocide* advisory opinion of 1951, the Court restated that '[A]rticle 68 of the Statute recognises that the Court has the power to decide to what extent the circumstances of each case must lead it to apply to advisory proceedings the provisions of the Statute which apply in contentious cases'.[41] Finally, the Court, in the 1971 *South West Africa* advisory opinion, described the advisory procedure as 'relatively unschematic'.[42] Article 68 is therefore a 'permissive rule'[43] that enables the Court to 'pick and

36 Statute of the International Court of Justice, Article 68.

37 Quintana Aranguren (n. 3) 1245.

38 International Court of Justice, *Rules of Court*, Rule 102(2).

39 Shabtai Rosenne, *The Law and Practice of the International Court, 1920–1996*, vol 3 (3rd edn, Brill/Nijhoff 1997) 1676.

40 *Interpretation of Peace Treaties with Bulgaria, Hungary and Romania* (n. 24) 72.

41 *Reservations to the Convention on Genocide* (Advisory Opinion) [1951] ICJ Rep 15, 19. See also Quintana Aranguren (n. 3) 1245.

42 *Legal Consequences for States of the Continued Presence of South Africa in Namibia* (n. 11) 26 [38]. See also Rosenne (n. 39) 1676.

43 Hugh Thirlway, 'The International Court of Justice 1989–2009: At the Heart of the Dispute Settlement System?' (2010) 57(3) *Netherlands International Law Review* 347, 388.

choose from the toolbox of its contentious procedure when dealing with advisory matters'.[44]

It is important to note that not every article in the Statute that is applicable to contentious proceedings is applicable to advisory proceedings. Certain procedural institutions would not be applicable because they are too dependent on certain core factors that define contentious proceedings and that distinguish them from advisory proceedings. For instance, advisory proceedings do not have parties, whereas contentious proceedings are governed by this feature, seeking to resolve disputes between two state litigants. Thus, there are some procedural aspects that are logically applicable to contentious proceedings because parties are involved – but could not apply in advisory proceedings. For instance, third-party intervention (governed by Articles 62 and 63 of the ICJ Statute) finds no place in advisory proceedings where parties do not exist. Another example is Article 53 of the ICJ Statute, explaining the consequences of the non-appearance of a party.[45]

Nonetheless, the rules that govern witness participation do not fall under this caveat as they are not dependent on the feature of parties in contentious cases. Although it could be argued that these issues are closely tied to questions of evidence, which are not present in advisory proceedings, the absence of the term 'evidence' in the context of advisory proceedings does not mean that evidence is either unnecessary or undesirable. In reality, there are certain fact-intensive advisory questions – for example, *Wall*, *Obligations of States in respect of climate change* or *Policies and Practices of Israel* – in which certain procedural tools, such as witness testimony, would be useful.

Therefore, Judge de Castro adopted a very restrictive reading of Article 68 in the *Western Sahara* advisory opinion, when he concluded that the Court is unable to apply fact-finding tools to advisory proceedings. To him, 'even if article 68 of the Statute is interpreted in the broadest manner, it would not seem that in advisory proceedings the Court is entitled'.[46] Under a more open interpretation of Article 68, there is no reason why this would not be possible; the matter is within the Court's

[44] Jean-Pierre Cot and Stephan Wittich, 'Article 68' in Andreas Zimmermann et al (eds), *The Statute of the International Court of Justice: A Commentary* (3rd edn, OUP 2019) 1868. See also Quintana Aranguren (n. 3) 1245.

[45] Quintana Aranguren (n. 3) 1245.

[46] *Western Sahara* (n. 12) 138 (Separate opinion of Judge de Castro).

discretion, and the only obvious obstacle would be clauses that could not practically apply.

The Court has, in the past, analogously applied Articles 48–52 in advisory proceedings. In the *Judgment No.2867 of the Administrative Tribunal of the International Labour Organisation upon a Complaint Filed against the International Fund for Agricultural Development* (IFAD) advisory opinion, the Court resorted to Article 49 of the Statute and called upon one of the organisations involved to produce certain documents.[47] This advisory opinion was requested by IFAD and concerned the validity of a judgment rendered by the International Labour Organisation Administrative Tribunal (ILOAT). The ILOAT judgment was the outcome of a dispute between IFAD and its employee of Venezuelan nationality, Ana Teresa Saez García. In 2011, the Court's Registrar requested the IFAD to produce copies of its employment contract with Ms. García for the years 2005 and 2006, and the IFAD responded accordingly. It provided the contract, as well as other subsequent employment contracts. It also requested the Court to authorise it to present additional observations and documents to the Court in relation to the employment contracts.[48] The judgment specifies that the request of the Court was an application of its powers under Article 49 of the Statute. This article is part of the group of articles – between Articles 48 and 52 – addressing the gathering of evidence by the Court. It reads that '[t]he Court may, even before the hearing begins, call upon the agents to produce any document or to supply any explanations'.[49]

It is perhaps more understandable that the Court would apply articles on acquiring evidence in advisory proceedings reviewing the validity of the decisions of administrative tribunals; such cases were in fact contentious cases brought under the heading of advisory opinions, as the parties concerned were an individual and an international organisation, neither of whom had *locus standi* at the World Court (see Chapter 4). But the application of fact-finding tools in the Statute has been considered in other advisory proceedings by the Court's predecessor. In certain cases, the PCIJ considered the appointment of experts,

[47] *Judgment No. 2867 of the Administrative Tribunal of the International Labour Organisation upon a Complaint Filed against the International Fund for Agricultural Development* (Advisory Opinion) [2012] ICJ Rep 10, 19 [15].

[48] Ibid.

[49] Statute of the International Court of Justice, Article 49.

pursuant to its Statute's Article 50. The advisory opinion on the *Jurisdiction of the European Commission of the Danube between Galatz and Braila*[50] is an example. This case stemmed from a conflict between France, Great Britain, and Italy against Romania with regards to the competence of the European Commission of the Danube. Romania denied that the European Commission had jurisdiction in the sector from Braila to Galatz.[51] Here, the Permanent Court acknowledged that the facts that needed examination had already been investigated by the Special Committee appointed by the League of Nations. For this reason, it was not necessary to make new investigations and enquiries.[52] This means that it deemed itself competent to use the fact-finding tools at its disposal, if necessary.

In the light of the above, the articles related to witness testimony can be applied in advisory proceedings.[53] Indeed, although advisory opinions are not as high in number as judgments on contentious matters, it is still important for the Court to integrate relevant individuals in advisory proceedings on matters that concern them to meet standards of both technocracy and democracy that are used to measure its legitimacy.

3.2 Individuals as *amici curiae*

This section will examine the instances in which the Court has been confronted with requests for *amicus curiae* participation from individuals. To do so, it will explore the Court's more elaborate confrontations with *amicus curiae* from non-governmental organisations (NGOs), who often defend, *inter alia*, vulnerable individuals. It argues that while the Court's increased openness to civil society in theory is noteworthy, it raises numerous questions about its actual engagement with such entities in practice.

Non-state actors have made attempts to be *amici curiae* before the Court in contentious proceedings such as *Asylum (Colombia v. Peru)*,[54]

[50] *Jurisdiction of the European Commission of the Danube between Galatz and Braila* (Advisory Opinion) [1927] PCIJ Series B.

[51] Ibid 28.

[52] Ibid.

[53] Christian J. Tams, 'Article 50' in Andreas Zimmermann et al (eds), *The Statute of the International Court of Justice: A Commentary* (3rd edn, OUP 2019) 1438–39.

[54] Correspondence (8 October 1949), 227–28.

Gabčikovo-Nagymaros Project (Hungary/Slovakia),[55] and *Jurisdictional Immunities (Germany v. Italy)*.[56] However, certain similar incidents in advisory proceedings are the focus of this section.

As aforementioned, there are no parties *per se* in advisory proceedings. However, when facing a request for an advisory opinion, the Court will decide which states or international organisations are permitted to provide information on the question. Indeed, Article 66(2) of the ICJ Statute reads as follows:

> The Registrar shall also, by means of a special and direct communication, notify any state entitled to appear before the Court or international organisation considered by the Court, or, should it not be sitting, by the President, as likely to be able to furnish information on the question, that the Court will be prepared to receive, within a time-limit to be fixed by the President, written statements, or to hear, at a public sitting to be held for the purpose, oral statements relating to the question.[57]

The priority accorded to states' interests is palpable in this clause, which confirms that states are *entitled* to appear before the Court – whereas international organisations are limited to those that the Court deems as capable of providing useful information.[58] Regardless, Article 66(2) – also confirmed in Article 105 of the Rules of Procedure – prohibits individuals from providing information. This was confirmed by former Registrar Stanislas Aquarone, who stated when describing the wording in Article 66(2) that *expressio unius est exclusio alterius*.[59] This famous adage, signifying that the express mention of one thing excludes all others, confirms that this clause had every intention to exclude entities that are neither states nor certain international organisations. Indeed, as the Court confirmed in the *Admissibility of Hearings of Petitioners by the Committee of South West Africa* (1956) advisory opinion, "unless

[55] Luigi Crema, 'Testing *Amici Curiae* in International Law: Rules and Practice' (2013) 22(1) *The Italian Yearbook of International Law Online* 91, 121; Eric De Brabandere, 'NGOs and the "Public Interest": The Legality and Rationale of *Amicus Curiae* Interventions in International Economic and Investment Disputes' (2011) 12(1) *Chicago Journal of International Law* 85, 94.

[56] Bruno Simma, 'Human Rights before the International Court of Justice: Community Interest Coming to Life?' in Christian J. Tams and James Sloan (eds), *The Development of International Law by the International Court of Justice* (1st edn, OUP 2013) 316, n. 63.

[57] Statute of the International Court of Justice, Article 66(2).

[58] Connie Peck and Roy S. K. Lee (eds), *Increasing the Effectiveness of the International Court of Justice: Proceedings of the ICJ/UNITAR Colloquium to Celebrate the 50th Anniversary of the Court*, vol 29 (Kluwer Law International 1997) 53.

[59] Correspondence (29 July 1970), 639.

individuals and other non-state bodies have been explicitly granted procedural rights before an international forum they will not be accorded."[60] Regardless, the Court has been confronted by requests for *amicus curiae* participation, a well-known practice in international litigation. It has also arguably been unreceptive to *amicus curiae* briefs from non-state actors – NGOs and individuals alike.

While no universal definition of *amicus curiae* participation exists, it is a practice whereby an entity that is not a party to the case submits a brief or makes an oral statement with respect to the law or the facts, upon its initiative, in order to assist the court or tribunal to conduct a better proceeding and conclude a better judgment. Whether an entity will be allowed to participate as *amicus curiae* depends, on the whole, on the interest of the court of tribunal – rather than the interest of the requesting entity.[61] While *amici curiae* were traditionally understood to be neutral bystanders providing information as independent experts,[62] the practice has evolved to accommodate *amici* strategically advocating for causes in the public interest.[63]

While unsurprising that *amicus curiae* intervention is a welcome practice before criminal and human rights bodies,[64] and various reform proposals in investor–state dispute settlement (ISDS) have advocated for it,[65] it has been met with hesitance before inter-state courts and tribunals.[66]

[60] *Admissibility of hearings of petitioners by the Committee on South West Africa* (Advisory Opinion) [1956] ICJ Rep 23. See also Peck and Lee (n. 58) 53.

[61] Lance Bartholomeusz, 'The *Amicus Curiae* before International Courts and Tribunals' (2005) 5(3) *Non-state Actors and International Law* 209, 275.

[62] See for example *Decision on Request for leave to file amicus curiae brief* (Judgment) [2014] ECCC Trial Chamber 2 [5].

[63] See for example ICSID Arbitration Rules, Rule 37(2)(c) – the *amicus* must have a 'significant interest in the proceeding'. See also Avidan Kent and Jamie Trinidad, 'Amicus Curiae Participation in International Proceedings: Forever Friends?' in Avidan Kent, Nikos Skoutaris and Jamie Trinidad (eds), *The Future of International Courts* (Routledge 2019) 236.

[64] European Convention on Human Rights, 213 UNTS 221, Article 36(2); Rules of Procedure of the Inter-American Court of Human Rights, Rule 44; See, for example, International Criminal Court, Rules of Procedure and Evidence, Rules 103, 149. See also Hannah Woolaver and Sarah Williams, 'The Role of the *Amicus Curiae* before International Criminal Tribunals' (2006) 6(2) *International Criminal Law Review* 151.

[65] See generally, Chen Yu, '*Amicus Curiae* Participation in ISDS: A Caution against Political Intervention in Treaty Interpretation' (2020) 35(1–2) *ICSID Review – Foreign Investment Law Journal* 223.

[66] Brian McGarry and Yusra Suedi, 'Judicial Reasoning and Non-state Participation before Inter-state Courts and Tribunals' (2022) 21(1) *The Law & Practice of International Courts and Tribunals* 123.

The practice was initially accepted at the International Tribunal for the Law of the Sea (ITLOS)[67] but subsequently refused in one instance.[68] Conversely, the subject has been controversial at the World Trade Organisation (WTO), with the Appellate Body accepting the procedure despite WTO Member States strongly opposing it.[69] It is therefore perhaps no surprise that the same reluctance has been noted by the World Court.

The Court has granted *amicus curiae* rights to an NGO on one occasion: in a 1950 advisory opinion entitled *International Status of South West Africa*. The UN General Assembly requested the Court to advise on the legal status of the territory named South West Africa when under colonial rule by the German Empire and subsequently South Africa, and known today as Namibia. Following the First World War, this territory was part of the League of Nations mandate system. However, after the League's dissolution after the Second World War, it was unclear what would become of this territory, as it did not automatically fall under the UN trusteeship system. Therefore, the question was posed to the Court, which, as per Article 66(2) of its Statute, set a deadline (20 March 1950) to receive written statements from states.[70]

On 7 March 1950, a request to provide information, in accordance with Article 66(2), was received by the Court from the International League of Human Rights. This was an NGO that later, in 1976, became the International League for the Rights of Man and that had been heavily involved in colonial questions since its establishment.[71] As well as asking for the simple right to provide information, this organisation also requested a deadline extension to do so.[72]

The International League of Human Rights was an NGO as opposed to an international organisation. The latter is generally understood to be an organisation of states established by a treaty, governed by international

[67] *Responsibilities and Obligations of States Sponsoring Persons and Entities with Respect to Activities in the Area* (Advisory Opinion) [2011] ITLOS, [13].

[68] *The "Arctic Sunrise" Case (Kingdom of the Netherlands v. Russian Federation)* (Order of 22 November 2013) [2013] ITLOS, [15]–[19].

[69] See World Trade Organisation, 'Participation in Dispute Settlement Proceedings' www.wto.org/english/tratop_e/dispu_e/disp_settlement_cbt_e/c9s3p1_e.htm#fnt2.

[70] *International Status of South West Africa* (n. 11) 128–30.

[71] Roger S. Clark, 'The International League for Human Rights and South West Africa 1947–1957: The Human Rights NGO as Catalyst in the International Legal Process' (1981) 3(4) *Human Rights Quarterly* 101, 102–3.

[72] Ibid.

law and with a legal personality distinct from that of its members.[73] The International League of Human Rights did not objectively fulfil these criteria. In the Court's eyes, however, it was deemed an international organisation and authorised to submit an *amicus curiae* brief.[74] The then-Registrar thus responded favourably:

> Your letter March 7 *re* advisory opinion South-West Africa *stop* Am instructed to let you know that International Court justice is prepared to receive from you before April 10 1950 a written statement of the information likely to assist Court in its examination of legal questions put to it in Assembly request concerning South-West Africa *stop* This information confined to legal questions must not include any statement of facts which Court has not been asked to appreciate stop Court does not contemplate resorting further to League for Rights of Man in present case.[75]

Despite this, the International League of Human Rights failed to meet the deadline[76] missing the ideal opportunity to 'impress the Court upon the advantages of such participation'.[77] In fact, its statement that it prepared to submit to the Court included many arguments as to why the Court should be more open to NGO participation in advisory proceedings.[78]

Despite this one authorisation, the Court rejected subsequent requests to submit *amicus curiae* briefs by the Federation of International Civil Servants' Associations in *Awards of United Nations Administrative Tribunal* (1954) upon the grounds that it was 'not authorised to receive written or oral statements (. . .) from a body such as your Federation'.[79] Shapiro, Rabinowitz & Boudin Attorneys at Law, motivated by the short-lived success of the International League for the Rights of Man, also made a request, justifying that the Rules of the Court 'are more flexible' and that the Court's predecessor heard private organisations.[80] The Court, however, declined receiving both written and oral statements, explaining that it was 'bound by the limitations set forth in [Article 66, paragraph 2,

[73] International Law Commission, Draft Articles on the Responsibility of International Organisations [2011] *Yearbook of the ILC*, vol II, Part Two, Article 2(a).
[74] Correspondence (29 July 1970), 638.
[75] Correspondence (19 December 1949), 327.
[76] Clark (n. 71) 118.
[77] Ibid 119.
[78] Ibid 120.
[79] Correspondence (16 December 1953), [390].
[80] Ibid [394]–[395].

of its Statute]'.[81] Even in these unique types of advisory proceedings reviewing decisions of certain administrative tribunals, and directly impacting individuals (see Chapter 4), non-state actors were *personae non gratae*. The International League of Human Rights tried its luck a second time twenty years later, when the Court was requested to provide an advisory opinion on the *Legal consequences for States of the continued presence of South Africa in Namibia (South West Africa) notwithstanding Security Council Resolution 276* (1971). Here, South Africa had not respected a Security Council resolution that had called upon it to withdraw its administration from the territory of South West Africa (today known as Namibia). The latter's mandate had terminated, and South Africa no longer had a right to administer it. The Court, in its advisory opinion, declared that South Africa's continued presence in the territory was illegal. The International League of Human Rights NGO sent its request on 10 November 1970[82] – requesting not only to provide a written statement but also to participate in oral proceedings – to which the Registrar responded one week later, stating that the Court would have to make a decision that the NGO should not expect before January 1971.[83] Eventually, the Court responded, stating that the judges were not willing to allow the NGO to participate.[84] Even when it reiterated and narrowed its request to the Registrar, the latter firmly clarified that the matter was closed.[85]

If the International League of Human Rights, confident in having a precedent that supported its participation in advisory proceedings, was rejected, then other organisations making the same request had little hope of success. One organisation that learned this lesson the hard way was the American Committee on Africa, affiliated with the International League of Human Rights. The Court rejected its request in the Namibia proceedings on the grounds that the American Committee on Africa was not an international organisation.[86] The Committee starkly addressed the President of the Court concerning this rejection, claiming that 'the refusal to accept its statement was unwarranted in law, inconsistent with prior practice, and incompatible with the best interests of the Court and

81 Ibid [397].
82 Correspondence (29 July 1970), 639–40.
83 Ibid 644.
84 Ibid 672
85 Ibid 678–79.
86 Ibid 647.

of the people of Namibia'.[87] Despite this, the Registrar reaffirmed the Court's refusal.[88]

The Court's stance on *amicus curiae* briefs by NGOs defending individuals' interests was affirmed in another advisory opinion, the *Legality of the Use by a State of Nuclear Weapons in an Armed Conflict* (1996), where the World Health Organisation sought to establish whether the use of nuclear weapons in an armed conflict would breach a state's international legal obligations.[89] Here, the Court refused a request by the International Physicians for the prevention of Nuclear War to submit information,[90] and the International Committee of the Red Cross – despite its unique status in international law – only had its views referenced in and annexed to Costa Rica's oral statement.[91]

However, during the *Legality of the Threat or Use of Nuclear Weapons* advisory proceedings of the same year, the Court became more receptive to *amicus curiae* briefs. The ICJ Registrar is said to have received a 'myriad of [*amicus curiae*] briefs and memoranda'[92] from NGOs. This is because the General Assembly's request for an advisory opinion was a result of their 'heavy and well organised lobbying'.[93] While it did not admit such briefs as part of the record in these cases, they were made available to members of the Court in their library.[94] Higgins explained that '[e]very judge knew from week to week what was coming in, and it was up to each judge to decide if he wished to go beyond the already voluminous official pleadings and to read these other materials'.[95] Certain judges commented on this phenomenon in their separate opinions, Judge Oda having the impression that the

87 Ibid 649.

88 Ibid 672.

89 *Legality of the Use by a State of Nuclear Weapons in Armed Conflict* (Advisory Opinion) [1996] ICJ Rep 66. See also Dinah Shelton, 'The Participation of Nongovernmental Organisations in International Judicial Proceedings' (1994) 88(4) *The American Journal of International Law* 611, 624.

90 Correspondence: Letter from Eduardo Valencia-Ospina (then-Registrar) to Mr. Barry L. Levy (28 March 1994).

91 Verbatim record 1995/33, [27], [31].

92 Rosalyn Higgins, 'Remedies and the International Court of Justice' in Rosalyn Higgins (ed), *Themes and Theories: Selected Essays, Speeches, and Writings in International Law* (OUP 2009) 894.

93 Ibid.

94 Ibid; Crema (n. 55) 122; Eduardo Valencia-Ospina, 'Court Clarification: Letters to the Editor' *International Herald Tribune* (Paris, 15 November 1995).

95 Ibid (Higgins) 894.

request 'originated in ideas developed by some NGOs',[96] while Judge Guillaume confirmed that the Court received 'thousands of letters inspired by these groups, appealing both to the Members' conscience and to the public conscience'.[97]

The confrontations with *amicus curiae* briefs in *Nuclear Weapons* arguably influenced the adoption of Practice Direction XII in July 2004,[98] as 'many non-governmental organisations advocated their inclusion – with some success, not in their own right, but via sympathetic governments'.[99] Practice Direction XII indicates that NGOs may submit written statements, which are treated as separate publications – as opposed to elements of the case file – that may be referred to by states and international organisations presenting written and oral statements. It reads as follows:

Practice Direction XII

1. Where an international non-governmental organisation submits a written statement and/or document in an advisory opinion case on its own initiative, such statement and/or document is not to be considered as part of the case file.
2. Such statements and/or documents shall be treated as publications readily available and may accordingly be referred to by states and intergovernmental organisations presenting written and oral statements in the case in the same manner as publications in the public domain.
3. Written statements and/or documents submitted by international non-governmental organisations will be placed in a designated location in the Peace Palace. All states as well as intergovernmental organisations presenting written or oral statements under Article 66 of the Statute will be informed as to the location where statements and/or documents submitted by international non-governmental organisations may be consulted.

This Practice Direction acknowledges that NGOs may fulfil a useful role by providing the Court with information that it would not otherwise

96 *Legality of the Threat or Use of Nuclear Weapons* (n. 10) 335 (Dissenting opinion of Judge Oda).
97 Ibid 287–88 (Dissenting opinion of Judge Guillaume).
98 Quintana Aranguren (n. 3) 1256–57.
99 Andreas Paulus, 'Article 66' in Andreas Zimmermann et al (eds), *The Statute of the International Court of Justice: A Commentary* (3rd edn, OUP 2019) 1818.

receive from states (pursuant to Article 66) or from the Secretary-General (pursuant to Article 65(2)).[100] However, there seems to be a contradiction in that this information, treated as 'publications readily available' and 'in the public domain' (paragraph 2), is 'placed in a designated location in the Peace Palace' that few are aware of (paragraph 3). Furthermore, no reference is made to the Court *itself* using the information for the purposes of its deliberations.[101] See Military and Paramilitary Activities in and against Nicaragua (Nicaragua v. United States of America) (Merits) (Judgment) [1986] ICJ Rep 14, 40–41 [63].

Indeed, despite the welcome engagement with civil society through the adoption of Practice Direction XII, there is no published evidence that the Court has consulted such briefs in practice. Former Registrar Eduardo Valencia-Ospina stated that 'all such documents are given consistent treatment', but the details of such treatment in practice are unknown.[102] Conversely, international criminal tribunals or human rights courts have been noted to openly engage with such briefs.[103] However, the Court's approach is presumably due to a mindfulness towards likely disapproving states.

The same approach of the Court holds true for individuals who have made attempts to act as *amici* themselves. This was demonstrated in the same context of the *South West Africa* cases. In the 1950 advisory proceedings (for the *International Status of South West Africa* advisory opinion), Mr. Gordon F. Muirhead submitted a statement of fact and a statement of law, which he asserted that he was forwarding on behalf of the advisor of the International League for the Rights of Man. However, the Registrar responded that the Court had no evidence from the organisation that this was the case and requested that this information emanate from the organisation itself.[104] Court was not willing to receive a document from an individual.

In the *Namibia* advisory proceedings, the Court received two requests from individuals. The first was from Professor Michael Reisman from Yale University Law School, who felt 'deeply concerned' and asserted that

[100] Ibid 1828.

[101] Markus Benzing, 'Evidentiary Issues' in Andreas Zimmermann et al (eds), *The Statute of the International Court of Justice: A Commentary* (3rd edn, OUP 2019) 1411.

[102] Valencia-Ospina (n. 94).

[103] International Criminal Court, *Rules of Procedure and Evidence*, Article 103 (2); *Lautsi v. Italy* App no 30814/06 (ECHR, 18 March 2011) 21–24 [50]–[55].

[104] Correspondence (19 December 1949), 328–29.

'critical issues are raised'.[105] For these reasons, his request to the Court was twofold: if the Court would accept a memorial from an individual, and if the Court would consider a document discussing the legality and admissibility of *amicus curiae* briefs.[106] The Registrar responded in a lengthy letter that seemed to be a personal correspondence as opposed to one in his official capacity. In his carefully justified response of rejection, he claimed – referring to the 1950 advisory opinion – that the Court had already rejected several individuals' *amicus curiae* requests in the past. He also used the context of the Court's jurisprudence in reviewing certain decisions from administrative tribunals to justify the extent to which the Court was not favourable to having individuals present oral statements.[107] The Registrar concluded by stating his belief that the Court would be 'unwilling to open the floodgates to what might be a vast amount of proffered assistance'.[108]

The second request in the 1970 advisory proceedings was from Reverend Michael Scott. While he had originally contacted the Court to deliver a statement on behalf of the American Committee on Africa, he seized the opportunity of liaison with the Registrar to also inquire if he could personally deliver an oral or written statement, due to his strong credentials and involvement in the subject matter.[109] The Registrar candidly responded that Article 66(2) of the Statute does not allow such information from individuals.[110]

In sum, the Court does not wish to involve NGOs and even less individuals. NGOs also can, pursuant to Practice Direction XII, submit such briefs – although their precise utility for the judges is unknown. NGOs could also theoretically be considered by the Court as international organisations for the purposes of Article 66(2), as was the International League of Human Rights. This would be an indirect way for concerned individuals to have their thoughts heard and to provide certain information that could be of use in the proceedings, related to the impact of the Opinion on civil society. The Court has seemingly expanded its understanding of 'international organisation' in the *Obligations of States in respect of climate change* proceedings by

[105] Correspondence (29 July 1970), 636.
[106] Ibid.
[107] See Chapter 4.
[108] Correspondence (29 July 1970), 639.
[109] Ibid 645.
[110] Ibid 647.

authorising certain entities whose status as a traditional international organisation can be questioned.[111] However, no literal interpretation of Article 66(2) nor of Practice Direction XII could invite the formal participation of individuals – as opposed to NGOs – appeasing its fear of the floodgates of their anticipated excessive unwarranted participation.

Despite this, the Court has surpassed the wording of Article 66(2) in the past to enable entities other than states and international organisations to furnish information in advisory proceedings. This stands in stark contrast to its hesitation to authorise witnesses (Section 3.1) and individuals as *amici curiae* in advisory proceedings (Section 3.2). The next section therefore explores the potential of the analogous extension of Article 66(2) to allow for individual participation.

3.3 The Analogous Extension of Article 66(2) of the ICJ Statute?

It has been thus far established that individuals could participate in advisory proceedings as witnesses, through the application of Articles 48–52 of its Statute via the umbrella clause of Article 68, allowing for the analogous application of rules from contentious proceedings (Section 3.1). Alternatively, while neither a Practice Direction nor Article 66(2) of the Court's Statute can authorise *amicus curiae* briefs from individuals (Section 3.2), I argue in this section that the analogous extension of Article 66(2) could theoretically allow individuals to furnish information if the circumstances so required.

There are two categories of states entitled to appear before the Court. Firstly, all members of the UN are *ipso facto* parties to the ICJ Statute, and are thus entitled to appear before it.[112] Secondly, states who are not members of the UN may become parties to the ICJ Statute, if the General Assembly and the Security Council so decide.[113] As for international organisations, the Court has the discretion to decide which ones would qualify and fruitfully contribute to the advisory proceedings.

[111] See, e.g., Danilo B. Garrido Alves, 'The Concept of International Organization in the practice of the International Court of Justice' (*EJIL Talk!*, 27 July 2023) www.ejiltalk.org/the-concept-of-international-organization-in-the-practice-of-the-international-court-of-justice/.

[112] United Nations Charter, Article 93(1).

[113] Ibid, Article 93(2).

However, in both the *Accordance with international law of the unilateral declaration of independence in respect of Kosovo* advisory opinion, and the *Legal Consequences of the Construction of a Wall in the Occupied Palestinian Territory* advisory opinion, the Court extended the framework of Article 66(2) to allow another type of entity to participate, who was neither a state nor an international organisation.

The *Kosovo* advisory opinion was the outcome after failed negotiations between the people of Kosovo, who wished to be an independent sovereign nation, and the government of Serbia. The latter sponsored a UN General Assembly resolution asking the ICJ whether the declaration of independence from the Kosovar people, claiming that Kosovo is an independent and sovereign state, was in accordance with international law.

At the stage of proceedings, the legal status of Kosovo was unclear. It was administered by the United Nations Interim Administration Mission in Kosovo ('UNMIK'), which was created via Security Council resolution 1244 (1999). While this resolution also temporarily suspended Serbia's exercise of sovereign authority over Kosovo,[114] it did not provide Kosovo's final status, which was left to be negotiated by the parties. Further, Kosovo was not a Member State of the UN nor a party to the ICJ Statute via a decision by the UN General Assembly and Security Council.[115] Therefore, it was not a 'state entitled to appear before the Court', as per Article 66(2) of the ICJ Statute.

When advisory proceedings began, the Court considered that the unilateral declaration of independence was the subject of the question submitted before it. Hence, the authors of this declaration were 'likely to be able to furnish information on the question', pursuant to Article 66(2). The Court therefore invited the authors of the declaration to make written contributions via its Order of 17 October 2008.[116] The authors of the unilateral declaration were democratically elected leaders of Kosovo who were members of the Kosovo Assembly.[117] Leaders of any country whose sovereignty is not in question would be regarded as state officials, whose furnishing of information to the Court would thus

[114] *Kosovo* (n. 12) 443 [97] and 444 [100].

[115] United Nations Charter, Article 93.

[116] *Accordance with International Law of the Unilateral Declaration of Independence by the Provisional Institutions of Self-Government of Kosovo* (Order) [2008] ICJ Rep 409, 410 [4].

[117] Written Contribution of the authors of the unilateral declaration of independence (7 April 2009), [6.01].

conform to Article 66(2). However, when the sovereignty and independence of the relevant entity are questioned and when the entity in question does not qualify as a 'State entitled to appear before the Court' in the sense of Article 66(2), then the leaders cannot be considered as state officials in the same manner. They may simply be considered as, at the very least, individuals.

Serbia was clearly opposed to the Court's invitation extended to the authors of the Kosovar declaration. It argued in its written statement that the information requested by the Court should be furnished by the UNMIK, as opposed to the authors themselves. Such permission by the Court 'constitutes a considerable departure from the previous practice of the Court, and raises significant issues under (. . .) Articles 34, 35, and 66, paragraph 2, of the Statute of the Court'.[118] While I agree with Serbia that this approach raised a significant issue under Article 66(2), it was not a considerable departure from the previous practice of the Court as it was not the first time that the Court applied an analogous extension of Article 66(2) to the benefit of individuals.

The first instance in which such an analogous extension of Article 66 (2) was applied was in the *Wall* advisory opinion. In this case, the Israeli government decided to construct a security fence as a measure of self-defence against terrorist attacks coming from the West Bank.[119] The UN General Assembly, concerned that this wall would result in permanent annexation and thus encumber Palestinian self-determination, asked the ICJ what legal consequences would arise from its construction, considering rules and principles of international law, the Fourth Geneva Convention of 1949 and relevant UN resolutions.[120]

During the advisory proceedings, the Court invited Palestine to furnish information under Article 66(2), 'referring to its somewhat special character as an observer to the UN General Assembly and as a co-sponsor of the resolution requesting the opinion'.[121] Today, Palestine would qualify as a 'State entitled to appear before the Court' under the meaning of Article 66(2). This is because although it is not a UN member, Palestine could become a party to the ICJ Statute pursuant to Article 93(2) of the Statute, following the adoption of UN General Assembly Resolution

[118] Written statement of Serbia (17 April 2009), [18].
[119] *Wall* (n. 12) 194 [138].
[120] *Wall* (n. 12) 136 [1].
[121] *Legal Consequences of the Construction of a Wall in the Occupied Palestinian Territory* (Order) [2003] ICJ Rep 428, 429.

67/19 of November 2012.[122] It was therefore eligible to furnish information as any other state entitled to appear before the Court in the *Policies and Practices of Israel* advisory opinion of 2024.

Therefore, the *Kosovo* and *Wall* advisory proceedings indicate that the Court is not restricted by the wording of Article 66(2) and can analogously extend it, if it so wishes. The basis on which these decisions were made remains in question. The Orders where these decisions were declared offer brief explanations that make no reference to any legal norms or general principles of law. Rather, the Court justifies its decision by citing the unique circumstances of each case, including the role of the entity in question and its potential to assist the Court. It is the latter element that seems to have been particularly seminal.[123] The equality of parties, studied in Chapter 4, may also justify their participation.[124] In brief, the broad discretion of the Court in advisory proceedings to apply an analogous extension of Article 66(2) may go beyond the letter of the law.

I see no issue with the Court's chosen course of action in these two instances. Indeed, the good administration of justice (Section 4.2) begs us to consider the involvement of non-state entities should the advisory question revolve around them.[125] The Court's decision was made to guarantee procedural fairness and meet standards of democracy, thereby ensuring procedural legitimacy.

Former Principal Legal Secretary of the ICJ, Hugh Thirlway, points out that the Court's approach in the aforementioned two advisory proceedings would only be problematic if we considered that Article 66(2) were a limitative clause that debarred it from obtaining information from any other entity.[126] According to former Registrar Stanislas Aquarone (Section 3.2), Article 66(2) *is* limitative (*expressio unius est exclusio*

[122] A/RES/67/19.

[123] Gleider I. Hernández, 'Non-state Actors from the Perspective of the International Court of Justice' in Jean D'Aspremont (ed), *Participants in the International Legal System: Multiple Perspectives on Non-state Actors in International Law* (Routledge 2011) 151.

[124] Gleider I. Hernández, *The International Court of Justice and the Judicial Function* (OUP 2014) 56.

[125] Robert Kolb, 'Les maximes juridiques en droit international public: Questions historiques et théoriques' (1999) 32(2) *Revue belge de droit international* 407; Aurélia Lelarge, 'L'émergence d'un principe de bonne administration de la justice internationale dans la jurisprudence internationale antérieure à 1945' (2009) 27 *L'Observateur des Nations Unies*.

[126] Thirlway (n. 43) 388.

alterius).[127] This tells us that the *Kosovo* and *Wall* cases must have been considered exceptional circumstances.

Yet, Thirlway also asks himself if the Court's discretionary practice was the 'thin end of the wedge', opening the door for individuals to be granted the same privilege, through an analogous extension of Article 66(2).[128] It is only natural that if this practice has been allowed twice, it may lead to claims for more openness in other relevant instances. However, the Court has consistently shown reluctance towards receiving such information from private persons – even where warranted. It had opportunities to do this in the five advisory proceedings where it was requested to judicially review the decisions of administrative tribunals, as examined in Chapter 4. Here, individuals – staff members of certain international organisations – were at the focal point of the dispute and had crucial information to provide to the Court. However, the Court did not apply an analogous extension of Article 66(2) in their favour. Instead, it requested for other actors permitted to furnish information – such as international organisations – to do so on their behalf. If it could not do so for such individuals with undisputed interest, involvement, and relevance in the proceedings before it, then it should come as no surprise that it would reject *amici curiae* from less implicated individuals, as examined in Section 3.2.

Furthermore, the measures in the Kosovo and Palestine proceedings were not taken in other cases where a population at the heart of a dispute undoubtedly could have provided useful information. For example, in *Obligations of States in respect of Climate Change*, the Court was asked about the legal consequences for states who have caused climate harm to '*peoples and individuals* of the present and future generations affected by the adverse effects of climate change'.[129] It is well known that this request was initiated by young students in the Pacific.[130] Their participation to offer information on the nature of their harm as a result of states' failed climate obligations would have assisted the Court in more acutely answering the question. Similarly, in the *International Status of South*

[127] Correspondence (29 July 1970), 639.

[128] Thirlway (n. 43) 388.

[129] *Obligations of States in respect of Climate Change* (Request for Advisory Opinion) [2023].

[130] A/77/PV.64, 3 ["I also wish to highlight the important role of the young law students in the Pacific who inspired this initiative and who brought it to the attention of the Vanuatu Government in 2019."]

West Africa advisory opinion (1950) where the UN General Assembly requested the Court to advise on the legal status of the territory, certain inhabitants of the territory certainly could have furnished pertinent information. A final example is in *Western Sahara*, where the Court was tasked with determining if Western Sahara was a territory belonging to no one at the time of colonisation by Spain and what the legal ties were between this territory and the Kingdom of Morocco and the Mauritanian entity. Such an investigation, particularly to answer the latter question, surely warranted participation from the people of the Western Saharan territory.

The Court's approach to individuals in this context indicates that it perceived Kosovo and Palestine not as a collective of individuals, but rather as territories whose status under international law had not been determined, who had made declarations of statehood, and who considered themselves as sovereign and independent states. These were *sui generis* cases unlikely to reoccur, reassuring the Court's fear of opening floodgates through its discretionary decision.

In sum, while it remains implausible in practice, the Court's wide discretion surpassing the letter of the law would allow it to – in theory – analogously apply Article 66(2) to relevant individuals. This would be a gateway for them to furnish information in such proceedings. But how compatible would this be with the spirit of Article 34(1) of the ICJ Statute?[131] It is recalled from Chapter 1 of this study that Article 34(1) is one of three pillars of the ICJ's jurisdiction, precasting the parameters of the Court and determining a number of other Articles in the Statute that were drafted upon its underlying logic.[132] The structure of the Court is largely based upon the assumption that only states can be parties in cases before it.[133] However, it is debatable whether this holds true for advisory proceedings, which carry distinct features from contentious proceedings. It can be argued that the state-centric constraints of Article 34(1) are pertinent only in the context of contentious proceedings, wherein the disputes are between actual parties. The context of advisory proceedings – where there are no parties, no binding decisions, and broader legal questions often of public interest – is too distinct for such a clause to have bearing.

131 Ibid.

132 See opening of Chapter 1.

133 Hernández (n. 124) 140–64, 154.

3.4 Conclusion

Advisory proceedings are theoretically more accommodating to individuals than contentious proceedings. Not only are there fewer governing rules, but the Court has large discretion as to the procedure when it is requested to produce an advisory opinion. This discretion may enable the Court to include individuals as witnesses, through the application of Articles 48–52 of its Statute via the umbrella clause of Article 68 (Section 3.1). While *amicus curiae* participation is limited to NGOs (Section 3.2), the Court could potentially allow individuals to furnish information through an analogous extension of Article 66(2) of the Statute (Section 3.3).

But would the Court exercise such prerogatives? The ICJ is generally much more restrictive towards non-state entities than its predecessor. The PCIJ showed considerable flexibility with regards to the types of entities from which it received documents or enabled to provide oral arguments. These non-state entities ranged from labour unions and trade union federations to political parties and minority groups.[134] The Permanent Court allowed many organisations that would not qualify today as 'international organisation[s]' in the sense of Article 66(2) to participate in proceedings. For instance, in its advisory opinion on *Designation of the Workers' Delegate for the Netherlands at the Third Session of the International Labor Conference* in 1922, the Permanent Court welcomed any international organisation that expressed a desire to be heard, receiving a memorandum from the Netherlands General Confederation of Trades Unions and allowing for other trade unions to participate.[135] The ICJ, in comparison, has been far more restrictive.[136]

The Court's hesitation regarding the inclusion of witnesses can be attributed to two main reasons. First, the Court has not faced many requests for advisory opinions, much less any that would require probing into facts. In situations where this has arisen, the practice has not been applied, in favour of a more cautious and non-controversial approach.

[134] Manley O. Hudson, *The Permanent Court of International Justice, 1920–1942: A Treatise* (The Macmillan Company 1943) 422–23.

[135] *Designation of the Workers' Delegate for the Netherlands at the Third Session of the International Labor Conference* (Judgment) [1922] PCIJ Series B, 11. See also *Interpretation of the Convention of 1919 concerning Employment of Women during the Night* (Advisory Opinion) [1932] PCIJ Series A/B.

[136] Paul C. Szasz, 'Enhancing the Advisory Competence of the World Court' in Leo Gross (ed), *The Future of the International Court of Justice*, vol 2 (Oceana Publications 1976) 507.

This can be understood from Judge Higgins' expression of relief that the question of using witness procedures in advisory proceedings was avoided by the Court in the *Legality of the Threat or Use of Nuclear Weapons* advisory opinion.[137] Second, the Court has demonstrated a general hesitation to exercise proper fact-finding mechanisms in contentious proceedings and would therefore be no different in advisory proceedings.

Regarding the analogous extension of Article 66(2) of the Statute, the Court has refrained from extending *amicus curiae* status to individuals, fearing it would open the floodgates. Good reasons plead for such an approach: in both Professor Reisman's and the American Committee on Africa's requests, they made reference to the 'precedent' established by the ICJ in accepting the International League of Human Rights to submit information in 1950. This reflects the 'thin end of the wedge' argument: on the one hand, it demonstrates the eagerness for non-state actors to rely on precedent to get their foot in the door and, on the other hand, may explain the Court's reluctance to establish any precedent that *could* open the floodgates. However, this fear is potentially unwarranted. Author Ruth Mackenzie opines that "the assumption of opening floodgates remains unproven in the face of the practice of international courts".[138] Indeed, there have been no public reports on an abundant number of NGOs submitting *amicus curiae* briefs since Practice Direction XII was published in 2004. Another related concern regarding the analogous extension of Article 66(2) of the Statute in favour of relevant individuals capable of providing pertinent information is that states may become more reluctant to turn to the Court to resolve their disputes as a result.[139] I am not fully convinced by this. As there are no parties in advisory proceedings, the spirit of antagonism feared by states (Section 1.2.4) would be absent. Furthermore, all states continue to be entitled to appear before the Court in advisory proceedings, unlike other actors, whose participation would depend on the Court's assessment of their ability to provide useful information. Finally, the Court is by no means bound to use all information presented to it.

137 Higgins (n. 34) 1369.

138 Ruth Mackenzie, 'The *Amicus Curiae* in International Courts: Towards Common Procedural Approaches?' in Tullio Treves et al, *Civil Society, International Courts and Compliance Bodies* (T.M.C. Asser Press 2005) 295–311. See also Paulus (n. 99) 1823, n. 96.

139 Ingrid Rossi, *Legal Status of Non-Governmental Organisations in International Law* (Intersentia 2010) 294. See also Paulus (n. 99) 1823, n. 96.

More frequently and openly receiving the views of private persons, who are concerned and affected by the outcome of advisory opinions, increasingly matters. The value of such participation lies in the democratic standards used to measure the Court's legitimacy in such proceedings. Such input is especially important for advisory opinions, which often impact a broad community of states and individuals.

4

Staff Members

> Questions may now properly be asked whether the system established in 1946 meets the present day principle of equality of access to courts and tribunals. While the Court is not in a position to reform this system, it can attempt to ensure, so far as possible, that there is equality in the proceedings before it.[1]

Until June 2016, the International Court of Justice (ICJ, the Court) occasionally dealt with distinct types of requests for advisory opinions in which individuals, working for certain international organisations, were directly involved as unofficial parties. These international civil servants, unsatisfied with the decisions rendered by the administrative tribunal dealing with their matters, were able to have these decisions re-examined by the Court. The reason for the failure of this type of advisory proceeding before the Court was primarily due to its inability to adequately adapt its procedural mechanisms to fully uphold the principle of equality between the parties.

Despite this practice being abolished, it drew much attention to the access and procedural inclusion of individuals before the World Court, testing the degree to which the latter could accommodate the needs of people at the centre of such disputes. For this reason, revisiting the practice and its challenges is valuable for this study. I argue in this chapter that the Court was indeed the incorrect forum for such concerned individuals seeking redress, due to its own Statute barring access to individuals and therefore entailing a permanent inequality of the parties. However, while the Court was handling such disputes, there were overlooked ways to adjust its procedural mechanisms to enable the concerned staff member to be even further integrated in proceedings

[1] *Judgment No. 2867 of the Administrative Tribunal of the International Labour Organisation upon a Complaint Filed against the International Fund for Agricultural Development* (Advisory Opinion) [2012] ICJ Rep 10, 29–30 [44].

and stand as an equal party to its employer. This was to be achieved through a wider interpretation of the principle of the good administration of justice.

The chapter will first expound three features of this unique type of advisory proceeding reviewing decisions of certain administrative tribunals (Section 4.1). It will then explain the notion of the equality of parties (Section 4.2), before assessing the Court's procedural adjustments in light of the two subtypes of the principle of the equality of parties: equality of access (Section 4.3) and equality of arms (Section 4.4). Section 4.5 concludes.

4.1 Features of Advisory Proceedings Reviewing Decisions of Certain Administrative Tribunals

Three features of this type of advisory proceeding must be understood: the choice of the advisory function, the concept of judicial review, and the types of administrative tribunals involved in such proceedings.

The first feature is the existence of an underlying contentious dispute between an international organisation and its concerned staff member. While the Court was arguably tasked with reviewing a decision as opposed to settling a dispute between two parties,[2] this dispute was still unavoidably at the core of the proceedings. The reason why such contentious cases were brought to the Court in the form of requests for advisory opinions is that Article 34(1) of the Court's Statute denies individuals and international organisations *locus standi* in contentious cases (see Chapter 1). Advisory proceedings, on the other hand, do not formally have parties (see Chapter 3).[3] However, this effectively turns an obviously contentious case into a non-contentious proceeding.[4]

While it has been argued in proceedings before the Court that the individual is *not* one of the 'parties' to the proceedings,[5] the procedure of recourse to the ICJ is a 'second instance' of sorts – a protraction of the

[2] Eric De Brabandere, 'Individuals in Advisory Proceedings before the International Court of Justice: Equality of the Parties and the Court's Discretionary Authority' (2012) 11(2) *The Law and Practice of International Courts and Tribunals* 253, 254.

[3] See also *Judgments of the Administrative Tribunal of the ILO upon Complaints Made against UNESCO* (Advisory Opinion) [1956] ICJ Rep 77, 157 (Dissenting opinion of Judge Córdova).

[4] Ibid (Dissenting opinion) 163; *Judgment No. 2867* Advisory Opinion (n. 1) 65 [40] (Separate opinion of Judge Cançado Trindade).

[5] *Judgment No. 2867* Advisory Opinion (n. 1) 28 [41].

original dispute between an individual and an international organisation.[6] Therefore, the Court has acknowledged the rights of the individuals concerned in its case law,[7] and has categorically stated that the dispute is one between the individual and the international organisation, in its 2012 *IFAD* advisory opinion.[8] This acknowledgment of the underlying dispute in the advisory context is due to the importance of the principle of the equality of parties in this context, as will be seen in Section 4.2.

This shoehorning of a dispute between an individual and an international organisation into the confines of an advisory proceeding raises other questions. Advisory opinions are traditionally not binding but – given the nature of the dispute – would the opinion be automatically binding on the relevant actors?[9] Another question raised is the impact that the advisory opinion would have on the original procedure of the administrative tribunal. To what degree would it override the original decision?[10] Addressing such questions lies beyond the scope of this study, but they nonetheless highlight the unique nature of these proceedings.

The second unique feature characterising advisory proceedings reviewing decisions of certain administrative tribunals is the existence of a decision by an administrative tribunal. UN tribunals are designed to resolve disputes between an institution and its staff members. In the lifespan of the ICJ, it has reviewed only five decisions from administrative tribunals: three from the United Nations Administrative Tribunal (UNAT)[11] and two from the Administrative Tribunal of the

[6] *ILOAT 1956* Advisory Opinion (n. 3) 164 (Dissenting opinion of Judge Córdova).

[7] *Effect of Awards of Compensation Made by the U.N. Administrative Tribunal* (Advisory Opinion) [1954] ICJ Rep 47, 62; *Application for Review of Judgment No. 158 of the United Nations Administrative Tribunal* (Advisory Opinion) [1973] ICJ Rep 166, 171–72 [14]; *Application for Review of Judgment No. 273 of the United Nations Administrative Tribunal* (Advisory Opinion) [1982] ICJ Rep 325, 333 [20].

[8] *Judgment No. 2867* Advisory Opinion (n. 1) 28–29 [42].

[9] Constitution of the International Labour Organisation (ILO) (1 April 1919), Article 37(1) suggests that this is the case.

[10] See Dražen Petrović, 'Wrong Address? Advisory Opinion of the ICJ on the Judgment No. 2867 of the ILOAT upon a Complaint Filed against the International Fund for Agricultural Development' in Rüdiger Wolfrum, Maja Sersic, and Trpimir M. Šošić (eds), *Contemporary Developments in International Law: Essays in Honour of Budislav Vukas* (Brill/Nijhoff 2016) 744.

[11] *UNAT 1973* Advisory Opinion (n. 7) 166; *UNAT 1982* Advisory Opinion (n. 7); *Application for Review of Judgment No. 333 of the United Nations Administrative Tribunal* (Advisory Opinion) [1987] ICJ Rep 18.

International Labour Organization (ILOAT).[12] Both had jurisdiction over a broad range of UN Specialized Agencies and other international organisations.[13]

The UNAT was established on 24 November 1949 through General Assembly Resolution 351(IV)A. The original UNAT Statute within this resolution did not provide for judicial review, its Article 10(2) stating that UNAT decisions were 'final and without appeal'.[14] But between 1952 and 1953, several UN Secretariat staff members were terminated by the Secretary-General without their consent, and they appealed to the UNAT against their dismissal. The UNAT upheld their appeal and required that they be compensated, but certain Member States of the General Assembly refused, arguing that there was no obligation to do so. The General Assembly therefore requested an advisory opinion from the ICJ on whether the Assembly was legally entitled to refuse to give effect to the awards of compensation made by the UNAT.[15] In its 1954 advisory opinion entitled *Effect of Awards of Compensation made by the United Nations Administrative Tribunal Advisory Opinion*, the Court stated that since UNAT decisions cannot be reviewed, its decisions were binding on the General Assembly. However, its Article 11 could be amended to 'provide for a means of redress by another organ'.[16] Following this advisory opinion, the UNAT Statute was amended in 1955 through General Assembly Resolution 957(X) to allow an unsatisfied party to seize the ICJ for review.[17] The UNAT was abolished by the General Assembly in 1995[18] and replaced by two tribunals: the United Nations Dispute Tribunal (UNDT), which hears claims in the first instance, and the United Nations Appeals Tribunals (UNApT), which acts as an appellate instance instead of the ICJ.[19]

[12] *ILOAT 1956* Advisory Opinion (n. 3) 77; *Judgment No. 2867* Advisory Opinion (n. 1) 10.

[13] Membership to the ILOAT available at: International Labour Organisation, 'Organisations Recognising the Jurisdiction' (*ILO Administrative Tribunal*) www.ilo.org/tribunal/membership/lang–en/index.htm.

[14] A/RES/351(IV)A, Article 10.

[15] Kaiyan Homi Kaikobad, *The International Court of Justice and Judicial Review: A Study of the Court's Powers with Respect to Judgments of the ILO and UN Administrative Tribunals* (Kluwer Law International 2000) 114.

[16] *UNAT 1954* Advisory Opinion (n. 7) 47.

[17] A/RES/957(X), Article 11.

[18] A/RES/50/54.

[19] August Reinisch and Christina Knahr, 'From the United Nations Administrative Tribunal to the United Nations Appeal Tribunal – Reform of the Administration of

As for the ILOAT, it was created in 1927 as the successor of the Administrative Tribunal of the League of Nations.[20] Just like the UNAT, its creation has its origins in a dispute over competence,[21] based on the 'theory of the excess power of the international judge'.[22] The League Administrative Tribunal decided to give compensation to a staff member in a case (*Zoppino v. International Labour Office*), justifying its behaviour under Article II paragraph 1 of its Statute, providing for jurisdiction relating to contracts of employment of International Labour Organization (ILO) officials.[23] But the question was raised whether it had that competence or rather, whether it was the role of the Assembly of the League to take such measures. It was concluded by the League's Finance & Sub-Committee that the Tribunal did not have that competence and that it had 'exceeded its jurisdictional powers in trying to overrule the League'.[24]

Therefore, the ILOAT replaced the Administrative Tribunal of the League of Nations in 1927. Following this incident, it was believed that some modifications to the Administrative Tribunal's Statute should be made. The Chairman of the ILO's Governing Body suggested that '[p]rovision might perhaps be made for a "court of appeal", for example, the International Court of Justice'.[25] Therefore, after discussions by the Committee on Staff Questions and the Governing Body, the amendment to include Article XII was recommended to the ILO Labour Conference, which adopted it in October 1946:[26]

> 1. In any case in which the Executive Board of an international organisation which has made the declaration specified under article II, paragraph 5, of the Statute of the Tribunal challenges a decision of the Tribunal confirming its jurisdiction, or considers that a decision of the

Justice System within the United Nations' (2008) 12(1) *Max Planck Yearbook of United Nations Law* 447.

[20] *Report to the Eighth Ordinary Session of the Assembly of the League on the Work of the Council, on the Work of the Secretariat and on the Measures Taken to Execute the Decisions of the Assembly* (1 June 1927).

[21] Leo Gross, 'Participation of Individuals in Advisory Proceedings before the International Court of Justice: Question of Equality between the Parties' (1958) 52(1) *The American Journal of International Law* 16, 35.

[22] Ibid 33.

[23] *UNAT 1954* Advisory Opinion (n. 7) 47; Written Proceedings (15 February 1954), 61 (Memorandum by the International Labour Office).

[24] Kaikobad (n. 15) 102.

[25] *UNAT 1954* Advisory Opinion (n. 7) 47; Written Proceedings (n. 23), 71.

[26] Kaikobad (n. 15) 101–4.

> Tribunal is vitiated by a fundamental fault in the procedure followed, the question of the validity of the decision given by the Tribunal shall be submitted by the Governing Body, for an advisory opinion, to the International Court of Justice.
>
> 2. The opinion given by the Court shall be binding.[27]

Article XII of the ILOAT Statute was abolished in June 2016,[28] thus stripping the ICJ of its function of reviewing decisions of administrative tribunals.[29] While other administrative tribunals do exist, no other makes recourse to the ICJ. This is largely due to the significant challenges the Court faced in attempting to ensure procedural equality between the staff member concerned and the international organisation, which presented their dispute under the guise of advisory proceedings.

An understanding of the features explained in this section enables us to assess why the Court could not successfully ensure the procedural equality and inclusion of the individual in such proceedings (Sections 4.3 and 4.4). But before answering this question, this principle of the equality of parties must first be understood (Section 4.2).

4.2 The Principle of Equality of Parties

This chapter argues that a wider interpretation of the principle of the good administration of justice would have allowed for further measures to be taken to guarantee the principle of the equality of parties in these advisory proceedings. The principle of equality of parties (*audi alteram partem*) is a fundamental principle of judicial procedure.[30] The Court's Statute features this principle in its Article 35(2), where it states (in the context of *locus standi* of states) that 'in no case shall such conditions place the parties in a position of inequality before the Court'.[31] The principle of equality of parties has been enshrined in a number of international human rights conventions[32]

[27] *Resolution concerning the Statute of the Administrative Tribunal of the International Labour Organisation* (7 June 2016). See further *Judgment No. 3003* [2011] ILOAT.

[28] GB.326/PFA/12/1. See also ibid (*Resolution concerning the Statute of the Administrative Tribunal of the International Labour Organisation*).

[29] However, the ILO continues to request advisory opinions on more abstract legal questions to the Court. See *Right to Strike under ILO Convention No. 87* (Request for Advisory Opinion) [2023].

[30] Georgios Petrochilos, *Procedural Law in International Arbitration* (OUP 2004) [4.86].

[31] Statute of the International Court of Justice, Article 35(2) [hereafter, ICJ Statute].

[32] International Covenant on Civil and Political Rights, 999 UNTS 171, Article 14(1); European Convention on Human Rights, 213 UNTS 221, Article 6(1); American

and is considered a 'key element of human rights protection', according to the UN Human Rights Committee.[33] At the crux of this principle is the idea that a judicial settlement that does not prevent procedural arbitrariness *vis-à-vis* the parties' rights cannot be legitimate.[34] Upholding this principle is therefore key to meet standards of fairness used to assess the procedural legitimacy of the Court. It is considered to be a 'cardinal characteristic of a judicial process',[35] and an element within the wider notion of 'international due process'.

In the words of the Court, the principle of equality of parties forms part of 'the requirements of good administration of justice'.[36] This is one of the general principles governing the Court's procedural law employed by the latter to ensure effectiveness and efficiency in its decision-making.[37] The good administration of justice empowers the latter with a large breadth of discretion to make the necessary adjustments in order to carry out its procedural functions in the most optimal conditions.[38] It finds application in diverse circumstances[39] but has been observed as applying to preserve a variety of interests such as time, cost, judicial economy, and judicial integrity – and the equality of the disputing parties.[40]

Convention on Human Rights, 1144 UNTS 123; Universal Declaration of Human Rights, A/RES/217(III), Article 10.

33 UN Doc CCPR/GC/32 [2].

34 Charles T. Kotuby and Luke A. Sobota, *General Principles of Law and International Due Process: Principles and Norms Applicable in Transnational Disputes* (OUP 2017) 176.

35 Ibid.

36 *ILOAT 1956* Advisory Opinion (n. 3) 86. Other names include: "proper administration of justice", "better administration of justice" and "sound administration of justice".

37 Chester Brown, 'The Inherent Powers of International Courts and Tribunals' (2005) 76 *British Yearbook of International Law* 195, 231.

38 *Legality of Use of Force (Serbia and Montenegro v. Italy)* (Preliminary Objections) (Judgment) [2004] ICJ Rep 865, 880 [32]; *Mavrommatis Palestine Concessions* (Judgment) [1924] PCIJ Series A 16; *Application of the Convention on the Prevention and Punishment of the Crime of Genocide (Bosnia and Herzegovina v. Serbia and Montenegro)* (Counter-claims) (Order of 1997) [1997] ICJ Rep 243, 284 [18].

39 Andreas Zimmermann et al (eds), *The Statute of the International Court of Justice: A Commentary* (3rd edn, OUP 2019) 977; *Construction of a Road in Costa Rica along the San Juan River (Nicaragua v. Costa Rica)* (Joinder of Proceedings) (Order of 17 April 2013) [2013] ICJ Rep 184, 196 [20] (Separate opinion of Judge Cançado Trindade).

40 Julien Cazala, 'Good Administration of Justice' in *Max Planck Encyclopedia of Public International Law* (OUP 2019).

It is understood by the Court that procedural unfairness is detrimental to the good administration of justice.[41] However, a historical understanding of the good administration of justice is appropriate in the context of this study. The good administration of justice finds its origins in the notion of the denial of justice,[42] which was first developed in the Middle Ages to advocate for the rights of individuals to justice. It was historically applied in the context of an individual whose rights had been violated by a sovereign state who had then failed to uphold the individual's right to justice. For instance, both an 836 treaty between Sicard and the Neapolitans and another in 840 between Italian Emperor Lotar I and Doge Petris Tradenicus of Venice affirmed the rights of a private person who had suffered in the territory of a foreign state, and the foreign state failed to do justice. The exercise of reprisals was therefore limited by the notion of the denial of justice.[43] The good administration of justice was born to describe the antithesis of the denial of justice for individuals.[44]

A human-centred understanding of the good administration of justice has been adopted by the European Court of Human Rights, which authorises *amicus curiae* submissions 'in the interest of the proper administration of justice'.[45] While such standards are expected of a human rights court, it can be argued that a similar approach should be applied in proceedings before the World Court that focus on an individual staff member's rights against their employer.

The human-centred understanding of the good administration of justice may have led to more creative procedural efforts to uphold the principle of the equality of parties. This chapter proceeds to illustrate the ways in which this was not successfully achieved.

41 *Legality of Use of Force (Serbia and Montenegro v. Belgium)* (Provisional Measures) (Order of 2 June 1999) [1999] ICJ Rep 124, 139 [44]. See more generally Filippo Fontanelli and Paolo Busco, 'The Function of Procedural Justice in International Adjudication' (2016) 15(1) *The Law & Practice of International Courts and Tribunals* 1.

42 Aurélia Lelarge, 'L'émergence d'un principe de bonne administration de la justice internationale dans la jurisprudence internationale antérieure à 1945' (2009) 27(2) *L'Observateur des Nations Unies* 23, 27–28.

43 See Chittharanjan Felix Amerasinghe, *Local Remedies in International Law* (2nd edn, CUP 2004); Carlo Focarelli, 'Denial of Justice' in *Max Planck Encyclopedias of Public International Law* (OUP 2015); Hans W. Spiegel, 'Origin and Development of Denial of Justice' (1938) 32(1) *The American Journal of International Law* 63.

44 Lelarge (n. 42) 27–28.

45 European Convention on Human Rights, 213 UNTS 221 (4 November 1950), Article 36 (2).

In the context of the Court's advisory opinions reviewing decisions of certain administrative tribunals, equality of the parties comes into consideration at two different stages. The first stage is within the international organisation (the employer). Typically, such organisations have a Review Committee composed of Member States that decide if applications for a request for a review of the judgment of the Administrative Tribunal should be taken to the ICJ in the first place.[46] The latter has recognised inequality of the parties with regard to the Review Committee's procedure within the international organisation.[47] The second stage in which the equality of parties plays a role is before the Court itself, which is the focus of this chapter.

The issue of equality of the parties is one that the PCIJ had already dealt with in the past, in its 1935 advisory opinion entitled *Consistency of Certain Danzig Legislative Decrees with the Constitution of the Free City*.[48] This was a case between the Free City of Danzig and individuals representing three minority political parties. The latter submitted a petition to the Council of the League of Nations concerning certain legislative decrees of the Danzig state. The PCIJ decided that it would receive written statements from the Government of the Free City of Danzig, as well as from the individuals. However, it did not allow the individuals to participate in oral proceedings because this practice was uncommon in its advisory cases.[49] Judge Dionisio Anzilotti strongly dissented to this decision[50] and the then-Vice President Guerrero suggested removing 'any inequality between the parties, whoever they might be'.[51] In another instance in 1939, former officials of the Governing Commission of the Saar Territory complained to the League of Nations of the 'prejudice occasioned to them by the expiry of the powers of the Governing Commission' and that their right to be

46 Kaikobad (n. 15) 186.

47 *UNAT 1982* Advisory Opinion (n. 7) 340 [32]. See also ibid 218.

48 *Consistency of Certain Danzig Legislative Decrees with the Constitution of the Free City* (Advisory Opinion) [1935] PCIJ Series A/B, 161.

49 Gross (n. 21) 16.

50 *Consistency of Certain Danzig Legislative Decrees with the Constitution of the Free City* Advisory Opinion (n. 48) 65.

51 Report of the Special Committee on Review of Administrative Tribunal Judgments, *Participation of Individuals in Proceedings before the International Court of Justice, Memorandum Transmitted by the Secretary-General to the Special Committee on Review of Administrative Tribunal Judgments (1955)*, Tenth Session (A/2909) 43 [20]. See also Gross (n. 21) 16.

heard had not been respected.[52] During preparations to seize the PCIJ with the matter, the right to present written and oral statements to the Court was withheld, since the same possibility could not be given to the petitioners as well. The PCIJ presumably did not wish to grant the government officials greater opportunities of furnishing information to the Court than the petitioners themselves.[53]

In these unique types of advisory proceedings, the Court was challenged with upholding the principle of the equality of the parties: the individual (staff member), on the one hand, and the international organisation (employer), on the other hand. Now that the equality of parties has been understood, its two constituents – equality of access (Section 4.3) and equality of arms (Section 4.4) – will be assessed, in order to determine to what extent they were respected by the procedural mechanisms employed by the Court in these types of advisory proceedings, and if any other measures could have been innovated or considered.

4.3 Equality of Access: The Permanent Obstacle of the Statute

The first constituent of the principle of the equality of parties is the equality of access. The Court defined the concept of equality of access as follows: 'According to generally accepted practice, legal remedies against a judgment are equally open to either party. In this respect each possesses equal rights for the submission of its case to the tribunal called upon to examine the matter'.[54]

While the UNAT allowed both the wronged staff member *and* the international organisation to seize the Court,[55] the ILOAT Statute only allowed the international organisation to do so.[56] Judge Roberto Córdova dissented in 1956 that in not respecting the equality of access of the

[52] *Participation of Individuals in Proceedings before the International Court of Justice* (n. 51) 46.

[53] Ian Brownlie, 'The Individual before Tribunals Exercising International Jurisdiction' (1962) 11(3) *International and Comparative Law Quarterly* 701, 704–5.

[54] *ILOAT 1956* Advisory Opinion (n. 3) 85; *Judgment No. 2867* Advisory Opinion (n. 1) 29–30 [44].

[55] A/RES/957(X), Article 11.

[56] Statute of the Administrative Tribunal of the International Labour Organisation [hereafter, ILOAT Statute], Article XII read as follows (of the version last adopted on 11 June 2008); *Resolution concerning the Statute of the Administrative Tribunal of the International Labour Organisation* (n. 27); *Judgment No. 2867* Advisory Opinion (n. 1) 26–27 [38].

parties, it was impossible for the Court to administer justice in strict compliance with its basic principles.[57] On this issue, the Court stated in 2012 that 'questions may (. . .) properly be asked whether the system established in 1946 meets the present-day principle of equality of access to courts and tribunals' but that it is 'not in a position to reform this system'.[58]

The equality of access stems from two legal sources: the ILOAT Statute and the ICJ Statute. The problem with the equality of access is twofold: on the one hand, certain international organisations may not allow their staff members to seize the ICJ to review the organisation's decision, allowing only the organisation to do so. On the other hand, even if the organisation does allow the individual to seize the ICJ, the Court's own Statute does not allow this. There is therefore a dual problem, each of which shall be addressed in turn.

4.3.1 Access of the Injured Staff Member to the Court via Article XII, ILOAT Statute

Former Article XII of the ILOAT Statute only allowed the international organisation (the employer) but not the wronged staff member (the employee) to seize the ICJ to ask for an advisory opinion. If it so happened that the staff member was not satisfied with the decision of the ILOAT, they had no means to challenge the decision and seize the ICJ. This is because the ILOAT Statute did not give the individual this right. Judge Greenwood commented that 'I do not believe that it is acceptable today. This inequality is no technicality; it is a fundamental flaw in the system created by Article XII'.[59]

Concerns about this situation were already raised in 1956, when the Court considered whether the inequality of access constituted a compelling reason to refrain from delivering an advisory opinion.[60] It concluded that this was an inequality that was *antecedent* to the request for an advisory opinion, not an inequality before the Court itself.[61] The Court therefore considered that it was not affected by this inequality and decided to proceed. In his separate opinion, Judge Winiarski pointed

[57] *ILOAT 1956* Advisory Opinion (n. 3) 167 (Dissenting opinion of Judge Córdova).
[58] *Judgment No. 2867* Advisory Opinion (n. 1) 29–30 [44].
[59] *Judgment No. 2867* Advisory Opinion (n. 1) 95 [3] (Declaration of Judge Greenwood).
[60] *ILOAT 1956* Advisory Opinion (n. 3) 85.
[61] Ibid.

out that this was not compatible with the Court's judicial character.[62] Judge Helge Klaestad and Judge Córdova also disagreed with the Court's reasoning in this respect.[63]

Due to this controversy, the ILOAT abolished Article XII of its Statute in June 2016.[64] It had already pointed out in its Judgment No. 3003 of 2011 (the judgment that the ICJ then reviewed in its 2012 advisory opinion) that the procedure set forth in Article XII of the Annex to its Statute is 'fundamentally imbalanced to the detriment of staff members'.[65] It also pointed out that its Article XII was essentially different from the procedure under the UNAT, in that the latter permitted staff members, the international organisation in question, the Secretary-General, *and* Member States to seize the Court:

> The fact that recourse to the Court under Article XII is confined to the organisations and hence can only relate to judgments unfavourable to them, means that the possibility of obtaining a stay of execution would, by definition, only benefit the organisations themselves. This would doubly worsen the imbalance between the parties created by the Article XII procedure, to the detriment of the staff members.[66]

In 2015, in an internal document entitled *Workload and effectiveness of the Tribunal*, the ILO stated that '[u]rgent consideration should (. . .) be given to repealing Article XII of the Statute along with the formalisation of the procedure for the review of judgments developed in the Tribunal's case law' and requested the ILO Director-General 'to prepare draft amendments to the Tribunal's Statute relating to Article XII'.[67] The ILO Governing Body stated the following in its *Proposed amendments to the Statute of the Tribunal*: 'Given that the review procedure is open only to defendant organisations and not to aggrieved staff members, it is generally recognised today that Article XII of the Statute and Article XII of the Annex fail to meet the overriding principle of equality of access to courts and tribunals. The provision has been vividly criticised by the International Court of Justice as anachronistic (. . .)'.[68] On 7 June 2016, Article XII was formally deleted from the ILOAT Statute.

62 Ibid 108 (Separate opinion of Judge Winiarski).

63 Ibid 111 (Separate opinion of Judge Klaestad) and 167–68 (Dissenting opinion of Judge Córdova).

64 GB.325/PFA/9/1(Rev.) [30].

65 *Judgment No. 3003* [2011] ILOAT 17 [40].

66 Ibid [43].

67 GB.325/PFA/9/1(Rev.) (n. 64).

68 GB.326/PFA/12/1 (n. 28) 1 [3].

This decision affected 11 UN specialised agencies and the International Atomic Energy Agency,[69] all of whose staff members would turn to the ILOAT if wronged by their employer. During discussions, the employers' groups and worker spokesperson approved of the idea to remove Article XII, and the Africa group also supported the decision upon the condition that the option of a review system would feature in the ILOAT Rules of Procedure.[70] Contrarily, the proposal to abolish Article XII was strongly refuted by the *Union syndicale fédérale des services publics européens et internationaux* and the Federation of International Civil Servants' Association.

The violation of the equality of access could have easily been remedied via an amendment of Article XII of the ILOAT Statute. Indeed, Article XI of the ILOAT Statute states that '[t]he present Statute may be amended, after consultation with the Tribunal, by the International Labour Conference or such other organ of the International Labour Organization as the Conference may determine.'[71] An amendment of Article XII allowing for the staff member to seize the ICJ would place them at par with the international organisation. Both parties concerned would have the same access to the Court. However, only half of the problem would have been resolved, as the inequality of access is also a feature of the ICJ Statute.

4.3.2 Access of the Injured Staff Member to the Court via Its Statute

The Court has stated that the inequality reflected in Article XII of the ILOAT Statute is not an inequality *before the Court* itself.[72] But this does not mean that the Court is free from the problem of inequality of access before it. Indeed, even if the ILOAT Statute allowed equal access, the ICJ Statute was still another hurdle for the disgruntled staff member.

Article XII was deliberately drafted with the goal of preventing individuals from seizing the Court *because* of Article 34(1) of the ICJ Statute. Indeed, the Court itself has explained,

> Under Article 34, paragraph 1, of the Statute of the Court 'only States may be parties in cases before the Court'. In Article XII it was sought to avoid

[69] Ibid 3 [3].
[70] GB.326/PV [653]–[655].
[71] ILOAT Statute (n. 56).
[72] *ILOAT 1956* Advisory Opinion (n. 3) 85.

> this difficulty while nevertheless securing an examination by and a decision of the Court by means of a Request, emanating from the Executive Board, for an Advisory Opinion. To the Executive Board-and to it alone-was given the right of challenging a Judgment of the Administrative Tribunal.[73]

While judges and scholars alike have vividly criticised Article XII of the ILOAT as well as the ICJ's conduct and approach during such proceedings, little to no criticism has been made towards Article 34(1) of the ICJ Statute itself, which is at the core of the entire controversy. If this clause was not drafted as such and the individual had *locus standi* before the Court, then Article XII would not have been drafted accordingly, and the inequality between the parties would not exist. Ultimately, *this* is the true hindrance. Thus, modifying Article XII would have had to go hand in hand with modifying the ICJ Statute. Even if the ILOAT Statute gave individuals access to the ICJ, the latter's Statute itself would not and the two Statutes would stand in stark contradiction.

Scholar Leo Gross, in support of the amendment of Article 34(1), has stated that 'a great deal of traditional thinking was jettisoned by the General Assembly when it adopted the novel review procedure directly involving staff members. Probably no one will shed any tears if a little more of the same stuff goes overboard when an even greater traditional principle is at stake'.[74] However, as discussed in Chapter 1, this would not be possible for a number of reasons and, furthermore, the Court has explicitly stated that it is "not in a position to reform this system."[75] It thus found itself in face of an uncomfortable *fait accompli* that it had to remedy through the second component of the overarching principle of the equality of parties: the equality of arms.

4.4 Equality of Arms: New Procedural Mechanisms in Favour of the Injured Staff Member

The Court has made clear that while it is 'not in a position to reform this system [creating the inequality of access], it can attempt to ensure, so far as possible, that there is equality in the proceedings before it'."[76] Indeed, while the Court could not change the equality of access, it could – and

[73] Ibid 85. See also 111 (Separate opinion of Judge Klaestad).
[74] Gross (n. 21) 40.
[75] *Judgment No. 2867* Advisory Opinion (n. 1) 29–30 [44].
[76] Ibid.

did attempt to – change the equality of arms. However, it will be argued in this section that the Court did not fully exhaust the procedural mechanisms at its disposal to try and close the gap of inequality between the parties.

The principle of equality of arms means that parties must be treated equally from a procedural standpoint, having equal opportunity to present their case without being at a disadvantage to their opponent. This principle has been developed in the jurisprudence of international human rights courts.[77] It represents another aspect of the principle of equality of the parties, emphasizing that true equality requires more than merely door to the courthouse.

The issue regarding equality of arms arises from the fact that wronged staff members, who were originally parties to the proceedings before the administrative tribunals, were barred from appearing in a similar capacity at the Peace Palace. As a result, they were excluded from these proceedings despite having a clear and justified legal interest in the case. Indeed, Article 66(2) of the ICJ Statute[78] states the following:

> The Registrar shall also, by means of a special and direct communication, notify any *state entitled to appear before the Court or international organisation considered by the Court*, or, should it not be sitting, by the President, as likely to be able to furnish information on the question, that the Court will be prepared to receive, within a time-limit to be fixed by the President, written statements, or to hear, at a public sitting to be held for the purpose, oral statements relating to the question.[79]

As examined in Chapter 3, this provision permits governments and international organisations to participate in advisory proceedings, but not private parties (Section 3.3). In these proceedings reviewing decisions of certain administrative tribunals, however, the Court took it upon itself to tweak and contrive procedures in order to uphold the principle of the equality of arms,[80] reassuring private parties that '[a]ny absence of equality (...) inherent in the terms of Article 66 of the Statute of the

77 *Judgment No. 2867* Advisory Opinion (n. 1) 84–87 [92]–[100] (Separate opinion of Judge Cançado Trindade).

78 *UNAT 1973* Advisory Opinion (n. 7) 179–80 [34].

79 ICJ Statute, Article 66(2) (emphasis added).

80 Anna Riddell and Brendan Plant, *Evidence before the International Court of Justice* (British Institute of International and Comparative Law 2009) 368.

Court is capable of being cured by the adoption of appropriate procedures which ensure actual equality in the particular proceedings'.[81] In so doing, the Court has always been guided by its duty to remain faithful to the requirements of its judicial character.[82]

The Court took two principal measures to preserve and guarantee the equality of arms: first, an actor with access to the Court in advisory proceedings would arrange to transmit the views of the concerned staff members to the Court (Section 4.4.1). Second, since only states or international organisations could participate in oral proceedings, but not individuals, oral proceedings were barred from proceedings altogether, in order to equalise the parties in the procedure before the Court (Section 4.4.2). Both measures are examined more closely here.

4.4.1 *Transmitting the Staff Member's Documents*

In advisory proceedings of this nature, there have been two authorities who were tasked with transmitting documents from the individual to the ICJ: the UN Secretary-General in the case of UNAT and the international organisation (employer) in the case of ILOAT.

The Secretary-General was involved in the transmission of documents in advisory proceedings reviewing decisions made by the UNAT. This is because the UNAT Statute's Article 11, in its paragraph 2 *in fine*, stated that the Secretary-General would arrange to transmit to the Court the views of the wronged staff member.[83] This procedure was practised in the only three advisory proceedings involving UNAT brought to the Court's docket: *Application for Review of Judgment No. 158 of the UNAT case* (1973), *Application for Review of Judgment No. 273 of the UNAT case* (1982),[84] and *Application for Review of Judgment No. 333 of the United Nations Administrative Tribunal* (1987).[85] In 1955, the Secretary-General at the time considered this

[81] *UNAT 1973* Advisory Opinion (n. 7) 180 [35].

[82] Ibid 175 [24]; *ILOAT 1956* Advisory Opinion (n. 3) 84; *Constitution of the Maritime Safety Committee of the Inter-Governmental Maritime Consultative Organisation* (Advisory Opinion) [1960] ICJ Rep 150, 153; *Western Sahara* (Advisory Opinion) [1975] ICJ Rep 12, 21 [23].

[83] A/RES/957(X).

[84] *UNAT 1982* Advisory Opinion (n. 7) 327 [6] and [8].

[85] *UNAT 1987* Advisory Opinion (n. 11) 20.

role his 'responsibility to assure as far as possible an equality of rights for the staff member concerned'.[86]

The Court was satisfied with the Secretary-General's role in facilitating the staff member's participation, as the staff member was not dependent on the international organization (employer), unlike in ILOAT proceedings.[87] Regardless, this system involving the Secretary-General bore the risk of delays, as seen in the 1982 advisory proceeding: the staff member argued that the procedure resulted in a six-week delay in communication between himself and the Court.[88]

The alternative means of transmitting the staff member's documents was through the international organisation in dispute with its staff member. Unlike the UNAT, which explicitly provided in its Article 11 (2) that the Secretary-General would transmit the individual's documents to the Court,[89] the ILOAT Statute made no such explicit provision. The ICJ therefore developed the practice of relying on the international organisation in its 1956 and 2012 cases involving the ILOAT.[90]

The setback in this approach is that the staff member had to rely on the goodwill of the international organisation to transfer the documents. In the 1956 advisory opinion, this was criticised by Judges Klaestad, Córdova, and Muhammad Zafrulla Khan.[91] The process was different from that involving the Secretary-General, who was more compelled to act in good faith given his role in the UN and his lack of legal interest in the case. The international organisation, on the other hand, was the other 'party' in the dispute *against* the individual and was therefore not guaranteed to act in good faith. In the Court's 2012 *IFAD* advisory opinion, the International Fund for Agricultural Development (IFAD) did not comply in transmitting the documents of the relevant staff member, Ms. Ana Teresa Saez García.[92] The Court conveyed 'the failure of IFAD to inform Ms. Saez García in a timely way of the procedural requests it was making to the Court'[93] and 'IFAD's initial failure to

[86] *Report of the Special Committee on Review of Administrative Tribunal Judgments*, A/C.5/L.635 (17 October 1955) 3 [8].

[87] *UNAT 1973* Advisory Opinion (n. 7) 180 [35].

[88] *UNAT 1982* Advisory Opinion (n. 7); Written Statements (30 November 1981), 132.

[89] A/RES/957(X).

[90] *ILOAT 1956* Advisory Opinion (n. 3) 77; Written Statements (1 April 1956), 170–83.

[91] Ibid 110 (Separate opinion of Judge Klaestad); 116 (Dissenting opinion of Judge Córdova); 114 (Separate opinion of Judge Muhammad Zafrulla Khan).

[92] *Judgment No. 2867* Advisory Opinion (n. 1) 17 [3] and 30 [45].

[93] Ibid 30 [46].

transmit to the Court certain communications from Ms. Saez García'.[94] Judge Greenwood also commented in his separate opinion that 'IFAD's approach to the proceedings, of which the Court (in paragraph 46 of the Opinion) has rightly been critical, amounted to treating Ms. Saez García as a spectator rather than a participant in proceedings whose outcome would have a direct and substantial effect upon her'.[95] Due to this incident, the filing of all necessary documents was not completed until 15 months after the request for the advisory opinion,[96] which was of much concern to the Court.[97]

I believe there were unexplored ways to equalise the roles of the 'parties' and prevent the international organization from being responsible for submitting the individual's documents. For instance, instead of the international organisation submitting its own documents as well as those for the other party, a neutral third party could have served as the transmitting organ for both parties. While the Secretary-General assumed this role, the delays highlighted the need for a neutral third party, appointed specifically for the purpose of participating in the proceedings, and thus able to respond more efficiently. This could be a professional from the UN Secretariat or Ombudsman and Mediation Services, or a representative of another international organisation. This entity could have also been available to transmit any written communications between the parties and the Registry of the Court. The presence of this neutral actor would have prevented both the international organisation and the wronged staff member from directly transmitting their documents before the Court, thereby successfully placing the parties on an equal footing at the Peace Palace.

4.4.2 *The Absence of Oral Hearings in Advisory Proceedings*

As discussed earlier, one way the Court has attempted to address the inequality of arms is by allowing the individual to transmit documents indirectly. However, it was also suggested that a suitable alternatives could have been considered. The second means of redress in response to the inequality of arms practised by the Court was the prohibition of oral proceedings.

94 Ibid.
95 Ibid 95–96 [4] (Declaration of Judge Greenwood).
96 Ibid 30 [46].
97 Ibid 31 [48]

While Article 66(2) of the ICJ Statute assumes that there may be a written and an oral component in advisory proceedings, Article 105(2)(b) of the Court's Rules states that the Court shall 'decide whether oral proceedings shall take place at which statements and comments may be submitted to the Court under the provisions of Article 66 of the Statute, and fix the date for the opening of such oral proceedings'.[98] This indicates that oral proceedings are generally not *sine qua non*, and written submissions may be adequate in providing sufficient information for the Court to give an advisory opinion.[99] The Court also commented in its 1973 *Application for Review of Judgment No. 158 of the United Nations Administrative Tribunal* advisory opinion that there is no 'general principle of law' requiring oral hearings to take place[100] and that 'True, certain judges considered that the absence of oral proceedings constituted either an insuperable or a serious obstacle to the Court's complying with the request for an advisory opinion. But that view was not shared by the Court'.[101]

Thus, oral proceedings are, in theory, dispensable. In fact, there were no oral hearings in the first instance proceedings between the international organisation and the staff member before the ILOAT. In this sense, in not providing oral proceedings, the ICJ was not robbing the 'parties' of a procedural mechanism that was offered to them in the first stage of their dispute. The proposal to eliminate oral hearings was first introduced during the first review of an administrative tribunal's decision before the ICJ, and has been applied in all five such cases. In the 1956 *Judgments of the Administrative Tribunal of the ILO upon Complaints Made against UNESCO* advisory opinion,[102] the individuals involved – Mr. Peter Duberg, Mr. David Leff, Mrs. Wilcox, and Mrs. Bernstein[103] – were not granted the right to appear before the Court, and as a result, neither was UNESCO. The Court stated that 'although no oral proceedings were held, the Court is satisfied that adequate information has been made available to it'.[104] However, it should be noted that the Court has always held oral proceedings, with these five cases being the only

[98] Juan José Quintana Aranguren, *Litigation at the International Court of Justice: Practice and Procedure* (Brill/Nijhoff 2015) 1258.
[99] Kaikobad (n. 15) 201.
[100] *UNAT 1973* Advisory Opinion (n. 7) 181.
[101] Ibid 180 [35].
[102] *ILOAT 1956* Advisory Opinion (n. 3) 80.
[103] Ibid 81.
[104] Ibid 86.

exceptions.[105] It is reasonable to assume that if there were no issue of inequality between the parties, the Court would have no justification for prohibiting oral hearings.[106]

Doing away with oral hearings was not free from criticism by dissenting ICJ judges such as Judges Hermann Mosler,[107] Isaac Forster, Nagendra Singh,[108] and Klaestad.[109] Then-Secretary-General Javier Perez de Cuellar even stated in his report that such a process 'does violence to the judicial procedures of the Court'.[110] The Court itself stated in its 1982 advisory opinion that it was 'depriving itself of a very useful procedure'.[111]

Given the formal and structured nature of oral proceedings at the Court, one could argue that their absence would result in little loss.[112] However, the exercise of oral hearings is significant to meet standards of democracy necessary to uphold the Court's procedural legitimacy (see Section I.1.2). Oral hearings can also enhance such legitimacy by meeting standards of technocratic expertise, in at least three ways.

Firstly, oral hearings may elucidate certain misunderstandings generated from written documents. They are considered to be the means by which the Court may obtain clarification of the issue before it.[113] In this sense, they may allow the Court to obtain the fullest possible argument from the parties.[114] In some circumstances, cases are so intricate that only oral hearings can disentangle the difficulties.[115] This was acknowledged in the 1987 advisory opinion (*Application for Review of Judgment No. 333 of the United Nations Administrative Tribunal*), where Judge Stephen Schwebel dissented that 'had oral arguments taken place, certain significant factual uncertainties might have been resolved'.[116]

105 Quintana Aranguren (n. 98) 1258.
106 Ibid.
107 *UNAT 1982* Advisory Opinion (n. 7) 380 (Separate opinion of Judge Mosler).
108 *UNAT 1973* Advisory Opinion (n. 7) 215 (Declaration of Judges Forster and Nagendra Singh).
109 *ILOAT 1956* Advisory Opinion (n. 3) 110 (Separate opinion of Judge Klaestad).
110 A/C.5/34/31.
111 *UNAT 1982* Advisory Opinion (n. 7) 339 [30].
112 Paul C. Szasz, 'Enhancing the Advisory Competence of the World Court' in Leo Gross (ed), *The Future of the International Court of Justice* vol II (Oceana Publications 1976) 530.
113 *ILOAT 1956* Advisory Opinion (n. 3) 108 (Separate opinion of Judge Winiarski).
114 Gross (n. 21) 31.
115 Kaikobad (n. 15) 202.
116 *UNAT 1987* Advisory Opinion (n. 11) 132 (Dissenting opinion of Judge Schwebel).

Secondly, oral hearings may allow judges to obtain missing information.[117] Judge Gros, dissenting to the 1973 advisory opinion (*Application for Review of Judgment No. 158 of the United Nations Administrative Tribunal*), believed that an intermediate stage was necessary before adjudicating because the staff member in the case had limited factual information in his case file.[118] This would allow the staff member to receive a full picture of the affair. This stage was also important for the Court; Judge Khan described that the Court had deprived itself of obtaining valuable assistance in the discharge of one of its judicial functions.[119] Indeed, it has been claimed that 'there would have been an investigation as a phase separate from the adjudication only if the Court had considered (. . .) that an enquiry and additional explanations were required before going ahead'.[120] The Court was therefore sacrificing an important process in the investigations.

Thirdly, oral hearings remove doubt as to whether the written statements reflect the individual's views. For example, in the 1973 case (*Application for Review of Judgment No. 158 of the United Nations Administrative Tribunal*), the ICJ President doubted whether Mr. Mohamed Fasla's statement, transmitted to the Court via the Secretary-General, 'accurately represented Mr. Fasla's views. The President therefore decided on 25 October 1972 that the written statement (. . .) might be amended by the filing of a corrected version of the statement of Mr. Fasla's views, and fixed 5 December 1972 as the time-limit for this purpose'.[121] This slowed down proceedings considerably, whereas the alternative of oral proceedings, allowing the individual to express their views directly, could have resolved this issue. It could possibly have done so more successfully than written statements, given the opportunity to ask questions and seek clarifications in case of any lingering doubt. Here, oral hearings are what make the difference in a process that otherwise consists of two rounds of potentially redundant written submissions (before the administrative tribunal and then before the ICJ).[122]

117 *UNAT 1973* Advisory Opinion (n. 7) 215 [26] (Declaration of Judges Forster and Nagendra Singh).

118 Kaikobad (n. 15) 202.

119 *ILOAT 1956* Advisory Opinion (n. 3) 114 (Separate opinion of Judge Muhammad Zafrulla Khan).

120 *UNAT 1973* Advisory Opinion (n. 7) 266–67 [38] (Dissenting opinion of Judge Gros).

121 Ibid 168 [7]–[8].

122 Szasz (n. 112) 530.

However, it must be noted that oral hearings may only be barred with the consent of UN Member States. While Article 105(2)(b) of the Court's Rules does give the Court discretion to decide if oral proceedings will take place, the Registrar must notify Member States of its decision.[123] Consequently, the Court finds itself in the uncomfortable position of relying on states to cooperate with this decision[124] and, as put by then-UN Secretary-General Perez de Cuellar, '[T]he entire procedure is thus at the mercy of any State that might insist on its right to make an oral statement under Article 66(2) of the ICJ Statute (which would result in the type of inequality of arms *vis-à-vis* the applicant that would almost surely cause the Court to abort the proceeding)'.[125] In contrast, an individual has no such power to insist on holding an oral hearing; this was made particularly clear when the interested staff member in the 1973 advisory proceedings (*Application for Review of Judgment No. 158 of the United Nations Administrative Tribunal*) insisted through letters to the Court that oral proceedings be held, to no avail.[126]

Other solutions could have been explored that would have enabled the Court to maintain oral hearings while placing the parties at more of an equal standing. This would involve both parties being represented in another format which would be acceptable in the Court's procedure.

First, the Court could have authorised the relevant staff members to make a statement in oral hearings, pursuant to Article 66(2) of its Statute. As examined in Chapter 3, the Court has exercised its discretion to allow relevant entities beyond states to furnish information. Despite the Court's observed reticence, this theoretically could have been a viable option to ensure the equality of parties.

Second, in line with proposals submitted in other chapters of this study, both sides – the staff member and the organisation – could have been heard as witnesses.[127] This is a delicate and controversial suggestion as the Court has not clearly established that the procedures regarding witnesses applicable in contentious cases could also be

123 ICJ Statute, Article 66(2); International Court of Justice, *Rules of Court*, Article 105(2)(b).

124 Joanna Gomula, 'The International Court of Justice and Administrative Tribunals of International Organisations' (1991) 13(1) *Michigan Journal of International Law* 83, 117.

125 A/C.5/34/31.

126 *UNAT 1973* Advisory Opinion (n. 7) 215 (Declaration of Judges Forster and Nagendra Singh).

127 Clarence Wilfred Jenks, *The Prospects of International Adjudication* (Stevens 1964) 144.

applied in advisory proceedings (see Chapter 3). It is also questionable whether the international organisation would accept to be 'down-graded' from being authorised to provide information in its own capacity pursuant to Article 66(2), to a witness. The Court might take issue with this as well: In the 2003 *Armed Activities* case, when Uganda requested to summon the Minister of Defence of the Republic of Uganda and a senior military officer in the Uganda People's Defence Forces as witnesses, the Court opined that it would not be appropriate. It stated that the participation of such individuals should not take the form of witness testimony.[128] The same reasoning could potentially apply to international organisations. However, the witness procedure remains a possible option.

Another possibility would be for two UN representatives to be appointed to appear before the Court, one representing the organisation and the other representing the staff member. These two representatives would play the role of counsel, specially designated to present and clarify issues for their clients.[129] Further, similar to the proposal for the transmission of written documents, the parties' views could have been communicated by an ombudsman. This was proposed for UNAT proceedings before the Court by a number of members of the UN Sixth Committee of the General Assembly.[130]

There were also possibilities for the individual to be represented in oral hearings by another entity entitled to appear before the Court. For instance, the Secretary-General could have represented the individual concerned; a suggestion made in scholarship[131] and by Judge Schwebel in 1987, who dissented that 'counsel selected by the application could be introduced as the Secretary-General's special representative to express the applicant's views'.[132] Despite possible delays in oral hearings (due to the abovementioned delays with the transmission of written documents), this was a procedurally viable option.

Although the Federation of International Civil Servants' Associations could be considered as the staff member's representative, it is doubtful that the Court would qualify this as an international organisation in the

[128] *Armed Activities on the Territory of the Congo (Democratic Republic of the Congo v. Uganda)* (Judgment) [2005] ICJ Rep 168, 178 [15].

[129] Szasz (n. 112) 529.

[130] Doc. A/C.6/48/SR.36, 3 (Ireland), 4 (Australia), 5 (Iran), 6 (United Kingdom), and 8 (France).

[131] Szasz (n. 112) 180 fn 179.

[132] *UNAT 1987* Advisory Opinion (n. 11) 132 (Dissenting opinion of Judge Schwebel).

sense of Article 66(2) of its Statute (Section 3.2). Although the PCIJ did hear organisations such as the International Federation of Trade Unions, the International Confederation of Christian Trade Unions, and International Organisation of Industrial Employers in successive ILO cases,[133] its successor became much more reserved, only allowing the International League for the Rights of Man in once instance, upon the premise that it was indeed an international organisation, as discussed in Chapter 3. It is therefore unlikely that any association would be permitted to represent the staff member in question, but another suitable representative from an international organisation would still be a viable option for the individual.

4.5 Conclusion

There are several reasons why the Court was an initially seen as an attractive forum for reviewing the decisions of administrative tribunals on disputes between certain international organisations and their staff members. First, its predecessor (the PCIJ) required to perform judicial review.[134] Second, these unique types of requests for advisory opinions nourished the Court's position as the principal judicial organ of the UN. Indeed, in reviewing the decisions of administrative tribunals, the Court was tasked with giving judicial advice on legal questions related to international institutional law,[135] particularly on activities of importance in the UN system of which it is part.[136] An indication that the Court placed importance on this task is that it never declined to deal with such requests, although it had the discretion to do so.[137] While the reasons for refusal include it not wishing to compromise 'the requirements of its judicial character",[138] or "compelling reasons',[139] the Court has stated that '[i]t is equally well established that the reply of the Court to a request

[133] Jenks (n. 127) 144.

[134] See International Civil Aviation Convention, 15 UNTS 295, Articles 84 and 86; International Air Services Transit Agreement, 84 UNTS 389, Article II Section 2; International Air Transport Agreement, Article IV Section 3.

[135] Kaikobad (n. 15) 295–96.

[136] Ibid 296.

[137] ICJ Statute, Article 65(1). See also *Accordance with International Law of the Unilateral Declaration of Independence in Respect of Kosovo* (Advisory Opinion) [2010] ICJ Rep 403, 415–16 [29].

[138] *ILOAT 1956* Advisory Opinion (n. 3) 84.

[139] Ibid 86; *UNAT 1973* Advisory Opinion (n. 7)183; *UNAT 1982* Advisory Opinion (n. 7) 347; *UNAT 1987* Advisory Opinion (n. 11) 31.

for opinion represents its participation in the activities of the United Nations and, in principle, should not be refused'.[140] Indeed, rejecting such an advisory opinion would 'imperil the working of the regime established by the Statute of the Administrative Tribunal for the judicial protection of officials',[141] according to the Court. The ICJ has thus considered all judicial review requests, even the *Application for Review of Judgment No. 273 of the United Nations Administrative Tribunal* advisory opinion of 1982, in which the Court admitted that there were indeed compelling reasons to decline giving an advisory opinion.[142]

Another benefit was the ability of this system to uphold fundamental principles of due process such as that of the faculty to 'appeal'. Although the principle of finality – stipulating that the decision rendered by a court is final – is paramount in international adjudication, it is limited by the faculty of appeal.[143] While ICJ has made clear that it is not a court of appeal, nor are such processes appeals,[144] the general idea of the injured party having the option to recourse to a sort of 'second instance' is still relevant in this context. In the words of one author, '[I]t is generally in the interests of international justice for the party aggrieved by an erroneous decision to have the means of correcting it. Otherwise, the finality of proceedings might lead to "perpetuating judicial errors" and may in fact hinder the proper administration of justice'.[145] *In casu*, the natural outcome of abolishing the practice of requesting the ICJ to review the ILOAT's decision is that the latter's judgments are final, and there is no procedure allowing the parties to challenge its judgments,[146] as stipulated in Article VI(1) of the ILOAT Statute.[147] They are thus binding on the parties, pursuant to the principle of *res judicata*.

Requesting to have the administrative tribunal's decision reviewed by the ICJ had seemingly been well-sought by staff members: while the ILOAT does not have clear statistics, it was reported in 1994 that 92

140 *UNAT 1987* Advisory Opinion (n. 11) 31–32 [25]; *UNAT 1973* Advisory Opinion (n. 7) 166 [40].
141 *ILOAT 1956* Advisory Opinion (n. 3) 77, 86.
142 *UNAT 1982* Advisory Opinion (n. 7) 347–48 [45].
143 Chester Brown, *A Common Law of International Adjudication* (OUP 2007) 153.
144 *UNAT 1973* Advisory Opinion (n. 7) 166 [14], [38], [47]–[48]; *ILOAT 1956* Advisory Opinion (n. 3) 98–99. See also *ILOAT 1956* Advisory Opinion (n. 3) 156 (Dissenting Opinion of Judge Córdova).
145 Brown (n. 143) 156.
146 A/C.6/94/2, 12.
147 *Judgment No. 442* [1981] ILOAT [2]–[3].

applications had been made from staff members to UNAT.[148] However, the Committee on Applications for Review of Administrative Tribunal Judgments provided for a filtering mechanism, resulting in only three being referred to by the Court.[149] As the Court had made clear that its task was that of a judicial review and not an appeal, it could be argued that judicial review is typically discretionary in its nature and not a right of the individual, contrary to an appeal. Despite this, removing this possibility for staff members could arguably interfere with certain general principles of law and procedural guarantees to which they are entitled, such as the right to effective remedy and the guarantee of due process.[150]

Notwithstanding these reasons in support of maintaining this procedure of review of administrative decisions by the Court, the structural and internal adversities that arose when the Court was faced with such cases were manifest. The structural adversities included the management of what were fundamentally contentious cases under the auspices of the advisory function between two non-state actors, and the ensuing complications. The internal adversities included whether it was appropriate to rule on questions of international administrative law, whether to review the merits of the administrative tribunal's decision, and most importantly, the multiple ramifications from the inequality between the parties, in written and oral proceedings.[151] The problems with respect to the inequality of the parties fundamentally stemmed from the fact that individuals have no *locus standi* to the Court. This was the source of inherent inequality of the parties in the entire review system.[152]

It seems unwarranted to dismantle the Court's Statute for a type of case that only reached the Court's docket on five occasions. The Court was ultimately not intended to address matters between individuals and staff members. History supports this: during the meeting of the Washington Committee of Jurists in 1945, the Venezuelan delegation proposed that the Court 'should be able to set itself up as a court of appeal for questions coming in first instance under the jurisdiction of other international administrative courts which may be created'.[153] This

[148] A/C.6/94/2 (n. 146) 3.
[149] Ibid; *UNAT 1973* Advisory Opinion (n. 7) 176–77 [27].
[150] See Antônio Cançado Trindade, *The Access of Individuals to International Justice* (OUP 2011) 64.
[151] *Judgment No. 2867* Advisory Opinion (n. 1) 69 [50] (Separate opinion of Judge Cançado Trindade); Kaikobad (n. 15) 287–89.
[152] Ibid (Kaikobad) 287–89.
[153] UNX.341.13 U51 vol III 231 [16].

amendment was ultimately rejected,[154] and Judge Córdova argued in his dissenting opinion of 1956 that this stands as clear evidence that the drafters of the Statute did not envision this function for the Court.[155] Venezuela's vision nonetheless came to fruition, due to international organisations delegating the Court with a function that went beyond the parameters of its own Statute. Fortunately, the terms of the Statute were broad enough to permit the Court to give advisory opinions akin to judicial review.[156] However, the Court made it clear in 2012 that it was uncomfortable with such a procedure, prompting the ILO to discontinue it.[157]

The Court was correct to question 'whether the system established in 1946 meets the present-day principle of equality of access to courts and tribunals'; it most certainly did not. The Court was also right in stating that it was 'not in a position to reform this system'.

But did the Court 'attempt to ensure, *so far as possible*, that there is equality in the proceedings before it'?[158] This chapter has argued that it did not. Articles 34(1) and 66(2) carry the unfortunate promise that the parties would have never truly been equal in an absolute sense. Due to the wording of the Statute, the equality of access will persist, despite any adaptations made with regard to the equality of arms. Yet, this chapter aimed to demonstrate that there were other potential solutions the Court did not consider to address the inequality of arms. Beyond the measures already taken, additional possibilities existed to adapt to the circumstances and narrow the inequality gap as much as possible. The Court, master of its own procedure, had the ability to implement these measures, which would have reflected a wider interpretation of the good administration of justice.

The short-lived practice of reviewing administrative tribunals' decisions was a robust and remarkable reminder that the Court is consistently faced with issues concerning individuals. Through challenges such as this one, it was invited to question whether the modest degree to which individuals participate in proceedings before it is appropriate. The system of reviewing decisions of UN administrative tribunals, according to a

[154] *ILOAT 1956* Advisory Opinion (n. 3) 107 (Separate opinion of Judge Winiarski).

[155] *ILOAT 1956* Advisory Opinion (n. 3) 160–61 (Dissenting opinion of Judge Córdova).

[156] Kaikobad (n. 15) 30.

[157] Judge Peter Tomka, 'Speech' (Sixty-Seventh Session of the General Assembly of the United Nations, 1 November 2012) 6. www.icj-cij.org/files/press-releases/0/17150.pdf; *Judgment No. 2867* Advisory Opinion (n. 1) 95 [3] (Declaration of Judge Greenwood).

[158] *Judgment No. 2867* Advisory Opinion (n. 1) 29–30 [44] (emphasis added).

former UN Secretary-General, was 'not established primarily for the purpose of giving applications, or even executive heads, another level of appeal (. . .) its purpose was to enable States to challenge judgments which they considered were for some reason as unacceptable (. . .)'.[159] The entire procedure was designed to grant more rights to states, rather than to individuals. Regardless of why this system was established, it was ultimately dismantled due to the consistent violation of the individual's procedural rights as a key stakeholder in the process.[160] This alone highlights the discrepancy between the increasing presence, relevance, and needs of individuals in international law and the Court's infrastructure. Through these types of advisory proceedings, it was proven that the Court's exercise of its procedural mechanisms does not copiously live up to required standards in today's international legal system.

[159] Doc. A/C.6/49/2, 11 [35]. See also Kaikobad (n. 15) 285 and 297.
[160] *Judgment No. 2867* Advisory Opinion (n. 1) 27 [39].

5

Remarks on Law

Part I explored the extent to which individuals are integrated in the proceedings of the Court. It looked beyond contentious disputes concerning a state litigant's compliance with a multilateral human rights treaty, focusing instead on other thematic contexts in contentious and advisory proceedings where individuals are at the centre of the case. Explaining how historically the individual fell short of being granted *locus standi* (Chapter 1), it turned to diplomatic protection proceedings (Chapter 2), advisory proceedings (Chapter 3) and the involvement of individuals in advisory proceedings regarding the review of the decisions of administrative tribunals (Chapter 4). Each chapter emphasised the gap between the degree to which the individual is in focus, on the one hand, and the degree to which they are procedurally included, on the other hand. In brief, the individual is procedurally involved in such contexts to a minor extent. I offer some reflections on the reasons for this.

5.1 A Culture of State-Centrism

The key reason explaining this approach is the culture of state-centrism developed by both state litigants and the Court. Professor Susan Marks has argued that the term 'state-centrism' may take three forms. First, it is the technique by, and reason for which, international law is disregarded by states.[1] Second, it may reflect an undue preoccupation with states as opposed to non-state actors.[2] Third, a state-centric approach is one that places 'too much emphasis on state sovereignty in the validation and application of international legal norms'.[3]

[1] Susan Marks, 'State-Centrism, International Law, and the Anxieties of Influence' (2006) 19 (2) *Leiden European Journal of International Law* 339, 345.
[2] Ibid 343.
[3] Ibid 340.

The preoccupation with states as opposed to non-state actors – such as individuals – is visible through the observations made in Part I. Indeed, states and non-state actors are classically distinguished by their legal status, capabilities, and resources on the international plane. The drafting of Article 34(1) would unknowingly define the milieu of the Peace Palace as one exclusively reserved for sovereign states and suggest that individuals have no place within those walls. At least partially because of this, the attitude of states has been set in stone: they are attached to their sovereignty and quite resistant to any type of potential interference with it.[4]

Although two viable options recurring in Part I were oral witness testimony or the inclusion of an individual in a government's delegation, these are far from being exploited by state litigants. For instance, in the context of diplomatic protection, despite the individual's central role in reality, state litigants limit their involvement to providing evidence for written pleadings. Yet, in such instances, the injured individuals could stand as witnesses or make statements as part of the states' delegation.

The relationship between states and non-state actors is more intertwined than the dichotomy at the World Court would suggest. Indeed, Marks reflects that there is a tendency to consider the state as if they 'had a reality and an agency all of their own', failing to acknowledge the extent to which states are already present within the other, and vice versa.[5] However, this dichotomy is maintained in the Court's culture not only due to state litigants' choices but also due to the Court's approach to its procedural mechanisms (Section 5.2) and fears (Section 5.3).

5.2 A Passive Approach to Procedural Mechanisms

Article 30 of the ICJ Statute confirms that it 'shall frame rules of carrying out its functions. In particular, it shall lay down rules of procedure'.[6] The freedom to determine its own procedural mechanisms was deliberately left to the Court by its Statute's drafters.[7] Furthermore, it has confirmed

[4] Sir Arthur Watts, 'Enhancing the Effectiveness of Procedures of International Dispute Settlement' (2001) 5 *Max Planck Yearbook of United Nations Law* 21.

[5] Marks (n. 1) 341.

[6] Statute of the International Court of Justice, Article 30 [hereafter, ICJ Statute].

[7] Hugh Thirlway, 'Article 30' in Andreas Zimmermann et al (eds), *The Statute of the International Court of Justice: A Commentary* (3rd edn, OUP 2019) 517.

that state litigants are 'under a duty to comply with all decisions as to procedure, which [it] is specifically empowered to make'.[8]

The Court therefore has ample power to manage evidence, in particular oral witness evidence in contentious proceedings involving individuals – whether it is one key injured individual in the context of diplomatic protection or an entire community. Indeed, both the state litigants *and* the Court are empowered to request witnesses. Furthermore, the Court has the power to analogously apply Articles 48–52 of its Statute where it feels that this is necessary to acquire evidence from private persons in advisory proceedings. In such proceedings, where the Court reviewed decisions of certain administrative tribunals on disputes between certain international organisations and their injured staff members, the Court had the power to guarantee the equality of parties and place the staff member on par with the international organisation in a number of innovative ways that were not fully exploited. The Court is also responsible for allowing *amicus curiae* submissions in advisory proceedings, and even in contentious ones.

Yet, in a myriad of contexts, the Court does not sufficiently exploit the procedural mechanisms at its disposal. It has very rarely used its powers to request additional documents, appoint experts or witnesses, or make site visits.[9] This has been criticised by many judges in their dissenting opinions.[10] The Court's 'hands-off' attitude is likely due to its underlying belief that its primary function is the respect of states' wishes and that its own powers to manage its procedural mechanisms are secondary. This finds its roots in the principle of sovereignty: states that have chosen the Court as a means to resolve their disputes have the prerogatives to frame the case as they wish, to present the evidence that they wish to present,

[8] *Land, Island and Maritime Frontier Dispute (El Salvador/Honduras: Nicaragua intervening)* (Judgment) [1992] ICJ Rep 350, 581–82 [371].

[9] For more on powers of international courts regarding evidence, see Chester Brown, *A Common Law of International Adjudication* (OUP 2007) 102–18.

[10] Some examples include: *Oscar Chinn* (Judgment) [1934] PCIJ Series A/B 109 (Individual opinion of Judge Anzilotti); *Barcelona Traction Light and Power Company Ltd. (Belgium v. Spain)* (Preliminary Objections) (Judgment) [1964] ICJ Rep 6, 80 (Separate opinion of Judge Bustamante); *Case concerning the Temple of Preah Vihear (Cambodia v. Thailand)* (Merits) (Judgment) [1962] ICJ Rep 6, 100 [55] (Dissenting opinion of Judge Wellington Koo); *Kasikili/Sedudu Island (Botswana/Namibia)* (Judgment) ICJ Rep 1045, 1072–73 [43]; *Military and Paramilitary Activities in and against Nicaragua (Nicaragua v. United States of America)* (Merits) (Judgment) [1986] ICJ Rep 14 [132] (Dissenting opinion of Judge Schwebel); *Oil Platforms (Islamic Republic of Iran v. United States of America)* (Judgment) [2003] ICJ Rep 161, 322–23 [52] (Separate opinion of Judge Owada).

and to decide how they aspire to have the proceedings handled. They may have perhaps even chosen the Court as the appropriate venue to settle their dispute *because* of their satisfaction with the Court's procedural framework and their ability to 'steer the wheel' in this sense, during proceedings. This approach therefore contributes to the culture of state-centrism. The Court's deference to states finds grounds in states' roles as the sole clients and funders of the Court (through the General Assembly).

However, a more proactive Court that still yields to states' demands is a viable prospect. Typically, the consultations held between governments and the President and the Registry before the course of proceedings – and the 'Notes for Parties' sent from the Registrar with any particular instructions and information – are opportune moments for the Court to prompt states to consider involving individuals through witness testimony. This is more straightforward than amending Practice Directions, which may easily be ignored.[11] Furthermore, in the scope of communication between parties and the Court, the latter may organise communication with the parties at the initiation of proceedings before written pleadings have been submitted. This approach allows the Court to better prepare itself if it anticipates that witnesses will be summoned.[12]

The Court has taken great strides to adapt its procedural mechanisms to its needs since its inception.[13] Anything done in favour of integrating individuals would merely be a continuation of the procedural adaptations in other areas that it has seamlessly made over the years.[14] In the words of international lawyer Wilfred Jenks, '[W]e must not underestimate the procedural resources specifically provided for in the Statute and already used, the procedural innovations and developments not specifically provided for in the Statute which have proved possible within its terms. Nor must we belittle the extent or effectiveness of the remedies available by the existing procedures'.[15]

[11] 'A Dialogue at the Court: Proceedings of the ICJ/UNITAR Colloquium Held on the Occasion of the Sixtieth Anniversary of the International Court of Justice' (2006) Registry of the Court UNITAR(063)/I16/2006, 25.

[12] Anna Riddell and Brendan Plant, *Evidence before the International Court of Justice* (British Institute of International and Comparative Law 2009) 76.

[13] Georges Abi-Saab, 'De l'évolution de la Cour internationale: Réflexions sur quelques tendances récentes' (1992) *Revue générale de droit international public* 273.

[14] Fernando Lusa Bordin, 'Procedural Developments at the International Court of Justice' (2021) 20 *The Law and Practice of International Courts and Tribunals* 395.

[15] Clarence Wilfred Jenks, *The Prospects of International Adjudication* (Stevens 1964) 125.

5.3 Fears

The Court's culture of state-centrism can also be attributed to several concerns it holds. Firstly, it fears being overwhelmed with evidence and information if individuals were more fully integrated into its procedures. Indeed, initiating the inclusion of witnesses, accepting states' demands for potentially large amounts of witnesses or accepting *amicus curiae* briefs could strain the Court's judicial economy, the 'efficient management of the judicial office as regards human, financial or instrumental resources'.[16] This reflects the Court's concern to avoid unnecessary effort or expense.[17] This fear of floodgates is amplified by the 'thin end of the wedge' phenomenon, where one seemingly insignificant procedural action will set a precedent with potentially negative repercussions. However, this can be controlled with a more active approach to procedural mechanisms, as discussed earlier.

A second fear that the Court may have is the fear of favour. Chapter 2 discussed the growing practice of evidenced videotaped statements from victims, seen in *Chagos* and *DRC v Uganda* and attempted in *Jadhav*. The procedural inclusion of individuals may be perceived as a tool of courtroom persuasion. Indeed, Professor Philippe Sands described Elysé's intervention as a statement of impact[18] and that she was there to 'tell her story (. . .) in the hope that her account might encourage the fourteen judges in a direction that could allow her to return to the place of her birth'.[19] Courtroom persuasion stems from the common law tradition, where the Aristotelian *pathos* device is employed to engage sympathy and therefore persuade decision-makers. Judges – particularly those from a civil law background – may fear that considering such statements would detract from their task of applying the law without concern for other non-legal considerations, which will be discussed in more depth in Part II.

This culture of state-centrism has been reinforced by two key concerns: preserving both the Court's uniqueness and its tradition. First, the Court is distinguished on the international stage by its procedural exclusion of individuals. Elsewhere, individuals have infiltrated international

[16] Fulvio Maria Palombino, 'Judicial Economy', *Max Planck Encyclopedia of Public International Law* (2020).

[17] Jonathan Wallace, *Webster's New World Law Dictionary*. Susan Ellis Wild, ed. (Wiley Hoboken 2006).

[18] Verbatim record 2018/20, 71–72 [4] (Philippe Sands).

[19] Philippe Sands, *The Last Colony: A Tale of Exile, Justice and Britain's Colonial Legacy* (Weidenfeld & Nicolson 2022) 3.

judicial fora in several ways. They are parties before human rights and international criminal courts, and may be parties in investor–state arbitration,[20] before the Iran–US Claims Tribunal[21] or before the International Tribunal for the Law of the Sea (ITLOS)'s Seabed Disputes Chamber.[22] Thus, the exclusion of individuals may stem from a desire to preserve the Court's unique character. Second, the Court's adherence to its traditions has upheld its state-centric approach. Like any court, whether domestic or international, the World Court is deeply rooted in its traditions. One ICJ judge has described that there is 'almost a pride in maintaining the rigidity and maintaining the way things were done 70 years ago'.[23]

However, procedural inclusion of individuals through the avenues discussed in Part I would not affect the Court's unique character, as its restriction of standing to states would remain unchanged. In some contexts, such as when reviewing decisions of certain administrative tribunals (Chapter 4), ensuring the equality of parties would reflect an application of the good administration of justice. In this sense, tradition cannot always be said to be helpful and, in the words of a judge, 'if [the Court] changed or modernised a bit, that wouldn't hurt really'.[24]

However, the culture of state-centrism may be challenged by a subtle shift in recent practice, where state litigants have arranged for relevant individuals to attend hearings, even if they did not actively participate. For example, a delegation of Chagossians were present during the Chagos oral hearings.[25] Similarly, during the oral hearings in the *Application of the Convention on the Prevention and Punishment of the Crime of Genocide (The Gambia v. Myanmar)* provisional measures phase,[26] H.E. Mr. Abubacarr Tambadou, then Attorney General and Minister of

[20] See, for example, International Centre for Settlement of Investment Disputes Convention, Article 25(1).

[21] Declaration of the Government of the Democratic Popular Republic of Algeria Concerning the Settlement of Claims by the Government of the United States and the Government of the Islamic Republic of Iran (19 January 1981) Article III(3).

[22] United Nations Convention on the Law of the Sea, 1833 UNTS 3, Articles 187(d), 291(2); Statute of the International Tribunal for the Law of the Sea, 1833 UNTS 561, Rule 20(2).

[23] Nienke Grossman, 'Julia Sebutinde: An Unbreakable Cloth' in Josephine Jarpa Dawuni and Akua Kuenyehia (eds), *International Courts and the African Woman Judge: Unveiled Narratives* (Routledge 2019) 47.

[24] Ibid 47.

[25] Sands (n. 19) 1.

[26] Although this contentious case falls outside the scope of this study, this example is important to illustrate this trend.

Justice of The Gambia, addressed the Court, stating, 'I am also pleased that The Gambia's delegation today includes members of the Rohingya community, including those who have travelled from the refugee camps in Bangladesh'.[27] Should this practice continue by state litigants, it might encourage more inclusion taking other forms in future.

Beyond state litigants, the Court could also take proactive measures to procedurally integrate individuals, as this would enhance its legitimacy from the perspective of social idealism. Each chapter in Part I demonstrated that the absence of individuals in proceedings where they are directly impacted may have repercussions on the Court's legitimacy, insofar as one or a combination of these standards are strained.

The Court's legitimacy may also stem from an ability to adapt to developments in the environment in which it operates. As discussed in the Introduction, the international legal order is now characterised by its multiplicity of actors. An inability to adapt to this reinforces a perception that the Court is isolated and disconnected from reality. It can be argued that legitimacy is only in the eyes of the Court's constituencies: UN organs, state litigants, and the wider international community with an 'interest in the proper application and development of international law'.[28] From the perspective of social idealism, the wider international community includes not only states but also individuals.

5.4 A Word on Transparency

Part I focused on the integration of individuals in certain proceedings before the Court. However, another means to complement – or compensate for the lack of – such practices is by enhancing transparency. Transparency and participation should not be confused; an institution may be transparent without enabling or enhancing participation of actors other than states. Transparency has become an increasing concern in international adjudication due to the interpenetration of human rights and the growing role of the individual in the international legal system.

Overall, the Court has good practices in transparency – especially compared to other inter-state adjudicatory bodies, such as at the World

[27] Verbatim record 2019/18, 16–17 [1].

[28] André Nollkaemper, 'The Court and Its Multiple Constituencies: Three Perspectives on the Kosovo Advisory Opinion' in Marko Milanovic and Michael Wood (eds), *The Law and Politics of the Kosovo Advisory Opinion* (OUP 2015) 219.

Trade Organisation (WTO).[29] Written parties' submissions are not disclosed while the case is pending,[30] meaning that neither state litigant may disclose pleadings to their citizens during proceedings.[31] However, they are made public on or after oral proceedings with the parties' consent.[32] Oral hearings are made open to the public unless the Court or both parties decide otherwise[33] and are streamed live on the internet, thereby allowing concerned individuals to follow them wherever they are in the world.[34] External media crews may not record the entire hearings but are permitted during the first minutes of oral hearings.[35] Deliberations at the Court are highly confidential, as is the composition of the drafting committee, which is a common feature in all national and international courts.[36]

Yet, in view of further enhancing transparency towards procedurally excluded individuals, the Court could enhance its public relations efforts by explaining its judgments to broader audiences. For example, the Registrar could answer questions of the press after the public delivery of a judgment.[37] Former Registrar Eduardo Valencia-Ospina, however, opposed this suggestion, arguing in 1997 that more emphasis should be put on the needs and interests of the parties and that public interest cases are less intense than criminal cases brought before other courts.[38]

29 At the WTO, written and oral pleadings are confidential. See Panagiotis Delimatsis, 'Institutional Transparency in the WTO' in Andrea Bianchi and Anne Peters (eds), *Transparency in International Law* (CUP 2013) 112–41.

30 International Court of Justice, *Rules of Court*, Article 53 [hereafter, *Rules of Court*].

31 Correspondence (28 September 1949) 628–29 ["it would be inconsistent with the proper administration of justice to expose the pleadings to public, perhaps even to polemical, discussion before the hearing."].

32 *Rules of Court*, Article 53(2).

33 ICJ Statute, Article 46; *Rules of Court*, Article 59.

34 They are streamed on UN Web TV, available at: http://webtv.un.org/.

35 International Court of Justice, 'Media Services' www.icj-cij.org/en/media-services cl A.4.

36 Thore Neumann and Bruno Simma, 'Transparency in International Adjudication' in Andrea Bianchi and Anne Peters (eds), *Transparency in International Law* (CUP 2013) 457–62.

37 Keith Highet, 'Problems in the Preparation of a Case: Perceptions of the Parties and the Court – Presentation' in 'A Dialogue at the Court: Proceedings of the ICJ/UNITAR Colloquium Held on the Occasion of the Sixtieth Anniversary of the International Court of Justice' (2006) Registry of the Court UNITAR (063)/I16/2006 126.

38 Eduardo Valencia-Ospina, 'Financing, Administering and Making Known the Work of the Court' in 'A Dialogue at the Court: Proceedings of the ICJ/UNITAR Colloquium Held on the Occasion of the Sixtieth Anniversary of the International Court of Justice' (2006) Registry of the Court UNITAR(063)/I16/2006 216.

This statement does seem accurate or reflective of the Court's current docket. Communities have been known to organise separate events alongside oral hearings to explain the significance of the dispute for their lives.[39] There are notable public interest dimensions in many cases on the Court's docket, and it has been documented that many cases are instigated by non-state actors.[40] Enhancing transparency practices in this direction could compensate for the absence of the individual in certain proceedings before the Court.

Bringing Part I to a close, the monograph turns to Part II, which addresses the degree to which the individual is considered in the practice of the World Court.

[39] E.g., Impunity Watch (@ImpunityWatch), 'Live from the Hague: Syrian Survivors of Torture and Families of Individuals Detained and Disappeared are Convening a Side-event as a "Right to Reply" to the Two Days of Oral Interventions at the #ICJ and What the Case Means to Them' (Twitter/X, 11 October 2023) https://x.com/ImpunityWatch/status/1712087915260420481?s=20.

[40] Michael A. Becker, 'Pay No Attention to that Man behind the Curtain: The Role of Civil Society and Other Actors in Decisions to Litigate at the International Court of Justice' (2023) 26 *Max Planck Yearbook of United Nations Law Online* 90.

PART II

The Individual in the Practice of the International Court of Justice

6

Maritime Disputes

> The Court, in assessing the extent of the lateral maritime boundary (. . .) is aware of the importance that fishing has had for the coastal populations of both Parties.[1]

When maritime entitlements between neighbouring coastal states overlap in the Exclusive Economic Zone (EEZ) or the continental shelf, Articles 74 and 83 of the United Nations Convention on the Law of the Sea (UNCLOS) provide that such issues shall be resolved 'by agreement on the basis of international law, as referred to in Article 38 of the Statute of the International Court of Justice, in order to achieve an equitable solution'.[2] The International Court of Justice (ICJ, the Court) is one of the institutions available to UNCLOS parties to resolve their disputes, pursuant to UNCLOS's Article 287. The Court has developed extensive practice in maritime boundary disputes, definitively delimiting overlapping maritime claims to identify the maritime areas in which coastal states may exercise sovereign rights. In some boundary disputes, the Court has delimited (i.e. drawn) maritime boundaries, while in others, it has simply ascertained if a state has sovereignty over a disputed maritime zone, without necessarily delimiting a boundary.[3] This chapter considers both approaches.

Maritime boundary disputes may carry repercussions for the livelihoods of coastal populations requiring access to the fishing resources of certain waters. There are two main types of fishing activities of benefit to coastal populations: industrial and traditional (or artisanal) fishing. Industrial fishing is typically carried out by vessels catching tonnes of

[1] *Maritime Dispute (Peru v. Chile)* (Judgment) [2014] ICJ Rep 3, 45 [109].

[2] See United Nations Convention on the Law of the Sea, 1833 UNTS 3, Articles 74 and 83.

[3] E.g., *Maritime Delimitation in the Black Sea (Romania v. Ukraine)* (Judgment) [2009] ICJ Rep 61; *Fisheries Jurisdiction (United Kingdom v. Iceland)* (Merits) (Judgment) [1974] ICJ Rep 3.

fish for the state. Traditional fishing is smaller in scale, carried out by communities of coastal inhabitants for their livelihood.[4] While industrial fishing activities may be considered, this chapter mainly focuses on traditional fishing. Maritime boundary disputes yield significant disruption for traditional fishing activities, which are of social and cultural importance to coastal populations.[5] It may also result in the internal displacement of coastal populations to sustain their livelihoods.

Despite these potential repercussions on coastal populations, such considerations are seldom reflected in the Court's judicial reasoning. This chapter questions whether the Court's approach aligns with the object and purpose of the UNCLOS to 'promote the *economic and social advancement* of all *peoples* of the world, in accordance with the Purposes and Principles of the United Nations as set forth in the Charter'.[6] In other words, is it effectively supporting the UN regime? (Section I.1.1) Furthermore, is it upholding outcome legitimacy by making just decisions for coastal populations? (Section 1.1.2). In this chapter, I identify the distinct contexts in maritime disputes where concerns for local populations are raised in states' arguments but ultimately dismissed by the Court. I observe that the overarching reason underpinning the Court's approach is its adherence to formalism (Section 6.1). I first argue that this approach is appropriate when determining the pre-existence of a maritime boundary before proceeding with delimitation (Section 6.2). However, when adjusting a provisional line in maritime boundary delimitation, I argue that the principle of equity can play a greater role in promoting a fuller consideration of the needs of local populations (Section 6.3). The approach of dismissing concerns for local populations – and more specifically, their historic fishing rights – has also taken place beyond the delimitation process, when attributing sovereignty to a maritime zone (Section 6.4). In this context, I argue that reframing the understanding of stability can allow for historic fishing rights to be

4 FAO, 'Guidelines for the Routine Collection of Capture Fishery Data' in FAO Fisheries Technical Paper No. 382 prepared at the FAO/DANIDA Expert Consultation (Bangkok 1998) (FAO, Rome 1999) 1, 105; *Second stage of the proceedings between Eritrea and Yemen (Maritime Delimitation) (Eritrea/Yemen)* (Award) (1999) XXII RIAA 335, 360 [106]; Polite Dyspriani, 'Traditional Fishing Rights: Analysis of State Practice' (2011) United Nations Office of Legal Affairs Division for Ocean Affairs and the Law of the Sea.

5 Vandick S. Batista, Nidia N. Fabré, Ana C. M. Malhado and Richard J. Ladle, 'Tropical Artisanal Coastal Fisheries: Challenges and Future Directions' (2014) 22(1) *Reviews in Fisheries Science & Aquaculture* 1, 3.

6 UNCLOS, preamble cl 7 (emphasis added).

upheld and therefore for the needs of local populations to be considered. I then conclude (Section 6.5).

6.1 Formalism and the World Court

The Court's approach to maritime boundary disputes is largely anchored in formalism, a normative theory that dictates how international law should be applied. In this section, I explain some relevant features of formalism to understand the Court's approach to maritime boundary disputes developed in the remaining sections of this chapter.

First, formalism pleads for an exclusive application of law without consideration for non-juridical elements. It thereby distinguishes law from non-law, insisting that judges must only refer to the law to make their decisions.[7] This perspective assumes that the law, on one hand, and all other considerations, on the other, are autonomous and mutually exclusive. Accordingly, extra-legal considerations such as morality, substantive values, politics or humanitarian, or social or economic factors are outside of the scope of judicial activities and thus immaterial. According to formalism, amalgamating law with such elements would rob it of its objectivity, neutrality, and credibility.[8] Closely related is the distinction between *lex lata* and *lex ferenda*: any approach other than a strict reading of the black-letter law will result in what the law ought to be, as opposed to what it is.[9] This position was well expressed by the Court in *South West Africa (Liberia v. South Africa; Ethiopia v. South Africa)*:

> Throughout this case it has been suggested, directly or indirectly, that humanitarian considerations are sufficient in themselves to generate legal rights and obligations, and that the Court can and should proceed accordingly. The Court does not think so. It is a court of law, and can take account of moral principles only insofar as these are given a sufficient expression in legal form. Law exists, it is said, to serve a social need; but precisely for that reason it can do so only through and within the limits of its own discipline. Otherwise, it is not a legal service that would be rendered.[10]

[7] Andrea Bianchi, *International Law Theories: An Inquiry into Different Ways of Thinking* (OUP 2016) 24.

[8] Ibid 27.

[9] Ibid 26.

[10] *South West Africa (Liberia v. South Africa; Ethiopia v. South Africa)* (Second Phase) (Judgment) [1966] ICJ Rep 6, 34 [49]. See also *South West Africa (Liberia v. South Africa; Ethiopia v. South Africa)* (Preliminary Objections) (Judgment) [1962] ICJ Rep 319, 466 (Joint dissenting opinion of Sir Percy Spender and Sir Gerald Fitzmaurice). The Court has

It is demonstrated in this chapter (Sections 6.2 and 6.3) that the Court rejects the consideration of coastal populations to adjust its delimited maritime boundary due to its reticence to apply what it considers to be 'non-law'.

The second relevant feature of formalism is its objective to 'provide predictability in the behaviour of law-making authorities', such as the ICJ.[11] It therefore implies that international judges have little choice in law application; their task is to apply jurisprudence to fortify an international legal system of norms.[12] In the context of maritime disputes, the desire for predictability has led to the development of the principle of stability of boundaries. The Court has placed great emphasis on this principle, refusing to consider other elements that could somehow jeopardise it.[13] It has clearly stated that 'Whether it is a land frontier or a boundary line in the continental shelf that is in question, the process is essentially the same, and inevitably involves the same element of stability and permanence, and is subject to the rule excluding boundary agreements from fundamental change of circumstances'.[14] Stability was reportedly the underlying objective behind outsourcing delimitation to international courts and tribunals; the International Tribunal for the Law of the Sea (ITLOS) explained in *Bangladesh/Myanmar* that international courts and tribunals were tasked with maritime delimitation to develop 'a body of case law (. . .) which has reduced the elements of subjectivity and uncertainty in the determination of maritime boundaries (. . .)'.[15]

Thus, in *Continental Shelf (Tunisia/Libyan Arab Jamahiriya)*, Tunisia claimed that fishing resources must be taken into account as supplementing its national economy in eking out its survival as a country.[16] The Court carefully explained that it was unable to take such factors into

also said elsewhere that it does not decide on matters of policy: *Whaling in the Antarctic (Australia v. Japan: New Zealand intervening)* (Judgment) [2014] ICJ Rep 226, 254 [69].

11 Jean d'Aspremont, *Formalism and the Sources of International Law: A Theory of the Ascertainment of Legal Rules* (OUP 2011) 18–19.

12 Ibid 19.

13 This is also the case in territorial disputes (see Chapter 7). See *Case concerning the Temple of Preah Vihear (Cambodia v. Thailand)* (Merits) (Judgment) [1962] ICJ Rep 6, 34; *Territorial Dispute (Libyan Arab Jamahiriya/Chad)* (Judgment) [1994] ICJ Rep 6, 37 [72]–[73].

14 *Aegean Sea Continental Shelf (Greece v. Turkey)* (Judgment) [1978] ICJ Rep 3, 35–36 [85].

15 *Delimitation of the Maritime Boundary in the Bay of Bengal (Bangladesh/Myanmar)* (Judgment) [2012] ITLOS Rep 4, 64 [226].

16 *Continental Shelf (Tunisia/Libyan Arab Jamahiriya)* (Judgment) [1982] ICJ Rep 18, 77 [106].

account to delimit the continental shelf areas because '[t]hey are virtually extraneous factors since they are variables which unpredictable national fortune or calamity, as the case may be, might at any time cause to tilt the scale one way or the other. A country might be poor today and become rich tomorrow as a result of an event such as the discovery of a valuable economic resource'.[17] It has explained in other judgments that resource-related criteria are treated cautiously and not considered to be relevant circumstances in maritime delimitation.[18] Fishing activities fall under the same category, in the view of the Court.

It is observed in this chapter that the Court's refusal to apply 'non-law' and its concern for predictability prohibit it from adjusting a provisional line in maritime boundary delimitation (Section 6.3). When determining sovereignty over a disputed maritime zone (without necessarily delimiting a boundary), the Court also prioritises stability by not upholding arguments related to historic fishing rights in maritime zones (Section 6.4). These reflect its broad formalist approach to international law, which is challenged in this chapter. This is because this approach can lead to unjust outcomes for coastal populations. From the perspective of social idealism, this can impact the legitimacy of the decision (Section I.1.2). An approach that does not consider such populations can also call the effectiveness of the Court into question (Section I.1.1). However, while the Court adopts a similar approach when determining the pre-existence of a boundary before exercising delimitation, I argue that this is appropriate in this context (Section 6.2).

6.2 Determining a Pre-existing Boundary

Before delimiting a maritime boundary, the Court may first seek to determine whether the parties have already agreed on a boundary. If no such agreement exists, the Court will then proceed to delimit the maritime boundary itself. It is observed in this section that while the Court may support state litigants factoring in their coastal populations when drawing a straight baseline, for example, it will not make the same consideration when deciding whether parties have already agreed on a boundary and when determining the extent of that boundary. This, I argue, is appropriate given the objectivity of the latter exercise.

[17] Ibid 77–78 [107].

[18] *Black Sea* (n. 3) 125–26 [198]; *Territorial and Maritime Dispute (Nicaragua v. Colombia)* (Judgment) [2012] ICJ Rep 624, 706 [223].

In the 2014 *Maritime Dispute (Peru v. Chile)* judgment, the Court had to delimit the boundary between the two states' maritime zones in the Pacific Ocean. The applicant Peru argued that access to the waters off the coast of Southern Peru was of critical importance to the local population and the country.[19] It requested the Court to recognise a maritime zone lying within 200 nautical miles of Peru's coast and thus appertaining to Peru. Chile, on the other hand, considered this maritime zone to be part of the high seas. Peru's main argument was that, in order to avoid friction and incidents with Chile due to the absence of a delimited maritime boundary, Peruvian fishermen's activities had been limited on a provisional basis to the line of latitude and the zone of tolerance established in the 1954 Agreement on a Special Zone.[20] Peru has therefore 'exhibited considerable self-restraint',[21] but now crucially needed definitive delimitation to provide its coastal population with an equitable access to the maritime resources of the disputed area.[22]

The Court, therefore, had to determine whether Peru did, in fact, own the said maritime zone lying within 200 nautical miles of its coast. Through analysing evidence, it first found that the parties had tacitly acknowledged the existence of an all-purpose pre-existing maritime boundary.[23] Then, to determine the extent of this boundary – and more specifically, whether the boundary extended to the 200-nautical mile limit – it analysed the relevant practice of the parties in the early and mid-1950s.[24]

At the time, the state parties contended that the areas lying off their coasts were rich in marine resources, and expressed the fear that 'large foreign fishing fleets exhausting resources necessary for the livelihood of coastal populations', which the Chilean diplomat considered 'tragic'.[25] The Court also took note of the location of the most important fishing ports at the time for both parties – Ilo for Peru and Arica for Chile (120 km north-west and 15 km south of the seaward terminus of the land boundary, respectively).[26] Ultimately, however, it concluded that the extent of the resources that would be important for fishing out to

19 Memorial of Peru (20 March 2009) 59–60 [2.31].
20 Ibid.
21 Ibid.
22 Ibid 60 [2.32].
23 *Maritime Dispute (Peru v. Chile)* (n. 1) 41 [100]–[102].
24 Ibid 44 [108].
25 Ibid 42 [105]–[106].
26 Ibid 44 [108].

200 nautical miles '[was] not see[n] as of great significance'.[27] What it *did* consider significant was that such boats would not cross the parallel beyond a point approximately 57 nautical miles from the starting point of the maritime boundary.[28] It therefore considered that fishing for coastal populations, while important, was not relevant in its assessment. The movement of the boats was what provided evidence to the Court to conclude that the boundary did not extend beyond 80 nautical miles from the coast.[29]

Indeed, 'at the time when they acknowledged the existence of an agreed maritime boundary between them, [Peru and Chile] were unlikely to have considered that it extended all the way to the 200-nautical-mile limit'.[30] This serves as indication that, regardless of the protests or concerns that state parties may raise with respect to the needs of their coastal populations, the process of establishing a pre-existing maritime boundary remains fact-based and evidence-driven. Akin to my assessment in Chapter 7 on effective control in territorial disputes, peoples' actions are only considered as evidence for a specific task, if relevant, without considerations for their needs.

Elsewhere, the Court has demonstrated support for state litigants who, themselves, factor in the needs of their coastal populations when tasked with a drawing exercise. In the 1951 *Anglo-Norwegian Fisheries* case, Norway unilaterally enacted a 1935 decree delimiting its northern coast using straight baselines. The objective of the decree was to reserve certain fishing grounds situated off its northern coast for the exclusive use of its own fishermen. In defence of its decree, Norway argued that Norwegian fishermen living along the northern coast (the Lopphavet basin) had exclusively fished there throughout history. It therefore advocated for the traditional fishing rights of the communities living at the coast and the requirement to protect their interests. According to Norway, the fishing zone as delimited was necessary to safeguard the interests of these communities.[31] The Court recognised that these '[fishing] grounds were known to Norwegian fishermen and exploited by them from time immemorial'[32] and decided that 'Such rights, founded on the vital needs of the

[27] Ibid 44 [109].
[28] Ibid 44 [108].
[29] Ibid 71 [196]–[197].
[30] Ibid 45 [111].
[31] *Fisheries Case (United Kingdom v. Norway)* (Judgment) [1951] ICJ Rep 116, 127 and 142.
[32] Ibid 142.

population and attested by very ancient and peaceful usage, *may legitimately be taken into account in drawing a line* which, moreover, appears to the Court to have been kept within the bounds of what is moderate and reasonable'.[33]

The focus of this case was on the lawfulness of straight baselines, which states can draw of their own accord, as opposed to the determination of a pre-existing maritime boundary, which cannot be drawn by a state unilaterally. Nonetheless, this case shows the Court's approval for the state litigant's consideration of local fishermen's needs. Where the Court engages in a similar drawing exercise (to determine the pre-existence of a maritime boundary), however, it is more mindful of the objectivity required by the task at hand. In my view, this is the correct approach for this particular task. While states may wish to exercise their sovereignty by considering fishing when unilaterally drawing their own lines, the Court's foundational drawing tasks should be an objective fact-based – and not need-based – process.

In *Maritime Dispute (Peru v. Chile)*, the Court first reached the conclusion that the pre-existing boundary spanned 80 nautical miles and then delimited the maritime boundary to determine its course from that point on.[34] To reach the conclusion that the pre-existing boundary spanned 80 nautical miles, the Court could only rely on existing relevant evidence indicating what that boundary looked like. Similarly, delimiting the rest of its course beyond 80 nautical miles was the act of drawing the provisional line, which is the first stage of the maritime boundary delimitation process.

Indeed, when delimiting a maritime boundary, the Court has developed a general methodology in its jurisprudence. The first stage is usually the delimitation of a provisional line. The second stage of maritime delimitation requires the Court to consider whether certain factors – referred to as 'relevant circumstances' – necessitate adjusting the provisional line to achieve an equitable result.[35] The final stage, in Exclusive Economic Zone (EEZ) and continental shelf delimitation, is to verify that this line does not lead to an inequitable result (disproportionality test).[36]

[33] Ibid 127.

[34] *Maritime Dispute (Peru v. Chile)* (n. 1) 71–73 [198].

[35] The term "relevant circumstances" is used in EEZ and continental shelf delimitation. In the territorial sea, they are called "special circumstances" (see UNCLOS, Article 15).

[36] *Black Sea* (n. 3) 101–3 [116]–[122].

Massimo Lando observes that '[E]stablishing a provisional equidistance line[] should be approached as [an] objective exercise[]. Conversely, adjusting the provisional equidistance line and the assessment of disproportionality ensure that the boundary achieves an equitable solution'.[37] The judicial process of the Court has distinguished between drawing lines and adjusting them. The Court may therefore draw provisional line in maritime delimitation (stage one), and then adjust the latter in light of needs of local populations, for example (stage two). In the delimitation exercise, there was an opportunity to raise concerns related to local populations as a relevant circumstance.[38] The adjustment of the provisional line for relevant circumstances in maritime boundary delimitation, examined in further detail below, is where consideration of local populations is more appropriate and has more potential.

6.3 Maritime Boundary Delimitation

The Court can consider coastal populations as a relevant circumstance in stage two of the maritime delimitation process, necessitating the adjustment of the provisional line to achieve an equitable result. The Court can also consider coastal populations as a factor in stage three, when assessing the overall test for the equitableness of the boundary (disproportionality test). This involves conducting a final check that there is 'no great disproportionality of maritime areas (. . .) by comparison to the ratio of coastal lengths'.[39]

Arguments relating to the fishing activities of coastal populations have come before the Court in different forms. First, states have indicated the importance of natural resources, the access to which provides food and energy and is therefore an important source of wealth for both governments and local populations. This was raised and rejected in *Territorial and Maritime Dispute (Nicaragua v. Colombia)*, for example.[40]

A second argument is that fishing activities should be considered as evidence of the state's conduct or effective control (*effectivités*) over a certain contested maritime zone, which should be factored into the delimitation of a contested boundary (Section 7.2). For instance, in *Black Sea*, Ukraine argued that its behaviour (providing licences for

[37] Massimo Lando, *Maritime Delimitation as a Judicial Process* (CUP 2019) 30.

[38] Ibid 65–66 [181]–[182].

[39] Ibid 103 [122].

[40] *Territorial and Maritime Dispute (Nicaragua v. Colombia)* (n. 18) 706 [223].

fishing practices and intercepting illegal fishing boats) constituted maritime *effectivités* and proved its sovereignty over the fishing zone extending up to the disputed line.[41] The *acte à titre de souverain* ('act as the sovereign') with respect to fishing should therefore be considered as a relevant circumstance.[42] The Court, echoing the findings of an arbitral tribunal that 'resource-related criteria have been treated more cautiously' in international adjudication, stated in this case that it '[did] not see (. . .) any particular role for the State activities invoked (. . .)'.[43]

Both arguments place more emphasis on the state's interests: natural resources benefit states more generally, while fishing activities are raised as a conduct of states and evidence of their sovereignty. A third argument, which will be the focus of this section, squarely addresses the needs of local populations. In several instances, state litigants have argued that coastal populations' ability to fish and acquire resources necessary for their livelihood should be a relevant circumstance, warranting the adjustment of the provisional line drawn in the first stage of the maritime delimitation process. However, the Court has only upheld this argument and adjusted the provisional line accordingly in one instance. This is because of its formalistic approach (Section 6.1) and a concern for the stability of boundaries.

I argue in this section that the principle of equity can play a greater role in promoting a fuller consideration of the needs of coastal populations. I first explain the principle of equity (Section 6.3.1). I then observe how the Court developed its jurisprudence consistently dismissing state litigants' claims related to their populations (Section 6.3.2). Finally, I reflect on the appropriateness of this approach in light of the principle of equity (Section 6.3.3).

6.3.1 The Principle of Equity

Equity is the concept of fairness and reasonableness in the administration of justice.[44] As the Court described, 'Equity as a legal concept is a direct emanation of the idea of justice'[45] offering a 'bridge to justice where the

[41] Counter-Memorial of Ukraine (19 May 2006) 216–19 [8.58]–[8.65].
[42] *Black Sea* (n. 3) 124 [193].
[43] Ibid 125–26 [198].
[44] Elihu Lauterpacht, *Aspects of the Administration of International Justice* (Grotius Publications 1991) 117–52.
[45] *Continental Shelf (Tunisia/Libyan Arab Jamahiriya)* (n. 16) 60 [71].

law itself is not able to adequately respond'.[46] It has been applied to maritime boundary disputes as early as 1909. Indeed, in *Award on the Grisbådarna*, a dispute over the maritime boundary in the Grisbådarna fisheries zone between Norway and Sweden, an arbitral tribunal considered traditional fishing activities in its delimitation task. The arbitral tribunal stated that the demarcation assigning the Grisbådarna to Sweden was carried out in light of the following circumstances: the fact that lobster fishing had been carried out for a much longer time, to a much larger extent, and by a much greater number of Swedish fishermen than Norwegian ones; that lobster fishing was the most important fishing and what gives the banks their value as a fishing area; Swedes were the first to fish for lobsters; and fishing was more important to the inhabitants of Koster (Sweden) than Hvaler (Norway).[47] In so doing, the arbitral tribunal applied the principle of equity to directly respond to the real interest of the parties on the rich lobster fisheries of the Grisbådarna Banks.[48]

In contemporary international adjudication, equity has been approached with caution mainly due to its conflation with adjudication *ex aequo et bono*. Equity and adjudication *ex aequo et bono* are often confused in practice, and it is unhelpful that the terms are sometimes used interchangeably. Some distinctions may be drawn between them.[49] There are several ways to implement the principle of equity, largely depending on the type of equity being discussed: equity may denote a means for filling the gaps in international law (equity *praeter legem*), be considered as an intrinsic attribute of the rules of law (equity *infra legem*), or be used in derogation from the law, to remedy its social inadequacies (equity *contra legem*).[50] Only the latter type of equity, *contra legem*, is tantamount to adjudication *ex aequo et bono*.[51] This type of adjudication allows the Court to base its

[46] Thomas Cottier, *Equitable Principles of Maritime Boundary Delimitation: The Quest for Distributive Justice in International Law* (CUP 2015) 8. See also Masahiro Miyoshi, *Considerations of Equity in the Settlement of Territorial and Boundary Disputes*, vol 2 (Martinus Nijhoff Publishers 1993) 11–13.

[47] *The Grisbådarna case (Norway/Sweden)* (1909) (Award) PCA XI RIAA 147, 161.

[48] Robert Kolb, *Case Law on Equitable Maritime Delimitation: Digest and Commentaries*, vol 38 (Martinus Nijhoff Publishers 2003) 8. See also René Waultrin, 'Un conflit de limites maritimes entre la Norvège et la Suède: L'affaire des Grisbådarna' (1910) 17 *Revue générale de droit international public* 77.

[49] See also Miyoshi (n. 46) 14–16.

[50] Andreas Zimmermann et al (eds), *The Statute of the International Court of Justice: A Commentary* (3rd edn, OUP 2019) 874.

[51] Ibid 794 and 797.

decisions on considerations which are not necessarily legal in character.[52] When adjudicating *ex aequo et bono*, the Court would not apply international law but would take other considerations into account instead of the law, in the pursuit of fairness or justice.[53]

It is unclear whether, and to what extent, an *ex aequo et bono* decision would differ from a decision based on equity *contra legem* in practice, apart from the procedural requirement that *ex aequo et bono* can only be exercised with the explicit agreement of the parties, as stipulated by Article 38(2) of the Statute.[54] However, from a conceptual standpoint, the notions of equity *contra legem* and adjudication *ex aequo et bono* are essentially the same, although the Court has never used the term 'equity *contra legem*' in its jurisprudence. One can understand, however, that when it refers to adjudication *ex aequo et bono*, the term may effectively be substituted for equity *contra legem*.

While the Court has explicitly shown disapproval for adjudication *ex aequo et bono*, it has applied the principle of equity in some instances. When doing so, it has been careful to clarify that it is not deciding *ex aequo et bono*[55] – the difference being that equity is applicable as an element of law and does not require the parties' consent.[56] The Court, in other words, is clarifying that it is not applying the principle of equity *contra legem*. This reasoning suggests that the Court refers to equity that is in conformity with the law; in other words, *praeter legem* (for filling the gaps in international law) or equity *infra legem* (as an intrinsic attribute of the rules of law).[57]

Despite the claim that the Court has never decided *ex aequo et bono*,[58] it is unclear what type of equity is being applied in most cases. *North Sea*

[52] For this reason, it has been called "the model of juridical vacuum" by one author. See Cottier (n. 46) 205.

[53] Markus Kotzur, 'Ex aequo et bono' in *Max Planck Encyclopedia of Public International Law* (OUP 2009).

[54] *Case of Free Zones of Upper Savoy and the District of Gex* (Order) [1930] PCIJ Series A, 10; *Continental Shelf (Tunisia/Libyan Arab Jamahiriya)* (n. 16) [71]; *Delimitation of the Maritime Boundary in the Gulf of Maine Area (Canada/United States of America)* (Judgment) [1984] ICJ Rep 246, 278 [59]; *Frontier Dispute (Burkina Faso/Mali)* (Judgment) [1986] ICJ Rep 554, 567–68 [28].

[55] *Continental Shelf (Tunisia/Libyan Arab Jamahiriya)* (n. 16) 60 [71]; *North Sea Continental Shelf (Federal Republic of Germany/Denmark; Federal Republic of Germany/Netherlands)* (Judgment) [1969] ICJ Rep 3, 48–49 [88]; *Continental Shelf (Libyan Arab Jamahiriya/Malta)* (Judgment) [1985] ICJ Rep 13, 38–39 [45].

[56] *Frontier Dispute (Burkina Faso/Mali)* (n. 54) 575–76 [42].

[57] Miyoshi (n. 46) 117–42 (equity *infra legem*), 146–71 (equity *praeter legem*).

[58] Zimmermann (n. 50) 882.

Continental Shelf, for example, was notable for explicitly introducing equity in maritime delimitation.[59] However, the judgment only refers to the general principle of equity without specifying which type had been employed.[60] Judge Ammoun gave assurances in his separate opinion that equity *praeter legem* (for filling the gaps in international law) had been applied.[61] Yet in a 1978 letter to Elihu Lauterpacht, Sir Gerald Fitzmaurice, another judge involved in the North Sea Continental Shelf cases, stated that, in the context of discussing the cases, 'a Tribunal is precluded by its Statute (. . .) from deciding *ex aequo et bono, but is in fact doing just that*, it cannot avow it, and has to take refuge in silence'.[62] This suggests that *ex aequo et bono* may have in fact been applied in *North Sea Continental Shelf*.

The Court's reticence to adjudicate *ex aequo et bono* (equity *contra legem*) reflects the underlying approach of formalism and the fear of inviting consideration for extra-legal factors. I will demonstrate in Section 6.3.3 that in the context of maritime boundary delimitation, the proposed application of equity to consider coastal populations is not an *ex aequo et bono* exercise (equity *contra legem*) – rather, it is part and parcel of the legal process. Before doing so, it is important to understand how the Court's position with respect to local populations emerged in its jurisprudence (Section 6.3.2).

6.3.2 *The 'Catastrophic Repercussions' Threshold*

It is important to understand how the Court developed its jurisprudence dismissing state litigants' claims related to their populations. The Court established its position in *Delimitation of the Maritime Boundary in the Gulf of Maine Area (Canada/United States of America)* (1984). In this case, Canada and the United States of America (US) requested a Chamber of the Court to delimit the maritime boundary dividing their continental shelf and fisheries zones in the Gulf of Maine on the East Coast of North America.[63] Once it drew the provisional boundary line (stage one), the Chamber had to decide

[59] Catharine Titi, *The Function of Equity in International Law* (OUP 2021) 41.
[60] See, e.g., *North Sea Continental Shelf* (n. 55) 46–47 [85], 48–49 [88].
[61] Ibid 151–52 [56] (Separate opinion Ammoun).
[62] Lauterpacht (n. 44) 125 n. 19.
[63] The precise delimited area is described by the Court in its judgment: *Gulf of Maine* (n. 54) 268 [29].

whether this line was equitable in light of relevant circumstances, and if anything could justify its adjustment. Both Canada and the US had placed significant emphasis on the importance of fishing activities, '*in extenso*'.[64] The Chamber acknowledged that they 'exchanged a lengthy argument' on various matters related to fishing, for instance, the nationality of the first fishermen in this area had, the importance of fisheries for various economic industries in the region, the dependence of their populations on such fisheries, and the negative impacts of an unfavourable delimitation on the nations' economies.[65]

The US also emphasised that its historic fishing presence in the area (see Section 6.4) should be considered as a relevant circumstance in the maritime boundary delimitation.[66] Canada, on the other hand, emphasised socio-economic arguments also largely connected to fishing practices, insisting that 'any single maritime boundary should ensure the maintenance of the existing fishing patterns that are in its view vital to the coastal communities of the region in question'.[67] Fishing was clearly the central part of this dispute.

The Chamber, however, held that the 'crux of the matter lies elsewhere' and that while fishing considerations require the examination of political and economic considerations, the Chamber must achieve a result on the basis of law; not *ex aequo et bono* ('from equity and conscience').[68]

In this assessment, the Chamber proceeded to reject both parties' arguments regarding fishing activities. However, the Chamber then penned down a reservation, which would come to be known as the 'catastrophic repercussions' doctrine:

> What the Chamber would regard as a legitimate scruple lies rather in concern lest the overall result, even though achieved through the application of equitable criteria and the use of appropriate methods for giving them concrete effect, should unexpectedly be revealed as radically inequitable, that is to say, as likely to entail *catastrophic repercussions for the livelihood and economic well-being of the population of the countries concerned*.[69]

[64] Ibid 277–278 [58].
[65] Ibid.
[66] Ibid 340–41 [233]. See also Memorial of the United States of America (27 September 1982) 5 [8], 6 [12], 7 [18], 57 [157].
[67] *Gulf of Maine* (n. 54) 341 [234].
[68] Ibid 278 [59].
[69] Ibid 342 [237] (emphasis added).

In the view of the Court, this was not the situation in the present case,[70] despite its acknowledgement that the 'obvious' socio-economic impact of Canada's fisheries on the communities inhabiting in certain counties of Nova Scotia was 'undeniable'.[71] However, the decision to discard arguments related to fishing activities proved problematic, causing significant disruption to historic fishing patterns in the boundary area.[72] For example, the incompatible views between the US and Canada on fisheries management on either side of the boundary caused major obstacles to subsequent reciprocal access arrangements.[73] This was to be expected, given the important fishery interests of these countries,[74] demonstrated, for instance, through their joint proposal at the Second United Nations Conference on the Law of the Sea in 1960 of a six-mile territorial sea and a six-mile fishing zone with protection of traditional fishing rights for ten years.[75] The parties made several attempts to negotiate the question of fisheries access in the region, only bringing it to The Hague after impasse.[76] Overall the judgment 'drew heavy criticisms from both Canada and the United States'.[77] Local populations were not considered a factor when assessing the overall equitableness of the boundary due to the Chamber's concerns to produce a decision grounded in law rather than equity.

The Chamber's approach in *Gulf of Maine* can be compared with the 1993 *Jan Mayen* case; both applied the 'catastrophic repercussions' threshold, but only in the latter was it met. In *Jan Mayen*, Denmark and Norway were in dispute over the delimitation of their fishing zones and continental shelf areas between Greenland (a country within the Kingdom of Denmark) and the Norwegian island of Jan Mayen, in the northern Atlantic Ocean. The dispute boiled down to a conflict over access to fishery resources.[78] Both parties placed emphasis on this in their

[70] Ibid 343 [238].
[71] Ibid 342 [236].
[72] Glen J. Herbert, 'Fisheries Relations in the Gulf of Maine Implications of an Arbitrated Maritime Boundary' (1995) 19(4) *Marine Policy* 301, 303.
[73] Ibid 303.
[74] Douglas M. Johnston, *Canada and the New International Law of the Sea*, vol 54 (University of Toronto Press 1985) 5.
[75] S. P. Jagota, *Maritime Boundary*, vol 9 (Martinus Nijhoff Publishers 1985) 25.
[76] Herbert (n. 72) 308.
[77] Leonardo Bernard, 'The Effect of Historic Fishing Rights in Maritime Boundaries Delimitation' (Presented at the Tenth LOSI Conference, Seoul, May, 2012) 1, 13–14.
[78] *Maritime Delimitation in the Area between Greenland and Jan Mayen (Denmark v. Norway)* (Judgment) [1993] ICJ Rep 38, 71–72 [75].

pleadings: Denmark argued that the Inuit population of Greenland depended on sealing and whaling on the Greenland east coast, while Norway contended that the disputed waters between Greenland and Jan Mayen have been the scene of whaling, sealing and fishing by Norwegian coastal communities.[79] The Court acknowledged the parties' emphasis on the 'traditional character of the different types of fishing carried out by the populations concerned'[80] and the importance of fishing for their respective economies.[81]

After drawing the provisional line, the Court had to consider whether any relevant circumstances justified an adjustment. It made reference to the 'catastrophic repercussions' doctrine established in the *Gulf of Maine* case but reached a different conclusion.[82] In its view, the provisional line was too far to the west for Denmark (i.e. Greenland) to be assured of equitable access to the only fish commercially exploited in the area: the capelin stock (a migratory type of fish found in the autumn and summer south of the disputed areas).[83] Greenland fishermen would therefore not have been able to access capelin stocks in certain months of the year due to drifting ice – unless the boundary had been shifted to the east. It therefore adjusted the median line eastwards to ensure equitable access to the capelin fishery resources 'for the vulnerable fishing communities concerned'.[84] This conclusion has been described as 'unique in modern maritime boundary delimitation'.[85]

One may question why the argument of 'catastrophic repercussions' was upheld in this case but discarded in *Gulf of Maine*. In my view, the Court regarded the circumstances in *Jan Mayen* as exceptional and more grave compared to those in the *Gulf of Maine* case.

First, the coastal communities of Greenland were heavily dependent on fishing the seasonal capelin fish, in sharp contrast to Jan Mayen, which had no permanent fishing community.[86] Second, the lack of any other known form of resource exploitation, such as hydrocarbon, made

[79] Ibid 46 [15] and 71 [74].
[80] Ibid 71–72 [75].
[81] Ibid.
[82] Ibid.
[83] The capelin stock is defined in: *Jan Mayen* (n. 78) 72 [76]. The Court's conclusion is found in 46 [14] and 70 [73].
[84] Ibid 71–72 [75]–[76]. See also Stephen Fietta and Robin Cleverly, *A Practitioner's Guide to Maritime Boundary Delimitation* (OUP 2016) 86.
[85] Fietta and Cleverly (n. 84) 342.
[86] Fietta and Cleverly (n. 84) 342.

fishing the only valuable natural resource in the disputed area.[87] By contrast, in *Gulf of Maine*, fisheries were not the only natural resource of concern in the disputed area, as hydrocarbon exploration had also been undertaken in the past.[88] In fact, other factors had been raised – such as hydrocarbons, defence, navigation,[89] or the water column reposing on the seabed of the delimitation area[90] – in contrast to the *Jan Mayen* case where fishing activities were the central issue of the dispute. Therefore, while both disputes were centred on fisheries, it appears that the US and Canada's dependence on fisheries was less critical, urgent, and all-encompassing than in the *Jan Mayen* case. The relevant circumstances in the latter case warranted application of the 'catastrophic repercussions' doctrine established in the *Gulf of Maine* case.[91]

The severity of the situation was apparent in *Jan Mayen* as the Court was unreceptive to all proposed extra-legal considerations, categorically stating its refusal to consider population-related and socio-economic factors in the adjustment of the provisional line. Denmark claimed that Jan Mayen had no settled population, contrary to Greenland's population of 55,000, six percent of which live in the region abutting the delimitation area.[92] It also contended that Greenland's principle economic activity was fishing and that Jan Mayen's fishing interests are in fact Norway's, as there are no fishermen in Jan Mayen.[93] Finally, Denmark also asked the Court to consider a cultural factor: the attachment of the people in Greenland to their land and the surrounding sea would make it difficult for them to accept its cutback.[94] In response to these concerns, the Court stated,

> The question is whether the size and special character of Jan Mayen's population, and the absence of locally based fishing, are circumstances which affect the delimitation. The Court would observe that the attribution of maritime areas to the territory of a State, which, by its nature, is destined to be permanent, *is a legal process based solely on the possession by the territory concerned of a coastline.*[95]

[87] Ibid 85.
[88] *Gulf of Maine* (n. 54) 279 [61] and 343 [239].
[89] Fietta and Cleverly (n. 84) 247.
[90] *Gulf of Maine* (n. 54) 275 [49].
[91] *Jan Mayen* (n. 78) 71–72 [75].
[92] Ibid 73 [79].
[93] Ibid.
[94] Ibid [79].
[95] Ibid 73–74 [80] (emphasis added).

Referring to *Continental Shelf (Libyan Arab Jamahiriya/Malta)*, where it concluded that relative economic positions of states are irrelevant in maritime delimitation,[96] the Court concluded that there was no reason to consider either the limited nature of the population of Jan Mayen, or socio-economic factors.[97] The shifting of the median line to accommodate local populations therefore indicates the perceived severity of this situation.

The *Gulf of Maine* and *Jan Mayen* judgments therefore indicate that, in strict circumstances, local populations may be considered as relevant circumstances to adjust the provisional line in maritime boundary delimitation. It is worth mentioning that it can be debated whether such adjustments were considered in stage two or in stage three of the process.[98] In *Gulf of Maine*, it could be interpreted that the Chamber considered geographical features as relevant circumstances (stage two) but resource-related factors (including fishing considerations) in stage three of the maritime boundary delimitation process: to test the boundary's overall equitableness. This is because it clarified that delimitation is first and foremost to be determined in relation to geographical features in the area, after which 'other criteria' may be considered in order for the boundary to be equitable.[99] One scholar considers that the Chamber only turned to fishing concerns *after* considering relevant circumstances, although the reasons for this distinction are not clear.[100] Similarly, in *Jan Mayen*, it could be argued that local populations were considered not in stage two but rather to assess disproportionality of the provisional line and its overall equitableness (stage three).[101]

Regardless, subsequent case law has shed more light on the requirements of the 'catastrophic repercussions' doctrine. First, Kenya argued in *Maritime Delimitation in the Indian Ocean (Somalia v. Kenya)* that the livelihood and economic well-being of its fisherfolk would suffer greatly if the relevant equidistance line were not adjusted.[102] One of the reasons given by the Court in dismissing this argument was that it was required to '[c]onsider the well-being of the populations on both sides of the

[96] *Continental Shelf (Libyan Arab Jamahiriya/Malta)* (n. 55) 41 [50].
[97] *Jan Mayen* (n. 78) 73–74 [80].
[98] Lando (n. 37) 246.
[99] Ibid 278 [59].
[100] Ibid 198.
[101] *Jan Mayen* (n. 78) 67 [65].
[102] *Maritime Delimitation in the Indian Ocean (Somalia v. Kenya)* (Judgment) [2021] ICJ Rep 206, 262 [153].

delimitation line'.[103] This indicates that unless one side is significantly disadvantaged, the Court will not feel compelled to consider the well-being of one state's populations over that of the other.

Second, the Court's assessment also appears to rely on how many people would be affected. In *Somalia v. Kenya*, it also rejected Kenya's argument as '17 out of 19 fish landing sites are located near or at the Lamu Archipelago and would therefore be unaffected by an equidistance line. Only two landing sites are close to the land boundary terminus'.[104] In contrast, Greenland had a population of 55,000 in *Jan Mayen*.[105] This perhaps indicates that a more significant number of people must be affected by the delimitation for the Court to consider it a relevant circumstance.

Third, the doctrine demands that a high level of evidence be provided by the relevant state litigant. The Court observed in *Black Sea* that Ukraine had not submitted evidence that any delimitation line other than that claimed by it would entail catastrophic repercussions.[106] A series of arbitral awards rendered since *Gulf of Maine* have confirmed that the burden of proof rests with the state invoking local populations as a relevant circumstance. In *Award of the Arbitral Tribunal in the second stage of the proceedings between Eritrea and Yemen* (1999), fishing activities and concerns for their local populations comprised an enormous part of the parties' arguments in the Phase II Award. The tribunal came to the conclusion that the threshold had not been met due to a lack of evidence.[107]

Similarly, in the *Barbados/Trinidad and Tobago* arbitration (2006), Barbados requested that fishing activities should be taken into account in the delimitation of the boundary due to its great importance for Barbadian fisherfolk and the country's economy.[108] The arbitral tribunal, however, decided that not enough conclusive evidence had been submitted by Barbados for it to uphold its claim that any denial of access to Tobago would entail 'catastrophic repercussions'.[109] It stated that 'determining an international maritime boundary between two states on the basis of traditional fishing on the high seas by nationals of one of those

[103] Ibid 263–64 [159].
[104] Ibid.
[105] *Jan Mayen* (n. 78) 46 [14].
[106] *Black Sea* (n. 3) 125–26 [198].
[107] *Second stage of the proceedings between Eritrea and Yemen* (n. 4) 346 [48] and 352 [72]–[73].
[108] *Barbados v. Trinidad and Tobago* (2006) (Award) XXVII RIAA 147, 216–17 [247].
[109] Ibid 82–83 [264]–[266]. See also Igor V. Karaman, *Dispute Resolution in the Law of the Sea*, vol 72 (Martinus Nijhoff Publishers 2012) 224–29.

States is altogether exceptional'.[110] Finally, in *Bay of Bengal Maritime Boundary Arbitration between Bangladesh and India* (2014), the arbitral tribunal decided that Bangladesh, arguing about the importance of fishing in the Bay of Bengal for its population, did not provide sufficient evidence that this would warrant the adjustment of the provisional delimitation line.[111] In brief, in a series of subsequent arbitral awards, the lack of evidence has been stated as a principal reason for its rejection as a relevant circumstance.

In sum, the absence of extreme circumstances such as those in *Jan Mayen* has resulted in arbitral tribunals rejecting access to fishing resources as a relevant circumstance (or as a factor when assessing the overall test for the equitableness of the boundary) meeting the 'catastrophic repercussions' threshold and thus, meriting the adjustment of a maritime boundary.[112]

6.3.3 *The Appropriateness of This Approach in Light of the Principle of Equity*

The Court's restrictive approach can be explained by its adherence to formalism, explained earlier (Section 6.1). It believes that consideration for local populations somewhat derogates from the legal process. Indeed, the Court stated in *Gulf of Maine* above that the consideration of local populations in maritime delimitation would steer the Court away from achieving a result 'on the basis of law' and qualify as *ex aequo et bono*.[113] The Court appears to make a strict separation between law and 'other considerations', stating that maritime delimitation 'is a *legal process* based solely on the possession by the territory concerned of a coastline',[114] which would exclude considerations linked to society, the economy, or culture for example. Conversely, it considers that geographical circumstances do not fall under adjudication *ex aequo et bono*. In this section, I first argue that consideration of local populations in maritime delimitation would be an application of the principle of equity – which forms an integral part of the maritime boundary delimitation process. I then

[110] Ibid 80 [269].
[111] *Bay of Bengal Maritime Boundary Arbitration between Bangladesh and India (Bangladesh v. India)* (2014) (Award) XXXII RIAA 1, 126 [424].
[112] Fietta and Cleverly (n. 84) 342.
[113] *Gulf of Maine* (n. 54) 278 [59].
[114] *Jan Mayen* (n. 78) 73–74 [80] (emphasis added).

submit that geographical circumstances – prioritised by the Court – can lead to overly superficial and occasionally insufficient outcomes and are just as contrary to formalism as other considerations.

First, the consideration of local populations in maritime delimitation would be an application of the principle of equity – which forms an integral part of the maritime boundary delimitation process – and not *ex aequo et bono*. The consideration of local populations and the potential injustice caused to them by depriving them of access to fishing resources necessary for their livelihoods, infringing on their cultural and traditional practices, or even possibly causing them to relocate is a matter of justice falling under the ambit of equity. Indeed, as explained before, equity can function as individualised justice, making adjustments 'with a care for the specific case' in a way that would achieve fairness.[115]

The type of equity to be applied is equity in conformity with the law. If maritime boundary delimitation is described as 'a legal process',[116] equity is inherently part of this process, integrating equitable considerations such as the needs of local populations into the legal framework rather than opposing it. Equity is 'the very content of the applicable rules' in maritime delimitation.[117] The second and third stages in the maritime delimitation process emphasise its significance. The Court stated in the *North Sea Continental Shelf* cases that delimitation was 'not a question of applying equity simply as a matter of abstract justice, but of applying a rule of law which itself requires the application of equitable principles'.[118] Equity is therefore not only perceived as a rule of law[119] but is enshrined in Articles 74 and 83 of UNCLOS (presented at the opening of this chapter) as the objective of maritime delimitation ('in order to achieve an equitable solution'[120]). The Court itself noted in *Continental Shelf (Tunisia/Libyan Arab Jamahiriya)* that 'it is virtually impossible to achieve an equitable solution in any delimitation without taking into account the particular relevant circumstances in the area'.[121]

[115] Titi (n. 59) 71.
[116] *Jan Mayen* (n. 78) 73–74 [80] (emphasis added).
[117] *Fisheries Jurisdiction (United Kingdom v. Iceland)* (n. 3) 33 [78]; *Fisheries Jurisdiction (Federal Republic of Germany v. Iceland)* (Merits) (Judgment) [1974] ICJ Rep 175, 202 [69].
[118] *North Sea Continental Shelf* (n. 55) 46–47 [85].
[119] Joseph Charles Witenberg and Jacques Desrioux, *L'organisation judiciaire, la procédure et la sentence internationales: Traité pratique* (Pedone 1937) 304.
[120] See UNCLOS, Articles 74 and 83; Fietta and Cleverly (n. 84) 53.
[121] *Continental Shelf (Tunisia/Libyan Arab Jamahiriya)* (n. 16) 60–61 [71]–[72].

As equity is an inherent part of the legal delimitation process, the equitable consideration of local populations is the mere application of equity in conformity with the law and not a *contra legem* exercise. A certain regard beyond black-letter and into the repercussions of the law's application for the affected people is an exercise that is part and parcel of the law itself. In other words, considering such relevant circumstances is part of – and not in derogation of – the legal exercise. One author has commented that maritime boundary delimitation is therefore 'the main legal test as to whether and to what extent public international law is, in a given and difficult context, able to discharge distributive justice' and 'bring about the fair distribution of resources under the inequitable foundations of maritime zones and among unequal nations'.[122] Equity is a strong component underpinning and guiding the process, as indicated by stages two and three. This should be given due regard.

Second, while the Court views consideration for local populations as somewhat deviating from the legal process, resembling adjudication *ex aequo et bono*, it nonetheless accepts relevant circumstances of a geographical nature to adjust the provisional line. I submit that geographical circumstances can lead to overly superficial and occasionally insufficient outcomes and are just as contrary to formalism as other considerations.

'Relevant circumstances' generally fall into two categories: geographic (disparity in relevant coastal lengths,[123] distorting effects of islands, rocks, promontories, and other small features,[124] the presence of enclaves and semi-enclaves,[125] *inter alia*[126]), and non-geographic circumstances (conduct of the parties,[127] exploration and exploitation activities,[128] security considerations,[129] navigational interests,[130] natural resources,

[122] See Cottier (n. 46) 4–5. For more about equity as law, see Lauterpacht (n. 44) 120–36.

[123] Fietta and Cleverly (n. 84) 72.

[124] Ibid 73.

[125] Ibid 81.

[126] See ibid 68.

[127] *Continental Shelf (Tunisia/Libyan Arab Jamahiriya)* (n. 16) 83–86 [117]–[121]; *Continental Shelf (Libyan Arab Jamahiriya/Malta)* (n. 55) 28–29 [24]–[25]; *Gulf of Maine* (n. 54) 303–12 [126]–[154]; *Jan Mayen* (n. 78) 75–77 [82]–[86]; *Land and Maritime Boundary between Cameroon and Nigeria (Cameroon v. Nigeria: Equatorial Guinea intervening)* (Judgment) [2002] ICJ Rep 303, 447–48 [304]; *Black Sea* (n. 3) 123–26 [189]–[198].

[128] *Gulf of Maine* (n. 54) 342 [237]; *Jan Mayen* (n. 78) 71–72 [75]–[76].

[129] *Continental Shelf (Libyan Arab Jamahiriya/Malta)* (n. 55) 42 [51]; *Jan Mayen* (n. 78) 74–75 [81]; *Black Sea* (n. 3) 127–28 [202]–[204].

[130] *Arbitration regarding the Delimitation of the Maritime Boundary between Guyana and Suriname* (2007) (Award) XXX RIAA 1, 84–86 [303]–[307].

hydrocarbon resources and exploitation, or fishing resources). The unlimited potential for relevant circumstances[131] and their expansion over the years has resulted in international courts and tribunals seemingly weighing them against each other in a way that has not only 'distance[d] relevant circumstances from the delimitation process'[132] according to Professor Malcolm Evans, but has possibly disadvantaged the consideration of local populations.

The geographical configuration of coasts is 'not an element open to modification by the Court but a fact on the basis of which the Court must effect the delimitation'.[133] For this reason, it is considered to be more of a stable and permanent factor to consider. Prioritising geographical considerations is also perceived by the Court to be of a 'more neutral character'.[134] Therefore, geographical features are considered to be a part of the legal process, while non-geographical features, such as fishing resources for local populations, fall within the scope of adjudication *ex aequo et bono*. The Court seldom considers local populations in maritime disputes, as it views such considerations as conflicting with the principle of boundary stability. This emphasis on stability has effectively transformed maritime boundary delimitation into a predominantly geographical process.

However, such an approach might render the process overly superficial. The three-pronged delimitation process, which incorporates considerations to ensure equity, suggests that geographical circumstances alone may not always suffice to achieve an equitable outcome. The real-life effects of delimiting a boundary purely on the basis of geographical circumstances may occasionally lead to an inequitable outcome. The Chamber of *Gulf of Maine*, for instance, did acknowledge that delimitation purely on the basis of geographical considerations may lead to catastrophic repercussions. As Cottier has observed,

> [T]he Chamber agrees that delimitation on the basis of surface-related, geographical principles and circumstances may well affect related industries and even create catastrophic repercussions for the livelihood of industries and populations. The ex post test indicates the importance of

[131] *North Sea Continental Shelf* (n. 55) 50 [93].

[132] See Malcolm D. Evans, 'Maritime Delimitation and Expanding Categories of Relevant Circumstances' (1991) 40(1) *The International and Comparative Law Quarterly* 1, 33.

[133] *Cameroon/Nigeria* (n. 127) 443–45 [295].

[134] *Gulf of Maine* (n. 54) 327 [194].

> socio-economic aspects as an overriding final test, against which a geographical delimitation has to stand in order to qualify as an equitable result. It implies that geographic equity can turn out to neglect such interests and therefore can be inequitable. In other words, geographic principles are not sufficiently reliable per se.[135]

Sole regard for geographical circumstances is considered to suffice to ensure long-lasting peace between states. However, thc *Jan Mayen* case indicates that such peace and stability extend beyond the satisfaction of states to the people facing repercussions of judicial decisions. A court cannot be said to achieve this if human security and protection have been jeopardised. This is why equity plays a significant role in maritime delimitation, and so it should. In certain circumstances, it can serve as a 'corrective force, seeking to reconcile the geometric constructions with the human realities'.[136] For these reasons, I submit that concerns for stability must be balanced with equity where the latter can ensure greater stability, permanence, and peace in the specific context.

Finally, neither geographical nor non-geographical considerations are legal *per se*. In the second stage of the maritime delimitation process, geographical features are classified as relevant circumstances—extralegal factors that justify adjusting the line to achieve equity. In this sense, they are no more legal than non-geographical features, or any other relevant circumstance. Relevant circumstances, by their very nature, steer away from formalism as they invite extra-legal factors – whether geographical or non-geographical – to be considered. The mere existence of relevant circumstances acknowledges that the process is not meant to be purely legal by default.

At the very least, the Court can draw from its practice in territorial disputes (Chapter 7) and the practice of arbitral tribunals to uphold and protect fishing activities *post scriptum*, despite its decision in the maritime boundary dispute.[137] *Award of the Arbitral Tribunal in the second stage of the proceedings between Eritrea and Yemen* (1999) provides an example of such a practice. Indeed, despite the arbitral tribunal refusing to apply the 'catastrophic repercussions' doctrine in that case, it acknowledged, in the first stage of the Award focused on territorial sovereignty, that its findings entailed 'the perpetuation of the traditional fishing regime in the region' and therefore required Yemen to 'ensure that the

135 Cottier (n. 46) 586.
136 Kolb (n. 48) 16.
137 Fietta and Cleverly (n. 84) 87.

traditional fishing regime of free access and enjoyment for the fishermen of both Eritrea and Yemen shall be preserved for the benefit of the lives and livelihoods of this poor and industrious order of men'.[138]

It then reaffirmed, in stage two of proceedings on the maritime delimitation, that the traditional fishing regime recognises certain associated rights (such as free passage for fishermen through waters, including to enter relevant ports and sell and market fish) and exists 'for the benefit of the fishermen of both countries throughout the region'.[139] Accordingly, the traditional fishing regime '[did] not depend, either for its existence or for its protection, upon the drawing of an international boundary' by the Arbitral Tribunal.[140] Similar conclusions were drawn in the *Abyei arbitration (Government of Sudan / The Sudan People's Liberation Movement/Army)*, where the tribunal reaffirmed that 'traditional rights, in the absence of an explicit agreement to the contrary, have usually been deemed to remain unaffected by any territorial delimitation'.[141] In *Eritrea/Yemen*, traditional fishing rights were extended through the EEZs of both states, with no limitations imposed by maritime boundary rules. This was made possible as, in that case, the arbitral tribunal was empowered to take into account other pertinent factors aside from UNCLOS, therefore allowing it to go beyond traditional fishing as it would exist therein.[142] Notwithstanding instructions in Special Agreements, the judges on the bench of the World Court often have the possibility to take into account other pertinent factors in their deliberations. In the spirit of this arbitral award, mention can therefore be made of the need of the parties to preserve the traditional fishing regime, so as to ensure free access and enjoyment for all fishermen.

6.4 Historic Fishing Rights

Contrary to Section 6.3 addressing the stages of maritime boundary delimitation, this section focuses on disputes where the Court ascertains

138 *Territorial Sovereignty and Scope of the Dispute (Eritrea and Yemen)* (1998) (Award) XXII RIAA 209, 329–30 [526].

139 *Second stage of the proceedings between Eritrea and Yemen* (n. 4) 361 [109].

140 Ibid 361 [110].

141 *Arbitration regarding the Delimitation of the Abyei Area between the Government of Sudan and the Sudan People's Movement/Army* (2009) (Award) XXX RIAA 145, 408–10 [753]–[760] and 412 [766].

142 *Second stage of the proceedings between Eritrea and Yemen* (n. 4) Annex 1, Article 2(3).

if a state has sovereignty over a maritime zone without drawing a maritime boundary. In this context, another scenario allowing for the consideration of fishing activities and their importance for local populations is when such activities are argued to be historic fishing rights. In this section, I identify the reasons for the Court's reticence to uphold historic fishing rights in this context, including a concern for stability. I argue that reframing the understanding of stability can allow for a greater balance to be struck and, therefore, for the needs of coastal populations to be considered.

Given that traditional fishing has, by definition, been practised by coastal populations for generations, it qualifies as their historic right. The basic concept of historic fishing rights holds that nationals of one state have the right to traditionally fish in another state's jurisdiction due to the historic longevity of this practice. Traditional fishing rights are private rights by nature and are acquired by use and time. However, 'the interest of the State in the fisheries enjoyed by its nationals, and the protection which it provides them with, provide such private activities with a public underpinning and make possible the establishment of a mixed (private/public) prescriptive title'.[143]

State litigants have invoked their populations' traditional fishing as a historic right to be considered in the Court's assessment of the sovereignty over a contested maritime zone. As clarified by the arbitral tribunal in the *South China Sea* arbitration, historic rights 'may [be a claim to] sovereignty, but may equally include more limited rights, such as fishing rights or rights of access, that fall well short of a claim of sovereignty'.[144] States typically make such claims to sovereign rights in the other state's EEZ or to invoke the alleged right of a state and its nationals to access and exploit living resources in another state's EEZ.[145]

In this section, I observe that while the Court has stated that '[h]istoric titles must enjoy respect and be preserved as they have always been by long usage',[146] it has yet to uphold a claim to sovereignty nor has it found that one state's population has a right to fish in the maritime zones of

[143] Kolb (n. 48) 17.

[144] *South China Sea Arbitration (Philippines v. China)* (2016) (Award) XXXIII RIAA 153, 271 [225] (emphasis added).

[145] This, however, is subject to certain conditions determined by the coastal State, pursuant to UNCLOS, Article 61(1).

[146] *Continental Shelf (Tunisia/Libyan Arab Jamahiriya)* (n. 16) 73 [100].

another state. I reflect on the reasons for this here, which include a concern for stability.

First, historic fishing rights are rarely upheld by the Court because opportunities to do so have been few and far between. Indeed, historic fishing rights are challenging for state litigants to invoke due to the burden of proof. This was seen in *Alleged Violations of Sovereign Rights and Maritime Spaces in the Caribbean Sea (Nicaragua v. Colombia)* (2022), where the Court rejected Colombia's third counterclaim that Nicaragua failed to respect the traditional and historic fishing rights of the inhabitants of the San Andrés Archipelago, including the indigenous Raizal people, in the waters in which they were allegedly entitled to exercise said rights.[147] To reach this conclusion, the Court considered whether there was a customary rule of international law under which the Raizales were entitled to fish in the relevant maritime zones. Colombia had provided eleven affidavits to prove the existence of this long-standing fishing practice. Although the Court acknowledged the need for 'some flexibility' in considering their probative value,[148] it expressed caution in giving weight to affidavit evidence and ultimately judged that the eleven affidavits did not sufficiently establish its claim.

Judge *ad hoc* McRae argued in his dissenting opinion that the Raizales are indigenous fishermen and their claimed rights were therefore indigenous rights, which warranted special attention.[149] He also argued that the standard the Court set for establishing traditional fishing rights was essentially one that could never be reached.[150] Although Judge Xue made a declaration emphasising the importance of traditional fishing rights, and particularly their recognition and protection under customary international law,[151] she ultimately agreed with the decision to reject the counterclaim. The majority view of the judges to reject it indicates the bench's reluctance to uphold traditional historic fishing rights in assessing the sovereignty of a maritime zone.

Second, historic fishing rights have also yet to be upheld because their importance decreased with the emergence of the EEZ. Traditional fishing rights have been addressed by the international community

[147] *Alleged Violations of Sovereign Rights and Maritime Spaces in the Caribbean Sea (Nicaragua v. Colombia)* (Counter-Claims) (Order) [2017] ICJ Rep 289, 302 [40].

[148] *Alleged Violations of Sovereign Rights and Maritime Spaces in the Caribbean Sea (Nicaragua v. Colombia)* (Judgment) [2022] ICJ Rep 266, 350 [221].

[149] Ibid 450–53 [55]–[64] (Dissenting opinion of Judge McRae).

[150] Ibid 453 [65].

[151] Ibid (Declaration of Judge Xue), especially 404 [2], 407 [9], 408 [12].

since before the adoption of UNCLOS in 1982. In 1958, the First Law of the Sea Conference (UNCLOS II) adopted a resolution recognising the preferential requirements of a state whose people are overwhelmingly dependent on coastal fisheries for their livelihood or economic development, or who engage in local fishing in small boats and are dependent on coastal fisheries for the animal protein in their diet.[152] The *travaux préparatoires* of Article 6 of the 1958 Convention on the Continental Shelf (one of the four conventions adopted at UNCLOS II) indicate that such fishing rights were 'special circumstances' influencing the delimitation of the continental shelf.[153] However, with the steady emergence of the concept of the EEZ regime, traditional fishing activities were gradually marginalised by states.[154]

The Court seems to have followed this approach of minimising the importance of historic fishing rights. In *Gulf of Maine*, discussed earlier, the Chamber noted the US's emphasis that its historic fishing presence in the area – which the Chamber described as 'somewhat akin to the invocation of historic rights, though that expression has not been used'[155] – should be a considered circumstance in the maritime boundary delimitation.[156] The Chamber explained that while the US, as the coastal state, may have been able to achieve an actual *de facto* predominance for its fisheries at certain places and times, the situation radically altered after the coastal states set up EEZs. Such *de facto* predominance could no longer constitute a valid ground for its claiming of the incorporation into its own exclusive fishery zone of an area which had legally become Canada's.[157]

Third, despite their decreased importance, any number of states may make historic fishing claims on the same disputed waters, and no single state can claim an exclusive fishing right. In the recent *South China Sea* arbitration, for instance, both China and the Philippines claimed historic

[152] Jagota (n. 75) 25; Arthur H. Dean, 'The Second Geneva Conference on the Law of the Sea: The Fight for Freedom of the Seas' (1960) 54(4) *The American Journal of International Law* 751; D. W. Bowett, 'The Second United Nations Conference on the Law of the Sea' (1960) 9(3) *International and Comparative Law Quarterly* 415.

[153] *Continental Shelf (Tunisia/Libyan Arab Jamahiriya)* (n. 16) 122–24 [79]–[84] (Separate opinion of Judge Eduardo Jiménez de Aréchaga).

[154] Huan-Sheng Tseng and Ching-HsiewnOu, 'The Evolution and Trend of the Traditional Fishing Rights' (2010) 53 *Ocean & Coastal Management* 270, 275.

[155] *Gulf of Maine* (n. 54) 340–41 [233].

[156] Ibid. See also Memorial of the United States of America (27 September 1982) 5 [8], 6 [12], 7 [18], 57 [157].

[157] *Gulf of Maine* (n. 54) 341–42 [235].

fishing rights in the same fishing grounds.[158] This would put the Court in a difficult position to decide between competing claims. While this has yet to occur, in the *Fisheries Jurisdiction* cases the Court dealt with competing claims between historic fishing rights, on the one hand, and other similar rights protecting local populations, on the other hand. There, the Court did not prioritise historic fishing rights either.

Indeed, the *Fisheries Jurisdiction* cases suggest that historic fishing rights do not automatically supersede all other considerations and are not absolute rights. While these were not maritime boundary delimitation disputes, the conclusions reached about historic fishing rights could also apply to such disputes. In these cases, the UK and Germany challenged Iceland's assertion of an exclusive fishing zone extending 50 nautical miles.[159] This assertion directly impacted the rights of British and German nationals who had historically fished in these waters. Iceland, however, justified its preferential rights on the grounds of its local populations as well. It claimed that its economy depended almost entirely on fishing in the vicinity of its coasts, and for this reason, 'the population of Iceland has followed the progressive impoverishment of fishing grounds with anxiety'.[160] Given that fishing equipment was much less efficient than it is today, Iceland advocated that measures to protect fisheries ought to be extended in proportion to the growing efficiency of fishing equipment.[161]

The Court recognised that Iceland did have 'preferential fishing rights' in the maritime areas adjacent to its fishing zone but also that the UK and Germany had 'traditional fishing rights' in the same maritime areas.[162] The Court explained that neither right is absolute:

> [T]he preferential rights of a coastal State are limited according to the extent of its special dependence on the fisheries and by its obligation to take account of the rights of other States and the needs of conservation; the established rights of other fishing States are in turn limited by reason of the coastal State's special dependence on the fisheries and its own

[158] Stefan Talmon and Bing Bing Jia (eds), *The South China Sea Arbitration: A Chinese Perspective* (Hart Publishing 2014) 48.

[159] *Fisheries Jurisdiction (United Kingdom v. Iceland)* (n. 3) 7–8 [11]. See also Knut Reese, 'The Making of a Case for the International Court of Justice – Icelandic Fishing Rights' (1973) 6(3) *Comparative and International Law Journal of Southern Africa* 394.

[160] *Fisheries Jurisdiction (United Kingdom v. Iceland)* (n. 3) 10–11 [20].

[161] Ibid 10–11 [20].

[162] Ibid 29–30 [67]–[69].

> obligation to take account of the rights of other States, including the coastal State, and of the needs of conservation.[163]

Accordingly, the Court concluded that both states had an obligation to recognise the other's rights and that '[t]he most appropriate method for the solution of the dispute is clearly that of negotiation'.[164] The parties were thus under mutual obligation to undertake negotiations to find an equitable solution in good faith. This demonstrates that historic fishing rights are in no way absolute. The Court's judgment required Iceland to respect the historic fishing rights of the citizens of Germany and the UK and thus reaffirmed the importance of traditional fishing rights of third states. However, Iceland's preferential rights also had to be respected by Germany and the UK.

The non-absolute nature of historic fishing rights was also indicated in *Gulf of Maine*, examined earlier, where the US claimed historic fishing rights and the Court did not give it any more consideration than it did to Canada's socio-economic arguments relating to fishing activities.[165] Indeed, there is no hierarchy between one type of fishing right and the other. The non-absolute nature of historic fishing rights is perhaps not too surprising if we consider that during the UNCLOS II negotiations, a proposal of a six-nautical mile fishing zone subject to traditional fishing rights for ten years was not adopted by the plenary.[166]

The fourth reason why the Court has yet to uphold historic fishing rights when assessing the sovereignty of a maritime zone is because they are exceptional in nature and cannot contravene the UNCLOS. Indeed, historic fishing rights often serve as an exception to the rules laid down in the UNCLOS in practice, most commonly because those rights existed before its adoption.[167] For instance, Article 15 of the UNCLOS provides that the delimitation rule for the territorial sea does not apply 'where it is necessary by reason of historic title or other special circumstances to delimit the territorial seas of the two States in a way which is at variance therewith',[168] and the heated negotiations about fishery limits in light of

[163] Ibid 30–31 [71].
[164] Ibid 31–32 [73].
[165] *Gulf of Maine* (n. 54) 278 [59], 340–41 [233], 341–42 [235].
[166] Jagota (n. 75) 27.
[167] Dyspriani (n. 4) 2.
[168] UNCLOS, Article 15.

the breadth of the territorial sea during UNCLOS II indicate that fishing rights were targeted in these provisions.[169]

Further to this, historic fishing rights cannot supersede UNCLOS in cases of incompatibility, as indicated in the *South China Sea* arbitration. This means that the Court would not be able to uphold historic fishing rights if they contravened any clause in UNCLOS. Indeed, the arbitral tribunal did not doubt that China had historic rights giving it certain privileges in such waters, but explained that China's adherence to UNCLOS had changed this situation and meant that it accepted to relinquish 'the rights it may have held in the waters allocated by the Convention to the exclusive economic zones of other States'.[170] This reasoning was inspired by the Court's response to the US's arguments about its historic fishing presence in the area, in *Gulf of Maine*.[171] The Tribunal explained that the *South China Sea* arbitration differed from the *Fisheries Jurisdiction* cases as the latter involved the UK and Germany asserting a right of access to Icelandic waters, rather than disputing Iceland's EEZ rights, as China did.[172] Historic fishing rights are therefore interpreted within the framework and limitations imposed by UNCLOS, which 'supersedes earlier rights and agreements to the extent of any incompatibility'.[173] China's historic rights were 'contrary to the Convention and without lawful effect to the extent that they exceed the geographic and substantive limits of China's maritime entitlements under the Convention'.[174]

A final and most relevant reason why the Court has not upheld historic fishing rights may be a concern for stability. Historic fishing reflects an activity carried out by a coastal population whose presence could change or evolve over time. In this sense, they could represent less permanence than geographical features in maritime disputes. Therefore, following a similar logic to that applied to territorial disputes (Chapter 7), the Court may be reluctant to draw conclusions based on possibly migrating populations in inter-state disputes. However, international law recognises stability as a characteristic of historic fishing. As the arbitral tribunal stated in the *South China Sea* award,

169 Jagota (n. 75) 25–27.
170 *South China Sea Arbitration* (n. 144) 285 [257].
171 *Gulf of Maine* (n. 54) 341–42 [235].
172 *South China Sea Arbitration* (n. 144) 285–86 [258].
173 Ibid 278–79 [246].
174 Ibid 612–13 [1203 B(2)].

> The legal basis for protecting artisanal fishing stems from the notion of vested rights and the understanding that, having pursued a livelihood through artisanal fishing over an extended period, generations of fishermen have acquired a right, akin to property, in the ability to continue to fish in the manner of their forebears. Thus, traditional fishing rights extend to artisanal fishing that is carried out largely in keeping with the longstanding practice of the community, in other words to 'those entitlements that all fishermen have exercised continuously through the ages.' [. . .][175]

More broadly, with respect to vested rights referred to in this passage, international law has long recognised the stability of private rights such as historic fishing rights. Indeed, as the Permanent Court of International Justice (PCIJ) made clear, 'Private rights acquired under the existing law do not cease on a change of sovereignty'.[176] Therefore, historic fishing rights are characterised by their stability due to the longevity of this practice. They therefore reflect stability that aligns with the Court's approach in such disputes and should be considered where appropriate.

To conclude, given the difficulties that arise when states invoke such rights as arguments in their pleadings, and the challenging characteristics of such historic fishing rights, they have yet to be upheld by the Court in its assessment of sovereignty over a disputed maritime zone.[177] However, the arbitral tribunal stated in *Grisbådarna* as early as 1909, in reference to Sweden's historic fishing rights, that 'it is a well-established principle of the law of nations that the state of things that actually exists and has existed for a long time should be changed as little as possible'.[178] It would therefore be advisable for the Court, a proponent for the principle of stability, to embrace historic fishing rights in all of their permanence where relevant.

6.5 Conclusion

Local populations are rarely factored into the legal reasoning of the Court in maritime disputes. The Court has dismissed states litigants' arguments regarding the concerns for their fishing populations to influence the determination of a pre-existing boundary (Section 6.2). The desires or needs of local populations have always been rejected as relevant

175 Ibid 467 [798].
176 *German Settlers in Poland* (Advisory Opinion) [1923] PCIJ Series B 36.
177 Cottier (n. 46) 485.
178 *The Grisbådarna case* (n. 47) 161.

circumstances (or as a factor when assessing the overall test for the equitableness of the boundary) save in *Jan Mayen*, due to the exceptional severity of the situation (Section 6.3). The Court, although acknowledging the general value of historic fishing rights, has yet to uphold them as an argument in a maritime dispute (Section 6.4). From the perspective of social idealism, concerned with a greater balance between states and individuals, such outcomes can be considered unjust, calling into question the legitimacy of the decision (Section I.1.2).

The overarching explanation for the approach observed in this chapter is the Court's application of formalism (Section 6.1). While I have argued that such an approach is appropriate when determining the pre-existence of a boundary (Section 6.2), the principle of equity could find application when adjusting the provisional line in maritime delimitation, to consider local populations impacted by this process (Section 6.3). While formalism and concerns for stability have hindered this, I have noted that equity is integral to the legal process. Moreover, the prioritisation of geographical circumstances is no less contrary to legal formalism than other relevant circumstances, may sometimes yield superficial outcomes, and may occasionally fall short in to adequately resolving the relevant dispute. Finally, I have identified and challenged the Court's reluctance to uphold arguments related to historic fishing rights, as they reflect the stability and permanence valued by the Court (Section 6.4).

Debates on the nature of law—whether as predictable and constant or as equitable and just—both within and beyond the context of maritime boundary disputes, reflect the broader intellectual tension between stability and change that has shaped international legal discourse since time immemorial.[179] Resolving such tensions and striking a satisfactory balance is a delicate, case-by-case task. However, while law must be stable, it 'cannot stand still'.[180] In this chapter, I have proposed ways to reconcile the need for change with the need for stability in maritime boundary disputes to better serve the local populations impacted by such judgments of the World Court.

179 Titi (n. 59) 74.
180 Roscoe Pound, *Interpretations of Legal History* (CUP 1923) 1.

7

Territorial Disputes

> A territorial change means not just a transference of a portion of the earth's surface and its resources from one regime to another; it usually involves, perhaps more importantly, a decisive change in the nationality, allegiance and way of life of a population.[1]

Territorial land disputes are means for states to reinforce their territorial integrity. The principle of territorial integrity in international law assures a geographical space for a government to exercise its authority and therefore reinforces state sovereignty.[2] Finalising the space in which a state may exercise its sovereignty, through stabilising its territorial boundaries, is therefore critical to states. Such boundaries can be defined as 'the imaginary lines on the surface of the earth which separate the territory of one State from that of another, or from unappropriated territory, or from the Open Sea'.[3]

There are two types of territory-related disputes that may appear before the International Court of Justice (ICJ, the Court): 'frontier disputes' or 'delimitation disputes' are centred on delimiting or clarifying the particularities of a line itself, while 'disputes as to attribution of territory' focus on the areas divided by the line.[4] While the Court elucidates that their difference is in the 'degree as to the way the operation in question is carried out', it admits that there is 'not so much a difference in kind'[5] between them. Thus, both types of disputes will be examined in this chapter.

1 Robert Y. Jennings and Marcelo Kohen, *The Acquisition of Territory in International Law with a New Introduction by Marcelo G. Kohen* (Manchester University Press 2017) 16.
2 Lassa Francis Lawrence Oppenheim, *International Law: A Treatise*, vol I (3rd edn, Longmans, Green and Company 1920) 564.
3 Ibid [253].
4 *Frontier Dispute (Burkina Faso/Republic of Mali)* (Judgment) [1986] ICJ Rep 554, 563–64 [17].
5 Ibid.

Inhabitants form a critical part of any territory. The first criterion of statehood in the 1933 Montevideo Convention on the Rights and Duties of States is 'a permanent population'.[6] A lack of inhabitants on a territory may be an indication that it is *terra nullius*: belonging to no one.[7] The Court has clarified that state sovereignty comprises not only control over territory but also control over people.[8]

As individuals form an important part of a territory, they are likely affected when territorial boundaries change. In the words of former ICJ President Rosalyn Higgins, 'When a state delimits its territorial boundaries, grants nationality under its own rules and asserts territorial and extended jurisdiction over its nationals, individuals are manifestly affected.'[9] Indeed, handing down a judgment regarding a territorial dispute is only the beginning of the story for a state's population, as several changes may thereafter occur on the ground. For instance, nationals may become foreigners, certain residents may have their status altered, and private property may become foreign instead of domestic, thereby requiring new rules of governance. Transferring property from one nation to another would be negotiated, and people may have to be compensated for losing their properties.[10] For instance, in *Land and Maritime Boundary between Cameroon and Nigeria (Cameroon v. Nigeria: Equatorial Guinea intervening)*, the Court, *inter alia*, ordered a transfer of sovereignty of the Bakassi peninsula from Nigeria to Cameroon. This has impacted Bakassians identifying as Nigerian who have been killed, disenfranchised, or become internally displaced persons.[11] As one author explained when describing this dispute,

[6] Montevideo Convention on the Rights and Duties of States, 165 LNTS 19 ["Montevideo Convention"].

[7] *Western Sahara* (Advisory Opinion) [1975] ICJ Rep 12, 38–39 [79]–[80]; *Legal Status of Eastern Greenland* (Judgment) [1933] PCIJ Series A/B, 22.

[8] *Sovereignty over Pedra Branca/Pulau Batu Puteh, Middle Rocks and South Ledge (Malaysia/Singapore)* (Judgment) [2008] ICJ Rep 12, 40 [79].

[9] Rosalyn Higgins, 'Conceptual Thinking about the Individual in International Law' (1978) 4(1) *British Journal of International Studies* 1, 1.

[10] Hephzibah Egede, 'The ICJ Bakassi Decision: The Rights of the Indigenous Communities and Populations in the Bakassi Peninsula' in Edwin Egede and Mark Igiehon (eds), *The Bakassi Dispute and the International Court of Justice: Continuing Challenges* (Routledge 2018) 91.

[11] 'Cameroon forces "kill 97 Nigerian fishermen" in Bakassi' *BBC News* (14 July 2017). www.bbc.co.uk/news/world-africa-40607306; Anietie Akpan, 'Bakassi Returnees' Two-Decade Grueling Sojourn in "New Bakassi"' *The Guardian* (1 May 2022) https://guardian.ng/sunday-magazine/bakassi-returnees-two-decade-grueling-sojourn-in-new-bakassi/.

> There is an abundance of facts to support a claim that the people of Bakassi dreaded the unwelcome consequences of being dislocated from their comfortable connection to Nigeria. The Bakassi was not simply about a physical space or resources contained in that area. It was also about human beings. There should be a marked distinction between cases where a state engages in a boundary dispute to protect its territory and assets and where it engages in a dispute that pertains to an inhabited territory.[12]

In this chapter, I argue that such implications for individuals are seldom considered in territorial disputes and propose ways to do so. Such adjustments are encouraged to fulfill the demands of justice under social idealism, serving as a basis for evaluating the legitimacy of judgments. I first observe that the Court traditionally resolves territorial disputes with reference to a firm hierarchy of titles, few of which allow for the consideration of individuals (Section 7.1). Titles are modes of acquisition through which states will establish their sovereignty over a piece of land[13] – in other words, the legal or factual conditions that prove a state's wilful territorial sovereignty.[14] I then consider how the title of *effectivités* could potentially allow for the consideration of individuals (Section 7.2) and acknowledge that their rights and needs have been mentioned by the Court as an afterthought in certain judgments (Section 7.3). Finally, I analyse the reasons for the Court's approach (Section 7.4) and argue that the principle of equity could play a stronger role in allowing for the consideration of individuals in territorial disputes (Section 7.4). Section 7.5 concludes.

7.1 Legal Titles and Local Populations: A Mismatch

The most preferred titles by the Court are legal titles. The main difference between legal titles and the other main category of title, *effectivités*

[12] Eemeka Duruigbo, 'Should Nigeria Have Sought Revision of the Bakassi Decision by the International Court of Justice?' in Edwin Egede and Mark Igiehon (eds), *The Bakassi Dispute and the International Court of Justice: Continuing Challenges* (Routledge 2018) 25.

[13] Marcelo G. Kohen, 'Titles and *effectivités* in Territorial Disputes' in Marcelo G. Kohen and Mamadou Hébié (eds), *Research Handbook on Territorial Disputes in International Law* (Edward Elgar Publishing 2018) 145.

[14] *Burkina Faso/Republic of Mali* (n. 4) [17]–[18]; Malcolm Shaw, 'The International Court of Justice and the Law of Territory' in Christian J. Tams and James Sloan (eds), *The Development of International Law by the International Court of Justice* (1st edn, OUP 2013) 154–55.

(Section 7.2), is that the latter is concerned with the *display* of authority – certain practices proving and establishing the existence of sovereignty[15] – while legal titles rely on the *source or root* of territorial jurisdiction.[16] Indeed, emanating from legal acts, legal titles typically take the form of 'a document endowed by international law with intrinsic legal force for the purpose of establishing territorial rights'.[17] While there are many kinds of legal titles, the most valued of them by the Court is a boundary treaty.[18]

There are many reasons why boundary treaties are the most preferred legal titles. Treaties, more generally, are featured in Article 38 of the ICJ Statute, which compels the Court to consider them as a source of international law. They also reflect state consent, which is a paramount principle in the eyes of the Court.[19] Thus, to question the content of the treaty if presented would be tantamount to questioning and obstructing the parties' desires.[20]

Boundary treaties are of particular value to the Court in the context of such disputes because they solidify territorial stability in a number of ways. First, in terms of *ratione temporis*, such treaties are timeless in that their consequences will continue even if the treaty itself ceases to exist, as stated by the Court in *Territorial Dispute (Libyan Arab Jamahiriya/ Chad).*[21] Second, in terms of *ratione personae*, boundary treaties create objective borders that are valid *erga omnes*, creating rights binding upon third states.[22] Third, the common requirement for parties to register treaties with the United Nations Secretariat, pursuant to Article 102 of

15 Kohen (n. 13) 145.

16 Ibid.

17 *Burkina Faso/Republic of Mali* (n. 4) [54].

18 *Land, Island and Maritime Frontier Dispute (El Salvador/Honduras: Nicaragua intervening)* (Judgment) [1992] ICJ Rep 350, 389–90 [45].

19 E.g., *Land, Island and Maritime Frontier Dispute (El Salvador/Honduras: Nicaragua intervening)* (Application to Intervene) (Judgment) [1990] ICJ Rep 92, 132–33 [94]; *East Timor (Portugal v. Australia)* (Judgment) [1995] ICJ Rep 90, 102 [29]; *Anglo-Iranian Oil Co. (United Kingdom v. Iran)* (Judgment) [1952] ICJ Rep 93, 102–3; *Maritime Delimitation and Territorial Questions between Qatar and Bahrain (Qatar v. Bahrain)* (Judgment) [1994] ICJ Rep 112 [25]; *Oil Platforms (Islamic Republic of Iran v. United States of America)* (Judgment) [2003] ICJ Rep 161, 182–83 [42]; *Armed Activities on the Territory of the Congo (New Application: 2002) (Democratic Republic of the Congo v. Rwanda)* (Order of 10 July 2002) [2002] ICJ Rep 219, 241 [57].

20 Brian Taylor Sumner, 'Territorial Disputes at the International Court of Justice' (2004) 53 (6) *Duke Law Journal* 1779, 1804.

21 *Territorial Dispute (Libyan Arab Jamahiriya/Chad)* (Judgment) [1994] ICJ Rep 6, 37 [73].

22 *Territorial Sovereignty and Scope of the Dispute) (Eritrea and Yemen)* (1998) (Award) PCA Case No. 1996-04, [153].

the UN Charter, gives a greater degree of certainty and transparency. These elements guarantee peace and long-term stability for states.[23] The Court has explained the importance it places on such stability: 'Whether it is a land frontier or a boundary line in the continental shelf that is in question, the process is essentially the same, and inevitably involves the same element of stability and permanence and is subject to the rule excluding boundary agreements from fundamental change of circumstances'.[24]

While certain treaties may confer rights upon individuals (see Section 9.1), the focus of boundary treaties is naturally not the inhabitants of the state parties. Therefore, given that the Court prioritises such treaties, it is no surprise that individuals are often sidelined in the Court's judicial reasoning in the exercise of territorial boundary delimitation.

The second type of legal title prioritised by the Court in territorial disputes is the principle of the intangibility of boundaries inherited from colonisation, more commonly referred to as *uti possidetis juris.* This principle aims to 'secur[e] respect for the territorial boundaries at the moment when independence [was] achieved'.[25] Colonial powers will have typically adopted bilateral or unilateral instruments – for instance, a decree by one leader of a colony – or joint declarations or agreements between two colonial powers defining a boundary.[26] The principle of *uti possidetis juris* transforms such delimitations into international frontiers.[27]

Like boundary treaties, most colonial agreements treated by the Court make no reference to the inhabitants of the disputed territory. Therefore, the principle of *uti possidetis juris* does not allow individuals to be considered in the Court's legal reasoning in the context of territorial boundary disputes. Furthermore, this process of 'freez[ing] the territorial

[23] *Libyan Arab Jamahiriya/Chad* (n. 21) 37 [72]; *Case concerning the Temple of Preah Vihear (Cambodia v. Thailand)* (Judgment) [1962] ICJ Rep 6, 34.

[24] *Aegean Sea Continental Shelf (Greece v. Turkey)* (Judgment) [1978] ICJ Rep 3, 35–36 [85]. For more on the principle of stability in territorial disputes, see Géraldine Giraudeau, *Les différends territoriaux devant le juge international: entre droit et transaction* (Martinus Nijhoff Publishers 2013) 281–339.

[25] *Burkina Faso/Republic of Mali* (n. 4) 566 [23]. See also Philippe Couvreur, 'Notes sur le "droit" colonial français dans la mise en oeuvre du principe de *l'uti possidetis juris* par la Cour internationale de Justice' in Maurice K. Kamga and Makane Moïse Mbengue (eds), *Liber amicorum [en l'honneur de] Raymond Ranjeva: l'Afrique et le droit international; variations sur l'organisation internationale* (Pedone 2013) 111–24.

[26] Hugh Thirlway, 'Territorial Disputes and Their Resolution in the Recent Jurisprudence of the International Court of Justice' (2018) 31(1) *Leiden Journal of International Law* 117, 132.

[27] *Burkina Faso/Republic of Mali* (n. 4) 566 [23].

title'[28] focuses on the colonial power's boundaries prior to the independence of the modern-day state and not indigenous boundaries of the first people settled on the land. The designated Chamber of the Court recalled in *Land, Island and Maritime Frontier Dispute (El Salvador/Honduras: Nicaragua intervening)* (1992) that 'when the principle of the *uti possidetis juris* is involved, the *jus* referred to is not international law but the constitutional or administrative law of the pre-independence sovereign'.[29] Hence, when El Salvador argued that the *uti possidetis* boundaries should be drawn based on those of the earlier Indian settlement ('poblaciones'), the Chamber refuted this.[30] The emphasis of such legal titles is on the will of the colonial sovereigns dominating the territory in question as opposed to local populations.

In the Court's spirit of ensuring stability, the rationale behind the *uti possidetis juris* principle was the need for stability and security after decolonisation, particularly in African nations.[31] While understandable, the principle has still been criticised for undermining local populations. Makau Mutua has argued that this form of territorial boundary delimitation does not respect the real configuration of African populations. In his view, in instances where 'European map-makers split one nation in two states (. . .), the fate of the people was discussed as though they were two separate and alien entities, in defiance of reality on the ground'.[32] Furthermore, the application of this principle is problematic insofar as it legitimises *a posteriori* the administrative decisions made in grave violation of the rights and freedoms of colonised populations.[33] In this vein, Judge Mohamed Bennouna contemplates whether 'contemporary international law can rely on law produced by such an institution, even

[28] Ibid [30]; *Frontier Dispute (Benin/Niger)* (Judgment) [2005] ICJ Rep 90, 109 [26].

[29] *El Salvador/Honduras: Nicaragua intervening* (n. 18) 558–59 [333].

[30] Ibid 392–93 [50].

[31] Makane Moïse Mbengue, 'Delimitation and Demarcation of Borders in Africa: History, Problems and Prospects' in Pierre D'Argent (ed), *Droit des frontières internationales: Journées Franco-Allemandes = The Law of International Borders* (Pedone 2016) 87–101; Inge Van Hulle, 'Imperial Consolidation through Arbitration: Territorial and Boundary Disputes in Africa (1870–1914)' in Ignacio de la Rasilla and Jorge E. Viñuales (eds), *Experiments in International Adjudication: Historical Accounts* (1st edn, CUP 2019) 55–75.

[32] Makauwa Mutua, 'Why Redraw the Map of Africa: A Moral and Legal Inquiry' (1995) 16 (4) *Michigan Journal of International Law* 1113, 1119.

[33] *Frontier Dispute (Burkina Faso/Niger)* (Judgment) [2013] ICJ Rep 45, 95 (Declaration of Judge Bennouna); Robert McCorquodale and Raul Pangalangan, 'Pushing Back the Limitations of Territorial Boundaries' (2001) 12(5) *European Journal of International Law* 867.

though it involved only administrative boundaries which, moreover, attached little importance to the populations concerned and their historical and sociological relationships'.[34]

In sum, legal titles such as treaties and colonial instruments applied through the principle of *uti possidetis juris* do not leave much room for the consideration of individuals, as they reflect the desires of past and present sovereign powers at the expense of local populations. Beyond legal titles, however, *effectivités* present more prospects for inclusion.

7.2 The Potential of *Effectivités*

Contrary to the legal titles examined before (Section 7.1), *effectivités* has given individuals a platform of sorts in the Court's jurisprudence on territorial disputes.[35] *Effectivités* is the exercise of effective possession by an authority of the state on the basis of its sovereignty. Contrary to legal titles, relying on a legal *source* to prove the state's sovereignty, *effectivités* relies on the state's *actions* and practice that demonstrate its authority over the relevant territory. It includes any 'actual continuous and peaceful display of state functions',[36] such as, but not limited to, 'legislative acts or acts of administrative control, acts relating to the application and enforcement of criminal or civil law, acts regulating immigration, acts regulating fishing and other economic activities, naval patrols as well as search and rescue operations'.[37] The Permanent Court of International Justice (PCIJ) explained in *Eastern Greenland* that alongside such a display of authority, 'the intention and will to act as sovereign' is required.[38]

[34] *Frontier Dispute (Burkina Faso/Niger)* (Declaration of Judge Bennouna) (n. 33).

[35] Marcelo Kohen and Mara Tignino, 'Do People Have Rights in Boundaries' Delimitations?' in Laurence Boisson de Chazournes, Christina Leb, and Mara Tignino (eds), *International Law and Freshwater* (Edward Elgar Publishing 2013) 98.

[36] *Island of Palmas (or Miangas) (The Netherlands/The United States of America)* (1928) (Award) II RIAA 829, 10.

[37] *Territorial and Maritime Dispute (Nicaragua v. Colombia)* (Judgment) [2012] ICJ Rep 624, 655 [80]. See also *Territorial and Maritime Dispute between Nicaragua and Honduras in the Caribbean Sea (Nicaragua v. Honduras)* (Judgment) [2007] ICJ Rep 659, [176]–[208]; *Sovereignty over Pulau Ligitan and Pulau Sipadan (Indonesia/Malaysia)* (Judgment) [2002] ICJ Rep 625, 683 [137]–[141]; *Minquiers and Ecrehos (France/United Kingdom)* (Judgment) [1953] ICJ Rep 47, 65–69.

[38] *Legal Status of Eastern Greenland* (n. 7) 45-46.

Acts of individuals can serve as evidence of a state's sovereignty over the relevant territory. An example where *effectivités* was recognised to this end was in *Sovereignty over Pedra Branca/Pulau Batu Puteh, Middle Rocks and South Ledge (Malaysia/Singapore)* (2008). Here, Malaysia claimed that its title to Pedra Branca/Pulau Batu Puteh was confirmed by the ties of loyalty existing between the Sultanate of Johor and a nomadic 'people of the sea' named the Orang Laut. These people were reported to have engaged in 'various activities such as fishing and piratical activities in the waters in the Straits of Singapore, including in the area of Pedra Branca/ Pulau Batu Puteh'.[39] Malaysia provided evidence – writings of British officials in Singapore – that the Straits of Singapore were these peoples' habitat that they frequently visited[40] and that they were subjects of the King of Johor, appointed by the latter.[41] Due to the high probative value given to these sources, the Court concluded that Malaysia had the original title over Pedra Branca/Pulau Batu Puteh.[42]

Therefore, *effectivités* is seemingly, as a state litigant once said, '[t]he only satisfactory way of dealing with the emotively real and ethically unavoidable question of the link between man and the land'.[43] However, this title carries two main problems when considering its ability to integrate individuals into the Court's legal reasoning in territorial disputes.

First, *effectivités* is secondary to legal titles. Despite this showcase of the behaviour of individuals in the assessment of territorial sovereignty, the Court has always stood by the primacy of legal title over effective control.[44] This means that if both a legal title and *effectivités* are presented, and the legal title and *effectivités* state different rights, then preference is given to the legal title.[45] For instance, the Court rejected

[39] *Malaysia/Singapore* (n. 8) 37 [70].

[40] Ibid 37 [71].

[41] Ibid 37–38 [72]–[73].

[42] Ibid 38–39 [74]. However, the Court ultimately concluded that Pedra Branca/Pulau Batu Puteh belonged to Singapore through acquisitive prescription.

[43] Memorial of the Republic of El Salvador (1 June 1988) [7.17].

[44] Marcelo G. Kohen, 'La relation titres/effectivités dans la jurisprudence récente de la Cour internationale de Justice (2004-2012)' in Denis Alland et al (eds), *Unité et diversité du droit international: ecrits en l'honneur du professeur Pierre-Marie Dupuy* (Martinus Nijhoff Publishers 2014) 599–614.

[45] *Burkina Faso/Republic of Mali* (n. 4) 586–87 [63]. See also *El Salvador/Honduras: Nicaragua intervening* (n. 18) 398 [61]; *Land and Maritime Boundary between Cameroon and Nigeria (Cameroon v. Nigeria: Equatorial Guinea intervening)* (Judgment) [2002] ICJ Rep 303, 353–54 [68]; *Benin/Niger* (n. 28) 148–49 [141]; *Case concerning Sovereignty over Certain Frontier Land (Belgium/Netherlands)* (Judgment) [1959] ICJ Rep 209, 229–30.

Thailand's claims of sovereignty over the temple in *Preah Vihear*, allegedly manifested through a number of acts of effective control subsequent to a 1904 boundary treaty with France attributing sovereignty to Cambodia.[46]

Effectivités only serves to confirm the right derived from a legal title if the latter is 'obscure'[47] or 'doubtful',[48] therefore failing to provide a clear solution regarding the disputed territory.[49] For example, the Court turned to *effectivités* in *El Salvador/Honduras* after noting that the legislative and administrative texts provided were 'confused and conflicting'.[50] *Effectivités* may also override legal titles where the latter is lacking.[51] For instance, in *Sovereignty over Pulau Ligitan and Pulau Sipadan (Indonesia/Malaysia)* (2002), the Court only considered *effectivités* after having decided that neither of the parties had provided a legal title.[52] Finally, *effectivités* may also be considered where a contending state proves that it acquiesced effective control over a disputed territory, despite the existence of a treaty attributing original sovereignty to another state (acquisitive prescription).[53] Therefore, despite *effectivités* taking individuals into account, it is only a subsidiary consideration.

The second limitation to *effectivités* is its preoccupation with the state's authority as opposed to the individual's desires. The activities of individuals are not assessed to arrive at a solution that factors their needs or desires into account. Rather, they serve as 'evidence of the intention of that Government to act as sovereign (...) involving a manifestation of State authority in respect of [the relevant territory]'.[54] The Court clearly stated in *Indonesia/Malaysia* that 'activities by private persons cannot be seen as *effectivités* if they do not take place on the basis of official regulations or under governmental authority'.[55] The mere presence of

[46] *Temple of Preah Vihear* (n. 23) 27–29. See also *Kasikili/Sedudu Island (Botswana/Namibia)* (Judgment) [1999] ICJ Rep 1045, 1087 [63], 1095 [75], 1096 [79], [80].

[47] See *Burkina Faso/Niger* (n. 33) [78].

[48] *Benin/Niger* (n. 28) 148–49 [141].

[49] *El Salvador/Honduras: Nicaragua intervening* (n. 18) 566 [347]; Ibid.

[50] *El Salvador/Honduras: Nicaragua intervening* (n. 18) 55–59 [333]. See also *Nicaragua v. Colombia* (n. 37) 649 [55].

[51] *Libyan Arab Jamahiriya/Chad* (n. 21) 38–39 [76]; *Benin/Niger* (n. 28) 108–10 [25]–[27], 127 [76]–[77], 128 [82].

[52] *Indonesia/Malaysia* (n. 37) 678–79 [127].

[53] *Cameroon v. Nigeria: Equatorial Guinea intervening* (n. 45) 352–53 [67]; *Malaysia/Singapore* (n. 8) 50–51 [121].

[54] *France/United Kingdom* (n. 37) 71.

[55] *Indonesia/Malaysia* (n. 37) 683 [140] and 683–84 [142].

individuals is therefore insufficient to be considered by the Court – only their presence *à titre de souverain* would yield value.[56]

Thus, the Court rejected Indonesia's argument that Indonesian fishermen used the waters around Ligitan and Sipadan, as these activities did not constitute acts *à titre de souverain* reflecting the intention and will of Indonesia.[57] Similarly, in *Kasikili/Sedudu Island (Botswana/Namibia)* where Namibia invoked its title on the grounds of *effectivités* in two instances to claim its sovereignty over the island, the Court found in both instances that there was nothing showing that the presence of the Masubia people was linked to territorial claims by the Caprivi authorities.[58] It noted that it was 'not uncommon for the inhabitants of border regions in Africa to traverse such borders for purposes of agriculture and grazing, without raising concern on the part of the authorities on either side of the border'.[59] The acts of individuals in and of themselves are therefore insufficient to establish *effectivités*, reflecting the theory of agency.[60]

As it stands, the peoples' consent and acceptance to be ruled by the claiming state litigant is in fact an implicit element in the Court's assessment. They, for instance, pay taxes imposed by the state litigants or use buildings that the state litigants claim to have built. This receptivity indicates their acceptance of the state's authority and therefore allegiance to that state. This, however, is not explicitly acknowledged nor examined in territorial disputes. As I have argued elsewhere, the Court could, in determining the application of *effectivités*, go further than assume the peoples' allegiance due to their passive acceptance of the state's actions.[61] It could verify that the individuals in question have

[56] *Malaysia/Singapore* (n. 8) 50–51 [121]; Ibid 683–84 [142]. See also Mariano Aznar, 'The Human Factor in Territorial Disputes' in Marcelo Kohen and Mamadou Hébié (eds), *Research Handbook on Territorial Disputes in International Law* (Edward Elgar Publishing 2018) 308.

[57] *Indonesia/Malaysia* (n. 37) 683 [140]–[141].

[58] *Botswana/Namibia* (n. 46) 1094–95 [74], 1103–4 [94], 1105–6 [98].

[59] Ibid [74].

[60] Ian Brownlie, *Principles of Public International Law* (7th edn, OUP 2008) 138 ("Acts by private persons purporting to appropriate territory for the State of which they are nationals may be ratified by the State … based upon [a theory of] agency in private law"); Angelo Piero Sereni, 'Agency in International Law' (1940) 34(4) *The American Journal of International Law* 638.

[61] Yusra Suedi, 'Self-Determination in Territorial Disputes before the International Court of Justice: From Rhetoric to Reality?' (2022) 36(1) *Leiden Journal of International Law* 161.

exhibited allegiance and a desire to be governed by that state and explicitly affirm this.

For example, in *El Salvador/Honduras*, the Chamber noted that '[i]n the absence of legislative instruments formally defining provincial boundaries, not only the grants to Indian communities but also land grants to private individuals afford some evidence which might indicate where the boundaries were thought to be or ought to be'.[62] In this case, the private individuals must have consented to the granting state's authority even if no mention was made of this in the analysis of *effectivités* by the Court. It is not only the state's intention to govern a people but also the latter's desire to be governed by the state, which has value in the claim of *effectivités*. Similarly, in *Malaysia/Singapore*, if there were any reason to believe that the Orang Laut did not accept the sovereignty of the Sultanate of Johor, the *effectivités* of Malaysia would likely not have been upheld. However, this step of the reasoning is omitted in judgments in territorial disputes, which only place emphasis on the state. My proposal is to not only analyse the Sultan of Johor's authority over the Orang Laut but also to consider if the Orang Laut accepted such authority and, if so, explicitly state this.

This subtle shift does not compromise the principle of stability of boundaries as the Court is already foregoing such stability when resolving a territorial dispute on the grounds of a state litigant's *effectivités*, due to the absence or inadequacy of a boundary treaty. The state's territorial integrity also remains unaffected insofar as *effectivités* still aims to affirm the state's sovereignty. However, this proposal implies that if, when assessing the peoples' desires in the examination of *effectivités*, they do not align with the state's acts *a titre de souverain*, then *effectivités* would not be upheld as a valid title in the given context. In such a scenario, the Court would still have other more subsidiary means to resolve the territorial dispute pursuant to its practice, such as the principle of equity explored later (Section 7.6).[63]

In summary, examining a state's *effectivités* over a territory—and, by extension, the actions of individuals—is the primary means by which the latter are incorporated into the framework established by the Court for addressing territorial disputes. Despite its subsidiary nature, a shift in

[62] *El Salvador/Honduras: Nicaragua intervening* (n. 18) 394 [54].

[63] Yusra Suedi, 'Man, Land and Sea: Local Populations in Territorial and Maritime Disputes Before the International Court of Justice' (2021) 20(1) *Law and Practice of International Courts and Tribunals* 30, 44–52.

legal reasoning during its application can allow the desires of local populations to be considered in territorial disputes before the Court. This proposal does not completely address the marginalisation of individuals in territorial disputes before the Court, nor does it prioritise them in such cases. However, it offers a way to acknowledge peoples' aspirations without upending the established jurisprudence that has shaped the Court's steadfast approach.

7.3 Forsaken Titles

Legal titles and *effectivités* are the two main categories of title considered by the Court in territorial disputes. As observed earlier, neither directly reflects human concerns. However, state litigants have occasionally invoked other arguments allowing for local populations to be considered in the dispute, such as human concerns and history, respectively. This section illustrates such instances, noting that such titles have been rejected by the Court as they fail to fit in the well-established title system developed in its jurisprudence.

First, states have plainly expressed concern for the human dimensions of the case to advocate for the rights of their inhabitants in territorial disputes. In *El Salvador/Honduras*, for example, El Salvador explicitly requested for the appointed Chamber to consider the 'human factor' in hopes of impacting the Chamber's legal reasoning in its delimitation of the territorial boundary. Explaining how the disputes would impact its local populations, it pleaded on the grounds of 'reasons of crucial human necessity',[64] arguing that factoring in human considerations was 'indispensable in the best interests of the requirements of authentic international justice'.[65] It therefore asked the Chamber 'to ensure that the duly considered judgment is appropriate for the destiny and necessities of the persons whose lives are bound up in the matter'.[66] The Chamber, however, responded that its task was 'to declare what areas are, and what are not, already part of the one State and the other. If Salvadorians have settled in areas of Honduras, neither that fact, nor the consequences of the application of Honduran law to their properties, can affect the matter'.[67]

64 Memorial of the Republic of El Salvador (1 June 1988) [7.16].
65 Ibid.
66 Ibid [7.2].
67 *El Salvador/Honduras: Nicaragua intervening* (n. 18) 419 [97].

A similar example where human concerns invoked by state litigants were rejected by the Court was in *Frontier Dispute (Burkina Faso/Niger)* (2013), where Niger argued extensively that populations should be taken into account in the delimitation of the territorial boundary. It argued that the 1927 Arrêté and Erratum that the Court was anticipated to rely on to resolve the dispute 'raised problems for the nomadic populations'[68] given that they are not sufficiently precise to fix the frontier at issue.[69] Furthermore, Niger submitted that the territorial colonial partitions constituted a 'socially disruptive factor' which provoked 'population movements motivated by the preservation of communal or cultural identities, or the safeguard of interests'.[70] While the Court did not directly factor in such considerations, it used a map produced by the French *Institut géographique national* (IGN map)[71] as a reflection of the colonial *effectivités*[72] in its resolution of the dispute, pursuant to the parties' request.[73] Given that the map was drawn on the basis of information, provided by the local authorities[74] and consultations with village chiefs and local people,[75] on the boundaries of their cantons,[76] it was deemed by Judge Antônio Augusto Cançado Trindade to be 'the appropriate frontier line therein from the perspective of the relations between people and territory'.[77]

Human concerns aside, state litigants have also made historical claims as title. This title is typically rooted in the idea that a certain state possessed a certain territory first or for a significant period of time. It therefore sheds light on a community who historically inhabited the disputed territory. However, the Court has typically discarded these arguments if it has been able to rely on legal titles or, eventually, *effectivités*. In *Preah Vihear*, the Court, satisfied with the 1904 Boundary

68 *Burkina Faso/Niger* (n. 33) 101–2 [13] (Separate opinion of Judge Cançado Trindade).
69 Memorial of Niger (20 April 2011) [2.1-4].
70 Ibid [6.6].
71 *Burkina Faso/Niger* (n. 33) 75–76 [67] and 105 [24] (Separate opinion of Judge Cançado Trindade).
72 Memorial of Niger (20 April 2011) [68].
73 *Burkina Faso/Niger* (n. 33) 75–76 [67] and 105 [24] (Separate opinion of Judge Cançado Trindade).
74 Ibid 116 [58] (Separate opinion of Judge Cançado Trindade).
75 Ibid 117 [61] (Separate opinion of Judge Cançado Trindade).
76 Ibid 116 [58] (Separate opinion of Judge Cançado Trindade).
77 Ibid 132 [102] (Separate opinion of Judge Cançado Trindade).

Treaty, explicitly stated that it was unable to regard other arguments relied on by the parties 'of a physical, historical, religious and archaeological character' as legally decisive.[78] In *Territorial dispute (Libya/Chad)*, Libya had submitted to the Court that prior to French colonialism, part of the disputed territory (the "Borderlands") was already inhabited by peoples under Libyan dominance,[79] but the presence of a treaty eclipsed this argument.[80] As explained earlier (Section 7.1), in *El Salvador/ Honduras*, El Salvador argued that the *uti possidetis* boundaries should be drawn based on the indigenous delimitation of the early Indian settlement ('poblaciones'), as opposed to the Spanish colonial administration's boundaries.[81] The Court, however, rejected any historical titles pre-dating the parties' independence in 1821.[82] In brief, historical claims have yet to be upheld by the Court in a territorial dispute.

State litigants have therefore expressed concerns for their people in various ways. French jurist Pierre-Marie Dupuy has commented that doing so benefits not only the local populations but also the litigants themselves: '[S]i, devant la Cour internationale de Justice ou tout autre tribunal international, un Etat était demain amené à défendre sa souveraineté sur la portion d'un fleuve ou d'un lac, il le fera d'autant mieux sur le plan juridique qu'il pourra s'appuyer sur le droit de sa population à l'eau.'[83]

The rejection of both human concerns and historical claims indicates that the Court is trapped within the parameters of the notion of legal title. Beyond the parties' arguments, the consideration of populations will depend on their inclusion in legal sources recognised as legitimate by the Court. Arguments and titles raised outside of the title system have no place in the Court's decision-making in territorial disputes.

78 *Temple of Preah Vihear* (n. 23) 15.

79 Memorial written by the Great Socialist People's Libyan Arab Jamahiriya (26 August 1991), [3.36].

80 *Libyan Arab Jamahiriya/Chad* (n. 21) 21–26 [40]–[52].

81 *El Salvador/Honduras: Nicaragua intervening* (n. 18) 392–93 [49]–[50].

82 Ibid 392–93 [50] and 544–46 [307]. See also Sumner (n. 20) 1799.

83 Pierre-Marie Dupuy, 'Le droit à l'eau, un droit international?' (2006) European University Institute Department of Law Working Paper 2006/06. See also Aznar (n. 56) 334. Author's translation: If tomorrow, before the International Court of Justice or any other international tribunal, a State were to defend its sovereignty over the portion of a river or a lake, it would be better off relying on the right of its population to water, from a legal perspective.

7.4 P.S.: Questions, Rights and Needs

While the Court may not acknowledge historical claims nor human concerns, its inquiry into the human dimensions of the dispute through questions during oral proceedings has been noteworthy. For example, in the oral proceedings of *Burkina Faso/Niger*, Judge Cançado Trindade asked the parties to indicate, with precision, to what extent will the fixing of the frontier have a bearing on the nomadic populations in the relevant areas.[84] Burkina Faso responded that the reduction of pastoral spaces posed by international borders may cause difficulties to the nomads, but in the instant case, any frontier that is determined between it and Niger will have no detrimental effect on the populations (nomads or otherwise) living in the border area.[85] Niger, on the other hand, replied that while the authorities of both states do not rigorously apply the regulations for the movement of populations, this forms part of the *modus vivendi* between them (arrangement allowing for peaceful coexistence).[86] Judge Cançado Trindade concluded from this that 'any frontier to be determined does not seem likely to have an impact on the population, as long as both States continue to guarantee the free movement to the nomads and semi-nomads, and their living conditions do not change as a consequence of the fixing of the frontier (by the Court)'.[87]

The practice of asking questions indicates a certain interest from the judges on the bench in the fate of such populations and hints to a possible discussion in the judges' deliberations. The practice also suggests that if the parties not provide this information *proprio motu*, the Court can inquire into the potential impact of boundary delimitation on the local populations of one or both countries.

Given the rarity of this practice and reliance on the interests of specific judges, a more common approach has been for the Court to acknowledge individual rights and needs of populations *post scriptum*, directing state litigants to address the repercussions of its judgments. The affirmation of individual rights *post scriptum* has been observed in four instances. First,

[84] Verbatim record 2012/26, 59–60 (Judge Cançado Trindade).

[85] Replies of Burkina Faso and Niger to the questions put by Judge Cançado Trindade at the end of the public sitting held on 17 October 2012 (translation) (16 November 2012), [16]–[17], [19].

[86] Ibid 6.

[87] *Burkina Faso/Niger* (n. 33) 114 [47] (Separate opinion of Judge Cançado Trindade); Verbatim record 2018/20, 86 [37] (Judge Gaja).

refuting El Salvador's human-centric claims explained before (Section 7.3), the appointed Chamber noted in *El Salvador/Honduras* that

> The situation may arise in some areas whereby a number of the nationals of one Party will, following the delimitation of the disputed sectors, find themselves living in the territory of the other, and property rights apparently established under the laws of the one Party will be found to have been granted over land which is part of the territory of the other. The Chamber has every confidence that such measures as may be necessary to take account of this situation will be framed and carried out by both Parties, in full respect for acquired rights, and in a humane and orderly manner.[88]

Second, although it was decided in *Kasikili/Sedudu Island* that the island forms part of the territory of Botswana,[89] the Court decided that there should be unimpeded access for the craft of the nationals and flags of the parties in the two channels of the river around the island irrespective of sovereignty on an equal treatment basis.[90] This followed Botswana stressing its policy on free navigation during the oral hearings.[91]

Third, in resolving the *Cameroon v. Nigeria* dispute, the Court was required to delimit the vicinity surrounding the Cameroonian village of Turu,[92] which had expanded onto Nigerian territory over time,[93] and the boundary in the vicinity of the Nigerian village of Kotcha, which had spread over onto the Cameroonian side of the boundary.[94] Predictably applying the treaty before it (the Thomson-Marchand Declaration) to resolve the matter, it stated that 'It is instead up to the Parties to find a solution to any resultant problems, with a view to respecting the rights and interests of the local population'.[95] It later stated in the judgment that 'the implementation of the present Judgment will afford the Parties a beneficial opportunity to cooperate in the interests of the population concerned, in order notably to enable it to continue to have access to educational and health services comparable to those it currently

88 *El Salvador/Honduras: Nicaragua intervening* (n. 18) 400 [66].

89 *Botswana/Namibia* (n. 46) 1106 [101].

90 Ibid 1107–8 [103]. See also 1112 (Declaration of Judge Abdul Koroma), 1110 (Declaration of Judge Ranjeva), and 1148–51 [25]–[35] (Separate opinion of Judge Kooijmans).

91 Ibid 1106–7 [102].

92 More specifically, the watershed from Ngosi to Humsiki (Roumsiki)/Kamale/Turu (the Mandara Mountains).

93 *Cameroon v. Nigeria: Equatorial Guinea intervening* (n. 45) 369 [104]; Rejoinder of Nigeria (4 January 2001), [7.135].

94 Ibid (*Cameroon v. Nigeria*) 373 [121].

95 Ibid 373–74 [123].

enjoys'.[96] This resulted in the establishment of a mixed commission to protect the right of affected populations through the Greentree Agreement.[97] Its Article 3 accords rights to Nigerian nationals of the Bekassi Peninsula that must be respected by Cameroon.[98]

The fourth example where the Court acknowledged populations' rights *post scriptum* is in *Frontier Dispute* (*Benin/Niger*) (2005) where Benin had argued that its people on the Nigerian bank had the acquired right to use the waters of the Niger River and that such rights should not be interfered with.[99] The Court, following the precedent established by its predecessor that private rights acquired under existing law do not cease on a change of sovereignty,[100] ruled that 'the determination in regard to the attribution of islands effected above is without prejudice to any private law rights which may be held in respect of those islands'.[101]

Beyond recalling individual rights or inviting state litigants to pay attention to them *post hoc*, the Court requested on one occasion for state litigants to have due regard for populations' needs. It stated in *Burkina Faso/Niger* that 'each Party, in exercising its authority over the portion of the territory under its sovereignty, should have due regard to the needs of the populations concerned, in particular those of the nomadic or semi-nomadic populations, and to the necessity to overcome difficulties that may arise for them because of the frontier. The Court notes the cooperation that has already been established on a regional and bilateral basis between the Parties in this regard, in particular under Chapter III of the 1987 Protocol of Agreement and encourages them to develop it further'.[102] The Court therefore likely considers that in certain cases,

[96] *Cameroon v. Nigeria: Equatorial Guinea intervening* (n. 45) 452 [316]. It also stated: "The Court takes note with satisfaction of the commitment thus undertaken in respect of these areas where many Nigerian nationals reside" ([317]).

[97] Laurence Boisson de Chazournes and Antonella Angelini, '"After the Court Rose": The Rise of Diplomatic Means to Implement the Pronouncements of the International Court of Justice' (2012) 11 *Law and Practice of International Courts and Tribunals* 1; Affef Ben Mansour, *La mise en oeuvre des arrêts et sentences des juridictions internationales* (Larcier 2011) 496–97.

[98] Greentree Agreement, 12 June 2006, Article 3. See also Egede (n.10) 80.

[99] Memorial of the Republic of Benin (27 August 2003) [2.182] and [3.4]; Reply of the Republic of Benin (17 December 2004), [0.13]; Verbatim record 2005/1, 20 [1.23] (M. Biaou).

[100] *Certain German Interests in Polish Upper Silesia* (Judgment) [1926] PCIJ Series A, 42; *German Settlers in Poland* (Advisory Opinion) [1923] PCIJ Series B, 6, 36.

[101] *Benin/Niger* (n. 28) 140–41 [118].

[102] *Burkina Faso/Niger* (n. 33) 90–92 [112].

reminding the parties to consider local populations can help mitigate the negative repercussions of its judgment.

7.5 Reasons for the Court's Approach

It has been established at this stage that the link between the legitimacy of territorial title and the fate of the residing population is seldom underlined in the Court's judgments.[103] A robust system has been woven into the Court's jurisprudence, where legal titles, such as treaties, take precedence (Section 7.1). Only in the absence of such titles will the Court turn to *effectivités* (Section 7.2) where various acts by individuals may be valuable only as proof of the government's *acte de souverain* over the territory in question. They serve more as a means of establishing the state's sovereignty, rather than reflecting where individuals themselves feel a sense of belonging. This system leaves little room for other arguments such as human concerns or historical claims, although states have occasionally raised them (Section 7.3). However, such arguments have yet to be considered, with the Court only acknowledging individuals' rights and needs *post scriptum* (Section 7.4).

It should be mentioned that the opportunities for the Court to address the repercussions on local populations are generally limited to states raising such concerns in their pleadings. Indeed, the Court is not authorised to raise such concerns upon its own initiative but is bound by the principle of *non ultra petita* ('not beyond the request'). This principle holds that the Court may not decide more than it has been asked to and may not innovate outside of the parties' submissions.[104] The Court has recognised the principle in its own jurisprudence.[105] It implies that unless

[103] Kohen and Tignino (n. 35) 100.

[104] *Request for Interpretation of the Judgment of 20 November 1950 in the Asylum Case (Colombia v. Peru)* (Judgment) [1950] ICJ Rep 395, 402. See also *Oil Platforms* (n. 19) 221 [7] (Declaration of Vice-President Ranjeva); Gerald Fitzmaurice, *The Law and Procedure of the International Court of Justice* (Grotius Publications 1986) 531; Friedlich Rosenfeld, '*Iura Novit Curia* in International Law' in Franco Ferrari et al (eds), *Iura Novit Curia in International Arbitration* (JurisNet LLC 2018) 453; Hugh Thirlway, *The International Court of Justice* (OUP 2016) 85–86.

[105] *Pulp Mills on the River Uruguay (Argentina v. Uruguay)* (Judgment) [2010] ICJ Rep 14, 72–73 [168]; *Continental Shelf (Libyan Arab Jamahiriya/Malta)* (Judgment) [1985] ICJ Rep 13, 23–24 [19]; *France/United Kingdom* (n. 37) 52; *Barcelona Traction Light and Power Company Ltd. (Belgium v. Spain)* (Second Phase) (Preliminary Objections) (Judgment) [1970] ICJ Rep 3, 34 [40].

state litigants raise concerns about their local populations in their pleadings, the Court may not take up the matter on its own accord. While state litigants have done so on many occasions presented in this chapter, the opportunity has not always presented itself for the Court to give due consideration to local populations.

However, in instances where such concerns have been raised, the Court has rejected them for two main reasons. The first reason is to respect the principle of the stability of boundaries (Section 6.1). The Court has made clear that the exercise of territorial delimitation has the objective 'to achieve stability and finality'.[106] This principle finds its origins in Article 62(2)(a) of the Vienna Convention on the Law of Treaties, which prohibits the invocation of a fundamental change of circumstances as a ground for terminating or withdrawing from a treaty establishing a boundary.[107] The International Law Commission specified that this principle had the objective of avoiding 'dangerous frictions' by allowing changes to be made to boundary treaties, which are 'instrument[s] of peaceful change'.[108]

While the principle of the stability of boundaries is important, the extent to which it should dictate the Court's delimitation process has been questioned in scholarship. Charles de Visscher stated in 1969 that it is the sole criterion for interpreting boundary treaties.[109] However, scholars have since challenged this, arguing that the exercise of delimiting territorial boundaries offers 'great flexibility' to judges,[110] who have a notably large discretionary power when delimiting territorial boundaries.[111] My view, supported by certain scholars, is that the principle of the stability of boundaries serves to resolve *preliminary* questions related to the function of the boundary, such as the legal nature of the delimitation, its legal effects, or its domain of application. However, it is not necessarily relevant to the actual delimitation process, that is deciding whether

[106] *Temple of Preah Vihear* (n. 23) 34. See also *Libyan Arab Jamahiriya/Chad* (n. 21) 37 [72]–[73].

[107] Vienna Convention on the Law of Treaties, 1155 UNTS 331, Article 62. See also Vienna Convention on Succession of States in respect of Treaties, 1946 UNTS 3, Article 11.

[108] Draft Articles on the Law of Treaties with commentaries [1966] *Yearbook of the ILC*, vol II, 259 [11].

[109] Charles de Visscher, *Problèmes de confins en droit international public* (Pedone 1969) 28.

[110] Giraudeau (n. 24) 281–82.

[111] Jacqueline Dutheil de la Rochère, 'Les procédures de règlement des différends frontaliers' in Société française du droit international, *La frontière* (Pedone 1980) 143.

the line should go here or there.[112] Massimo Starita reasons that 'Cela pour la simple raison que le but atypique des traités établissant des frontières (...) et le principe de sécurité qui l'accompagne semblent trop génériques pour aider l'interprète à choisir entre un tracé et un autre'.[113] It is therefore possible that the Court has occasionally applied the principle further than necessary.[114]

The second reason for the Court's approach to local populations in territorial disputes is its desire to respect formalism. As discussed in Chapter 6, legal formalism pleads for an exclusive application of law without consideration for non-juridical elements, such as morality, substantive values, politics or humanitarian, or social or economic considerations (Section 6.1). In the view of the Court, considering local populations in territorial disputes would contradict formalism, which is critical for a decision's objectivity, neutrality, and credibility.[115] In the context of territorial disputes, the Court has been careful to note that it has not stepped outside the legal realm to reach its decision where it may be suspected that it has done so.[116]

However, no formalist can deny the existence of the principle of equity (Section 6.3.1). Equity may be a tool to peacefully adapt laws at the drastic disservice of state litigants' local populations. Its mere existence confirms the viable coexistence between the law and other considerations.[117] Indeed, equity is often considered *alongside* stability in the process of delimitation, as one arbitral tribunal stated.[118] Resorting to it would appear to be innate to a court carrying 'justice' in its name.[119] The next section examines its potential application in the context of territorial disputes to the benefit of local populations.

[112] Giuseppe Nesi, 'Boundaries' in Marcelo Kohen and Mamadou Hébié (eds), *Research Handbook on Territorial Disputes in International Law* (Edward Elgar Publishing 2018) 231–32.

[113] Massimo Starita, 'L'interprétation des traités établissant la frontière' in Société française pour le droit international, *Droit des frontières internationales* (Pedone 2016) 73–76. Author's translation: "This for the simple reason that the atypical purpose of treaties establishing borders (...) and the principle of security which accompanies it seem too generic to help the interpreter choose between one line and another."

[114] Suedi (n. 63) 43. See also Giraudeau (n. 24) 291–98.

[115] Andrea Bianchi, *International Law Theories: An Inquiry into Different Ways of Thinking* (OUP 2016) 27.

[116] *Burkina Faso/Republic of Mali* (n. 4) [149].

[117] Giraudeau (n. 24) 342, 344–45.

[118] *Guyana v. Suriname* (2007) (Award) PCA Case No. 2004-04, 108 [334] (emphasis added).

[119] Andreas Zimmermann et al (eds), *The Statute of the International Court of Justice: A Commentary* (3rd edn, OUP 2019) 133.

7.6 The Principle of Equity as a Tool to the Benefit of Local Populations

Equity may provide greater consideration of local populations than would be possible if only legal titles were applied. It allows for individuals to be integrated into the hierarchical framework developed through the Court's jurisprudence on territorial disputes. Applying the principle of equity would typically result in a zone being split in half and equally attributed to each party. While the Court has stated that '[e]quity does not necessarily imply equality',[120] it has clarified that 'where there are no special circumstances the latter is generally the best expression of the former'.[121]

The Court has resorted to the principle of equity when it has had no other option and no evidence pointing to a legal title or effective control that could help it delimit the boundary. It has applied equity twice in the context of territorial disputes: in *Burkina Faso/Mali* (1986) where it divided the Soum pool equitably between the two states who had not submitted any evidence indicating where the boundary could run,[122] and in *Burkina Faso/Niger* (2013) to delimit a boundary river. Applying equity *infra legem*, it decided that 'the requirement concerning access to water resources of all the people living in the riparian villages is better met by a frontier situated in the river than on one bank or the other'.[123]

Both times, the Court claimed to be applying equity *infra legem* – considered as an intrinsic attribute of the rules of law. As explained in Chapter 6, equity may also denote a means for filling the gaps in international law (equity *praeter legem*) or be used in derogation from the law, to remedy its social inadequacies (equity *contra legem*).[124] This distinction is important to note, as it explains in part the Court's reluctance to apply it altogether.

Chapter 6 explained that the Court has explicitly shown disapproval for equity *contra legem* (Section 6.3.1). It has been careful to specify in the scarce instances of applying equity that it was not doing so *contra*

[120] *North Sea Continental Shelf (Federal Republic of Germany/Netherlands)* (Judgment) [1969] ICJ Rep 3, 49–50 [91].

[121] *Burkina Faso/Republic of Mali* (n. 4) 633 [150].

[122] *Burkina Faso/Republic of Mali* (n. 4) 633 [150] (see also [28] and [149]). See also Kohen and Tignino (n. 35) 103–4.

[123] *Burkina Faso/Niger* (n. 33) 85 [101].

[124] Zimmermann (n. 119) 874.

legem, as this is tantamount to *ex aequo et bono* where other considerations are taken into account *instead of* the law and not in parallel to it.[125] The Court would not wish for state litigants to feel like it was disregarding the applicable law.

It has therefore stated that it would be unjustified to resort to equity in order to modify a frontier that has already been defined by valid sources of international law – no matter what deficiencies may exist.[126] This stance is not ideal for local populations who may face repercussions from the Court's decision in a territorial dispute. However, the principle of equity can be employed in the context of territorial disputes in order to allow for the consideration of individuals. Unlike in maritime disputes where equity is 'the very content of the applicable rules',[127] equity in land territorial disputes is 'seen as an attribute of the rules to be applied'.[128]

There are ways to innovate the application of equity in light of the above. For instance, the consideration for the needs of local populations in territorial disputes could be a 'relevant circumstance', akin to the second stage of the maritime delimitation process (Section 6.2 *in fine*). One author has described the recognition of such rights in judgments such as *Burkina Faso/Niger* as 'a crystallization of a trend that consecrates [human rights] as a relevant circumstance in boundary delimitation cases'.[129] Human rights of relevance in the context of territorial disputes could include access to food, water, subsistence, and the rights of indigenous peoples. Dissenting in *Kasikili/Sedudu Island*, Judge Christopher Weermantry proposes that the Court 'should consider itself empowered to make a slight deviation from the strict geometric path indicated by the boundary treaty, but always preserving a balance between the entitlements of the two parties to the enjoyment of this precious asset'.[130] This is similar to the Court's practice in maritime delimitation, where it may adjust its provisional line upon the basis of relevant circumstances and must be sure that the line respects the principle of equity.

125 Ibid 794 and 797.

126 *Burkina Faso/Republic of Mali* (n. 4) 633 [149].

127 *Fisheries Jurisdiction (UK v. Iceland)* (Merits) (Judgment) [1974] ICJ Rep 3, 33 [78].

128 Zimmermann (n. 119) 880, fn 413.

129 Aznar (n. 56) 330–40.

130 *Botswana/Namibia* (n. 46) 1184 [92] (Dissenting opinion of Vice-President Weermantry).

Indeed, instead of only employing equity when no title is available in territorial disputes, it could be an overarching principle overseeing that the Court's adopted approach is fair and appropriate, as is also the case in maritime disputes. Thus, equity would be an element the Court will always check even after having applied a treaty or a colonial agreement through *uti possidetis*, to ensure that the applied law is 'flexible and responsive', in the words of Elihu Lauterpacht.[131] This aligns with the understanding of equity *infra legem*, which was described by the Court in *Burkina Faso/Mali* as 'a method of interpretation of the law in force, and one of its attributes'.[132] This type of equity would interpret and guide the delimitation exercise.

Such a proposal comes with three important caveats. First, the application of equity in territorial disputes could generally be applied to any legal title whose implementation would affect local populations to some extent. The Court could apply the 'catastrophic repercussions' doctrine established in maritime disputes, despite criticisms of this threshold (Section 6.3.2). For example, cases whereby entire populations are uprooted to another country could qualify as meeting this threshold, warranting equitable considerations to interpret the legal title in more justice and fairness.

Second, this exercise cannot be used to outright *contradict* the legal title in question. Judges must remain within the boundaries of law. This is because treaties, as sources of international law enshrined in Article 38 of the Court's Statute, reflect the paramount principle of state consent (Section 7.1).[133] To question the content of the treaty by violating it (*contra legem*) would be questioning the parties' wishes. The use of equity should therefore not change the sense of a clear text to create a new rule altogether that state litigants did not anticipate. Rather, it should be applied as far as possible to rectify justice through the interpretation of the relevant clauses of the legal title. This is a delicate exercise, nonetheless possible through the boundless discretion attributed to the Court in applying the principle of equity.[134]

[131] Elihu Lauterpacht, 'Equity, Evasion, Equivocation and the Evolution in International Law' (1977–78) 33 *Proceedings and Committee Reports of the American Branch of the International Law Association* 33, 46.

[132] *Burkina Faso/Republic of Mali* (n. 4) 567 [28].

[133] See n. 19.

[134] Maria De La Colina, *Judicial Discretion in International Law through the Recourse to Equity by the International Court of Justice* (Graduate Institute of International and Development Studies 2012) 70.

Third, the application of the principle of equity by the Court in favour of local populations would only be applicable if concerns for these populations were initially raised by the state litigants in their pleadings or, where relevant, in a Special Agreement. Otherwise, the Court would be perceived as overstepping. Such behaviour may cause states to take their distance if they perceive that the Court is taking excessive liberties within its assigned duties.

To conclude, the principle of equity is treated in the context of territorial disputes as an afterthought in the absence of other titles. But it can be applied alongside any title to guarantee more fairness. Therefore, if the application of a treaty or a colonial agreement through *uti possidetis* negatively impacts the relevant population (for example, causing catastrophic repercussions) and if concern for this has been expressed by the parties, then equity *infra legem* should be applied at the Court's discretion to control the damage as far as possible without contravening the title.

7.7 Conclusion

This chapter sought to outline how individuals are factored into the exercise of delimiting a contested territory. The overarching observation may be summarised as follows: 'Territorial disputes have been a *domain reservé* for states and their diplomatic lexicon. Solely states have invoked peoples' traditions, rights and fates in international adjudications. States have defended the former as a state's historic rights or needs, giving normally a "territorial look" instead of a "population approach"'.[135] Indeed, in territorial disputes, the Court sticks to its clearly developed system of hierarchised legal titles, which only involves individuals if they serve to prove an *acte de souverain* with regard to a sovereign state's effective control. Only equity, applied *ultima ratio*, can allow for individuals' needs to be considered. Thus, the Court's delimitation process in both territorial disputes is largely no more than a purely geometrical exercise.

In this chapter, I reflected on how both *effectivités* and the principle of equity can be enhanced to allow for greater inclusivity in territorial disputes. This is because reducing the resolution of such disputes to a purely geometrical exercise may cause strife to many human beings and

[135] Aznar (n. 56) 334.

therefore be characterised as unjust. This, in turn, calls into question the legitimacy of the decision from the approach of social idealism. In the words of Judge Weermantry,

> A court (. . .) cannot end its responsibilities with the mechanical exercise of a geometric delineation of boundaries on the ground. (. . .) [A] sacred site which is one and entire, (. . .) may need to be divided in two if merely geometrical considerations are to be followed. Likewise, a village may be separated from a grazing ground which for centuries had been integral to it, or the village itself may be divided into two parts whose residents thus became citizens of two different States, however closely they may be connected. It would be a diminution of a court's inherent jurisdiction if it were expected in such hypothetical circumstances to turn its glance away from these very real and vital problems and proceed with the task of delineation as if it were a purely geometrical exercise.[136]

This chapter opened by explaining that territorial disputes rightfully allow states to reinforce their sovereignty. However, it is not absurd to claim that individuals concerned by the outcome of territorial inter-state disputes should be considered in decisions that will affect their everyday lives. As Judge Bennouna has aptly stated, 'It is true that the Court, as the principal judicial organ of the United Nations, must contribute to the strengthening of peaceful relations between States (. . .). Nowadays, however, the search for peace among States also entails ensuring human security, namely respect for the fundamental human rights of the persons concerned and their protection, including by international justice. The exercise of sovereignty has thus become inseparable from responsibility towards the population. This new approach to sovereignty should certainly be present when the Court rules on the course of boundaries between States.'[137]

[136] *Botswana/Namibia* (n. 46) 1184 [91] (Dissenting opinion of Vice-President Weermantry).

[137] *Burkina Faso/Niger* (n. 33) 95 (Declaration of Judge Bennouna).

8

Environmental Disputes

> The environment is not an abstraction but represents the living space, the quality of life and the very health of human beings, including generations unborn.[1]

Compared to its extensive practice in territorial or maritime disputes, the International Court of Justice (ICJ, the Court) has had fewer opportunities to resolve environmental disputes between states. Since states acknowledged the scope of issues threatening the well-being of the planet that can only be tackled collectively, international environmental law has largely been developed through multilateral negotiations. However, there has been a recent surge in the judicialisation of international environmental issues. Not only have they been codified as sources of international law, but they have increasingly been the subject of disputes before international courts and tribunals, including the ICJ.

The judicialisation of international environmental law has provided ample opportunities for the Court to develop and clarify the law in this area. It has done so by identifying certain environmental principles – such as the duty to undertake environmental impact assessments (EIAs) or to prevent transboundary pollution – as customary international law.[2] It has also developed certain environmental law principles, such as the duty to prevent and of due diligence.[3] In making such assessments,

[1] *Legality of the Threat or Use of Nuclear Weapons* (Advisory Opinion) [1996] ICJ Rep 226, 241–42 [29]. See also *Gabčíkovo-Nagymaros Project (Hungary/Slovakia)* (Judgment) [1997] ICJ Rep 7, 77–78 [140] and *Pulp Mills on the River Uruguay (Argentina v. Uruguay)* (Provisional Measures) (Order of 13 July 2006) [2006] ICJ Rep 113, 132 [72].

[2] Daniel Bodansky, 'International Environmental Law' in Carlos Espósito and Kate Parlett (eds), *The Cambridge Companion to the International Court of Justice* (CUP 2023) 389–410.

[3] *Pulp Mills on the River Uruguay (Argentina v. Uruguay)* (Judgment) [2010] ICJ Rep 14, 55–56 [101], 59 [118], 79–80 [197], 82–83 [204]; *Certain Activities Carried Out by Nicaragua in the Border Area (Costa Rica v. Nicaragua)* and *Construction of a Road in*

opportunities have arisen for the Court to draw connections between the environmental matters and the people impacted by environmental harm. This, however, has rarely been undertaken.

An environment of sufficient quality must be maintained to circumvent undesirable effects on human health and living standards and thus violate certain human rights.[4] The connection between the environment and human rights has been increasingly affirmed by regional human rights bodies,[5] the UN Human Rights Council, and the UN General Assembly.[6] If any damage to the environment is potentially harmful towards human health and quality of life, then any complaint regarding harm to the environment that is brought to the Court will likely have the objective of protecting individuals whose human rights have been violated as a result of this harm. Thus, several environment-oriented cases that the Court has entertained, whether contentious or advisory, were brought to its docket in the spirit of protecting individuals, with governments submitting arguments regarding the protection of their own populations.[7] However, opportunities have been missed to draw emphasis on the victims of environmental degradation. Such emphasis is desirable from a socially idealist standpoint, which, *inter alia*, perceives individuals as central members of international society and aspires for just judicial decisions through greater balance between states and individuals. In this context, this translates into stronger acknowledgement that inter-state environmental disputes impact the rights, health, and well-being of people.

Scholars have taken increasing interest in the judicialisation of international environmental disputes.[8] However, this chapter argues that such judicialisation before the ICJ has not developed international

Costa Rica along the San Juan River (Nicaragua v. Costa Rica) (Judgment) [2015] ICJ Rep 665, 706 [104], 712 [121], 737 [217].

4 Pierre-Marie Dupuy and Jorge E. Viñuales, *International Environmental Law* (2nd edn, CUP 2018) 362; Alan Boyle and Michael R. Anderson (eds), *Human Rights Approaches to Environmental Protection* (OUP 1996) 1–24, 25–42, 43–70.

5 E.g., *The Environment and Human Rights* (Advisory Opinion) [2017] IACtHR, OC-23/17; *Marangopoulos Foundation for Human Rights (MFHR) v. Greece* (Decision on the Merits) [2007] ECSR, Complaint No. 30/2005; *Gbemre v. Shell Petroleum Development Company of Nigeria Ltd et al.* (Judgment) [2005] ACtHR, FHC/B/CS/53/05.

6 A/HRC/RES/48/13; A/76/L.75.

7 *Pulp Mills* (n. 3) 194–93 [158] (Separate opinion of Judge Cançado Trindade).

8 E.g., Justine Bendel, *Litigating the Environment: Process and Procedure before International Courts and Tribunals* (Edward Elgar Publishing 2023); Edgardo Sobenes, Sarah Mead and Benjamin Samson (eds), *The Environment through the Lens of International Courts and Tribunals* (Springer 2023); Joshua Paine, *The Functions of International Adjudication and International Environmental Litigation* (CUP 2024).

environmental law in a way favourable to victims of environmental degradation. First, certain promising human rights-focused environmental disputes were discontinued, indicating that other forms of peaceful dispute settlement remain more common in the environmental context (Section 8.1). Second, raising arguments in certain incidental proceedings in environmental disputes, such as counterclaims, have limited the potential for certain decisions to develop peoples' rights in environmental disputes (Section 8.2). Third, the Court's perceived judicial caution has limited its ability to clarify the role of local populations in environmental impact assessments (EIAs) (Section 8.3) and develop certain environmental principles in light of populations, such as the precautionary principle or the principle of intergenerational equity (Section 8.4). Section 8.5 concludes.

8.1 Protecting Victims of Environmental Degradation: Missed Opportunities

The first section presents environment-related contentious cases before the Court whereby states invoked arguments reflecting concern for their affected populations. It argues that the discontinuation of such disputes indicates that other forms of peaceful dispute settlement remain more common in the environmental context. Conversely, certain key environmental decisions rendered by the Court say very little about the relevant impacted populations, as they were not the focus of state litigants' arguments.

First, three cases where state litigants focused extensively on the repercussions of environmental damage for their citizens were discontinued: *Nuclear Tests (New Zealand v. France / Australia v. France)*, *Certain Phosphate Lands in Nauru (Nauru v. Australia)* and *Aerial Herbicide Spraying (Ecuador v. Colombia)*.

In *Nuclear Tests (New Zealand v. France / Australia v. France)*, both Australia and New Zealand instituted separate proceedings against France in 1973, as the latter wished to carry out nuclear tests in the atmosphere in the South Pacific region. Both Australia and New Zealand put forward the well-being of their populations as important arguments in their applications to institute proceedings. Indeed, Australia's decision to seize the Court reflected the conviction of the Australian people.[9] One

[9] *Nuclear Tests (Australia v. France)* (Application instituting proceedings) [1973] [9] and [14].

of Australia's principal arguments in its application instituting the proceedings was that France was violating its right and the right of its people, in common with other states and their peoples, to be free from atmospheric nuclear weapon tests by any country.[10] More specifically, Australia's motive was to protect the Australian peoples' health and well-being,[11] as it was concerned that the exposure of populations to radiation as a result of the nuclear tests would result in genetic mutations that would affect present and future generations.[12] Furthermore, Australia contended that its people had undergone psychological strain[13] and mental stress resulting from fear and anxiety that the nuclear tests posed.[14] Australia concluded that this was 'a cause of injury to them'.[15]

New Zealand adopted similar rhetoric in its application to institute proceedings. Speaking on behalf of the Cook Islands, Niue, and other Pacific territories in which it monitors levels of radioactivity,[16] it claimed that France's violation had caused harm, including apprehension, anxiety, and concern to its people.[17] It also stated in its application that there had been a 'progressive realisation of the dangers which [nuclear tests] present to life, to health and to the security of peoples and nations everywhere'[18] and that no nation has the right to 'pursue its security in a manner that puts at risk the health and welfare of other people'.[19]

Both Australia and New Zealand's approaches in this case place the individual at the centre of the motive to bring a case and reasons why the Court should uphold their claims. New Zealand argued that France's nuclear tests breached its peoples' rights to live free from radioactive material and, specifically, that such material should not cause them 'harm, including apprehension, anxiety and concern'.[20] As for Australia, it argued that France had breached its people's rights to be free from such tests and to decide whether to be exposed to such radiation.[21] However, the Court

10 Ibid [49].
11 Ibid [19] and [36].
12 Ibid [33]. See also Verbatim record 1973, 178, 180, 196, 226, 227. Australia also stated this in its application instituting proceedings: [34].
13 *Nuclear Tests (Australia v. France)* (Application instituting proceedings) (n. 9) [47].
14 Ibid [40], [44], [47]. This was also reiterated in: Verbatim record 1973, 177 and 180.
15 *Nuclear Tests (Australia v. France)* (Application instituting proceedings) (n. 9) [47].
16 *Nuclear Tests (New Zealand v. France)* (Application instituting proceedings) [1973] [13].
17 Ibid [28].
18 Ibid [23].
19 Ibid [24].
20 Ibid [28].
21 *Nuclear Tests (Australia v. France)* (Application instituting proceedings) (n. 9) [49].

did not end up rendering a judgment on the merits as France made several public statements announcing its intention to refrain from carrying out nuclear tests.[22] Characterised as unilateral statements, these sufficed for the Court to consider that the dispute had disappeared.[23] The case was, in essence, discontinued not by the parties involved but by the Court itself, which deemed a non-judicial, political approach—specifically, a unilateral statement—sufficient to resolve the dispute.

The *Certain Phosphate Lands in Nauru (Nauru v. Australia)* case, which was discontinued after the issuing of preliminary objections, inherently focused on the nexus between environmental law and human rights. Nauru seized the Court against Australia alleging that certain phosphate lands in Nauru that were mined by Australia (prior to Nauru's independence in 1968) were worked out, due to Australia's poor administration of the territory at the time.[24] Therefore, there was a violation of the Nauruan peoples' right to self-determination and sovereignty over its natural resources.[25] Nauru's principle argument was that Australia had breached the trusteeship obligations laid down in Article 5 (2)(1) of the Trusteeship Agreement, which guaranteed the promotion of the indigenous inhabitants' advancement towards independence[26] and the consideration of their customs, usages, rights, and interests.[27]

The phosphate industry was an important means for the Nauruan people to seek 'greater control over their own lives';[28] however, it was exploited by Australia and left in a useless state for habitation, agriculture, and other purposes necessary for the Nauruan people to live, until rehabilitation could be carried out. The repercussions of Australia's actions for the Nauruan people were emphasised in Nauru's Memorial.[29] In the opinion of Judge Antônio Augusto Cançado Trindade, this case placed emphasis on the long-term needs and future of the Nauruan people, revealing that 'the well-being of peoples is not

22 *Nuclear Tests (Australia v. France)* (Judgment) [1974] ICJ Rep 253, 271–72 [59].

23 Ibid [51].

24 *Certain Phosphate Lands in Nauru (Nauru v. Australia)* (Application instituting proceedings) [1989] [15].

25 *Certain Phosphate Lands in Nauru (Nauru v. Australia)* (Preliminary Objections) (Judgment) [1992] ICJ Rep 240, 243–44 [5].

26 Charter of the United Nations, 1 UNTS XVI, Article 76 [hereafter, UN Charter].

27 *Certain Phosphate Lands in Nauru* (Application instituting proceedings) (n. 24) [43].

28 *Nuclear Tests (New Zealand v. France)* (Application instituting proceedings) (n. 16) [13].

29 Memorial of the Republic of Nauru (20 March 1990) 144–52.

devoid of a temporal dimension'.[30] Had the Court rendered a judgment on the merits, it would have undoubtedly developed international law on the environment, human rights, and self-determination. However, Nauru and Australia notified the Court that they had reached a settlement and therefore discontinued proceedings.[31]

A final discontinued case placing people at its core was *Aerial Herbicide Spraying (Ecuador v. Colombia)*. Seizing the Court against Colombia for spraying toxic herbicides at locations near, at, and across their shared border,[32] Ecuador stated, 'the spraying had already caused damage to people, crops, animals and the natural environment on the Ecuadorian side of the frontier, and pose[d] a grave risk of further damage over time'.[33] In its application to institute proceedings, Ecuador also emphasised the severe impact on its communities and indigenous people.[34] This included health issues caused by exposure to the sprays,[35] damage to plants and crops that disrupted local farming needs,[36] and pollution of water sources, which harmed aquatic life and adversely affected river communities relying on rivers for domestic purposes.[37] For instance, Ecuador's population in the northern boundary areas 'reported serious adverse health reactions including burning, itching eyes, skin sores, intestinal bleeding and even death'.[38]

Furthermore, Ecuador pointed to the damage to plants and crops affected the farming needs of the local population[39] – the community of Las Salinas, for example.[40] It reported negative effects on the health and food security of border populations by polluting water sources and aquatic life, particularly for river communities who use rivers for

[30] *Pulp Mills* (n. 3) 196–97 [163]–[164] (Separate opinion of Judge Cançado Trindade).
[31] *Certain Phosphate Lands in Nauru (Nauru v. Australia)* (Order of 13 September 1993) [1993] ICJ Rep 322.
[32] *Aerial Herbicide Spraying (Ecuador v. Colombia)* (Application instituting proceedings) [2008] [2].
[33] Ibid [16].
[34] Ecuador stated in its Memorial that it is among the five Latin American countries with the largest indigenous populations, some of whom have lived for generations along the Ecuador-Colombia border – see Memorial of Ecuador (28 April 2009) 29 [2.18]. See also: *Aerial Herbicide Spraying* (Application instituting proceedings) (n. 32) [26].
[35] *Aerial Herbicide Spraying* (Application instituting proceedings) (n. 32) [4] and [14].
[36] Ibid [4] and [35].
[37] Ibid [29].
[38] Ibid [4].
[39] Ibid.
[40] Ibid [35].

domestic purposes.[41] Ecuador also reported that people have been forced to relocate as a consequence of the aerial spraying.[42] In Ecuador's Memorial, it included a number of witness statements to substantiate its claims of harm to individuals[43] and included a table listing the Ecuadorian communities, the provinces they come from, and the time period in which they were impacted by the aerial sprays.[44]

This case would have required the Court to examine whether Colombia had breached its obligations to prevent transboundary harm and to comply with international human rights law and the rights of indigenous peoples. Achieving this would have required a thorough evaluation of the presented evidence detailing how these populations were affected. However, the case was eventually discontinued on 13 September 2013, as the parties were able to come to a settlement through negotiation.[45]

In these three discontinued cases, state litigants prioritised their populations in their arguments. In contrast, the Court has issued other significant judgments in environmental law that are not centered on human impacts Rather, the impacts on such cases on state litigants' populations are briefly mentioned, and the legal question does not involve analysis related to local populations.

The first is *Certain Activities carried out by Nicaragua in the Border Area (Costa Rica v. Nicaragua)*, where Costa Rica claimed that Nicaragua had breached its international treaty obligations by committing several incursions on Costa Rican territory, including activities that caused environmental damage to the rainforests, wetlands, and, consequently, the Colorado and San Juan Rivers.[46] The proceedings for this case were joined with *Construction of a Road in Costa Rica along the San Juan River (Nicaragua v. Costa Rica)* (hereafter, the *Road* case).[47] In the latter case, Nicaragua protested to the Court that Costa Rica had carried out road

41 Ibid [29].

42 Ibid [36].

43 Memorial of Ecuador (28 April 2009) 29, 132, 181, 235, 320–78, 398–400.

44 *Aerial Herbicide Spraying* (Application instituting proceedings) (n. 32) [17].

45 *Aerial Herbicide Spraying (Ecuador v. Colombia)* (Order of 13 September 2013) [2013] ICJ Rep 278.

46 *Certain Activities Carried Out by Nicaragua in the Border Area (Costa Rica v. Nicaragua)* (Application instituting proceedings) [2010] [41].

47 *Construction of a Road in Costa Rica along the San Juan River (Nicaragua v. Costa Rica)* (Joinder of Proceedings) (Order of 17 April 2013) [2013] ICJ Rep 184.

construction works along the border, causing environmental damage to Nicaragua's territory.

Both state litigants made reference to the impact of the alleged breaches on their populations. In *Certain Activities*, Costa Rica claimed that Nicaragua had breached, *inter alia*, the SI-A-PAZ agreement (15 December 1990). This agreement sought to put into practice projects for national and sustained management of natural resources (with respect for the sovereign rights of each country), in order to improve the quality of life of the local populations and those of both countries in general.[48] It was signed partly because the border region between Costa Rica and Nicaragua is inhabited by marginalised rural groups that have been unable to achieve sustainable development due to a lack of financial resources and technical advice.[49] In the *Road* case, Nicaragua argued in its Memorial and filing for provisional measures that the construction of the road impacted upon the health of the riparian populations of the San Juan River.[50] Costa Rica, on the other hand, justified its decision to construct the road by claiming that it needed Costa Rican police to have direct and expeditious access to the border area in order to provide the local population with essential services.[51]

However, the Court's legal reasoning in resolving the dispute did not necessitate further consideration of local populations. While it was briefly mentioned that Nicaragua had breached Costa Rica's rights of navigation on the San Juan River,[52] the Court focused on interpreting the Treaty of Limits to determine whether Costa Rica had sovereignty over the disputed territory in *Certain Activities*.[53] The interpretation of sources was also the means to assess the breaches of Costa Rica's territorial sovereignty by Nicaragua.[54] In assessing whether the obligation to prevent significant transboundary harm had been breached in both the *Certain Activities* and *Road* cases, the Court focused on the relevant procedural and substantive obligations that related to the environmental damage.[55]

48 Memorial of Costa Rica (5 December 2011) vol I 126 [5.41] and vol II 253 Annex 22.
49 Ibid.
50 Memorial of Nicaragua (19 December 2012) 19 [2.14].
51 Memorial of Costa Rica (n. 48) 21–22 [2.2], 22–23 [2.4], 31–32 [2.20], 36 [2.25], 42 [2.37].
52 *Certain Activities/Construction of a Road Case* (n. 3) 716 [136].
53 See Chapter 6 for a critique of this approach.
54 This approach to determine sovereignty over a disputed territory is broadly critiqued in Chapter 6.
55 *Certain Activities/Construction of a Road Case* (n. 3) 705–12 [101]–[120].

To determine Costa Rica's substantive obligation not to cause transboundary environmental harm, the Court focused on the sediments dredged from the river and deposited on the Costa Rican bank of the San Juan River, as well as the damage caused to the Humedal Caribe Noreste wetland by the dredging programme.[56]

The second environmental case where state litigants' populations were only briefly mentioned is the *Gabčíkovo–Nagymaros (Hungary/Slovakia)* case. Here, the Court sought to resolve a dispute between the Republic of Hungary and the Czech and Slovak Federal Republic regarding the implementation and termination of a bilateral treaty regulating the construction and operation of the Gabčíkovo–Nagymaros Barrage System. This was 'the first case before the ICJ to be concerned with international environmental law in such a comprehensive manner',[57] and the 'heart of the dispute [was] the actual and anticipated environmental impacts of a major power project (. . .) between the capitals of two States'.[58] The two states had agreed, through a treaty, to construct works on their respective riverbanks in order to produce hydroelectricity and improve navigation along the Danube.[59] Hungary, however, suspended its works and then terminated the treaty due to its concern for the project's impact on the environment,[60] justifying its actions by relying on a state of necessity.[61]

In light of the confluence between environmental law and human rights, it may be interpreted that Hungary's motive to litigate was to safeguard its environment to the benefit of its population. Furthermore, the Court's confirmation that safeguarding the environment is an 'essential interest' of the state, pursuant to Article 33 of the Draft Articles on State Responsibility, signalled the importance of protecting the Hungarian citizens' human rights.[62] However, Hungary only briefly mentioned that it sought, *inter alia*, to repair the 'damages suffered by the Hungarian population on account of the

[56] Ibid 712 [119].

[57] Laurence Boisson de Chazournes and Makane Moïse Mbengue, 'Gabčíkovo-Nagymaros Project (Hungary/Slovakia) (1997)' in Eirik Bjørge and Cameron A. Miles (eds), *Landmark Cases in Public International Law* (Hart Publishing 2017) 435.

[58] Verbatim record 1997/2, 47 [3] (Gábor Vida).

[59] *Gabčíkovo-Nagymaros Project* (n. 1) 17–18 [15] and 20 [18].

[60] Ibid 25–27 [23] and 31 [32].

[61] Ibid 35–36 [40].

[62] Ibid 41 [53].

increase in the uncertainties weighing on its future *(pretium doloris)*'[63] and that its people had the fundamental rights to its natural resources.[64] Neither party's arguments lingered on the impact of the project on their populations nor did Hungary's requests require a people-focused assessment of any sort. The Court therefore did not dwell on this in its judgment, abiding by the principle of *non ultra petita* ('not beyond the request') (Section 7.5).

In sum, the discontinuation of environmental disputes yielding significance to victims of environmental degradation contextualises judicialisation as one of many ways to resolve environmental disputes in the international legal order. It also sheds light on the prevalence of other forms of peaceful settlement to resolve environmental disputes, such as negotiation. While the judicialisation of environmental disputes is increasing – especially in the wake of the climate crisis – the multiple avenues of dispute settlement might limit the potential for the World Court to develop the human rights–environmental law nexus to the benefit of individuals. Therefore, the judicialisation before the ICJ has not yet developed international environmental law in a way favourable to victims of environmental degradation.

8.2 The Limitations of Counterclaims

Even when arguments with both environmental and human impacts have been presented before the Court, and the cases were not discontinued, procedural obstacles have hindered the Court from developing its jurisprudence to the benefit of individuals. In *Alleged Violations of Sovereign Rights and Maritime Spaces in the Caribbean Sea (Nicaragua v. Colombia)*, for instance, Colombia raised a counterclaim that Nicaragua failed in its due diligence to protect the rights of the inhabitants of the San Andrés Archipelago, particularly the Raizales, to enjoy a healthy, sound, and sustainable environment.[65] The Court, however, decided by fifteen votes to one that this counterclaim was inadmissible.[66]

This dispute was a follow-up to the 2012 *Territorial and Maritime Dispute (Nicaragua v. Colombia)* case, where the Court was requested to

[63] Ibid 74 [127].
[64] Verbatim record 1997/2 (n. 58) 17 [11] (György Szénási).
[65] *Alleged Violations of Sovereign Rights and Maritime Spaces in the Caribbean Sea (Nicaragua v. Colombia)* (Counter-Claims) (Order) [2017] ICJ Rep 289, 297–98 [26].
[66] Ibid 314 [82].

assess which of the two states had sovereignty over a number of territorial and maritime features situated in the Caribbean Sea. The Court awarded all disputed territories to Colombia,[67] while its delimitation of the relevant maritime zones largely favoured Nicaragua.[68] After this judgment was rendered, Colombia enacted a 1946 Presidential decree proclaiming certain maritime boundaries in the Western Caribbean.[69] According to Nicaragua, this decree establishes jurisdictional rights over its maritime zones as confirmed by the Court and thus violates Nicaragua's sovereign rights over its maritime areas.[70] Nicaragua therefore seized the Court in November 2013. In Colombia's Counter-Memorial, in addition to defending its position with regard to the claims brought against it by Nicaragua, Colombia submitted counterclaims (which are, by definition, new claims linked to the principal claim). The second counterclaim was that Nicaragua violated its due diligence to protect the rights of the inhabitants of the San Andrés Archipelago, in particular the Raizales, to benefit from a healthy, sound, and sustainable environment.[71]

At this stage of proceedings, the Court was not tasked with deciding whether the Nicaragua had violated its due diligence to protect the rights of the inhabitants, but rather whether there was a direct connection, pursuant to Article 80 of the Rules of the Court, between Colombia's new counterclaim and Nicaragua's principal claims.[72] If it were to decide that the new counterclaim was valid, it would pave the way for determining, at a later stage of the proceedings (the merits), whether Nicaragua had breached its due diligence obligations.

Under Article 80(1) of the Rules of the Court, for a counterclaim to be admissible, it must fall within the Court's jurisdiction and be directly related to the subject matter of the opposing party's claim.[73] If these requirements are met, the Court 'may' entertain a

[67] *Territorial and Maritime Dispute (Nicaragua v. Colombia)* (Judgment) [2012] ICJ Rep 624, 718–20 [251].

[68] Ibid 680 [153], 716 [243], 718–20 [251]. See also Nienke Grossman, 'Territorial and Maritime Dispute (Nicaragua v. Colombia)' (2013) 107(2) *The American Journal of International Law* 396, 402.

[69] *Alleged Violations of Sovereign Rights and Maritime Spaces in the Caribbean Sea (Nicaragua v. Colombia)* (Application instituting proceedings) [2013] [11].

[70] Ibid [12]–[13].

[71] *Alleged Violations of Sovereign Rights and Maritime Spaces in the Caribbean Sea* (n. 65) 297–98 [26].

[72] Ibid 304 [46] and 313 [78].

[73] Statute of the International Court of Justice, Article 80(1).

counterclaim, the wording suggesting that it enjoys a certain measure of discretion.[74]

In the present case, with regard to this second counterclaim, the Court concluded that such a connection did not exist factually nor legally. It first reasoned that the facts underlying the counterclaims relate to Nicaragua's failure to protect and preserve the marine environment in the south-western Caribbean Sea (thereby affecting the Raizal community), while the principal claims are based on 'Colombia's Navy's alleged interference with and violations of Nicaragua's exclusive sovereign rights and jurisdiction in Nicaragua's EEZ'.[75] Furthermore, no legal connection existed, as Colombia invoked treaty and customary law regarding environmental protection in its counterclaim. Conversely, it referred to rules of treaty and customary law concerning the UNCLOS provisions on sovereign rights, jurisdiction, and duties of a coastal state within its maritime areas. The Court also determined that no legal connection existed, as it viewed the Parties as pursuing different legal objectives through their respective claims: Nicaragua initially sought to demonstrate that Colombia had violated its sovereign rights and jurisdiction within its maritime areas. In contrast, Colombia, through its counterclaim, aimed to establish that Nicaragua failed to fulfill its obligation to protect and preserve the marine environment in the south-western Caribbean Sea.[76]

Colombia's concerns were not inherently problematic. Rather, it was Colombia's decision to present them as counterclaims that explained their rejection. The requirements of Article 80(1) of the Rules of the Court posed a challenge for Colombia in raising a new claim at this stage of proceedings. This suggests that the judicialisation of environmental harm has limitations: certain procedures may prevent the development of peoples' rights in the environmental context if specific conditions are not met. In this sense, environmental judicialisation before the ICJ has further impeded the development of jurisprudence that could benefit victims of environmental degradation.

[74] *Alleged Violations of Sovereign Rights and Maritime Spaces in the Caribbean Sea* (n. 65) 322 [4] (Joint Opinion of Judges Tomka, Gaja, Sebutinde, Gevorgian and Judge *ad hoc* Daudet).

[75] *Alleged Violations of Sovereign Rights and Maritime Spaces in the Caribbean Sea* (n. 65) 301 [37].

[76] Ibid 301 [38].

8.3 People and Environmental Impact Assessments

It has thus far been observed that the judicialisation of environmental disputes to protect victims of environmental degradation has been challenging due to the discontinuance of promising cases (Section 8.1) and procedural obstacles (Section 8.2). However, even where promising opportunities have arisen, it is observed in this section that the Court has displayed notable judicial caution, often refraining from addressing questions directly relating to the role of local populations in the environmental dispute. This was notable in the *Pulp Mills on the River Uruguay (Argentina v. Uruguay)* case.

The *Pulp Mills* case is another critical dispute in which individuals' health and well-being formed a crucial part of the parties' arguments. Argentina seized the Court against Uruguay, which it accused of authorising and commissioning the construction of two pulp mills on the River Uruguay without notification,[77] thus violating the 1975 Statute of the River Uruguay.[78] Uruguay also allegedly failed to take precautionary measures, including conducting an environmental impact study.[79]

In this case, Argentina particularly advanced arguments on the negative effects of the pulp mills on its population, namely on human health, well-being, and livelihood.[80] Regarding human health, Argentina went to great lengths to demonstrate that the impacts of the pulp mills on the River Uruguay and on the air were hazardous to human health,[81] not to mention that they incurred civil unrest.[82] The rights of the Argentinian population were also emphasised during oral proceedings, where Argentina's counsel claimed that the rights at stake concerned the riverside populations, most directly affected by Uruguay's compliance with its

[77] *Pulp Mills* (n. 3) 53–54 [90].

[78] The 1975 Statute of the River Uruguay is a treaty between Argentina and Uruguay to "establish the joint machinery necessary for the optimum and rational utilization of the River Uruguay, in strict observance of the rights and obligations arising from treaties and other international agreements in force for each of the parties". *Pulp Mills* (n. 3) 32 [27].

[79] *Pulp Mills* (n. 3) 28 [22], 51–52 [82].

[80] *Pulp Mills on the River Uruguay (Argentina v. Uruguay)* (Application instituting proceedings) [2006] [15].

[81] Memorial of Argentina (15 January 2007) 6–7 [0.18], 74 [3.151], 81 [3.183], 82 [3.191], 85 [3.205], 134 [5.70], 134 [5.72], 146–47 [6.44]–[6.54], 150 [7.3]–[7.4], 156 [7.20], 160 [7.43], 162–63 [7.58], 165 [7.66], 170 [7.94], 185 [7.162], 191 [7.190], 192 [7.196]–[7.197]; *Pulp Mills* (Application instituting proceedings) (n. 80) [15]. For a critical perspective, see *Pulp Mills* (n. 3) 193 [155] (Separate opinion of Judge Cançado Trindade).

[82] *Pulp Mills* (Application instituting proceedings) (n. 80) [15].

international legal obligations.[83] The general well-being of the local population was also advanced by Argentina on a number of occasions.[84]

Furthermore, Argentina argued that the regions near the River Uruguay had been developed for tourism, a source of revenue for a large number of inhabitants; the pollution of the river was thus damaging to their livelihood.[85] Uruguay, on the other hand, responded that the pulp mills were not a menace to human health[86] – even going as far as advocating in its Rejoinder that social impact monitoring had indicated an improvement in the 'quality of life' in Fray Bentos and 'surrounding communities'.[87] The Court finally ruled that Uruguay had not breached any substantive obligations under Article 41 of the 1975 Statute of the River Uruguay.[88]

But unlike contentious cases seen earlier such as *Gabčíkovo-Nagymaros* or *Certain Activities/Road*, this case raised specific questions regarding aspects of environmental principles and their connection to people. As mentioned earlier, the Court has taken opportunities to consolidate certain environmental law principles as rules of customary international law. One of these principles is the duty to perform an environmental impact assessment (EIAs). Principle 17 of the Rio Declaration on Environment and Development (1992) states that '[e]-nvironmental impact assessment, as a national instrument, shall be undertaken for proposed activities that are likely to have a significant adverse impact on the environment and are subject to a decision of a competent national authority'.[89] This established practice in environmental law has the rationale of preventing environmental degradation, by enabling the state to evaluate the environmental consequences of a project and thus decide if the potentially negative impact outweighs the benefits.[90] The Court established in *Pulp Mills* and reaffirmed in *Certain*

83 Verbatim record 2006/46, 44 [19] and 45 [23] (Marcelo Kohen); 55 [21] (Laurence Boisson de Chazournes); 60 [11] (Alain Pellet).

84 Memorial of Argentina (n. 81) 77 [3.165] and 81 [3.186].

85 Ibid 4 [0.14], 147–49 [6.54]–[6.65], 162 [7.58].

86 It claimed that the project would have "no impacts on the health of the people in the area". See Counter-Memorial of Uruguay (20 July 2007) 30–31 [1.48] and 349 [5.33]–[5.34]. See also *Pulp Mills* (n. 3) 192–93 [154] (Separate opinion of Judge Cançado Trindade).

87 Rejoinder of Uruguay (29 July 2008) 220 [4.40].

88 *Pulp Mills* (n. 3) 101 [265].

89 A/CONF.151/26, Principle 17.

90 Sumudu Atapattu, *Emerging Principles of International Environmental Law* (Brill 2007) 289–90.

Activities/Road that the obligation to carry out an EIA is part of customary international law.[91]

While this was a welcome finding, ambiguity persists regarding the finer details of EIAs.[92] As Judge Bhandari opined in *Certain Activities/Road*, international environmental law is 'lamentably silent' on its exact contents.[93] More specifically, the Court was given an opportunity to clarify the role of local populations in the EIA process in *Pulp Mills*. Both Argentina and Uruguay claimed in their Memorials that conducting an EIA includes consulting the affected populations.[94] However, they disagreed on two key points. First, they disagreed on whether consulting affected populations as part of an EIA is an obligation under international law. The second point was the extent to which the affected populations must be consulted. I argue in this section that the Court's approach to such questions is marked by judicial caution.

Judicial caution is an approach or an attitude of 'prudence' when applying the law in force,[95] out of concern that judges may overstep their authority or render decisions with far-reaching implications. Sir Gerald Fitzmaurice observed that this may involve deciding the case at hand 'with the minimum of verbiage necessary for this purpose'.[96] While judges may still develop international law, Hersch Lauterpacht described that they may do so 'without admitting it; (...) while guided at the same time by existing law; (...) while remembering that stability and uncertainty are no less of the essence of the law than justice'.[97] In *Pulp Mills*, judicial caution was evident in the Court's handling of clarifying the role of local populations in EIAs.

Firstly, the Court demonstrated judicial caution in this case when asked to determine whether conducting an EIA entails an international

[91] *Pulp Mills* (n. 3) 82–83 [204]; *Certain Activities/Construction of a Road Case* (n. 3) 707–8 [106].

[92] Owen McIntyre, 'The Proceduralisation and Growing Maturity of International Water Law: *Case Concerning Pulp Mills on the River Uruguay (Argentina v Uruguay)*' (2010) 22 (3) *Journal of Environmental Law* 475, 486.

[93] *Certain Activities/Construction of a Road Case* (n. 3) 806 [47] (Separate opinion of Judge Bhandari).

[94] *Pulp Mills* (n. 3) 86–87 [215]; Counter-Memorial of Uruguay (n. 86) 306–7 [4.113].

[95] Hersch Lauterpacht, *The Development of International Law by the International Court* (CUP 1982) 75.

[96] Gerald Fitzmaurice, 'Hersch Lauterpacht – The Scholar as Judge' (1961) 37 *British Yearbook of International Law* 1.

[97] Lauterpacht (n. 95).

obligation to consult local populations. Argentina and Uruguay disagreed on this point. Argentina contended that the provision of the appropriate information and consultation with states concerned and the affected local population are integral parts of the principle.[98] According to Argentina, this obligation requires the state conducting the EIA to fulfill it before obtaining consent from the potentially affected state.[99] Thus, having failed to adequately consult the affected Argentinian populations, Uruguay violated its duty to perform an EIA.[100]

To support that the consultation of affected populations is an international legal obligation under the duty to carry out an EIA, Argentina cited a number of international legal sources:[101] the Convention on Environmental Impact Assessment in a Transboundary Context (Espoo Convention),[102] the African Commission on Human and Peoples' Rights,[103] the Inter-American Commission on Human Rights,[104] and Operational Policy 4.01 on Environmental Assessment of the International Finance Corporation (IFC).[105] These sources indicate that populations must participate in the process of assessing the impact on the environment and that their views must be taken into account. Argentina also referred to the World Bank Inspection Panel, which has underlined the importance of conducting timely and meaningful consultations with the concerned populations.[106] It also mentioned an example of the case taken up by the Aarhus Convention Compliance Committee (an innovation explained later in this chapter) concerning the construction of the Bystroe deep water navigation

98 Memorial of Argentina (n. 81) 85–86 [3.206]–[3.208]; Reply of Argentina (29 January 2008) 415 [4.101].

99 Reply of Argentina (n. 98) 415 [4.101].

100 Ibid 418 [4.105].

101 Memorial of Argentina (n. 81) 85–86 [3.206]–[3.208]; Convention on Environmental Impact Assessment in a Transboundary Context, 30 ILM 802, Arts 2(2), 2(6), 3(8), 4(2) [hereafter, Espoo Convention]; International Finance Corporation, 'Operational Policy 4.01 on Environmental Assessment' (1998) 4 [12] and 5 [14]; African Commission on Human and Peoples' Rights, 'The Social and Economic Rights Action Center and the Center for Economic and Social Rights v. Nigeria' COMM/A044/1 (27 May 2022) [53]; Inter-American Commission on Human Rights, 'Second Report on the Situation of Human Rights in Peru', OEA/SER.L/V/II 106 (2 June 2000) [26] and [39]; Inter-American Commission on Human Rights, 'Report on the Situation of Human Rights in Ecuador' OEA/Ser.L/V/II.96 (24 April 1997).

102 Espoo Convention, Articles 2(2), 2(6), 3(8), 4(2).

103 Memorial of Argentina (n. 81) 86 [3.207].

104 Ibid 86 [3.208].

105 Ibid 85 [3.206].

106 Reply of Argentina (n. 98) 415–17 [4.102].

canal. The Committee ruled that Ukraine had violated the Aarhus Convention, as it was fully aware of the concerns of the Romanian citizens and could have initiated the participation process through the Romanian authorities.[107] Argentina also made reference to Article 13 of the 2001 International Law Commission (ILC) Draft Articles on Prevention of Transboundary Harm from Hazardous Activities, and Principles 7 and 8 of the United Nations Environment Programme (UNEP) Goals and Principles.[108] Essentially, Argentina insisted that the public must have the possibility to examine all the pertinent details in order to guarantee its transparent participation.[109]

Uruguay, on the other hand, argued more generally that the EIA is a national – and not an international – procedure. It is not a joint procedure to be carried out in cooperation with other states.[110] It cited Principle 17 of the 1992 Rio Declaration on Environment and Development as well as the ILC's commentary on its draft Articles on Prevention of Transboundary Harm from Hazardous Activities, both of which describe the EIA as a national instrument or procedure in and by the state of origin.[111] Uruguay agreed that it must *notify* potentially affected states, pursuant to Principle 12 of the 1987 UNEP Goals and Principles of Environmental Impact Assessment (UNEP EIA Principles), but asserted that such states are not expected to *participate* in a national EIA because it is not an international process.[112] Uruguay also added that even if there were a right to participate, it would only be to the extent of providing information and making representations – but not providing prior approval.[113] Therefore, Uruguay denied that such an international obligation exists altogether – let alone an international obligation towards concerned populations.

The Court, after summarising the positions of the two parties in its judgment, curtly decided that 'no legal obligation to consult the affected populations arises for the Parties from the instruments invoked by Argentina'.[114] This was a manifestation of judicial caution, where the Court avoided the crux of the question. Argentina did not mean to argue

[107] Ibid 417–18 [4.104].
[108] *Pulp Mills* (n. 3) 87 [216].
[109] Reply of Argentina (n. 98) 415–17 [4.102].
[110] Counter-Memorial of Uruguay (n. 86) 293–94 [4.90].
[111] Ibid.
[112] Ibid.
[113] Ibid 294 [4.91].
[114] *Pulp Mills* (n. 3) 87 [216].

that Uruguay is bound by the specific instruments that Argentina mentioned. Of course, Uruguay could not be legally bound to consult affected populations on the basis of the Espoo Convention, as this is a United Nations Economic Commission for Europe (UNECE) convention that neither Argentina nor Uruguay has signed or ratified. Nor would Argentina argue that Uruguay is bound by anything established by the African Commission on Human and Peoples' Rights, or by non-legal sources such as the Operational Policy 4.01 on Environmental Assessment of the IFC or by the UNEP EIA Principles. Argentina could not have been saying that a legal obligation to consult affected populations arises for Uruguay from these sources.

Rather, Argentina meant to say that the consultation of affected populations has generally become an international legal obligation, most likely in the form of customary international law. This would justify the mentioning of these instruments by way of example to demonstrate the development of this practice by states, and/or their belief that this is a legal obligation (*opinio juris*). Thus, the Court was stating the obvious that no legal obligation arose from the instruments invoked. It chose a very narrow reading of the question in order to avoid responding to the real question, which was whether an international legal obligation to consult the affected populations *generally* existed. This more challenging question would have required the Court to identify the existence of a customary norm.

Apart from customary law, the Court could have also affirmed that consulting affected populations as part of an EIA constitutes an international obligation, based on Uruguay's unilateral statement. Judge *ad hoc* Raúl Emilio Viñuesa mentioned in his dissenting opinion that the Court did not address Uruguay's unilateral obligation to comply with established European standards. These standards mandate public consultation with local populations potentially affected by transboundary projects, ensuring their effective participation at an early stage.[115] Perhaps Uruguay had indeed made a unilateral declaration under international law that could have been examined by the Court, as such declarations are considered to be binding on the state that made it.[116] Thus, both types of international legal obligation – customary law and

[115] Ibid 282 [60] (Dissenting opinion of Judge *ad hoc* Vinuesa).

[116] *Nuclear Tests (Australia v. France)* (n. 22) [46]; Guiding Principles applicable to Unilateral Declarations of States Capable of Creating Legal Obligations with Commentaries [2006] *Yearbook of the ILC*, 2006, vol II, Part Two.

unilateral declarations – could have established that consulting the local populations is, indeed, an international legal obligation that Uruguay must respect. However, the Court, in its exercise of judicial caution, refrained from addressing this matter altogether.

The Court's second display of judicial caution emerged in addressing a point of contention between Uruguay and Argentina regarding the extent to which the affected populations must be consulted. Uruguay claimed in its Counter-Memorial that its EIA summary was made available for public comment from 7 December 2004 to 3 January, and a Public Meeting was held on 21 December 2004 to that end.[117] It also argued that it gave Argentina sufficient information about the second pulp mill (referred to as Botnia). For instance, on 9 December 2005, it gave an outline presentation on the evaluation of the medium prepared by MVOTMA (*Ministerio de Vivienda Ordenamiento Territorial y Medio Ambiente*), examining the impact of pulp mills on human communities, specifically examining populations. The presentation stated that Uruguay's implementation plan 'shall define concrete measures for the impacts on the environment from noise, disturbing odour, and effects on tourism, fishing and leisure activities in the area surrounding Fray Bentos'.[118]

Argentina retorted that Uruguay's decisions were based on unsatisfactory environmental assessments.[119] It argued that the Compliance Advisor/Ombudsman[120] of the World Bank's IFC reported that Uruguay's EIA did not adequately address the concerns of potentially affected local people.[121] Indeed, its method reflected a lack of consultation with the public.[122] The November 2005 report stated that Uruguay's consultation process seemed 'rushed', 'presented as a *fait accompli* to those being consulted', without 'sufficient acknowledgment of the legitimacy of concerns and fears of communities that are local to the project'.[123] It encouraged Uruguay to implement specific efforts to 'ensure that people who believe that they will be impacted are able to have trust in the process'.[124]

117 Counter-Memorial of Uruguay (n. 86) 316–17 [4.128].
118 Ibid 211–22 [3.100].
119 Memorial of Argentina (n. 81) 131 [5.62].
120 Compliance Advisor Ombudsman, 'About Us' www.cao-ombudsman.org/about-us.
121 Memorial of Argentina (n. 81) 131 [5. 62]; Reply of Argentina (n. 98) 417 [4.103].
122 Reply of Argentina (n. 98) 415–17 [4.102].
123 Ibid.
124 Ibid.

The Court, in addressing this question, noted all the instances in which Uruguay consulted the affected populations on both the Argentine and Uruguayan sides of the river: meetings with the participation of Argentine NGOs on 2 December 2003 in Rio Negro and on 26 May 2004 in Fray Bentos; a public hearing with inhabitants of Fray Bentos and nearby regions on 21 December 2004; and interviews conducted in Fray Bentos, Gualeguaychú, Montevideo, and Buenos Aires between June and November 2005 with civil society groups.[125] Upon the basis of these events, the Court concluded that consultation of the affected populations 'did indeed take place'.[126]

However, this bypassed the initial question. The parties were not in dispute that Uruguay had taken measures to consult affected populations, but rather whether Uruguay's actions were sufficient. For this, the objective was to know to what degree local populations are to be consulted for an EIA under international law and whether Uruguay had met this standard in the present case. Judge *ad hoc* Viñuesa described in his dissent that '[t]he Parties' disagreement concern[ed] the results of the consultation of the affected populations, the extent to which concerns raised were taken into consideration and whether the consultation was meaningful'.[127]

It is undisputed that public participation and consultation is a critical component of EIAs – even described by one author as 'its soul'.[128] Professor Alan Boyle commented that '[t]here should have been no difficulty persuading the Court (. . .) that public consultation is a necessary element of the EIA process (. . .)'.[129] The right of public participation in EIAs is well-recognised in international environmental law and considered a symbol of its 'democratisation'.[130] However, the extent to which local populations should be consulted is unclear in international environmental law. This raises further questions regarding the timing, manner, and duration of the consultation process.

[125] *Pulp Mills* (n. 3) 87 [217]–[218].

[126] Ibid 87–88 [219].

[127] Ibid 282 [59] (Dissenting opinion of Judge *ad hoc* Vinuesa).

[128] Neil Craik, *The International Law of Environmental Impact Assessment: Process, Substance and Integration* (CUP 2008) 31. See, more generally, on public participation and EIAs: 58, 80, 146–50, 198.

[129] Alan Boyle, 'Developments in the International Law of Environmental Impact Assessments and Their Relation to the Espoo Convention: Developments in International Law of EIA' (2011) 20(3) *Review of European Community & International Environmental Law* 227, 231.

[130] Atapattu (n. 90) 294, 353.

The question of when local populations should be consulted is particularly challenging. This is not helped by the fact that it is unclear at what stage an EIA should be carried out in international law. One issue to be clarified is whether an EIA should be carried out before any authorisations to commence the project are granted.

Argentina argued in its Memorial in *Pulp Mills* that 'without *prior* assessment there can be no meaningful notification and consultation in most cases of environmental risk'[131] and that 'the project sponsor supplies relevant material in a timely manner prior to consultation'[132] for such consultations to be meaningful. The Court ruled that Uruguay failed to give *prior* notification to CARU (*Comisión Administradora del Río Uruguay*), the binational commission tasked with monitoring the river pollution – and to Argentina, as required by Article 7 of the 1975 Statute.[133] The Court made it clear that with regard to CARU, the notification must be carried out in order for CARU to determine 'on a preliminary basis',[134] with the aim of obtaining 'initial environmental authorization and before the granting of that authorization'.[135] With regard to the state, the Court also clarified that 'the notification must take place before the State concerned decides on the environmental viability of the plan, taking due account of the environmental impact assessment submitted to it'.[136]

However, these conditions are strictly applicable to the 1975 Treaty in question. What does general international law say about when to carry out an EIA? Doctrine is not clear on this, but some lean towards the view that EIAs should be carried out before any authorisations to commence the project are granted.[137] This would mean that affected populations would be consulted as part of the EIA process, before the granting of an authorisation. Boyle explains that while it may normally take place before authorisation is granted, it may actually occur in several stages or

131 Memorial of Argentina (n. 81) 83 [3.198], referring to: Patricia W. Birnie and Alan E. Boyle, *International Law and the Environment* (2nd edn, OUP 2002) 133.

132 Memorial of Argentina (n. 81) 85–86 [3.206].

133 *Pulp Mills* (n. 3) 28 [22].

134 Ibid 56 [104].

135 Ibid 56–57 [105].

136 Ibid 59–60 [119].

137 Department of the Environment, Transport and the Regions, *Public Participation in Making Local Environmental Decisions: The Aarhus Convention Newcastle Workshop. Good Practice Handbook* (2000); Craik (n. 128) 31–32.

schemes – for instance, an initial assessment followed by a full one if the likelihood of harm is identified.[138]

In *Pulp Mills*, the Court acknowledged that Uruguay had indeed consulted the affected populations between June and November 2005.[139] However, Uruguay issued the initial environmental authorisations to construct the first pulp mill (referred to as CMB) on 9 October 2003 and to construct the second pulp mill (Botnia) on 14 February 2005.[140] It granted an authorisation for the first phase of construction of the Orion (Botnia) mill on 12 April 2005. Thus, authorisation to commence the project had already been granted before populations were consulted. Only one authorisation was granted after consultations had begun: on 5 July 2005: an authorisation to construct a port terminal for its exclusive use and to utilise the river bed for industrial purposes.[141] Therefore, populations should have been consulted prior to any action for it to be considered meaningful.[142] It was not, despite the Court's assertion to the contrary.[143] However, the Court's cautious approach, reflected in its use of the 'minimum of verbiage necessary',[144] left its reasoning leading to this conclusion unclear. Further elaboration on this point would have been helpful to clarify the ambiguous yet critical practice of conducting EIAs.

Timing is only one element in an assessment of the extent to which local populations should be consulted for an EIA. Other questions may also be raised, such as the extent of consultation, the method of consultation, and its duration. Regardless, the Court refrained from addressing these questions in its judgment due to its judicial caution. They are essential, given the importance of human rights in the international environmental regime.

8.4 People and Environmental Principles

Judicial caution has not been to EIAs alone. Opportunities have been lost to draw connections between people and two environmental principles

[138] Boyle (n. 129) 228.
[139] *Pulp Mills* (n. 3) 87 [218].
[140] *Certain Activities/Construction of a Road Case* (n. 3) 707–8 [106].
[141] Ibid 708 [107].
[142] *Pulp Mills* (n. 3) 282 [59], 283 [63], 283 [66] (Dissenting opinion of Judge *ad hoc* Vinuesa).
[143] Ibid 87–88 [219].
[144] Fitzmaurice (n. 96) 1.

that have been raised in disputes: the precautionary principle and the principle of intergenerational equity.

8.4.1 *The Precautionary Principle*

The precautionary principle holds that even when there is scientific uncertainty, states must adopt measures to prevent environmental damage.[145] It was notably formulated in Principle 15 of the 1992 Rio Declaration on Environment and Development: 'In order to protect the environment, the precautionary approach shall be widely applied by States according to their capabilities. Where there are threats of serious or irreversible damage, lack of full scientific certainty shall not be used as a reason for postponing cost-effective measures to prevent environmental degradation.'[146] Almost all environmental law instruments adopted since the Rio Declaration refer to the precautionary principle,[147] which is widely accepted in the international legal system.[148]

The precautionary principle must be distinguished from the preventive principle, which requires states to prevent *foreseeable* environmental harm[149] and therefore assumes that risks can be objectively assessed to avoid damage.[150] The precautionary principle, by contrast, assesses risks at an even earlier stage,[151] where there is scientific uncertainty,[152] and mandates environmental action in face of such uncertainty.[153]

The precautionary principle is a customary international norm. In the ITLOS Seabed Disputes Chamber's 2011 *Responsibilities and Obligations of States sponsoring persons and entities with respect to activities in the area* advisory opinion, the Chamber notes that the incorporation of this principle 'into a growing number of international treaties and other instruments (. . .) has initiated a trend towards making this approach part of customary international law'.[154] While the Chamber employs the

145 Atapattu (n. 90) 204.
146 A/CONF.151/26 (n. 89) Principle 15.
147 Atapattu (n. 90) 234–41.
148 Philippe Sands et al, *Principles of International Environmental Law* (4th edn, CUP 2018) 234.
149 Atapattu (n. 90) 206.
150 *Pulp Mills* (n. 3) 157–58 [55] (Separate opinion of Judge Cançado Trindade).
151 Atapattu (n. 90) 206.
152 Ibid 207.
153 *Pulp Mills* (n. 3) 157–58 [55] (Separate opinion of Judge Cançado Trindade).
154 *Responsibilities and Obligations of States Sponsoring Persons and Entities with Respect to Activities in the Area* (Advisory Opinion) [2011] 47 [135].

term 'approach' instead of 'principle', it recognises that the precautionary principle is in the process of customary crystallisation.

The precautionary principle must be distinguished from the EIA, examined earlier. The concepts are complementary, as they are both predicated on addressing uncertainty about environmental impact through influencing decision-making in environmental matters. However, they differ in their nature: the EIA is the concrete procedure by which states may respect the overarching precautionary principle. Thus, the EIA is a means by which the precautionary principle may be exercised. This is why, in *Request for an Examination of the Situation in Accordance with Paragraph 63 of the Court's Judgment of 20 December 1974 in the Nuclear Tests (New Zealand v. France) Case*, New Zealand aptly contended that the precautionary principle required an EIA 'as a precondition for undertaking the activities, and to demonstrate that there was no risk associated with them'.[155]

As EIAs are a means by which the precautionary principle is carried out, and EIAs require public participation, it can be understood that public participation is a component of the precautionary principle at large. In fact, no matter how states decide to implement the precautionary principle (through an EIA or through other means), public participation remains a critical component. This is because even in the wake of scientific uncertainty, local populations are key stakeholders who will bear the costs of any potential environmental threat. They are therefore expected to represent themselves and their interests.[156] This idea is expressed in Principle 10 of the Rio Declaration on Environment and Development:

> Environmental issues are best handled with participation of all concerned citizens, at the relevant level. At the national level, each individual shall have appropriate access to information concerning the environment that is held by public authorities, including information on hazardous materials and activities in their communities, and the opportunity to participate in decision-making processes. States shall facilitate and encourage public awareness and participation by making information widely available.

155 *Request for an Examination of the Situation in Accordance with Paragraph 63 of the Court's Judgment of 20 December 1974 in the Nuclear Tests (New Zealand v. France)* [1995] ICJ Rep 288, 298–99 [35].

156 Laurence Boisson de Chazournes, 'New Technologies, the Precautionary Principle and Public Participation' in Thérèse Murphy (ed), *New Technologies and Human Rights* (OUP 2009) 161, 179.

> Effective access to judicial and administrative proceedings, including redress and remedy, shall be provided.[157]

The EIA is a concrete procedure by which states may respect the overarching precautionary principle. Therefore, public participation and consultation – a core component of the EIA – is a feature in the implementation of the precautionary principle. While observed by Judge Cançado Trindade, however, this was not stated by the full bench in *Pulp Mills*.[158] Despite both parties invoking it,[159] it only noted that 'while a precautionary approach may be relevant in the interpretation and application of the provisions of the Statute, it does not follow that it operates as a reversal of the burden of proof'.[160]

The Court has generally been very reluctant to mention or develop the precautionary principle in its jurisprudence. While New Zealand explicitly brought this up in *New Zealand v. France*,[161] the Court did not address this matter in its Order.[162] In *Gabčíkovo-Nagymaros*, Hungary argued that the precautionary principle was applicable to Slovakia.[163] While the Court acknowledged that 'both Parties agree on the need to take environmental concerns seriously and to take the required precautionary measures, but they fundamentally disagree on the consequences this has for the joint Project',[164] it neither explicitly acknowledged nor developed this principle.[165] Nor did the Court take this opportunity in *Pulp Mills*. While New Zealand referred to the principle in *Whaling in the Antarctic (Australia v. Japan: New Zealand intervening)*, claiming that it entails reversing the burden of proof, the Court did not comment on

157 A/CONF.151/26 (n. 89) Principle 10.

158 *Pulp Mills* (n. 3) 193 [156] (Separate opinion of Judge Cançado Trindade). See also *Certain Activities/Construction of a Road Case* (n. 3) 776 [55] (Separate opinion of Judge Cançado Trindade).

159 Memorial of Argentina (n. 81) 82–83 [3.194]–[3.197], 113–14 [5.4], 117–20 [5.13]–[5.19], 178 [7.128], 179 [7.132]; Counter-Memorial of Uruguay (n. 86) 28–29 [1.45], 247–48 [4.7], 288–92 [4.79]–[4.87], 303–4 [4.106].

160 *Pulp Mills* (n. 3) 71 [164].

161 *Request for an Examination of the Situation in Accordance with Paragraph 63 of the Court's Judgment* (n. 155) 290 [5] and 298 [34].

162 Ibid 342–44 (Dissenting opinion of Judge Christopher Weeramantry); 412 (Dissenting opinion of Judge *ad hoc* Sir Geoffrey Palmer).

163 *Gabčíkovo-Nagymaros Project* (n. 1) 62 [97].

164 Ibid 68 [113].

165 *Pulp Mills* (n. 3) 161 [66] (Separate opinion of Judge Cançado Trindade). See also Sands et al (n. 148) 235–36.

this.[166] The opportunity was also not seized in the *Road* case, despite Nicaragua's claim that Costa Rica breached Article 3 of the Regional Agreement on the Transboundary Movement of Hazardous Wastes by failing to adopt and implement the precautionary approach to pollution outlined in that instrument.[167] The Court dismissed this claim on the ground that Nicaragua failed to prove how this instrument had been breached.[168]

Judge Cançado Trindade has commented that '[i]t escapes my comprehension why the ICJ has so far had so much precaution with the precautionary principle'.[169] In my view, the Court's general caution towards individual inclusion, combined with its reluctance to fully develop the precautionary principle, helps explain why it refrained from clarifying the principle's relationship with people. Doing so, however, would offer greater guidance to states on how to consult affected populations in their measures taken to prevent, mitigate, or avoid environmental degradation. This would be appropriate considering the strong implications that such measures may have for local populations. Given the widespread acceptance of the precautionary principle, recognising the human dimension and the participation of individuals in respect of this principle would carry more weight in international environmental law and complement such recognition with regard to EIAs.

8.4.2 The Principle of Intergenerational Equity

A second promising environmental principle for the protection of people, which the Court has yet to elaborate on, is the principle of intergenerational equity. This principle holds that people are not only beneficiaries of the environment but trustees or custodians with an obligation to preserve it for future generations.[170] The principle finds

[166] *Whaling in the Antarctic (Australia v. Japan: New Zealand intervening)* (Judgment) [2014] ICJ Rep 226, 240–41 [27].

[167] *Certain Activities/Construction of a Road Case* (n. 3) 737 [218].

[168] Ibid 737–38 [220].

[169] *Pulp Mills* (n. 3) 161 [66] (Separate opinion of Judge Cançado Trindade). See also Yann Kerbrat and Sandrine Maljean-Dubois, 'Les juridictions internationales et le principe de précaution, entre grande prudence et petites audaces' in Denis Alland et al (eds), *Unité et diversité du droit international: Écrits en l'honneur du Professeur Pierre-Marie Dupuy* (Martinus Brill/Nijhoff 2014) 929.

[170] Edith Brown Weiss, 'Intergenerational Equity', *Max Planck Encyclopaedia of Public International Law* (2021).

its origins in the 1972 Stockholm Declaration[171] and features sources such as the United Nations Framework Convention on Climate Change (UNFCCC)[172] and the Paris Agreement.[173] It refers to both relations between different living generational cohorts and presently living versus future unborn ones.[174] It therefore intimately and directly relates to people as victims of environmental degradation. While the importance of the principle has been emphasised in separate opinions of judges, the full bench has not incorporated it into its legal reasoning to reach its conclusions.

The principle of intergenerational equity has mainly been discussed in separate opinions of judges before the World Court. It was raised in the dissenting opinions of two minority judges in *New Zealand v. France.* This case followed the aforementioned *Nuclear Tests* judgment, wherein the Court stated that 'if the basis of this Judgement were to be affected, the Applicant could request an examination of the situation in accordance with the provisions of the Statute'.[175] New Zealand considered that the basis of the judgment was affected as France had, since this judgment, recommenced nuclear testing in the South Pacific – this time, conducting underground nuclear tests. The Court concluded that the basis of the *Nuclear Tests* judgment was atmospheric nuclear testing, and it was therefore not possible to reexamine the situation.[176]

The Court stated that it was unable to consider developments in international law in its legal reasoning – for instance, the conclusion of the Convention for the Protection of Natural Resources and Environment of the South Pacific Region.[177] However, two judges, in their dissenting minority opinions, argued that the basis of the *Nuclear Tests* judgment had been affected by developments in international environmental law, such as the growing recognition of the principle of intergenerational equity. Indeed, according to Judge Weermantry, New Zealand's affected rights '[did] not relate only to the rights of people

171 A/CONF.48/14, preamble cl 6; Articles 1 and 2.

172 United Nations Framework Convention on Climate Change, 1771 UNTS 107, Article 3.

173 Paris Agreement to the United Nations Framework Convention on Climate Change, 3156 UNTS 79, preamble cl 11.

174 Stephen Humphreys, 'Against Future Generations' (2022) 33(4) *European Journal of International Law* 1061, 1066.

175 *Nuclear Tests (Australia v. France)* (n. 22) 272 [60].

176 *Request for an Examination of the Situation in Accordance with Paragraph 63 of the Court's Judgment* (n. 155) 306 [63].

177 Ibid 306 [63].

presently in existence. The rights of the people of New Zealand include the rights of unborn posterity'.[178] Sir Geoffrey Palmer, in his dissent in the same case, stated that nuclear testing and accidents indicate that states are unwilling to act as 'good stewards for the environment' for future generations.[179] Had the Court considered such developments in international environmental law, its understanding of the basis of the *Nuclear Tests* judgments may have been different. Weermantry has referred to the principle of intergenerational equity in disputes beyond the environment: in *Jan Mayen*, where the Court adjusted its delimited line for equitable considerations (Section 6.3.2), he reflected that equity should develop a broader meaning, allowing for planetary resources to be shared by present and future generations.[180]

Judge Cançado Trindade is also known to have referred to the principle of intergenerational equity in his separate or dissenting opinions. In the *Whaling* case, Australia argued that Japan's whaling programme breached the International Convention for the Regulation of Whaling (ICRW), while Japan considered that its programme fell under an exception in Article VIII of the Convention, authorising states parties to issue permits to its nationals to kill whales for scientific research. Judge Cançado Trindade considered that the principle of intergenerational equity formed part of the foundations of his position,[181] as the ICRW's preamble acknowledged 'the interest of the nations of the world in safeguarding for future generations the great natural resources represented by the whale stocks'.[182] He argued that this principle had a long-term temporal dimension[183] and that it 'marks presence nowadays in a wide range of instruments of international environmental law, and indeed of contemporary public international law'.[184] It is, however, unclear in his dissenting opinion how the ICRW's preamble may have been factored into the Court's task to define 'scientific research' under

178 Ibid 341 (Dissenting opinion of Judge Weeramantry).
179 Ibid 420 [115] (Dissenting opinion of Judge Sir Geoffrey Palmer).
180 *Maritime Delimitation in the Area between Greenland and Jan Mayen (Denmark v. Norway)* (Judgment) [1993] ICJ Rep 38, 277 [242] (Separate opinion of Judge Weeramantry).
181 *Whaling in the Antarctic (Australia v. Japan: New Zealand intervening)* (n. 166) 349 [1] (Separate opinion of Judge Cançado Trindade).
182 International Convention for the Regulation of Whaling, 161 UNTS 72, preamble cl 1.
183 *Whaling in the Antarctic (Australia v. Japan: New Zealand intervening)* (n. 166) 362–63 [41]–[42] (Separate opinion of Judge Cançado Trindade).
184 Ibid 366–67 [47] (Separate opinion of Judge Cançado Trindade).

Article VIII and to assess whether lethal methods in Japan's whaling programme were necessary or reasonable.[185] Nonetheless, the dissent shed light on the development of the principle and its potential to factor into the Court's legal reasoning in environmental disputes.

While individual judges have commented on the importance of the principle of intergenerational equity for people, the Court has done so less frequently and more implicitly. When it has, the principle has not influenced the conclusions it has reached. For instance, the principle was merely alluded to in the *Legality of the Threat or Use of Nuclear Weapons* advisory opinion, which held relevance for victims of environmental degradation as a result of nuclear weapons. The original requested advisory opinion – *Legality of the Use by a State of Nuclear Weapons in Armed Conflict* – was more explicit and direct in its concern for peoples' health and well-being. The World Health Organization (WHO) asked the Court: 'In view of the health and environmental effects, would the use of nuclear weapons by a state in war or other armed conflict be a breach of its obligations under international law including the WHO Constitution?' The Court, however, rejected the request to provide an advisory opinion as it considered that the question was outside of the scope of WHO's activities: it was asking about the *legality* of the use of such weapons in view of their health and environmental effects, as opposed to the effects of the use of nuclear weapons on health.[186] Therefore, WHO request was impeded from going forward.

Nonetheless, the UN General Assembly took up the matter and requested an advisory opinion from the Court soon thereafter on the question: 'Is the threat or use of nuclear weapons in any circumstance permitted under international law?' Unlike WHO's question, this one made no reference to human health. However, the Court did note that in order to respond to the legal question, it must take account of the 'unique characteristics of nuclear weapons',[187] including, *inter alia*, that the radiation released would affect health over a very wide area, damage the environment, and cause genetic defects and illness in future generations.[188] It also stated that '[t]he environment is not an abstraction but represents

185 Makane Moïse Mbengue, 'Between Law and Science: A Commentary on the Whaling in the Antarctic case' (2015) 2 *QIL* 178, 179.

186 *Legality of the Use by a State of Nuclear Weapons in Armed Conflict* (Advisory Opinion) [1996] ICJ Rep 66, 76 [22].

187 *Nuclear Weapons* (Advisory Opinion) (n. 1) 226 and 244 [36].

188 Ibid 243 [35].

the living space, the quality of life and the very health of human beings, including generations unborn'.[189] These are clear acknowledgements for the principle of intergenerational equality and the ways in which environmental degradation can unjustly harm unborn populations. However, it was concluded that based on existing international law, the use of nuclear weapons could not be considered unlawful in all circumstances.[190]

In *Gabčíkovo–Nagymaros*, discussed earlier, the Court acknowledged the Project's impact upon and its implications for the environment.[191] It also acknowledged that the risks that mankind's interference with nature has led to risks for present and future generations, which have grown in awareness.[192] This can be interpreted as an application of the principle of intergenerational equity. However, the Court ultimately concluded that while Hungary's concerns for the environment related to its 'essential interest',[193] its suspension of their shared treaty could not be justified by necessity pursuant to Article 25 of the Draft Articles on State Responsibility.[194] Therefore, despite minor acknowledgement of the principle of intergenerational equity, this principle did not lead the Court to conclude that there was indeed an ecological necessity.

The principle of intergenerational equity was explicit in the request for an advisory opinion in *Obligations on Climate Change*. The Court was asked, 'What are the obligations of States under international law to ensure the protection of the climate system and other parts of the environment from anthropogenic emissions of greenhouse gases for States and for present and future generations?'. It was also asked what the legal consequences are for states that have caused significant harm not only to states but to 'peoples and individuals of the present and future generations affected by the adverse effects of climate change?'. This clearly invites more careful consideration for the principle of intergenerational equity. It also demonstrates the importance of framing legal questions in the advisory context in a way that refers to the human impacts of environmental degradation, thereby giving the Court permission to address such concerns.

[189] Ibid 241–42 [29]. See also *Gabčíkovo-Nagymaros Project* (n. 1) 77–78 [140] and *Pulp Mills* (n. 1) 132 [72].
[190] *Nuclear Weapons* (Advisory Opinion) (n. 1) 263 [97].
[191] *Gabčíkovo-Nagymaros Project* (n. 1) 77–78 [140].
[192] Ibid 77–78 [140].
[193] Ibid [53].
[194] Ibid [57].

8.5 Conclusion

There have not been many environmental disputes to appear before the Court and some key human-focused ones have been discontinued (Section 8.1). While opportunities have been impeded by counterclaim requirements (Section 8.2), other prospects to develop jurisprudence on individuals' rights in the environmental context have been noted, particularly regarding the scope and details of EIAs (Section 8.3). The Court has also had opportunities to create linkages between these rights and the principles of precaution and of intergenerational equity in its reasoning (Section 8.4). In brief, the development of international environmental law to the benefit of human beings has been limited before the Court.

In the context of the climate crisis, the judicialisation of environmental disputes will only continue to surge. Given the increasing recognition of the connections between the environment and the human experience, the human–environment nexus also continues to grow in the judicial context. In light of this, judicial caution might be difficult for the Court to sustain. A stronger acknowledgement of the relevance of individuals in environmental disputes, along with efforts to balance the interests of individuals and states in this context, would enable the Court to more effectively address global environmental challenges with no end in sight.

9

Sources

> Norms of international law have addressees. These include States but also individuals, physical or moral persons. It is the right of the latter to know and estimate the impact of international norms on their daily life.[1]

Two key sources of international law are treaties and customary international law.[2] At their heart is state practice: treaties are agreements between states, while customary international law results from consistent state practice by which states consider themselves bound. However, the International Court of Justice (ICJ, the Court) has recognised in certain decisions that such sources may confer rights and benefits for individuals. This chapter examines such decisions and observes that the Court adopts a more favourable approach to individuals in this area of its jurisprudence than to other subject areas examined in Part II of this book. Such measures taken by the Court reflect an acknowledgement of the relevance of such disputes for individuals in the pursuit of a greater balance between individuals and states. This chapter will first address rights conferred on individuals in treaties (Section 9.1), before turning to customary law (Section 9.2). Section 9.3 concludes.

9.1 Individual Rights Conferred upon Individuals in Treaties

A treaty is defined by the Vienna Convention on the Law of Treaties (VCLT) as follows: 'An international agreement concluded between States in written form and governed by international law, whether

[1] Laurence Boisson de Chazournes and Makane Moïse Mbengue, 'The *Amici Curiae* and the WTO Dispute Settlement System: The Doors Are Open' (2003) 2 *Law and Practice of International Courts and Tribunals* 205, 206.

[2] See Statute of the International Court of Justice, Article 38 [hereafter, ICJ Statute].

embodied in a single instrument or in two or more related instruments and whatever its particular designation.'[3]

Under the traditional positivist doctrine, individuals were not regarded as having rights and duties under international law. No international legal source conferring rights and duties to a state was directly applicable to individuals. Rather, individuals exercised rights and duties originating exclusively from municipal law. Indeed, '[t]he pure positivist doctrine was at the same time also in principle a dualistic doctrine'.[4] There was a clear distinction between municipal law and international law – the former governing the rights and the obligations of individuals in all circumstances and the latter excluding the individual entirely and only pursuing rights and duties of states.[5] Thus, in order for international treaties to create rights or duties for individuals, contracting states had to create these provisions into their domestic law.[6]

The role of the individual in the international legal system has evolved over time, and international treaty law has not been immune to this. The conferral of rights directly to individuals through treaties particularly expanded after the Second World War with the development of international human rights treaties, intended to confer such rights directly to them. However, the ICJ has interpreted relevant provisions of other international treaties, beyond the international human rights framework, as conferring rights on individuals.[7]

The Court's method of interpretation has varied from case to case. In the International Law Commission's (ILC) initial debates on treaty interpretation, two main approaches were recognised.[8] The first was the textualist approach: a literal interpretation based on the ordinary meaning of the text, governed by Article 31 of the VCLT ('shall be interpreted (. . .) in accordance with the ordinary meaning to be given to the terms of the treaty'). The second was the 'intentionalist' approach, focused on the

[3] Vienna Convention on the Law of Treaties, 1155 UNTS 331, Article 2.1(a) [hereafter, VCLT].

[4] Peter Pavel Remec, *The Position of the Individual in International Law According to Grotius and Vattel* (Springer 1960) 5.

[5] Ibid 4.

[6] Kate Parlett, *The Individual in the International Legal System: Continuity and Change in International Law* (CUP 2011) 15.

[7] See Carlos Manuel Vázquez, 'Treaty-Based Rights and Remedies of Individuals' (1992) 92 *Columbia Law Review* 1082.

[8] Mr de Luna [1964] *Yearbook of the ILC*, vol I, 276 [16]; Mr Bartos [1964] *Yearbook of the ILC*, vol I, 279 [64].

intentions of the drafters. While not always the case, these intentions can possibly be ascertained by considering the context of the treaty (contextual method), its object and purpose (teleological method), or its *travaux préparatoires* (historical method). There is no clear hierarchy between these latter methods to determine the drafters' intentions nor between the textualist and intentionalist approaches more broadly.[9]

The Court has never explicitly referred to its interpretative methodology using these terms, nor has it cited the VCLT in the course of its interpretation. However, the broader dichotomy of textualist and intentionalist approaches can be loosely identified in the Court's jurisprudence. For this reason, this chapter will analyse its treaty interpretation by reference to these two main approaches. I will argue that both the 'textualist' and 'intentionalist' approaches employed by the Court and its predecessor have allowed for the recognition of individuals' rights.

I will first address the 'intentionalist' interpretation employed by the Permanent Court of International Justice (PCIJ) in *Jurisdiction of the Court of Danzig* and by the Court in the 2009 *Dispute regarding Navigational and Related Rights (Costa Rica v. Nicaragua)* case (Section 9.1.1). I will then examine the 'textualist' approach of the Court in a series of cases pertaining to the Vienna Convention on Consular Relations (Section 9.1.2).

9.1.1 'Intentionalist' Interpretation by the PCIJ and the ICJ

To understand the Court's practice in 'intentionalist' interpretation, it is important to examine the practice of its predecessor. In 1928, the PCIJ rendered an advisory opinion titled *Jurisdiction of the Court of Danzig*.[10] This judgment addressed the question of whether individuals could be directly granted rights through an international treaty.

The source of the dispute was a 1921 Agreement between the newly established Government of Poland and the Free City of Danzig, a semi-autonomous city state that existed between 1920 and 1939. Both parties

[9] VCLT, Article 31; Draft Articles on the Law of Treaties with commentaries [1966] *Yearbook of the ILC*, vol II, 218; Alexander Orakhelashvili, *The Interpretation of Acts and Rules in Public International Law* (OUP 2008) 303–5.

[10] *Jurisdiction of the Courts of Danzig (Pecuniary Claims of Danzig Railway Officials who have passed into the Polish Service, against the Polish Railways Administration)* (Advisory Opinion) [1928] PCIJ Series B.

were the product of the Treaty of Versailles.[11] The 1921 Agreement between the two parties established that Poland would administer part of the railway system in Danzig. This Agreement was not incorporated into the national laws of Danzig nor of Poland.[12]

Due to their agreement, railway officials from Danzig were transferred into the Polish service. However, the railway officials opened a case at the court of the Free City of Danzig, demanding pecuniary claims against the Polish Railways Administration, the latter having violated a clause in the 1921 Agreement. The Government of Poland argued that the railway officials could not bring claims to the Danzig court based on the 1921 Agreement. Subsequently, the dispute between Poland and Danzig was taken to the High Commissioner for the Free City of Danzig, who also supported that the railway officials could not make claims based on the 1921 Agreement, because it was an international treaty concluded between two states and did not confer direct rights on individuals.[13]

The Government of the Free City of Danzig did not accept this decision and appealed to the Council of the League of Nations. Consequently, the Council sought an advisory opinion from the PCIJ to determine the validity of the decision. In other words, could individuals bring claims to a court based on the 1921 Agreement? Did this international treaty give direct rights to individuals?

The Free City of Danzig believed that the 1921 Agreement did confer rights directly on the railway officials, placing emphasis on the intention of the parties to confer these rights.[14] Conversely, the Polish government defended that it did not confer any rights directly upon the individuals and that they therefore could not make any claims to any court upon the basis of this Agreement. It further contended that any failure to fulfill its obligations under the Agreement would render it liable solely to the Government of Danzig, not to the individuals directly.[15]

The PCIJ relied on the intention of the contracting parties in order to answer the question 'whether the international agreement formed part of

[11] See Treaty of Versailles, UKTS 4, Articles 87 and 88 (for Poland) and Articles 102 and 103 (Danzig).

[12] Parlett (n. 6) 19.

[13] 'Jurisdiction of Danzig Courts in Actions Brought by Railway Officials against the Railway Administration', Decision of the High Commissioner (8 April 1927), English translation reproduced in: *Jurisdiction of the Courts of Danzig* Advisory Opinion (n. 10) Annex I.

[14] *Jurisdiction of the Courts of Danzig* Advisory Opinion (n. 10) 18.

[15] Ibid.

the contract of service of the Danzig officials'.[16] Possibly the most frequently quoted passage from the case is as follows:

> It may be readily admitted that, according to a well-established principle of international law, the *Beamtenabkommen* [international treaty], being an international agreement, cannot, as such, create direct rights and obligations for private individuals. But it cannot be disputed that the very object of an international agreement, according to the intention of the contracting Parties, may be the adoption by the Parties of some definite rules creating individual rights and obligations and enforceable by the national courts. That there is such an intention in the present case can be established by reference to the terms of the *Beamtenabkommen* [international treaty].[17]

Since the issuance of this decision, this passage has sparked considerable debate and opposing opinions in legal scholarship, with no clear resolution. On the one hand, certain scholars such as Hersch Lauterpacht claim that individuals may be conferred rights directly from international treaties.[18] This argument relies on the conclusion of the PCIJ elsewhere in the judgment that '[t]he wording and general tenor of the *Beamtenabkommen* [1921 Agreement] show that its provisions are directly applicable as between the officials and the Administration'[19] – bearing in mind that the 1921 Agreement had not been adopted in the domestic law of the Free City of Danzig nor of Poland. The PCIJ also clearly explains that 'the object of the [Agreement] is to create a special legal régime governing the relations between the Polish Railways Administration and the Danzig officials (. . .) [which] according to the intention of the contracting parties, is to be governed by the very provisions of the [Agreement]'.[20] Furthermore, in response to Poland's argument that Article 9 of the Agreement proves that 'the intention of the parties was to leave it to Poland to make all the regulations concerning the Danzig Railway officials', the PCIJ replied that this Article 'should not be construed in a manner which would make the applicability of [its] provisions (. . .) depend on their incorporation into a Polish

[16] Ibid.

[17] Ibid 17–18.

[18] Hersch Lauterpacht, *The Development of International Law by the Permanent Court of International Justice* (Longmans, Green and Company 1934) 52; Hersch Lauterpacht, 'The Subjects of the Law of Nations' (1947) 63(4) *Law Quarterly Review* 438.

[19] *Jurisdiction of the Courts of Danzig* Advisory Opinion (n. 10) 18.

[20] Ibid.

Regulation'.[21] Essentially, bearing in mind that the PCIJ stated that the 1921 Agreement conferred substantive rights to the individuals and knowing that this Agreement had not been incorporated into any national laws, then the 1921 Agreement must have created such rights for the individuals directly.

On the other hand, it was also argued that the individuals could not be conferred rights directly from international treaties. This view places emphasis on the phrase (in the passage quoted before) 'an international agreement, cannot, as such, create direct rights and obligations for private individuals', and interprets 'the adoption by the Parties of some definite rules creating individual rights and obligations and enforceable by the national courts' to mean rules of domestic law. Thus, individuals are subjects of municipal laws, and solely states are subjects of international law. This is in line with the positivist doctrine that prevailed during that period. PCIJ Judge Dionisio Anzilotti, the main proponent of this view, clearly explained that

> The opinion of the PCIJ does not say that a treaty, as such, can create rights and obligations for individuals, without the need for the rules and those things associated with the rules to be incorporated into internal law; it says only that the intention of the contracting parties can be that of adopting definite rules creating rights and obligations for individuals and capable of being applied by national tribunals.[22]

In my view, the 'definite rules' referred to in Anzilotti's passage are international rules directly applicable to individuals and not municipal rules on the domestic level. This is known through examining the context: the Court is explaining the law in relation to a situation whereby the 1921 Agreement was not, *in casu*, incorporated into domestic law. The Court is describing the Agreement, noting that, in some instances, the parties may intend to create definite international rules that can be directly applied to individuals without any municipal law being created. This is affirmed by the fact that the PCIJ did not at any point in the judgment go on to examine whether the relevant clauses in the 1921 Agreement had been adopted in municipal law in order to determine whether they apply, or not, to the officials. On the contrary, it says that '[n]either Party has disputed the fact that the *Beamtenabkommen*

[21] Ibid 20.

[22] Dionisio Anzilotti, *Cours de droit international* (L.G.D.J 1999) 133–34, 407–8.

has been actually put into effect in accordance with the intention of the contracting Parties'.[23] If the PCIJ was truly saying that municipal law is necessary in the *cas d'espèce* for the Agreement to apply to the individuals, then it would have examined if this were the case. Instead, it analysed the clauses and how they applied directly. It said 'taking into consideration the manner in which the Agreement has been applied' – the Agreement was not translated into municipal law.[24]

In response to this, Anzilotti argued that

> If, in this particular case, the [Permanent] Court did not consider it necessary to examine whether the rules outlined in the agreement had effectively been adopted, it is because the [Permanent] Court considered that the party which was obliged to adopt the said rules was not able, in any case, to take advantage of the fact that it had not executed its obligation, in order to avoid the duties imposed on it by the agreement as regards the other party.[25]

In other words, Poland had failed to meet its obligation to incorporate the rights from the 1921 Agreement into Polish law, and therefore, it could not argue that the individuals' rights did not exist in domestic law. Anzilotti is suggesting that due to these circumstances, the PCIJ deliberately ignored that the rights were not incorporated into Polish law. This partisan behaviour seems uncharacteristic of such an institution; it is difficult to believe that the PCIJ would wilfully turn a blind eye to the absence of domestic legislation and still conclude that the individuals in the present case derived rights via such a legislation that did not exist. However, the controversy surrounding the interpretation of the *Danzig* judgment is plausible. Lauterpacht describes that the PCIJ's 'departure from the established view was effected with such ingenious restraint that some have been led to believe that the decision of the Court amounts to a solemn affirmation of the established doctrine'.[26]

The *Danzig* judgment did not have any immediate transformative effect in the international legal system,[27] but in hindsight, it was the first authoritative statement addressing the possibility of individuals having their own rights conferred through a source of international law. This was arguably possible through the 'intentionalist' approach of

[23] *Jurisdiction of the Courts of Danzig* Advisory Opinion (n. 10) 20.
[24] Ibid 18.
[25] Anzilotti (n. 22) 133–34 and 407–8.
[26] Lauterpacht (1934) (n. 18) 52.
[27] Parlett (n. 6) 26.

interpretation, which appears to offer more flexibility to advance individuals' rights and interests than the 'textualist' approach where the interpreter is more confined to the strict letter of the law. However, as the *Danzig* case indicates, this mode of interpretation can be subject to ambiguity or cast doubt on the Court's reasoning.

This is further indicated in the 2009 *Dispute regarding Navigational and Related Rights (Costa Rica v. Nicaragua)*, where an 'intentionalist' approach was again employed decades later to the benefit of individuals – though not without ambiguity. In 2005, Costa Rica instituted proceedings against Nicaragua, asking the Court to determine the scope of Costa Rica's navigational rights in the San Juan River, located on the border between the two countries. To do so, the Court was tasked with the interpretation of the 1858 Treaty of Limits between both countries. This treaty had the purpose of fixing the course of the boundary between Costa Rica and Nicaragua from the Pacific Ocean to the Caribbean Sea.[28] It established that Nicaragua had sovereignty over the waters in the San Juan river but still gave Costa Rica navigational rights 'con objetos de comercio' ('for the purposes of commerce' according to Costa Rica and 'with merchandise of commerce' according to Nicaragua) on the lower course of the river.[29] In this case, the Court made two distinct interpretations in favour of individuals' rights on the basis of the drafters' intentions. These interpretations, however, gave rise to ambiguities.

First, the Court was asked to interpret the scope of the term 'commerce', to determine whether it strictly covered trade and goods, as Nicaragua contended, or extended to services, such as the transport of persons, tourists, and other individuals, as Costa Rica claimed.[30] Nicaragua argued that the 'intentionalist' approach should be applied 'to give the words used in the Treaty the meaning they had at the time the Treaty was concluded, not their current meaning, which can be quite different, because this is the only way to remain true to the intent of the drafters of the Treaty. . .'.[31] The Court explained that while it is indeed important to ascertain the meaning of a term when the treaty was drafted in order to 'shed light on the parties' common intention', a practice it has employed numerous times in the past, '[t]his does not however signify

[28] *Dispute regarding Navigational and Related Rights (Costa Rica v. Nicaragua)* (Judgment) [2009] ICJ Rep 213, 229 [19].

[29] Ibid.

[30] Ibid 240–41 [58]–[59].

[31] Ibid 240–41 [58].

that, where a term's meaning is no longer the same as it was at the date of conclusion, no account should ever be taken of its meaning at the time when the treaty is to be interpreted for purposes of applying it'.[32]

It elaborated that 'commerce' is a generic term whose meaning was likely to evolve over time and, given the 'continuing duration' of the treaty and its objective to achieve a permanent settlement between the parties, they presumably intended for the terms to have an evolving meaning.[33] It therefore adopted an evolutionary interpretation, defined by the ILC as '[A] meaning which is capable of evolving over time'.[34] It is not considered to be a separate type of interpretation outside of the VCLT framework, but rather 'the result of a proper application of the usual means of interpretation, as a means by which to establish the intention of the parties'.[35] It is therefore classified as a type of 'intentionalist' approach. Given that today, the term 'commerce' applies to the transport of persons, the members of the bench unanimously agreed that the right of navigation for purposes of commerce enjoyed by Costa Rica includes the transport of tourists.[36]

The Court has addressed evolutionary interpretation in past judgments, explaining that it is applicable to 'generic term[s]', as their 'meaning was intended to follow the evolution of the law and to correspond with the meaning attached to the expression by the law in force at any given time'.[37] Indeed, in *Pulp Mills on the River Uruguay (Argentina v. Uruguay)*, it recalled that 'there are situations in which the parties' intent upon conclusion of the treaty was, or may be presumed to have been, to give the terms used – or some of them – a meaning or content capable of evolving, not one fixed once and for all, so as to make allowance for, among other things, developments in international law'.[38] While this form of interpretation may allow for the conferral of rights to individuals through treaties, the task to interpret any term 'in accordance with the intentions of the parties at the time of its

[32] Ibid 242 [64].
[33] Ibid 243 [66]–[68].
[34] A/71/10, 187.
[35] Eirik Bjørge, *The Evolutionary Interpretation of Treaties* (OUP 2014) 2.
[36] *Costa Rica v. Nicaragua* (n. 28) 269 [156] (b).
[37] *Aegean Sea Continental Shelf (Greece v. Turkey)* (Judgment) [1978] ICJ Rep 3, 33 [77].
[38] *Pulp Mills on the River Uruguay (Argentina v. Uruguay)* (Judgment) [2010] ICJ Rep 14, 82–83 [204].

conclusion'[39] is not free from ambiguity. Judge *ad hoc* Guillaume described that '[a] real difficulty arises with that approach',[40] while Judge Skotnikov, in his separate opinion, argued that no evidence submitted by the parties showed that they intended to give an evolving meaning to the word 'commerce'.[41] Dawidowicz has questioned whether this method is truly satisfactory and appears to take full account of the common intention of the parties which, to him, is 'the main task of interpretation'.[42] Skotnikov, building on former ILC member Georg Nolte's work, opined that the subsequent practice of treaties should have been applied instead – although Bjørge warns that this may be restrictive compared to evolutionary interpretation.[43] Still, the 'recourse [that] must be had to presumptions' may make the Court's choices difficult to justify in some instances.[44] It also compromises the Court's prioritisation of stability insofar as if the word 'commerce' develops a new, different, or wider meaning in fifty years' time, the dispute resurface for further debate.

The second act of treaty interpretation favourable to individuals' rights made by the Court in *Navigational and Related Rights* occurred when it was asked to determine whether Article VI of the 1858 Treaty also governed activities of navigation carried out free of charge. Indeed, it was determined by the Court that the right of *free* navigation in this clause covered two types: those for commercial transactions or those where vessel passengers paid for the transport. However, many inhabitants of the villages on the Costa Rican bank regularly navigated their

[39] *Legal Consequences for States of the Continued Presence of South Africa in Namibia (South West Africa) notwithstanding Security Council Resolution 276 (1970)* (Advisory Opinion) [1971] ICJ Rep 16, 31-32 [53].

[40] *Costa Rica v. Nicaragua* (n. 28) 226 [15].

[41] Ibid 284 [5] (Separate opinion of Judge Skotnikov).

[42] Martin Dawidowicz, 'The Effect of the Passage of Time on the Interpretation of Treaties: Some Reflections on Costa Rica v. Nicaragua' (2011) 24(1) *Leiden Journal of International Law* 201.

[43] *Costa Rica v. Nicaragua* (n. 28) 284–85 (Separate opinion of Judge Skotnikov); Georg Nolte, 'Between Contemporaneous and Evolutive Interpretation: The Use of "Subsequent Practice" in the Judgment of the International Court of Justice Concerning the Case of Costa Rica v. Nicaragua' in Holger P. Hestermeyer et al (eds), *Coexistence, Cooperation and Solidarity* (Brill 2012) 1675–84; Georg Nolte, 'Introductory Report of the Study Group on Treaties over Time' in Georg Nolte (ed), *Treaties and Subsequent Practice* (OUP 2013) 169–209; Eirik Bjørge, 'The Means of Interpretation Admissible for the Establishment of the Intention of the Parties' in *The Evolutionary Interpretation of Treaties* (OUP 2014) 56–141.

[44] *Costa Rica v. Nicaragua* (n. 28) 297–98 [15] (Declaration of Judge *ad hoc* Guillaume).

vessels to meet the basic requirements of everyday life and thus were not subject to any fee. Were they also protected by the right to navigational freedom under Article VI of the 1858 Treaty? The Court responded that if one takes into account the provisions of the Treaty as a whole, and the way that the boundary is geographically fixed in the area, it may be insinuated that the parties wished to preserve this right for the Costa Rican inhabitants. The parties must 'be presumed, in view of the historical background to the conclusion of this Treaty and the Treaty's object and purpose as defined by the Preamble and Article I, to have intended to preserve' this right.[45] In coming to this conclusion, the Court claimed to have adopted an 'intentionalist' approach, claiming that 'while such a right cannot be derived from the express language of Article VI (. . .) [i]t cannot have been the *intention* of the authors of the 1858 Treaty to deprive the inhabitants of the Costa Rican bank of the river (. . .)'.[46]

The geographical circumstance that the Court is referring to is surely the fact that the border between Costa Rica and Nicaragua was set by the treaty to be on the Costa Rican side of the river. This is unusual, given that oftentimes, the border of two nations with a river running through it along the thalweg; the middle of the waterway. If the parties decided that the border should expressly be on the Costa Rican side and that Nicaragua should have full sovereignty of the river, there is no way Costa Rica would have accepted this without having the guarantee that its people could access the river. This appears to be a presumption, rather than something grounded in the evidence presented regarding the drafters' intentions. Ben Juratowitch argues that the Court pays lip service to Articles 31 and 32 of the VCLT but that the presumption does not stem from these provisions.[47] Nonetheless, it is a presumption to the benefit of the people of Costa Rica.

To conclude, the 'intentionalist' approach of interpretation gives freedom to advance individuals' rights and interests but leaves room for doubt. In *Danzig*, the PCIJ emphasised the intention of the state parties to the treaty as a necessary condition for individuals to be beneficiaries of rights derived from it (the 'intentionalist' approach).[48] In the

[45] Ibid 247 [79].

[46] Ibid.

[47] Ben Juratowitch, 'Individual Rights in Disputes between States' (Dialogues between International and Public Law, a conference organised by BIICL and Melbourne Law School, London, June–July 2016) 42–46.

[48] *Jurisdiction of the Courts of Danzig* Advisory Opinion (n. 10) 17–18.

Navigational and Related Rights judgment, the Court, in two instances, also relied on the intention of the parties: to determine that Costa Rica has free navigational rights on the San Juan River for commerce including transporting passengers and tourists[49] and that the inhabitants of the Costa Rican bank had the right to navigate the river to exercise the essential needs of everyday life.[50] However, as seen, all of these exercises of interpretation left room for doubt.

9.1.2 Textual Interpretation of the Vienna Convention on Consular Relations

Contrary to the 'intentionalist' approach, the Court has also employed the 'textualist' approach, drawing conclusions from literal interpretations of text in a treaty. This approach has led to the acknowledgement of individuals' rights directly conferred in the Vienna Convention on Consular Relations (VCCR) in particular.

The Court has dealt with a number of cases that required it to interpret Article 36(1)(b) of the VCCR, which reads as follows:

> 1. With a view to facilitating the exercise of consular functions relating to nationals of the sending State: (. . .) (b) if he so requests, the competent authorities of the receiving State shall, without delay, inform the consular post of the sending State if, within its consular district, a national of that State is arrested or committed to prison or to custody pending trial or is detained in any other manner. Any communication addressed to the consular post by the person arrested, in prison, custody or detention shall also be forwarded by the said authorities without delay. The said authorities shall inform the person concerned without delay of his rights under this sub-paragraph[.][51]

The Court has judged on the merits in three death penalty cases, in which it decided that individuals may acquire rights directly under international treaties: *LaGrand (Germany v. United States of America)*, *Avena (Mexico v. United States of America)*, and *Jadhav (India v. Pakistan)*. The *Vienna Convention on Consular Relations (Paraguay v. United States of America)* case also pertained to an interpretation of the same clause but was

[49] *Costa Rica v. Nicaragua* (n. 28) 246 [76].
[50] Ibid [156] (1) (a) (b) (c) and (f).
[51] Vienna Convention on Consular Relations and Optional Protocols, 596 UNTS 487.

discontinued on 10 November 1998.[52] This section focuses on individual rights, as distinct from human rights. While human rights are fundamental rights pertaining to every human being in the world and enshrined in a number of international human rights conventions, individual rights may be directly conferred to individuals but do not necessarily carry a human rights character. While all human rights are individual rights, not all individual rights are human rights.

In *LaGrand*, the Court ruled that by breaching its obligation to inform the LaGrand brothers of their rights under the VCCR, the United States of America (US) had violated their individual rights.[53] Distinction was made between individual rights and human rights, as Germany, defending the LaGrand brothers, submitted the argument that Article 36(1)(b) of the VCCR 'assumed the character of a human right' as well as conferring individual rights to them.[54] The Court, however, did not find it necessary to consider this additional argument as it had already characterised the clause as an individual right.[55] The interpretation that Article 36(1)(b) granted individual rights was largely supported by the bench, with the exception of Judge Oda who voted against it.[56]

These findings in the *LaGrand* case were reiterated by the Court in the *Avena* case, a dispute between Mexico and the US surrounding the death penalty sentences of 54 Mexican nationals in various US states. The ICJ upheld Mexico's claim that the US had violated Article 36(1)(b) of the VCCR. The slight distinction with the *LaGrand* case was that Mexico had seized the Court based on its own direct injury as opposed to its nationals' injuries (Section 2.1.1).[57] The Court therefore specified that the rights of states and individuals reflected in this clause were 'interdependent', in the sense that 'violations of the rights of the individual under Article 36 may entail a violation of the rights of the sending State, and that violations of the rights of the latter may entail a violation of the rights of the individual'.[58] In these proceedings as well, Mexico argued that 'the

[52] *Vienna Convention on Consular Relations (Paraguay v. United States of America)* (Order of 10 November 1998) [1998] ICJ Rep 426.

[53] *LaGrand (Germany v. United States of America)* (Merits) (Judgment) [2001] ICJ Rep 466, 494 [77].

[54] Memorial of the Federal Republic of Germany (6 September 1999) [4.93].

[55] *LaGrand* (n. 53) 494 [78].

[56] Ibid [128].

[57] *Avena and Other Mexican Nationals (Mexico v. United States of America)* (Judgment) [2004] ICJ Rep 12, 35–36 [40]. See also Chapter 2.

[58] Ibid.

right to consular notification and consular communication under the Vienna Convention is a fundamental human right that constitutes part of due process in criminal proceedings'.[59] The Court, however, stated that '[w]hether or not the Vienna Convention rights are human rights is not a matter that this Court need decide'.[60]

Most recently, the *Jadhav Case (India v. Pakistan)* was also centred on Pakistan's violation of Article 36(1)(b) in refusing to grant consular access to Mr. Kulbhushan Sudhir Jadhav before he was detained, tried and sentenced to death on 10 April 2017. On 17 July 2019, the Court ruled that Pakistan did not inform Mr. Jadhav of '*his rights*' under Article 36(1)(b) of the VCCR, and thus concluded that 'Pakistan breached its obligation to inform Mr. Jadhav of *his rights under that provision*'.[61] This reinforces the previous judgments and confirms that rights are indeed conferred to the individual through the treaty. The Court stated later in the judgment that 'the breaches by Pakistan (. . .) constitute internationally wrongful acts of a continuing character. Accordingly, the Court is of the view that Pakistan is under an obligation to cease those acts and to comply fully with its obligations under Article 36 of the Vienna Convention. Consequently, Pakistan must inform Mr. Jadhav without further delay of his rights under Article 36, paragraph 1 (b). . .'.[62] It accordingly ruled that the remedy in this case was to be effective review and reconsideration of the conviction and sentence of Mr. Jadhav.[63] In his separate opinion, Judge Antônio Augusto Cançado Trindade argued that this case provided the opportunity to examine individual rights under Article 36 of the VCCR as directly related to the human rights to due process of law and a fair trial.[64]

To conclude, the *LaGrand* judgment paid no attention to the intention of the state parties of the VCCR, but came to its conclusion after a bare reading of Article 36(1) (the 'textualist' approach), noting that, 'The clarity of these provisions, viewed in their context, admits of no doubt'.[65] Such an interpretative approach is often clearer than an 'intentionalist' approach and, as seen, may amount to the direct conferral of individuals' rights in treaties where the text permits it. However, the choice of which

[59] Ibid 60–61 [124].
[60] Ibid.
[61] *Jadhav (India v. Pakistan)* (Judgment) [2019] ICJ Rep 418, 446 [102] (emphasis added).
[62] Ibid 454 [134].
[63] Ibid 455–56 [138].
[64] *Jadhav* (n. 61) 475 [42] (Separate opinion of Judge Cançado Trindade).
[65] *LaGrand* (n. 53) 494 [77].

approach to adopt in a given context will not always be met with consensus. In *LaGrand*, Vice President Shi Jiuyong was not convinced that this provision conferred rights on individuals, opting for 'intentionalism' over 'textualism'. He contemplated that 'indiscriminate reliance on such a dictum in any circumstances ['textualism'] may not always be dependable or helpful in determining the true *intention* of the parties to a treaty'.[66]

9.1.3 Conclusion

The last century has seen an evolution in the Court's recognition of individual rights conferred in treaties. The *Danzig* judgment challenged the notion that the individual did not bear rights directly from international law, thereby questioning the entire concept of dualism in positivist international legal thinking that prevailed at the time.[67] For this reason, this case has become a landmark judgment, which arguably solidified the PCIJ's legacy. Nonetheless, the PCIJ – adopting 'intentionalist' interpretation and being cautious with its wording – left doubt as to whether it truly conferred individual rights through international treaties. The ICJ in the *LaGrand* case, however, adopted the 'textualist' approach and was clear in its wording, leaving no room for doubt.[68] This indicates that while the 'textualist' interpretation is a more certain method, allowing for the conferral of individual rights through international treaties, the 'intentionalist' approach has led to the same conclusion, albeit with greater controversy.

In the 2009 *Navigational Rights* case, the Court was intrepid in making evolutionary interpretation in one instance and presuming the drafters' intentions on another to come to conclusions that were very favourable for the Costa Rican people. The evolution of the Court's approach from cautious to candid in this respect is manifest. In fact, it is submitted that in *Navigational Rights*, the Court may have intentionally chosen to come to conclusions that would favour individuals. There are two key indicators that suggest this was the Court's approach.

[66] Ibid 519–20 [3] (Separate opinion of Vice President Shi) (emphasis added).

[67] Catherine Brölmann, 'The PCIJ and International Rights of Groups and Individuals' in Christian J. Tams and M. Fitzmaurice (eds), *Legacies of the Permanent Court of International Justice* (Martinus Nijhoff Publishers 2013) 139.

[68] Interestingly, however, the ICJ did not refer to the *Danzig* case in its 2001 judgment. Rather, in its paragraph 77, it referred to the *Acquisition of Polish Nationality* (Advisory Opinion) [1923] PCIJ Series B, 20 to substantiate its approach of "apply[ing clauses] as they stand."

First, given the judicial caution commonly exercised by the Court (Section 8.3), it would have been expected for the Court to adopt a more restrictive approach, pursuant to the PCIJ's *S.S. Wimbledon* case:

> The fact remains that Germany has to submit to an important limitation of the exercise of the sovereign rights which no one disputes that she possess over the Kiel Canal. This fact constituted *a sufficient reason for the restrictive interpretation, in case of doubt, of the clause which produces such a limitation*. But the Court feels obliged to stop at the point where the so-called restrictive interpretation would be contrary to the plain terms of the article and would destroy what has been clearly granted.[69]

The restrictive approach would have possibly been to interpret the scope of the freedom of navigation, and the term 'commerce', in a more limited manner. At the very least, it was expected for the Court to take a more balanced stance, claiming, for instance, that Nicaragua could deny visas to passengers in some specified exceptional cases.[70] It can be assumed that the adopted attitude of the Court was in order to preclude further disputes and definitively settle the matter between the parties (with the exception of its evolutionary interpretation of the term "commerce", which leaves ample room for the term's future evolution, potentially giving rise to new disputes). It is therefore possible that it wished to rule in a manner that would not be detrimental to the affected individuals in question.

Second, the Court came to a conclusion favourable to individuals in one instance in *Navigational and Related Rights* through no method of interpretation at all. The Court was asked to decide if Nicaragua had the right to require Costa Ricans, exercising the right of free navigation on the San Juan River to carry passports or obtain Nicaraguan visas.[71] The task of the Court was to determine if the scope of navigational freedom extends to requesting or denying a visa and on what grounds. This was a difficult task, as the 1858 Treaty was silent on this matter. The Court noted that '[t]he power of a State to issue or refuse visas is a practical expression of the prerogative which each State has to control entry by non-nationals into its territory'[72] and 'entails discretion'.[73] It also

[69] *S.S. "Wimbledon"* (Judgment) [1923] PCIJ Series A, 24–25.

[70] Marko Milanovic, 'The ICJ and Evolutionary Treaty Interpretation' (*EJIL Talk!* 14 July 2009) www.ejiltalk.org/the-icj-and-evolutionary-treaty-interpretation/

[71] *Costa Rica v. Nicaragua* (n. 28) 222 [13] (d). See also Memorial of Costa Rica (29 August 2006) [5.54]–[5.67]; Reply of Costa Rica (15 January 2008) [4.12]–[4.18]; Verbatim record 2009/6, 48–49 [37]–[40] (Lucius Caflisch).

[72] Verbatim record 2009/7, 44–46 [18]–[21] (Paul Reichler).

[73] *Costa Rica v. Nicaragua* (n. 28) 257–58 [115].

determined that the issue of visas raises the question of *who* is entitled to and who may benefit from the right of freedom of navigation for commercial purposes. It determined that it is the owners and operators of Costa Rican vessels, and passengers on such vessels even if they were not Costa Rica nationals.[74] Thus, imposing visa requirements on these people who enjoy the right of navigational freedom is a violation of this right.[75]

In my view, the determination of who could benefit from freedom of navigation was only one step of the legal reasoning. The next step should have then been to assess whether requiring a person who enjoys navigational freedom to have a visa – regardless of who it is – is, in fact, a violation of this right at all. In other words, does the right to freedom of navigation encompass, in its scope, the right to be free from visa requirements to navigate? Furthermore, on what interpretative grounds could this be determined, given that a 'textualist' approach was not an option? Could this be understood through examining the parties' intentions, or subsequent practice?[76] The Court did not broach the latter queries, nor did it provide a clear explanation for its decision. It is described to have 'creat[ed] bright line rules out of whole cloth'.[77] This is possibly why five members of the Court objected to this specific point[78] and why the separate opinion of Judge Bernardo Sepúlveda-Amor (sharing my position on this particular point) was submitted.[79] Therefore, aspects of the legal reasoning in *Navigational and Related Rights* and *Danzig* may indicate that there was a desire to progress individuals' rights conferred in international treaties. The last century has certainly seen an evolution in this regard.

9.2 Individuals as Beneficiaries of Customary Rights: A Mystifying Threshold

Beyond treaties, the Court has also conferred rights to individuals through the identification of customary international law. It has been required, in some cases, to identify customary international law, the

74 Ibid 257 [114].
75 Ibid 257–58 [114]–[115].
76 See ibid 284–85 [8]–[10] (Separate opinion Judge Skotnikov).
77 Milanovic (n. 70).
78 *Costa Rica v. Nicaragua* (n. 28) 269 [156] (d).
79 Ibid 274–77 [8]–[19] (Separate opinion of Judge Sepúlveda-Amor).

existence of which would confer rights to private persons in specific contexts. In this section, it is observed that the high threshold for the identification of bilateral custom has seemingly eased over time, ultimately benefiting individuals.

Customary international law is the settled, extensive, and virtually uniform practice of states coupled with their belief (*opinio juris*) that such practice amounts to a legal obligation.[80] While this implies a large number of states, it is also possible for bilateral rules binding just two states to be identified. This is referred to as local custom. In *Land, Island and Maritime Frontier Dispute (El Salvador/Honduras: Nicaragua intervening)*, Honduras even argued that even a 'trilateral local custom' could have established an agreement regarding joint sovereignty between itself, El Salvador, and Nicaragua.[81] The Court has clearly explained the concept of local custom in the *Right of Passage over Indian Territory (Portugal v. India)* case:

> Where therefore the Court finds a practice clearly established between two States which was accepted by the Parties as governing the relations between them, the Court must attribute decisive effect to that practice for the purpose of determining their specific rights and obligations. Such a particular practice must prevail over any general rules.[82]

The guidelines for the standard of proof required to identify local custom were established in the *Asylum (Colombia/Peru)* case, in which Peruvian national and political leader Victor Raúl Haya de la Torre had been accused of instigating a military rebellion and was granted diplomatic asylum in the Colombian Embassy in Peru. The Court was asked to decide, *inter alia*, whether Colombia was entitled to unilaterally decide whether the offence committed was a political offence or a common crime – a decision which would be binding on Peru, the territorial state. Colombia argued that it was entitled to do so, and such a decision was binding on Peru due to an existing local custom recognised by Latin American states.[83] In response, the Court clarified the standard of proof:

[80] *North Sea Continental Shelf cases (Federal Republic of Germany/Denmark; Federal Republic of Germany/Netherlands)* (Judgment) [1969] ICJ Rep 3, 43 [74] and 44 [77].

[81] Memorial of the Government of the Republic of Honduras (1 June 1998) [53]. See also *Land, Island and Maritime Frontier Dispute (El Salvador/Honduras: Nicaragua intervening)* (Judgment) [1992] ICJ Rep 351, 597–98 [399].

[82] *Right of Passage over Indian Territory (Portugal v. India)* (Merits) (Judgment) [1960] ICJ Rep 6, 43–44.

[83] Memorial submitted by the Government of the Republic of Colombia (10 January 1950) [15], [24], [29], [30], [31].

> The Party which relies on a custom of this kind must prove that this custom is established in such a manner that it has become binding on the other Party. The Colombian Government must prove that the rule invoked by it is in accordance with a constant and uniform usage practiced by the States in question, and that this usage is the expression of a right appertaining to the State granting asylum and a duty incumbent on the territorial State. This follows from Article 38 of the Statute of the Court, which refers to international custom "as evidence of a general practice accepted as law".[84]

In this case, the Court deemed that Colombia had not effectively proven that these conditions had been fulfilled. With regards to the requirement of constant and uniform usage practised by the relevant states, the Court noted that the evidence presented by Colombia 'disclose[d] so much uncertainty and contradiction, so much fluctuation and discrepancy (. . .)'.[85] The inconsistency made it impossible to discern any constant and uniform usage.[86] Furthermore, this case placed special emphasis on the importance of *opinio juris*, which is seemingly stricter in a bilateral context.

While the requirements to establish international and local custom are the same and both find their roots in Article 38 of the ICJ Statute, the standards of proof in order to bilaterally bind two states appear to be more rigorous. General customary international law is a more flexible law-making approach as it considers an undetermined number of states' behaviour reflecting the 'majority holding' with regard to a particular practice. On the other hand, local (bilateral) custom only involves two states and therefore depends on the particular activity of one state being accepted by the other. It requires the unequivocal acceptance of the two parties in order to take shape. The keystone principle of consent thus manifests itself more starkly in the context of local (bilateral) custom than with respect to general customary international law. One would therefore presume that local custom is indeed more difficult to establish.

However, in the *Right of Passage over Indian Territory (Portugal v. India)* case one decade later, the Court was satisfied that the conditions described in the *Asylum* case had been met. In this case, the Court had to ascertain the existence of a local custom between India and Portugal with

84 *Asylum (Colombia v. Peru)* (Judgment) [1950] ICJ Rep 266, 276.
85 Ibid 277.
86 Ibid.

regard to a right of passage of private persons, civil officials, and goods. Noting that the passage of private persons and civil officials was clearly defined and agreed upon by both parties, it found a 'constant and uniform practice allowing free passage between Daman and the enclaves' which had 'continued over a period extending beyond a century and a quarter unaffected by the change of regime in respect of the intervening territory which occurred when India became independent'.[87] This practice had therefore given rise to a right and a correlative obligation.[88] No further explanation was given with respect to its reasoning.

Similarly, the Court's approach to identifying custom relevant to individuals' rights in the aforementioned *Navigational and Related Rights* case indicates a progressive relaxation to the benefit of individuals. Beyond interpreting the 1858 Treaty of Limits, as analysed earlier, it was also requested by Costa Rica to determine whether Costa Rica's inhabitants had a customary right to subsistence fishing in the San Juan river.[89] The Court found that the riparian communities in Costa Rica had a customary right to subsistence fishing from the San Juan River. If we apply the criteria established in *Asylum (Colombia v. Peru)* and in *Right of Passage over Indian Territory (Portugal v. India)*, there was no evidence that Costa Rica's right to subsistence fishing had become binding on Nicaragua,[90] as Costa Rica never claimed before the case that it even had such a right.[91] Furthermore, there was no constant and uniform usage practised by states, as the Court itself stated that 'the practice, by its very nature, especially given the remoteness of the area and the small, thinly spread population, is not likely to be documented in any formal way in any official record'.[92] Thus, there was no documented practice attesting a customary fishing right.[93]

The Court, in its reasoning, explained that Nicaragua never protested the Costa Ricans fishing in the area.[94] Is acquiescence, however, enough to establish the *opinio juris* of the parties? There is no unanimous answer

[87] *Right of Passage over Indian Territory* (n. 82) 40.

[88] Ibid.

[89] *Costa Rica v. Nicaragua* (n. 28) 265 [140].

[90] Nicaragua strictly reiterated that it had "absolutely no intention of preventing Costa Rican residents from engaging in subsistence fishing activities". See ibid.

[91] Milanovic (n. 70).

[92] *Costa Rica v. Nicaragua* (n. 28) 265 [141].

[93] Yoshifumi Tanaka, 'Navigational Rights on the San Juan River: A Commentary on the *Costa Rica v. Nicaragua* Case' (2009) *Hague Justice Journal* 213.

[94] *Costa Rica v. Nicaragua* (n. 28) 265 [141].

in international law, although the ILC's 2018 Draft conclusions on identification of customary international law state in Article 10(3) that '[f]ailure to react over time to a practice may serve as evidence of acceptance as law (*opinio juris*), provided that states were in a position to react and the circumstances called for some reaction'.[95] The commentary to the draft conclusions specifies that two conditions must be met:

> First, it is essential that a reaction to the practice in question would have been called for: this may be the case, for example, where the practice is one that affects — usually unfavourably — the interests or rights of the State failing or refusing to act. Second, the reference to a State being "in a position to react" means that the State concerned must have had knowledge of the practice (which includes circumstances where, because of the publicity given to the practice, it must be assumed that the State had such knowledge), and that it must have had sufficient time and ability to act. Where a State did not or could not have been expected to know of a certain practice, or has not yet had a reasonable time to respond, inaction cannot be attributed to an acknowledgment that such practice was mandated (or permitted) under customary international law.[96]

In the present case, as the Court itself recognised the remoteness of the area and its small population,[97] the absence of protest could have simply derived from the lack of practical significance of the very small amount of fishing involved. There is no evidence that Nicaragua did not protest because it felt a sense of legal obligation that the riparian Costa Ricans had the right to fish.[98] It would therefore appear that the requirement for the establishment of local custom is not as high as would be expected. In this case, the Court demonstrated exceptional flexibility with regard to these criteria in order to uphold the fishing rights of the riparian communities.

To conclude, it is difficult to ascertain what the necessary standard of proof is for establishing local custom. In the sparse case law, progression can be noted by the Court from a high threshold to a more flexible approach granting individuals rights. As with the assessment with respect to treaty interpretation described earlier, the Court has seemingly been more receptive to identifying customary rights to the benefit of individuals in time – although few cases serve to establish a solidified pattern.

95 Draft conclusions on identification of customary international law [2018] *Yearbook of the ILC*, vol II, Part Two, Article 10 (3).
96 Ibid 140.
97 *Costa Rica v. Nicaragua* (n. 28) 265 [141].
98 Milanovic (n. 70).

Another related indicator of this is the Court's acknowledgment of individuals' behaviour as contributing to the formation of custom in *Navigational and Related Rights*. Customary law (international or local) is traditionally established by actions of states.[99] However, in the specific case, it is the practice of a local community of Costa Rican riparians – the affected individuals – that is being discussed. Indeed, the ILC explains that 'the acts of private individuals may sometimes be relevant to the formation or expression of rules of customary international law, but only to the extent that States have endorsed or reacted to them'.[100] It would therefore appear that in the present case, the Court recognised the existence of customary international law through the acts of local populations reflecting Costa Rica's effective control upon them. This draws a parallel to the conclusions drawn in Chapter 7 on territorial disputes: individuals may contribute to the formation of a legal title justifying the state's ownership of a piece of land, if the individuals' actions prove the state's sovereignty.

9.3 Conclusion

To conclude this chapter, the approaches identified by the Court when identifying sources of international law have allowed for the rights of populations to be acknowledged in the Court's jurisprudence and in the international legal system at large. The Court's findings have contributed to the undisputed fact that the VCCR confers individual rights, for instance, and its predecessor arguably advanced individuals' rights in *Danzig*. Its evolutionary interpretation of the word 'commerce' has also benefited a large scope of individuals. Furthermore, its recognition of the constant and uniform usage practised by Costa Rican riparians as amounting to custom was equally beneficial to individuals, as well as other conclusions drawn despite questions raised as to its reasoning.

The Court's recognition of individuals' rights conferred in treaties and customary law has therefore been favourable to individuals compared to other areas of its jurisprudence examined in the previous chapters in Part II of this study. Indeed, more rigid and detailed rules and processes governing substantive areas such as territorial (Chapter 7) or maritime disputes (Chapter 6) have been developed through years of jurisprudence, offering less discretion. This is possibly because the interpretation

[99] *Asylum* (n. 84) 276.
[100] *Costa Rica v. Nicaragua* (n. 28) 265 [140].

of treaties and the identification of custom are two of the most complex and mysterious tasks in international law.

Indeed, the Court has often been criticised for the mystery it generates when tasked with identifying sources of international law. Scholars have painstakingly tried to understand the Court's reasoning and method in its identification of custom – referred to by one author as 'secret custom'.[101] Similarly, scholars have noted the politics and challenges in treaty identification by the Court.[102] The Court's ambiguous approach to the identification and interpretation of international legal sources is therefore commonplace and not necessarily due to a particular desire to address individuals' concerns. Regardless of its intentions, this chapter shed light on the opportunities the Court has largely seized to conduct treaty interpretation and to identify customary law in a way favourable to affected individuals.

[101] Massimo Lando, 'Secret Custom *or* The Impact of Judicial Deliberations on the Identification of Customary International Law' (2022) 81(3) *The Cambridge Law Journal* 550–80. See also Stefan Talmon, 'Determining Customary International Law: The ICJ's Methodology between Induction, Deduction and Assertion' (2015) 26 (2) *European Journal of International Law* 417–43; Niels Petersen, 'The International Court of Justice and the Judicial Politics of Identifying Customary International Law' (2017) 28 (2) *European Journal of International Law* 357–85; Alberto Alvarez-Jiménez, 'Methods for the Identification of Customary International Law in the International Court of Justice's Jurisprudence: 2000 – 2009' (2011) 60(3) *International and Comparative Law Quarterly* 681–712; Rowan Nicholson, 'The International Court of Justice as a "Shortcut" to Identifying Custom' (2021) 20(3) *The Law & Practice of International Courts and Tribunals* 490–518.

[102] Joost Pauwelyn and Manfred Elsig, 'The Politics of Treaty Interpretation: Variations and Explanations across International Tribunals' in Jeffrey L. Dunoff and Mark A. Pollack (eds), *Interdisciplinary Perspectives on International Law and International Relations: The State of the Art* (CUP 2012) 445–74; Duncan French, 'Treaty Interpretation and the Incorporation of Extraneous Legal Rules' (2006) 55(2) *The International and Comparative Law Quarterly* 281–314.

10

Remarks on Practice

Part II of this monograph explored the extent to which individuals are considered in the legal reasoning of the Court. It did so by identifying contexts in which individuals are not at the centre of the dispute (as was the case in Part I) but would be affected by it, such as maritime disputes (Chapter 6), territorial disputes (Chapter 7), environmental disputes (Chapter 8), and the interpretations of treaties and identification of custom (Chapter 9).

It was observed that individuals are rarely considered in the Court's legal reasoning in such disputes. An exception lies in the interpretation of treaties and the identification of customary law, where the Court has, albeit sometimes ambiguously, contributed to the development of individuals' rights.

Generally, such consideration for individuals rests upon certain identified conditions: the Court must not overstep its assignment, contravene the principle of stability, or counter legal formalism.

The Court would not consider individuals *proprio motu* if there were no mention of them in state litigants' pleadings and limits itself to the evidence provided by the litigants[1] or respecting their requests in their Special Agreements.[2] They therefore set the boundaries for the pending judgment. While the Court may reject the litigants' submissions if it wishes,[3] it may not innovate outside of their submissions.[4] However, it

[1] E.g., *Pulp Mills on the River Uruguay (Argentina v. Uruguay)* (Judgment) [2010] ICJ Rep 14, 72–73 [168].

[2] E.g., in *Continental Shelf (Libyan Arab Jamahiriya/Malta)* (Judgment) [1985] ICJ Rep 13, 23–24 [19]; *Minquiers and Ecrehos (France/United Kingdom)* (Judgment) [1953] ICJ Rep 47, 52; *Barcelona Traction Light and Power Company Ltd. (Belgium v. Spain)* (Second Phase) (Preliminary Objections) (Judgment) [1970] ICJ Rep 3, 37 [49].

[3] E.g., *Case of Free Zones of Upper Savoy and the District of Gex* (Order) [1930] PCIJ Series A 138; PCIJ, *The Case of the S.S. Lotus* (Judgment) [1927] PCIJ Series A 31.

[4] Hugh Thirlway, *The International Court of Justice* (OUP 2016) 85–86.

was seen in many instances in Part II that state litigants often do raise concerns for their populations in their pleadings.

Reticence to contravene the principle of stability or to counter formalism largely explains the Court's approach in maritime (Chapter 6) and territorial boundary disputes (Chapter 7).[5] In the former chapter, it explains why the Court has rarely considered relevant circumstances to adjust a provisional line and has yet to consider historic fishing rights.[6] In the latter chapter, it is why boundary treaties are of particular value to the Court[7] and why the *uti possidetis* principle takes precedence over the principle of self-determination.[8]

A fishing practice characterised by its historical longevity and therefore considered to be stable should form part of the Court's application of the principle of stability. This reframing would allow for historic fishing rights to be upheld and, therefore, for the needs of local populations to be considered. As for the Court's adherence to formalism, it is still balanced by the principle of equity. The latter's existence acknowledges that the law is not always fair and that other relevant factors should be considered where they may allow for justice. In maritime boundary disputes, it was argued that equity does not encourage extra-legality and can play a greater role when adjusting a provisional line. In territorial boundary disputes, equity could also play a prominent role, extending beyond its traditional function as the last resort in the absence of other titles. The application of equity is both precise and appropriate, remaining true to its original conception and purpose. In the words of Professor Stephen Humphreys,

> [E]quity has, at its conceptual root, repeatedly centred on the human person, and it moreover shares an intimate, indeed foundational, relation with the notion of human rights, at least at the moment of the latter's conceptual emergence in the form of ideas about natural rights.[9]

In both contexts of territorial and maritime disputes, judges are thus encouraged to assess whether the outcome aligns with the core demands

[5] Yusra Suedi, 'Man, Land and Sea: Local Populations in Territorial and Maritime Disputes Before the International Court of Justice' (2021) 20(1) *Law and Practice of International Courts and Tribunals* 30.

[6] Leonardo Bernard, 'The Effect of Historic Fishing Rights in Maritime Boundaries Delimitation' (Presented at the tenth LOSI Conference, Seoul, May 2012) 19.

[7] *Territorial Dispute (Libyan Arab Jamahiriya/Chad)* (Judgment) [1994] ICJ Rep 6, 37 [72]; *Case concerning the Temple of Preah Vihear (Cambodia v. Thailand)* (Merits) (Judgment) [1962] ICJ Rep 6, 34.

[8] *Frontier Dispute (Burkina Faso/Republic of Mali)* (Judgment) [1986] ICJ Rep 554, 566–67 [25].

[9] Stephen Humphreys, 'Equity before "Equity"' (2023) 86(1) *Modern Law Review* 85.

of justice and to make the necessary adjustments if it does not. As argued in the introduction of this study, justice serves as a benchmark for evaluating judicial outcomes, representing a balance between states and individuals within the framework of social idealism. David D. Caron and Christian Tomuschat have argued that insisting on justice 'makes good sense in situations where the legal position, as inherited from the past, does not respond to the needs of times that have changed', but that the approach to change should be 'peaceful (...) that seeks to adapt a traditional legal framework to a present which demands a greater share of equity and justice'.[10] Such proposals have been made in the relevant chapters.

Beyond *non ultra petita*, stability, and formalism, one final reason for the Court's reticence is its caution to develop international law. In concluding Part II, I reflect that while the Court does not have a legislative function, it develops the law nonetheless through the clarifications and interpretations. It should not shy away from doing so, particularly where individuals are involved.

While the UN General Assembly proclaimed in its Resolution 171(II) A of 1947 that 'it is (...) of paramount importance that the Court should be utilised to the greatest practicable extent in the progressive development of international law',[11] neither the UN Charter nor the Court's Statute attributes it with a legislative function. Nor do the *travaux préparatoires* of the Statute indicate that the Court was intended to be a lawmaker. Conversely, Article 38 indicates that its function is 'to decide in accordance with international law', possibly implying pre-existing law.[12] The Court has supported this reading in its jurisprudence, stating, in the 1974 *Fisheries Jurisdiction* case, 'In the circumstances, the Court, as a court of law, cannot render judgment *sub specie legis ferendae*, or anticipate the law before the legislator has laid it down.'[13] It also clearly stated in the *Nuclear Weapons* advisory opinion that

> It is clear that the Court cannot legislate (...). Rather its task is to engage in its normal judicial function of ascertaining the existence or otherwise of legal principles and rules applicable (...). The contention that the giving

[10] David D. Caron and Christian Tomuschat, 'Article 2(3) UN Charter' in Andreas Zimmermann et al (eds), *The Statute of the International Court of Justice: A Commentary* (3rd edn, OUP 2019) 133.

[11] A/RES/171(II) A-C.

[12] Yuval Shany and Rotem Giladi, 'International Court of Justice' in Yuval Shany (ed), *Assessing the Effectiveness of International Courts* (OUP 2014) 168.

[13] *Fisheries Jurisdiction (United Kingdom v. Iceland)* (Merits) (Judgment) [1974] ICJ Rep 3, 23–24 [53].

> of an answer to the question posed would require the Court to legislate is based on a supposition that the present *corpus juris* is devoid of relevant rules in this matter. The Court could not accede to this argument; it states the existing law and does not legislate. This is so even if, in stating and applying the law, the Court necessarily has to specify its scope and sometimes note its general trend.[14]

However, developing the law can be borne out of various tasks. The Court has identified the legal status of already-existing law.[15] It has also clarified the meaning or provided interpretations.[16] Its design of criteria for ascertaining customary law and identifying treaties or recognising obligations *erga omnes* are only some examples[17] – as well as those apparent in Chapter 9 where the Court interpreted treaties and identified custom to the benefit of individuals. While none of these tasks involve legislating *stricto sensu*, the outcome has been the development of international law. As Hernández argues,

> To reduce the development of law down to the mere exposition of norms waiting to be discovered or 'exposed', as though they somehow exist objectively, and outside the hermeneutical process, is also a technique for judges to shield themselves from the accusation that they are engaging in law-creating rather than merely the interpretation of the law. Dispensing with that fallacy, whether judgments are a source of law or merely a means for the determination of the law, a court's interpretation nevertheless contributes to the creation of what it finds.[18]

The Court's clarifications and interpretations of law constitute a form of legal development, even though judges have characterised this process as incidental rather than intentional.[19]

[14] *Legality of the Threat or Use of Nuclear Weapons* (Advisory Opinion) [1996] ICJ Rep 226, 237–38 [18].

[15] E.g., *Questions Relating to the Obligation to Prosecute or Extradite (Belgium v. Senegal)* (Judgment) [2012] ICJ Rep 422, 457 [99] ["the prohibition of torture is part of customary international law and it has become a peremptory norm (*jus cogens*)"].

[16] *Reparation for Injuries Suffered in the Service of the United Nations* (Advisory Opinion) [1949] ICJ Rep 174, 185; *Reservations to the Convention on Genocide* (Advisory Opinion) [1951] ICJ Rep 15, 22–25, 29.

[17] Jean d'Aspremont, 'The International Court of Justice as the Master of the Sources' in *The Cambridge Companion to the International Court of Justice* (CUP 2021) 1; Sir Franklin Berman, 'The International Court of Justice as an 'Agent' of Legal Development?' in Christian Tams and James Sloan (eds), *The Development of International Law by the International Court of Justice* (OUP 2014) 7–21; *Barcelona Traction* (n. 2) 32 [33].

[18] Gleider Hernández, *The International Court of Justice and the Judicial Function* (OUP 2014) 90.

[19] Shany and Giladi (n. 12) 168.

This developing function, while not formally prescribed, is inevitable for two reasons. First, many judgments will be applicable to the wider network of states. This is obvious in advisory opinions often stemming from requests by the UN General Assembly. But even in contentious disputes, matters under consideration will likely be relevant to other prospective future state litigants. The Court's interpretation of multilateral treaties in bilateral disputes will impact all state parties to those treaties.[20] Moreover, both the Court and its predecessor have, at times, addressed or issued instructions to other states in their judgments on contentious disputes.[21]

Second, the gap created in the infrastructure of the international legal order positions the Court as a (reluctant) legislator. In the absence of a 'world government' or 'world parliament' producing binding law, and given the slow establishment of custom and of widely accepted multilateral treaties capable of developing international law, the World Court is looked at to perform somewhat of a legislative function.[22] These two circumstances contribute to the Court's incidental development of international law.

To conclude, to legislate outright and to demonstrate undue zeal and provide an authoritative narrative on broader issues may weaken the Court, as opposed to strengthen it, by causing states to take their distance if they perceive that the Court is taking excessive liberties within its assigned duties.[23] However, this is not what has been proposed in Part II, where, in numerous instances, state litigants have sought to draw the Court's attention to the relevance of their populations. Accommodating such concerns would involve an adjustment in the roles of stability and formalism within the judicial function. Additionally, while the Court does not have a formal law-making function, it develops international law nonetheless through its interpretations and clarifications and should not hesitate to do so when clarification is sought by state litigants on matters relating to the affected individuals in such disputes.

[20] E.g., *Application of the Convention on the Prevention and Punishment of the Crime of Genocide (Bosnia and Herzegovina v. Serbia and Montenegro)* (Judgment) [2007] ICJ Rep 43, 120 [183].

[21] E.g., *Corfu Channel (United Kingdom v. Albania)* (Merits) (Judgment) [1949] ICJ Rep 15, 28; *PS.S. "Wimbledon"* (Judgment) [1923] PCIJ Series A 22; *Case Relating to the Territorial Jurisdiction of the International Commission of the River Oder* (Judgment) [1929] PCIJ Series A 27.

[22] Alan E. Boyle and Christine Chinkin, *The Making of International Law* (OUP 2007) 116.

[23] Herch Lauterpacht, *The Development of International Law by the International Court* (CUP 1982) 75; Judge Joan Donoghue, 'The Role of International Courts in Global Governance' (Conference at the Graduate Institute of International and Development Studies, 8 October 2018) https://youtu.be/De4unNaIOjs (at 24:00 minutes).

11

Final Thoughts

> If parties turn to the ICJ, they cannot expect that special attention will be paid to the requirements of 'justice'.[1]

This study synthesised the broad scope of contexts in which individuals interact with the International Court of Justice (ICJ, the Court). Its approach was binary, exploring this relationship in terms of the Court's procedural mechanisms, on the one hand, and its legal reasoning and decision-making, on the other hand.

First, this study sought to assess the extent to which individuals are integrated in the procedural law of the Court (Part I). Looking beyond disputes on the violation of a multilateral human rights treaty or customary human rights obligations, it identified thematic areas where individuals are still at the heart of the dispute: diplomatic protection, advisory proceedings, and those reviewing the decisions of certain administrative tribunals. Rather than examining how the Court has developed the law in such disputes, it noted the ways in which individuals are starkly absent from proceedings, analysing the underlying reasons for this and exploring how they could be further integrated.

Second, the study explored the extent to which individuals are considered in decisions of the Court (Part II). It again looked beyond disputes on the violation of a multilateral human rights treaty or customary human rights obligations, where individuals are inherently considered. Instead, it turned to areas greatly dealt with by the Court where certain human dimensions may potentially be overlooked as they are not the principal focus of the dispute. It therefore focused on territorial, maritime, or environmental disputes, as well as disputes around treaty interpretation or custom identification. It was observed that states parties

[1] David D. Caron and Christian Tomuschat, 'Article 2(3) UN Charter' in Andreas Zimmermann et al (eds), *The Statute of the International Court of Justice: A Commentary* (3rd edn, OUP 2019) 133.

often raise concerns to the Court about the relevance of their populations. It was therefore discussed why, despite this, the Court does not factor in such considerations in its decision-making.

The conclusions reached may come as no surprise to *connaisseurs* of the Court: individuals are both integrated in the procedural law of the Court and considered in its decisions to a minor extent. While granting legal standing to individuals was considered during the establishment of the Court's predecessor, it was denied for fear of threatening state sovereignty (Chapter 1). This, however, did not lessen the types of disputes that would arrive at the Court's docket with a clear connection to one or several individuals. Diplomatic protection proceedings, for example, were the historical avenue enabling the protection of injured individuals (Chapter 2). Yet, the fiction characterising this practice would result in the absence of the individual in proceedings, despite his or her centrality to the dispute. A similar lack of initiative can be noted in advisory proceedings, where questions of interest to communities of individuals are often posed to the Court (Chapter 3). Despite the procedural avenues being available to the Court, I have argued that they have not been exercised by the latter. Conversely, it made attempts in advisory proceedings reviewing the decisions of certain administrative tribunals (Chapter 4), adjusting its procedural mechanisms to satisfy the principle of the equality of the parties. Yet, it was unable to go so far as to allow individuals to stand as equal parties to international organisations, or to use procedural discretion in other ways to more convincingly equalise the parties. This contributed to the relevant administrative tribunals removing their jurisdiction from the Court.

The conclusion is no different when examining how the Court considers individuals in its decisions (Part II). While state parties have brought arguments forward that coastal fishing populations should be factored in to determine if tacit agreements existed between parties on a maritime boundary, as a relevant circumstance in maritime boundary delimitation or as historic fishing rights, the Court has perceived such arguments as 'non-legal' and has prioritised the stability of boundaries (Chapter 6). The threshold for individuals to be considered as a relevant circumstance is exceptionally high and has only been met in one instance. In territorial disputes, the Court has only considered individuals' behaviour as evidence of the Court's sovereignty as opposed to a reflection of their own desires (Chapter 7). In both instances, equity, which would allow for the greater consideration of individuals, is an afterthought as opposed to an element of the legal reasoning.

In environmental disputes, opportunities to strengthen the nexus between human rights and environmental matters have also been missed, despite promising disputes being raised by states, direct questions being asked about the relevance of local populations, and relevant principles being invoked (Chapter 8). Only in the realm of the interpretation of treaties and the identification of customary law have initiatives been uniquely taken by the Court to recognise individuals' rights (Chapter 9).

What these procedural and substantive instances examined in this book show is that the relationship between the individual and the ICJ is not a distant or improbable subject of inquiry. On the contrary, each chapter has demonstrated the clear relevance of individuals in the matters under examination. Each chapter has also illustrated the attempts made by individuals, state litigants, or both for greater inclusion of individuals both in law and practice. Such attempts remain evident in new cases filed and requests for advisory opinions at the time of writing.

The natural question that arises is why such attempts have remained largely unfulfilled. Why have efforts to integrate individuals procedurally and substantively been so unsuccessful? This study has identified and analysed the specific reasons behind the reluctance of both the Court and state litigants.

This overall reticent approach can be rooted in the historical decision to limit *locus standi* before the Court to states. Indeed, the absence of the individual's *locus standi* has fostered a state-centred culture and mindset at the Peace Palace where emphasis is placed on states' interests, both procedurally and in legal reasoning. It has also meant that they have limited opportunities to express their views and that consideration for them in judgments will be at the goodwill of both state litigants and the Court. Procedural and substantive law are difficult to separate and 'react upon each other' in every legal system[2] and, to an extent, explains why the findings of this study have been largely analogous whether discussing the individual in the law or the practice of the ICJ.

This reluctance manifests itself in a multitude of ways explored in this book – including how the Court occasionally perceives disputes where individuals are in focus. Rosenne refers to the *Application of the Convention of 1902 Governing the Guardianship of Infants (Netherlands v. Sweden)*, where the Netherlands sued Sweden for allegedly violating the 1902 Convention on the guardianship of infants by placing a Dutch

[2] Clarence Wilfred Jenks, *The Prospects of International Adjudication* (Stevens 1964) 184.

child living in Sweden under a Swedish regime of protecting upbringing.[3] He explains that the case was originally entitled *Case concerning the Guardianship of an Infant* in the Court's General List, which emphasised the human being in the matter as opposed to implying that the case was a matter of 'abstract treaty interpretation'.[4]

A similar observation can be made in *Jurisdictional Immunities of the State (Germany v. Italy: Greece intervening)*. Leading up to this case, Italian courts had entertained civil claims brought against Germany by victims of Nazi crimes seeking reparation. Germany seized the Court claiming that Italy had failed to respect its jurisdictional immunity. The Court sided with Germany, after assessing whether immunity was applicable to acts committed by the armed forces of a state in the course of conducting an armed conflict.[5] Judge Yusuf criticised that the real-life situation of the Nazis demanded an examination not of this question but of whether the refusal of Italian courts to grant jurisdictional immunity to Germany constituted an internationally wrongful act.[6] The emphasis was therefore on the link between the denial of immunity by the Italian courts, on the one hand, and the lack of reparations, on the other hand.[7] In his view, the Court's focus was 'too abstract and formalistic' and best left 'for academic papers and scholarly discussions'.[8] This might, in part, be influenced by the Court's isolated character, as described by Philip Allott.[9]

Therefore, while much has been done and can be celebrated at the Court in both its jurisprudence and procedure, the main hindrance to any strengthening of the relationship between the individual and the Court lies in the willingness and creativity of state litigants and of the Court to navigate the contours crafted by Article 34(1) of the latter's Statute both in law and in practice.

I have argued that this can be done. In law, both state litigants and the Court have the power to summon witnesses, and state litigants may also

[3] *Case concerning the Application of the Convention of 1902 Governing the Guardianship of Infants (Netherlands v. Sweden)* (Judgment) [1958] ICJ Rep 55, 63.

[4] Shabtai Rosenne, 'Reflections on the Position of the Individual in Inter-state Litigation in the International Court of Justice' in Pieter Sanders (ed), *International Arbitration Liber Amicorum for Martin Domke* (Springer 1967) 240–51, 114.

[5] *Jurisdictional Immunities of the State (Germany v. Italy: Greece intervening)* (Judgment) [2012] ICJ Rep 99, 61.

[6] Ibid 291 [5] (Separate opinion of Judge Yusuf).

[7] Ibid [9].

[8] Ibid [7].

[9] Philip Allott, *Eunomia: New Order for a New World* (OUP 1990) 240.

give relevant individuals a platform as a part of their delegations during oral proceedings. In practice, I have argued that while the Court may not be able to go beyond state litigants' requests, it could make more of an effort to respond to such concerns when raised by states. I have challenged the Court's concerns for stability by arguing that its perception of this concept can be more accommodating. I have argued that its concerns for formalism might harm its legitimacy more than uphold it.

This stems from a social idealist approach to international law, which pleads for a greater balance between states and individuals, and places more emphasis on the role of the individual in the international legal order. Through this lens, it is argued that the Court's effectiveness and legitimacy are compromised through its current approach. The Court's effectiveness – the measurement of the degree to which a court accomplishes its specific objective aim – depends on its ability to adopt an all-encompassing approach to ensuring peace. It also depends on its ability to incorporate the UN Charter's people-focused preamble into this approach, as the principal judicial organ of the UN. Finally, it must confer legitimacy to the UN as a judicial custodian. This legitimacy stems from the fairness of its process and the just quality of its decisions. From a social idealist approach, both are at stake when examining the Court's relationship with individuals.

Admittedly, any assessment of legitimacy is a slippery slope and frustratingly intangible.[10] The same holds true for effectiveness and for yardsticks such as justice, fairness, and democracy. Such assessments are therefore inevitably subjective, especially when informed by an international legal theory. The delicate tensions between the state and the individual, stability and development of international law, law and justice, *lex lata* and *lex ferenda*, apology and utopia, and the role that the Court plays amidst them all, has shadowed me throughout the writing of this study and will, in all probability, remain a part of my thinking beyond,[11] for it is certainly not enough to only understand the functioning of the World Court in these respects. Rather, we must commit ourselves to understanding these debates in the wider context of international law. The scholarly efforts of this study have been put forth in this spirit.

[10] Brian McGarry and Yusra Suedi, 'Judicial Reasoning and Non-state Participation before Inter-state Courts and Tribunals' (2022) 21(1) *The Law & Practice of International Courts and Tribunals* 123, 142.

[11] Martti Koskenniemi, *From Apology to Utopia: The Structure of International Legal Argument* (CUP 2006).

BIBLIOGRAPHY

Primary Legal Sources

United Nations Documents

General Assembly Resolutions

United Nations General Assembly, 'Declaration on Principles of International Law concerning Friendly Relations and Cooperation among States in Accordance with the Charter of the United Nations', A/RES/2625(XXV) (24 October 1970)

'Establishment of a United Nations Administrative Tribunal', A/RES/351(IV)A (24 November 1949)

'The Human Right to a Clean, Healthy and Sustainable Environment', A/HRC/RES/48/13 (18 October 2021)

'The Human Right to a Clean, Healthy and Sustainable Environment', A/76/L.75 (26 July 2022)

'Need for Greater Use by the United Nations and Its Organs of the International Court of Justice', A/RES/171(II)A-C (14 November 1947)

'Procedure for Review of United Nations Administrative Tribunal Judgments: Amendments to the Statute of the Administrative Tribunal', A/RES/957(X) (8 November 1955)

'Request for an Advisory Opinion of the International Court of Justice on the Obligations of States in Respect of Climate Change', A/RES/77/276 (4 April 2023)

'Review of the Procedure Provided for under Article 11 of the Statute of the Administrative Tribunal of the United Nations', A/RES/50/54 (29 January 1996)

'Rio Declaration on Environment and Development', A/CONF.151/26 (12 August 1992)

'Status of Palestine in the United Nations', A/RES/67/19 (4 December 2012)

'Universal Declaration of Human Rights', A/RES/217(III) (10 December 1948)

International Law Commission Documents

Draft Articles on Diplomatic Protection, *Official Records of the General Assembly (2006)*, Sixty-First Session, Supplement No. 10 (A/61/10)

Draft Articles on Diplomatic Protection with Commentaries [2006] *Yearbook of the ILC*, vol II, Part Two

Draft Articles on the Law of Treaties with Commentaries [1966] *Yearbook of the ILC*, vol II

Draft Articles on the Responsibility of International Organizations [2011] *Yearbook of the ILC*, vol II, Part Two

Draft Articles on the Responsibility of States for Internationally Wrongful Acts with Commentaries [2001] *Yearbook of the ILC*, vol II, Part Two

Draft Conclusions on Identification of Customary International Law [2018] *Yearbook of the ILC*, vol II, Part Two

First Report on Diplomatic Protection, by Mr. John R. Dugard, Special Rapporteur, A/CN.4/506 and Add. 1 (7 March and 20 April 2000)

Guiding Principles Applicable to Unilateral Declarations of States Capable of Creating Legal Obligations with Commentaries [2006] *Yearbook of the ILC*, vol II, Part Two

Preliminary Report on Diplomatic Protection, by Mr. Mohamed Bennouna, Special Rapporteur, A/CN.4/484 (4 February 1998)

Report of the International Law Commission on the Work of Its Fifty-Second Session, A/55/10 (1 May–9 June and 10 July–18 August 2000)

Report of the International Law Commission on the Work of Its Sixty-Eighth Session, A/71/10 (2 May–10 June and 4 July–12 August 2016)

United Nations Specialised Agencies Documents

FAO, 'Guidelines for the Routine Collection of Capture Fishery Data' in FAO Fisheries Technical Paper No. 382 Prepared at the FAO/DANIDA Expert Consultation (Bangkok 1998) (FAO, Rome 1999)

ILO, Constitution of the International Labour Organisation (ILO) (1 April 1919)

Decision on the Ninth Item on the Agenda: Matters Relating to the Administrative Tribunal of the ILO Workload and Effectiveness of the Tribunal, GB.325/PFA/9/1(Rev.) (4 November 2015)

Decision on the Twelfth Item on the Agenda: Matters Relating to the Administrative Tribunal of the ILO Proposed Amendments to the Statute of the Tribunal, GB.326/PFA/12/1 (16 March 2016)

Minutes of the 326th Session of the Governing Body of the International Labour Office, GB.326/PV (10–24 March 2016)

Resolution Adopted by the Governing Body at Its 349th (Special) Session (International Labour Conference, 10 November 2023)

Resolution concerning the Statute of the Administrative Tribunal of the International Labour Organisation (International Labour Conference, 7 June 2016)

Reports and Minutes

United Nations Conference on International Organization, Proposed Draft of Article 34 Submitted by the Delegation of Venezuela, UNX.341.13 U51 Vol III (5 June 1945)

United Nations Dumbarton Oaks Proposals for a General International Organisation: To Be the Subject of the United Nations Conference at San Francisco (1945) 66 *Conference Series* Chapter VIII, Section A, [6]

United Nations Economic and Social Council, Commission on Human Rights Drafting Committee, 'Australia: Draft Proposals for an International Court of Human Rights', E/CN.4/AC.1/27 (10 May 1948)

United Nations General Assembly, 'Request for an Advisory Opinion of the International Court of Justice on the Obligations of States in Respect of Climate Change', A/77/PV.64 (29 March 2023)

United Nations Secretary-General, Complaints from Former Officials of the Governing Commission of the Saar Territory, Report by the Secretary-General, Doc. C.391.1939.V (12 December 1939)

Feasibility of Establishing a Single Administrative Tribunal: Report/by the Secretary-General, A/C.5/34/31 (9 November 1979)

Memorandum Submitted by the Secretary-General, UN Doc. A/AC.78/L.10 (13 April 1955)

Memorandum Transmitted by the Secretary-General to the Special Committee on Review of Administrative Tribunal Judgments, A/2909 (10 June 1955)

United Nations Sixth Committee, Summary Record of the 36th Meeting, A/C.6/48/SR.36 (23 November 1993)

United Nations Report of the Special Committee on Review of Administrative Tribunal Judgments, A/C.5/L.635 (17 October 1955)

United Nations Report on the Review of the Procedure Provided for under Article 11 of the Statute of the Administrative Tribunal of the United Nations, Doc. A/C.6/94/2 (17 October 1994)

United Nations Report to the Eighth Ordinary Session of the Assembly of the League on the Work of the Council, on the Work of the Secretariat and on the Measures Taken to Execute the Decisions of the Assembly (1 June 1927)

Other

Institut de droit international, Annuaire de l'Institut de droit international (Session d'Aix-en-Provence, 1954, vol 45(i))

United Nations Conference on the Human Environment, *Stockholm Declaration*, A/Conf.48/14 (16 June 1972)

League of Nations Documents

League of Nations, Covenant of the League of Nations (28 June 1919)

League of Nations Official Journal, vol I (February 1920)

League of Nations Official Journal, vol VII (November–December 1920)
League of Nations Official Journal (July 1923)
League of Nations Official Journal, vol X (1929)

International Court of Justice Documents

Correspondence: Letter from Eduardo Valencia-Ospina (then-Registrar) to Mr. Barry L. Levy (28 March 1994)

International Court of Justice, Practice Directions (31 October 2001, last amended 23 October 2023)

International Court of Justice, Rules of Court (14 April 1978)

The International Court of Justice: Handbook (6th edn, 2018)

Registry of the International Court of Justice and UNITAR, 'A Dialogue at the Court: Proceedings of the ICJ/UNITAR Colloquium Held on the Occasion of the Sixtieth Anniversary of the International Court of Justice' (2006) Registry of the Court and UNITAR(063)/I16/2006

Permanent Court of International Justice Documents

PCIJ Advisory Committee of Jurists, *Procès-verbaux of the Proceedings of the Committee* (16 June–24 July 1920)

United Nations, 'Report of the Informal Inter-Allied Committee on the Future of the Permanent Court of International Justice' (1945) 39 (1) Supplement: Official Documents *The American Journal of International Law* 1

Other Courts and Tribunals Documents

European Court of Human Rights, *Analysis of Statistics 2022* (Council of Europe, January 2023)

European Court of Human Rights, *Annual Report 2022* (Council of Europe, 2023)

ICSID Arbitration Rules (1 July 2022)

Inter-American Court of Human Rights, *Rules of Procedure* (16–28 November 2009)

International Criminal Court, *Rules of Procedure and Evidence* (2013)

International Treaties

Agreement between the Republic of Cameroon and the Federal Republic of Nigeria concerning the Modalities of Withdrawal and Transfer of Authority in the Bakassi Peninsula (Greentree Agreement) (12 June 2006)

American Convention on Human Rights, 1144 UNTS 123 (22 November 1969)

Charter of the United Nations, 1 UNTS XVI (24 October 1945)

European Convention on Human Rights, 213 UNTS 221 (4 November 1950)

International Air Services Transit Agreement, 84 UNTS 389 (7 December 1944)

International Air Transport Agreement 390 UNTS 1951 (7 December 1944)
International Centre for Settlement of Investment Disputes Convention 575 UNTS 159 (18 March 1965)
International Civil Aviation Convention, 15 UNTS 295 (7 December 1944)
International Covenant on Civil and Political Rights, 999 UNTS 171 (16 December 1966)
International Convention for the Regulation of Whaling, 161 UNTS 72 (2 December 1946)
Montevideo Convention on the Rights and Duties of States, 165 LNTS 19 (26 December 1934)
Optional Protocol I, International Covenant on Civil and Political Rights, 999 UNTS 171 (19 December 1966)
Paris Agreement to the United Nations Framework Convention on Climate Change, 3156 UNTS 79 (12 December 2015)
Protocol 14 to the European Convention for the Protection of Human Rights and Fundamental Freedoms Amending the Control System of the Convention, CETS 194 (13 May 2004)
Statute of the Administrative Tribunal of the International Labour Organisation (9 October 1946)
Statute of the International Court of Justice 33 UNTS 993 (18 April 1946)
Statute of the International Tribunal for the Law of the Sea, 1833 UNTS 561 (10 December 1982)
Statute of the Permanent Court of International Justice (16 December 1920)
Treaty of Versailles, UKTS 4 (28 June 1919)
Vienna Convention on Consular Relations and Optional Protocols, 596 UNTS 487 (24 April 1963)
Vienna Convention on the Law of Treaties, 1155 UNTS 331 (23 May 1969)
Vienna Convention on Succession of States in Respect of Treaties, 1946 UNTS 3 (23 August 1978)
United Nations Convention on the Law of the Sea, 1833 UNTS 3 (10 December 1982)
United Nations Framework Convention on Climate Change, 1771 UNTS 107 (9 May 1992)

Secondary Legal Sources

Books

Allott, Philip, *Eunomia: New Order for a New World* (OUP 1990)
The Health of Nations: Society and Law beyond the State (CUP 2002)
Amerasinghe, Chittharanjan Felix, *Diplomatic Protection* (OUP 2008)
Local Remedies in International Law (2nd edn, CUP 2004)

Anzilotti, Dionisio, *Cours de droit international* (LGDJ 1999)

Atapattu, Sumudu, *Emerging Principles of International Environmental Law* (Brill 2007)

Bagley, Tennent Harrington, *General Principles and Problems in the International Protection of Minorities: A Political Study* (Georg 1950)

Bendel, Justine, *Litigating the Environment: Process and Procedure before International Courts and Tribunals* (Edward Elgar Publishing 2023)

Bendel, Justine and Suedi, Yusra, *Public Interest Litigation in International Law* (Routledge 2023)

Ben Mansour, Affef, *La mise en oeuvre des arrêts et sentences des juridictions internationales* (Larcier 2011)

Bianchi, Andrea, *International Law Theories: An Inquiry into Different Ways of Thinking* (OUP 2016)

Birnie, Patricia W. and Boyle, Alan E., *International Law and the Environment* (2nd edn, OUP 2002)

Birnie, Patricia W., Boyle, Alan E. and Redgwell, Catherine, *International Law and the Environment* (4th edn, OUP 2021)

Bjørge, Eirik, *The Evolutionary Interpretation of Treaties* (OUP 2014)

Borchard, Edwin Montefiore, *The Diplomatic Protection of Citizens Abroad or the Law of International Claims* (The Banks Law Publishing Co. 1915)

Boyle, Alan E. and Anderson, Michael R. (eds), *Human Rights Approaches to Environmental Protection* (OUP 1996)

Boyle, Alan E. and Chinkin, Christine, *The Making of International Law* (OUP 2007)

Brown, Chester, *A Common Law of International Adjudication* (OUP 2007)

Brownlie, Ian, *Principles of Public International Law* (7th edn, OUP 2008)

Cançado Trindade, Antônio, *The Access of Individuals to International Justice* (OUP 2011)

The Application of the Rule of Exhaustion of Local Remedies in International Law: Its Rationale in the International Protection of Individual Right (CUP 1983)

Colette, Jean, *Les principes de droit des gens dans la jurisprudence de la Cour Permanente de Justice Internationale* (Berger-Levrault 1932)

Cottier, Thomas, *Equitable Principles of Maritime Boundary Delimitation: The Quest for Distributive Justice in International Law* (CUP 2015)

Craik, Neil, *The International Law of Environmental Impact Assessment: Process, Substance and Integration* (CUP 2008)

D'Aspremont, Jean, *Formalism and the Sources of International Law: A Theory of the Ascertainment of Legal Rules* (OUP 2011)

De la Colina, Maria, *Judicial Discretion in International Law through the Recourse to Equity by the International Court of Justice* (Graduate Institute of International and Development Studies 2012)

De Vattel, Emmerich, *The Law of Nations: Or, Principles of the Law of Nature, Applied to the Conduct and Affairs of Nations and Sovereigns* (CUP 2011)

De Visscher, Charles, *Problèmes de confins en droit international public* (Pedone 1969)

Crawford, James, *State Responsibility: The General Part* (CUP 2013)

Dupuy, Pierre-Marieand and Viñuales, Jorge E., *International Environmental Law* (2nd edn, CUP 2018)

Evans, Malcolm, *Religious Liberty and International Law in Europe* (CUP 1997)

Fietta, Stephen and Cleverly, Robin, *A Practitioner's Guide to Maritime Boundary Delimitation* (OUP 2016)

Fitzmaurice, Gerald, *The Law and Procedure of the International Court of Justice* (Grotius Publications 1986)

Franck, Thomas M., *Fairness in International Law and Institutions* (Clarendon Press 1998)

Giraudeau, Géraldine, *Les différends territoriaux devant le juge international: Entre droit et transaction* (Martinus Nijhoff Publishers 2013)

Gormley, W. Paul, *The Procedural Status of the Individual before International and Supranational Tribunals* (Springer 1966)

Hernández, Gleider, *The International Court of Justice and the Judicial Function* (OUP 2014)

Hudson, Manley, *The Permanent Court of International Justice, 1920–1942: A Treatise* (The Macmillan Company 1943)

Jagota, S. P., *Maritime Boundary*, vol 9 (Martinus Nijhoff Publishers 1985)

Jenks, Clarence Wilfred, *The Common Law of Mankind* (Praeger 1958)

A New World of Law? (Longmans, Green and Company 1969)

The Prospects of International Adjudication (Stevens 1964)

Jennings, Robert and Kohen, Marcelo Gustavo, *The Acquisition of Territory in International Law with a New Introduction by Marcelo G. Kohen* (MUP 2017)

Johnston, Douglas M., *Canada and the New International Law of the Sea*, vol 54 (University of Toronto Press 1985)

Kaikobad, Kaiyan Homi, *The International Court of Justice and Judicial Review: A Study of the Court's Powers with Respect to Judgments of the ILO and UN Administrative Tribunals* (Kluwer Law International 2000)

Karaman, Igor V., *Dispute Resolution in the Law of the Sea*, vol 72 (Martinus Nijhoff Publishers 2012)

Kjeldgaard-Pedersen, Astrid, *The International Legal Personality of the Individual* (OUP 2018)

Kolb, Robert, *Case Law on Equitable Maritime Delimitation: Digest and Commentaries/Jurisprudence sur les délimitations karitimes selon l'équité: Répertoire et commentaries*, vol 38 (Martinus Nijhoff Publishers 2003)

Kotuby, Charles and Sobota, Luke, *General Principles of Law and International Due Process: Principles and Norms Applicable in Transnational Disputes* (OUP 2017)

Lando, Massimo, *Maritime Delimitation as a Judicial Process* (CUP 2019)

Lauterpacht, Elihu, *Aspects of the Administration of International Justice, Hersch Lauterpacht* (Grotius Publications 1991)

Lauterpacht, Hersch, *The Development of International Law by the International Court* (CUP 1982)

The Development of International Law by the Permanent Court of International Justice (Longmans, Green and Company 1934)

Miller, David Hunter, *The Drafting of the Covenant* (W.S. Hein 2002)

Miyoshi, Masahiro, *Considerations of Equity in the Settlement of Territorial and Boundary Disputes*, vol 2 (Martinus Nijhoff Publishers 1993)

Motta, Giuseppe, *Less than Nations: Central-Eastern European Minorities after WWI* (Cambridge Scholars Publishing 2013)

Oppenheim, Lassa Francis Lawrence, *International Law: A Treatise* (3rd edn, Longmans, Green and Company 1920)

Orakhelashvili, Alexander, *The Interpretation of Acts and Rules in Public International Law* (OUP 2008)

Paine, Joshua, *The Functions of International Adjudication and International Environmental Litigation* (CUP 2024)

Palaco Caballero, Flor de Maria, *La cour internationale de Justice et la protection de l'individu* (Schulthess 2015)

Parlett, Kate, *The Individual in the International Legal System: Continuity and Change in International Law* (CUP 2011)

Peck, Connie and Lee, Roy (eds), *Increasing the Effectiveness of the International Court of Justice: Proceedings of the ICJ/UNITAR Colloquium to Celebrate the 50th Anniversary of the Court*, vol 29 (Kluwer Law International 1997)

Petrochilos, Georgios, *Procedural Law in International Arbitration* (OUP 2004)

Pomerance, Michla, *The Advisory Function of the International Court in the League and U.N. Eras* (Johns Hopkins University Press 1973)

Portmann, Roland, *Legal Personality in International Law* (CUP 2010)

Pound, Roscoe, *Interpretations of Legal History* (CUP 1923)

Quintana Aranguren, Juan José, *Litigation at the International Court of Justice: Practice and Procedure* (Brill/Nijhoff 2015)

Quoc Dinh, Nguyen et al, *Droit International Public* (6th edn, LGDJ 1999)

Remec, Peter Pavel, *The Position of the Individual in International Law according to Grotius and Vattel* (Springer 1960)

Riddell, Anna and Plant, Brendan, *Evidence before the International Court of Justice* (British Institute of International and Comparative Law 2009)

Rosenne, Shabtai, *The Law and Practice of the International Court, 1920–1996*, vol 3 (3rd edn, Brill/Nijhoff 1997)

Rossi, Ingrid, *Legal Status of Non-Governmental Organizations in International Law* (Intersentia 2010)

Salomon, André, *Le préambule de la Charte: Base idéologique de l'ONU* (des Trois Collines 1947)

Sands, Philippe, *The Last Colony: A Tale of Exile, Justice and Britain's Colonial Legacy* (Weidenfeld & Nicolson 2022)

Sands, Philippe et al, *Principles of International Environmental Law* (4th edn, CUP 2018)

Schramm, Bérénice Kafui, *La fiction juridique et le juge: Contribution à une autre herméneutique de la Cour internationale de justice* (Bruylant 2018)

Shany, Yuval, *Assessing the Effectiveness of International Courts* (OUP 2014)

Shaw, Malcolm, *International Law* (9th edn, CUP 2021)

Rosenne's Law and Practice of the International Court: 1920–2015, vol 3 (5th edn, Brill/Nijhoff 2016)

Simma, Bruno et al. (eds), The Charter of the United Nations: A Commentary (3rd edn, OUP 2012)

Sobenes, Edgardo et al. (eds), *The Environment through the Lens of International Courts and Tribunals* (Springer 2023)

Spiermann, Ole, *International Legal Argument in the Permanent Court of International Justice: The Rise of the International Judiciary* (CUP 2005)

Talmon, Stefan and Jia, Bing Bing (eds), *The South China Sea Arbitration: A Chinese Perspective* (Hart Publishing 2014)

Thirlway, Hugh, *The International Court of Justice* (OUP 2016)

Tiburcio, Carmen, *The Human Rights of Aliens under International and Comparative Law* (Brill/Nijhoff 2001)

Titi, Catherine, *The Function of Equity in International Law* (OUP 2021)

Wallace, Jonathan, *Webster's New World Law Dictionary* (Wild, Susan Ellis ed, Wiley Hoboken 2006).

Witenberg, Joseph Charles and Desrioux, Jacques, *L'organisation judiciaire, la procédure et la sentence internationales: Traité pratique* (Pedone 1937)

Zimmermann, Andreas et al (eds), *The Statute of the International Court of Justice: A Commentary* (3rd edn, OUP 2019)

Book Chapters

Aznar, Mariano, 'The Human Factor in Territorial Disputes' in Kohen, Marcelo and Hébié, Mamadou (eds), *Research Handbook on Territorial Disputes in International Law* (Edward Elgar Publishing 2018)

Benzing, Markus, 'Evidentiary Issues' in Zimmermann, Andreas et al (eds), *The Statute of the International Court of Justice: A Commentary* (3rd edn, OUP 2019)

Berman, Sir Franklin, 'The International Court of Justice as an "Agent" of Legal Development?' in Tams, Christian and Sloan, James (eds), *The Development of International Law by the International Court of Justice* (OUP 2014)

Bjørge, Eirik, 'The Means of Interpretation Admissible for the Establishment of the Intention of the Parties' in Bjørge, Eirik (ed), *The Evolutionary Interpretation of Treaties* (OUP 2014)

Bodansky, Daniel, 'The Concept of Legitimacy in International Law' in Wolfrum, R. and Röben, V. (eds), *Legitimacy in International Law* (Springer-Verlag 2008)

'International Environmental Law' in Carlos Espósito and Kate Parlett (eds), *The Cambridge Companion to the International Court of Justice* (CUP 2023)

'Legitimacy in International Law and International Relations' in Dunoff, J. L. and Pollack, M. A. (eds), *Interdisciplinary Perspectives on International Law and International Relations: The State of the Art* (CUP 2013)

Boisson de Chazournes, Laurence, 'New Technologies, the Precautionary Principle and Public Participation' in Murphy, Thérèse (ed), *New Technologies and Human Rights* (OUP 2009)

Boisson De Chazournes, Laurence and Mbengue, Makane Moïse, 'Gabčíkovo-Nagymaros Project (Hungary/Slovakia) (1997)' in Bjørge, Eirik and Miles, Cameron A. (eds), *Landmark Cases in Public International Law* (Hart Publishing 2017)

Brölmann, Catherine, 'The PCIJ and International Rights of Groups and Individuals' in Tams, Christian and Fitzmaurice, Malgosia (eds), *Legacies of the Permanent Court of International Justice* (Martinus Nijhoff Publishers 2013)

Buchanan, Allen, 'The Legitimacy of International Law' in Besson, S. and Tasioulas, J. (eds), *The Philosophy of International Law* (OUP 2010)

Caron, David D. and Tomuschat, Christian, 'Article 2(3) UN Charter' in Zimmermann, Andreas et al (eds), *The Statute of the International Court of Justice: A Commentary* (3rd edn, OUP 2019)

Cohen, Harlan Grant, Follesdal Andreas, Grossman, Nienke and Ulfstein, Geir, "Legitimacy and International Courts – A Framework" in Cohen, Harlan Grant, Follesdal, Andreas, Nienke, Andreas and Ulfstein, Geir (eds), *Legitimacy and International Courts* (CUP 2018)

Condorelli, Luigi, 'Protection diplomatique réussie et réparation due: Une glose' in Dupuy, Pierre-Marieet al (eds), *Unité et diversité du droit international: Écrits en l'honneur du Professeur Pierre-Marie Dupuy* (Nijhoff 2014)

Cot, Jean-Pierre and Wittich, Stephan, 'Article 68' in Zimmermann, Andreas et al (eds), *The Statute of the International Court of Justice: A Commentary* (3rd edn, OUP 2019)

Couvreur, Philippe, 'Notes sur le 'droit' colonial français dans la mise en oeuvre du principe de l'*uti possidetis juris* par la Cour internationale de Justice' in

Kamga, Maurice and Mbengue, Makane Moïse (eds), *Liber amicorum [en l'honneur de] Raymond Ranjeva: l'Afrique et le droit international; variations sur l'organisation internationale* (Pedone 2013)

D'Aspremont, Jean, 'The International Court of Justice as the Master of the Sources' in Carlos Espósito and Kate Parlett (eds), *The Cambridge Companion to the International Court of Justice* (CUP 2023)

Delimatsis, Panagiotis, 'Institutional Transparency in the WTO' in Bianchi, Andrea and Peters, Anne (eds), *Transparency in International Law* (CUP 2013)

De Zayas, Alfred, 'The International Judicial Protection of Peoples and Minorities' in Brölmann, Catherine, Lefeber, René and Zieck, Marjoleine (eds), *Peoples and Minorities in International Law* (Nijhoff 1993)

Dupuy, Pierre-Marie and Hoss, Cristina, 'Article 34' in Zimmermann, Andreas et al (eds), *The Statute of the International Court of Justice: A Commentary* (3rd edn, OUP 2019)

Duruigbo, Eemeka, 'Should Nigeria Have Sought Revision of the Bakassi Decision by the International Court of Justice?' in Egede, Edwin and Igiehon, Mark (eds), *The Bakassi Dispute and the International Court of Justice: Continuing Challenges* (Routledge 2018)

Egede, Hephzibah, 'The ICJ Bakassi Decision: The Rights of the Indigenous Communities and Populations in the Bakassi Peninsula' in Egede, Edwin and Igiehon, Mark (eds), *The Bakassi Dispute and the International Court of Justice: Continuing Challenges* (Routledge 2018)

Gaja, Giorgio, 'Quel préjudice pour un Etat qui exerce la protection diplomatique?' in Alland, Deniset al (eds), *Unité et diversité du droit international: Écrits en l'honneur du Professeur Pierre-Marie Dupuy* (Brill/Nijhoff 2014)

Grossmann, Nienke, 'Julia Sebutinde: An Unbreakable Cloth' in Josephine Jarpa Dawuni and Akua Kuenyehia (eds), *International Courts and the African Woman Judge: Unveiled Narratives* (Routledge 2019)

Hernández, Gleider, 'Non-State Actors from the Perspective of the International Court of Justice' in d'Aspremont, Jean (ed), *Participants in the International Legal System: Multiple Perspectives on Non-State Actors in International Law* (Routledge 2011)

Higgins, Rosalyn, 'Conceptual Thinking about the Individual in International Law' in Higgins, Rosalyn (ed), *Themes and Theories: Selected Essays, Speeches, and Writings in International Law* (OUP 2009)

'The Judicial Determination of Relevant Facts, Speech to the Sixth Committee of the General Assembly, 2 November 2007', in Higgins, Rosalyn (ed), *Themes and Theories: Selected Essays, Speeches, and Writings in International Law* (OUP 2009)

'Remedies and the International Court of Justice' in Higgins, Rosalyn (ed), *Themes and Theories: Selected Essays, Speeches, and Writings in International Law* (OUP 2009)

Janis, Mark, 'Individuals and the International Court' in Muller, David Raic and Thuránszky, J. M. (eds), *The International Court of Justice: Its Future Role After Fifty Years* (Brill 1996)

Karl, Wolfram, 'Article 69' in Zimmermann, Andreas et al (eds), *The Statute of the International Court of Justice: A Commentary* (3rd edn, OUP 2019)

Kato, Nobuyuki, 'The Role of Diplomatic Protection in the Implementation Process of Public Interests' in Komori, Teruo and Wellens, Karel (eds), *Public Interest Rules of International Law: Towards Effective Implementation* (Ashgate 2009)

Kent, Avidan and Trinidad, Jamie, '*Amicus Curiae* Participation in International Proceedings: Forever Friends?' in Kent, Avidan, Skoutaris, Nikos and Trinidad, Jamie (eds), *The Future of International Courts* (Routledge 2019)

Kerbrat, Yann and Maljean-Dubois, Sandrine, 'Les juridictions internationales et le principe de précaution, entre grande prudence et petites audaces' in Denis, Alland et al (eds), *Unité et diversité du droit international: Écrits en l'honneur du Professeur Pierre-Marie Dupuy* (Martinus Brill/Nijhoff 2014)

Kohen, Marcelo, 'La relation titres/effectivités dans la jurisprudence récente de la Cour internationale de Justice (2004–2012)' in Alland, Denis et al (eds), *Unité et diversité du droit international: Écrits en l'honneur du Professeur Pierre-Marie Dupuy* (Martinus Nijhoff Publishers 2014)

'Titles and *effectivités* in Territorial Disputes' in Kohen, Marcelo and Hébié, Mamadou (eds), *Research Handbook on Territorial Disputes in International Law* (Edward Elgar Publishing 2018)

Kohen, Marcelo and Tignino, Mara, 'Do People Have Rights in Boundaries' Delimitations?' in Boisson de Chazournes, Laurence, Leb, Christina and Tignino, Mara (eds), *International Law and Freshwater* (Edward Elgar Publishing 2013)

Koskenniemi, Martti, 'What Is International Law For?' in Evans, Malcolm (ed), *International Law* (5th edn, OUP 2018)

Lauterpacht, Hersch, 'The Subjects of International Law' in Lauterpacht, Elihu (ed), *International Law: Being the Collected Papers of Hersch Lauterpacht* (CUP 1970)

Mackenzie, Ruth, 'The *Amicus Curiae* in International Courts: Towards Common Procedural Approaches?' in Treves, Tullio et al (eds), *Civil Society, International Courts and Compliance Bodies* (TMC Asser Press 2005)

Mbengue, Makane Moïse, 'Delimitation and Demarcation of Borders in Africa: History, Problems and Prospects' in D'Argent, Pierre (ed), *Droit des frontières internationales: = The Law of International Borders Journée franco-allemande* (Pedone 2016)

Nesi, Giuseppe, 'Boundaries' in Kohen, Marcelo and Hébié, Mamadou (eds), *Research Handbook on Territorial Disputes in International Law* (Edward Elgar Publishing 2018)

Neumann, Thore and Simma, Bruno, 'Transparency in International Adjudication' in Bianchi, Andrea and Peters, Anne (eds), *Transparency in International Law* (CUP 2013)

Nollkaemper, André, 'The Court and Its Multiple Constituencies: Three Perspectives on the Kosovo Advisory Opinion' in Milanovic, Marko and Wood, Michael (eds), *The Law and Politics of the Kosovo Advisory Opinion* (OUP 2015)

Nolte, Georg, 'Between Contemporaneous and Evolutive Interpretation: The Use of "Subsequent Practice" in the Judgment of the International Court of Justice concerning the Case of *Costa Rica v. Nicaragua*' in Hestermeyer, Holger et al (eds), *Coexistence, Cooperation and Solidarity* (Brill 2012)

Nolte, Georg, 'Introductory Report of the Study Group on Treaties over Time' in Nolte, Georg (ed), *Treaties and Subsequent Practice* (OUP 2013)

Oellers-Frahm, Karin, 'Chapter XIV: The International Court of Justice, Article 92' in Simma, Bruno et al (eds), *The Charter of the United Nations: A Commentary* (3rd edn, OUP 2012)

Pauwelyn, Joost and Elsig, Manfred, 'The Politics of Treaty Interpretation: Variations and Explanations across International Tribunals' in Dunoff, Jeffrey L. and Pollack, Mark A. (eds), *Interdisciplinary Perspectives on International Law and International Relations: The State of the Art* (CUP 2012)

Pellet, Alain, 'La seconde mort d'Euripide Mavrommatis? Notes sur le projet de la C.D.I sur la protection diplomatique' in Angelet, Nicolas (ed), *Droit du pouvoir, pouvoir du droit: Mélanges offerts à Jean Salmon* (Bruylant 2007)

Petrović, Dražen, 'Wrong Address? Advisory Opinion of the ICJ on the Judgment No. 2867 of the ILOAT upon a Complaint Filed against the International Fund for Agricultural Development' in Wolfrum, Rüdiger, Sersic, Maja and Šošić, Trpimir (eds), *Contemporary Developments in International Law: Essays in Honour of Budislav Vukas* (Brill/Nijhoff 2016)

Rosenfeld, Friedlich, '*Iura Novit Curia* in International Law' in Ferrari, Franco et al (eds), *Iura Novit Curia in International Arbitration* (JurisNet LLC 2018)

Rosenne, Shabtai, 'Reflections on the Position of the Individual in Inter-State Litigation in the International Court of Justice' in Sanders, Pieter (ed), *International Arbitration Liber Amicorum for Martin Domke* (Springer 1967)

Santulli, Carlo, 'Entre protection diplomatique et action directe: la représentation (Éléments épars du statut international des sujets internes)' in Le Sujet en Droit International (Pedone 2005)

Scobbie, Iain, 'The Holiness of the Heart's Affection: Philip Allott's Theory of Social Idealism' in Orakhelashvili, Alexander (ed), *Research Handbook on the Theory and History of International Law* (Edward Elgar Publishing 2011)

'A View of Delft: Some Thoughts about Thinking about International Law' in Evans, Malcolm (ed), *International Law* (5th edn, OUP 2018)

Shany, Yuval and Giladi, Rotem, 'International Court of Justice' in Shany, Yuval, *Assessing the Effectiveness of International Courts* (OUP 2014)

Shaw, Malcolm, 'The International Court of Justice and the Law of Territory' in Tams, Christian and Sloan, James (eds), *The Development of International Law by the International Court of Justice* (1st edn, OUP 2013)

Simma, Bruno, 'Human Rights before the International Court of Justice: Community Interest Coming to Life?' in Tams, Christian and Sloan, James (eds), *The Development of International Law by the International Court of Justice* (1st edn, OUP 2013)

Sivakumaran, Sandesh, 'The International Court of Justice and Human Rights' in Joseph, Sarah and McBeth Adam (eds), *Research Handbook on International Human Rights Law* (Edward Elgar 2010)

Szasz, Paul, 'Enhancing the Advisory Competence of the World Court' in Gross, Leo (ed), *The Future of the International Court of Justice*, vol 2 (Oceana Publications 1976)

Thirlway, Hugh, 'Article 30' in Zimmermann, Andreas et al (eds), *The Statute of the International Court of Justice: A Commentary* (3rd edn, OUP 2019)

Tams, Christian J., 'Article 50' in Andreas, Zimmermann et al (eds), *The Statute of the International Court of Justice: A Commentary* (3rd edn, OUP 2019)

Tho Pesch, Sebastian, 'The Influence of Human Rights on Diplomatic Protection: Reviving an Old Instrument of Public International Law' in Weiss, Norman and Thouvenin, Jean-Marc (eds), *The Influence of Human Rights on International Law* (Springer 2015)

Van Hulle, Inge, 'Imperial Consolidation through Arbitration: Territorial and Boundary Disputes in Africa (1870–1914)' in de la Rasilla, Ignacio and Viñuales, Jorge (eds), *Experiments in International Adjudication: Historical Accounts* (1st edn, CUP 2019)

Articles in Peer-Reviewed Scientific Journals

Abi-Saab, Georges, 'De l'évolution de la Cour internationale: Réflexions sur quelques tendances récentes' (1992) *Revue générale de droit international public* 273

Alston, Philip, 'Against a World Court for Human Rights' (2014) *Ethics & International Affairs* 28(2) 197

Alvarez-Jiménez, Alberto, 'Methods for the Identification of Customary International Law in the International Court of Justice's Jurisprudence: 2000–2009' (2011) *International and Comparative Law Quarterly* 60(3) 681

Bartholomeusz, Lance, 'The *Amicus Curiae* before International Courts and Tribunals' (2005) 5(3) *Non-State Actors and International Law* 209

Batista, Vandick S., Fabré, Nidia N., Malhado, Ana C. M. and Ladle, Richard J., 'Tropical Artisanal Coastal Fisheries: Challenges and Future Directions' (2014) 22(1) *Reviews in Fisheries Science & Aquaculture* 1

Becker, Michael A., 'Pay No Attention to that Man behind the Curtain: The Role of Civil Society and Other Actors in Decisions to Litigate at the International Court of Justice' (2023) 26 *Max Planck Yearbook of United Nations Law Online* 90

Berman, Nathaniel, '"But the Alternative Is Despair": European Nationalism and the Modernist Renewal of International Law, (1993) 106 (8) *Harvard Law Review* 1792

Bodansky, Daniel, 'The Legitimacy of International Governance: A Coming Challenge for International Environmental Law?' (1999) 93(3) *American Journal of International Law* 596

Boisson de Chazournes, Laurence and Angelini, Antonella, '"After The Court Rose": The Rise of Diplomatic Means to Implement the Pronouncements of the International Court of Justice' (2012) 11 *Law and Practice of International Courts and Tribunals* 1

Boisson de Chazournes, Laurence and Mbengue, Makane Moïse, 'The *Amicus Curiae* and the WTO Dispute Settlement System: The Doors Are Open' (2003) 2 *Law and Practice of International Courts and Tribunals* 205

Bordin, Fernando Lusa, 'Procedural Developments at the International Court of Justice' (2021) 20 *The Law and Practice of International Courts and Tribunals* 395

Bowett, D. W., 'The Second United Nations Conference on the Law of the Sea' (1960) 9(3) *International and Comparative Law Quarterly* 415

Boyle, Alan, 'Developments in the International Law of Environmental Impact Assessments and Their Relation to the Espoo Convention: Developments in International Law of EIA' (2011) 20(3) *Review of European Community & International Environmental Law* 227

Brown, Chester, 'The Inherent Powers of International Courts and Tribunals' (2005) 76 *British Yearbook of International Law* 195

Brownlie, Ian, 'The Individual before Tribunals Exercising International Jurisdiction' (1962) 11(3) *International and Comparative Law Quarterly* 701

Cançado Trindade, Antônio, 'Origin and Historical Development of the Rule of Exhaustion of Local Remedies in International Law' (1976) *Revue belge de droit international* 499

Clark, Roger, 'The International League for Human Rights and South West Africa 1947–1957: The Human Rights NGO as Catalyst in the International Legal Process' (1981) 3(4) *Human Rights Quarterly* 101

Crema, Luigi, 'Testing *Amici Curiae* in International Law: Rules and Practice' (2013) 22(1) *The Italian Yearbook of International Law Online* 91

Dawidowicz, Martin, 'The Effect of the Passage of Time on the Interpretation of Treaties: Some Reflections on *Costa Rica v. Nicaragua*' (2011) 24 (1) *Leiden Journal of International Law* 201

Dean, Arthur H., 'The Second Geneva Conference on the Law of the Sea: The Fight for Freedom of the Seas' (1960) 54(4) *The American Journal of International Law* 751

De Brabandere, Eric, 'NGOs and the "'Public Interest": The Legality and Rationale of *Amicus Curiae* Interventions in International Economic and Investment Disputes' (2011) 12(1) *Chicago Journal of International Law* 85

'Individuals in Advisory Proceedings before the International Court of Justice: Equality of the Parties and the Court's Discretionary Authority' (2012) 11(2) *The Law and Practice of International Courts and Tribunals* 253

Donoghue, Joan E., 'The Effectiveness of the International Court of Justice' (2014) 108 *Proceedings of the Annual Meeting (American Society of International Law)* 114

Dutheil de la Rochère, Jacqueline, 'Les procédures de règlement des différends frontaliers' in *Société française du droit international* (Pedone 1980)

Evans, Malcolm D., 'Maritime Delimitation and Expanding Categories of Relevant Circumstances' (1991) 40(1) *The International and Comparative Law Quarterly* 1

Fink, Carole, 'The League of Nations and the Minorities Question' (1995) 157(4) *World Affairs* 197

Fitzmaurice, Gerald 'Hersch Lauterpacht – The Scholar as Judge' (1961) 37 *British Yearbook of International Law* 1

Fontanelli, Filippo and Busco, Paolo, 'The Function of Procedural Justice in International Adjudication' (2016) 15(1) *The Law & Practice of International Courts and Tribunals* 1

French, Duncan, 'Treaty Interpretation and the Incorporation of Extraneous Legal Rules' (2006) *The International and Comparative Law Quarterly* 55 (2), 281

Gaja, Giorgio, 'The Approach of the International Court of Justice to Injuries Suffered by Individuals' (2017) 103(125–30) *Boletim da Sociedade Brasileira de Direito Internacional* 571

'The Position of Individuals in International Law: An ILC Perspective' (2010) 21(1) *European Journal of International Law* 1

Gomula, Joanna, 'The International Court of Justice and Administrative Tribunals of International Organisations' (1991) 13(1) *Michigan Journal of International Law* 83

Gross, Leo, 'Participation of Individuals in Advisory Proceedings before the International Court of Justice: Question of Equality between the Parties' (1958) 52(1) *The American Journal of International Law* 16

Grossman, Nienke, 'Legitimacy and International Adjudicative Bodies' (2009) 41 (1) *George Washington International Law Review* 107

'Territorial and Maritime Dispute (*Nicaragua v. Colombia*)' (2013) 107(2) *The American Journal of International Law* 396

Hambro, Edward and Turlington, Edgar, 'Individuals before International Tribunals' (1941) 35 *Proceedings of the American Society of International Law* 22

Herbert, Glen J., 'Fisheries Relations in the Gulf of Maine Implications of an Arbitrated Maritime Boundary' (1995) 19(4) *Marine Policy* 301

Higgins, Rosalyn, 'Conceptual Thinking about the Individual in International Law' (1978) 4(1) *British Journal of International Studies* 1

'Human Rights in the International Court of Justice' (2007) 20(4) *Leiden Journal of International Law* 745

Hilpold, Peter, 'The League of Nations and the Protection of Minorities – Rediscovering a Great Experiment' (2013) 17 *Max Planck Yearbook of United Nations Law* 87

Humphreys, Stephen, 'Against Future Generations' (2022) 33(4) *European Journal of International Law* 1061

'Equity before "Equity"' (2023) 86(1) *Modern Law Review* 85

Jennings, Robert, 'The International Court of Justice after Fifty Years' (1995) 89(3) *The American Journal of International Law* 493

Jones, Mary Gardiner, 'National Minorities: A Case Study in International Protection' (1949) 14 *Law and Contemporary Problems* 599

Kingsbury, Benedict and Maisley, Nahuel, 'Infrastructures and Laws: Publics and Publicness' (2021) 17(1) *Annual Review of Law and Social Science* 353

Kjeldgaard-Pedersen, Astrid, 'The Influence of the Concept of International Legal Personality in the Drafting of the Statute of the Permanent Court of International Justice' (2014) 16(1) *Journal of the History of International Law* 9

Koessler, Maximilian, 'Government Espousal of Private Claims before International Tribunals' (1946) 13(2) *University of Chicago Law Review* 180

Kolb, Robert, 'Les maximes juridiques en droit international public: questions historiques et théoriques' (1999) 32(2) *Revue belge de droit international* 407

Lando, Massimo, 'Secret Custom *or* The Impact of Judicial Deliberations on the Identification of Customary International Law' (2022) *The Cambridge Law Journal* 81(3) 550

Lauterpacht, Elihu, 'Equity, Evasion, Equivocation and the Evolution in International Law' (1977–78) 33 *Proceedings and Committee Reports of the American Branch of the International Law Association* 33

Lauterpacht, Hersch, 'The Revision of the Statute of the International Court of Justice' (2002) 1(1) *The Law & Practice of International Courts and Tribunals* 55

'The Subjects of the Law of Nations' (1947) 63(4) *Law Quarterly Review* 438

Lelarge, Aurélia, 'L'émergence d'un principe de bonne administration de la justice internationale dans la jurisprudence internationale antérieure à 1945' (2009 27(2) *L'Obsevateur des Nations Unies* 23

Leys, David, 'Diplomatic Protection and Individual Rights: A Complementary Approach' (2016) 54 *Harvard International Law Journal* 2

Marks, Susan, 'State-centrism, International Law, and the Anxieties of Influence' (2006) 19(2) *Leiden European Journal of International Law* 339

Mazower, Mark, 'Minorities and the League of Nations in Interwar Europe' (1997) 126(2) *Daedalus* 47

Mbengue, Makane Moïse, 'Between Law and Science: A Commentary on the Whaling in the Antarctic case' (2015) 2 *Questions of International Law* 178

McCorquodale, Robert, 'An Inclusive International Legal System' (2004) 17(3) *Leiden Journal of International Law* 477

McCorquodale, Robert and Pangalangan, Raul, 'Pushing Back the Limitations of Territorial Boundaries' (2001) 12(5) *European Journal of International Law* 867

McGarry, Brian, 'Obligations *Erga Omnes (Partes)* and the Participation of Third States in Inter-State Litigation' (2023) 22(2) *The Law & Practice of International Courts and Tribunals* 273

McGarry, Brian and Suedi, Yusra, 'Judicial Reasoning and Non-State Participation before Inter-State Courts and Tribunals' (2022) 21(1) *The Law & Practice of International Courts and Tribunals* 123

McIntyre, Owen, 'The Proceduralisation and Growing Maturity of International Water Law: Case concerning Pulp Mills on the River Uruguay (*Argentina v Uruguay*)' (2010) 22(3) *Journal of Environmental Law* 475

Milano, Enrico, 'Diplomatic Protection and Human Rights before the International Court of Justice: Re-Fashioning Tradition?' (2005) 35 (1) *Netherlands Yearbook of International Law* 85

Mutua, Makau, 'Why Redraw the Map of Africa: A Moral and Legal Inquiry' (1995) 16(4) *Michigan Journal of International Law* 1113

Nicholson, Rowan, 'The International Court of Justice as a "Shortcut" to Identifying Custom' (2021) 20(3) *The Law & Practice of International Courts and Tribunals* 490

Nwokolo, Ndubuisi N., 'Peace-Building or Structural Violence? Deconstructing the Aftermath of Nigeria/Cameroon Boundary Demarcation' (2020) 29(1) *African Security Review* 41

Orrego Vicuña, Francisco, 'Changing Approaches to the Nationality of Claims in the Context of Diplomatic Protection and International Dispute Settlement' (2000) 15(2) *ICSID Review – Foreign Investment Law Journal* 340

'Individuals and Non-State Entities before International Courts and Tribunals' (2001) 5(1) *Max Planck Yearbook of United Nations Law Online* 59

Paulus, Andreas, 'Article 66' in Zimmermann, Andreas et al (eds), *The Statute of the International Court of Justice: A Commentary* (3rd edn, OUP 2019)

Pellet, Alain, 'The Second Death of Euripide Mavrommatis? Notes on the International Law Commission's Draft Articles on Diplomatic Protection' (2008) 7(1) *The Law & Practice of International Courts and Tribunals* 33

Pergantis, Vasileios, 'Towards a "Humanization" of Diplomatic Protection?' (2006) 66(2) *Zeitschrift für ausländisches öffentliches Recht und Völkerrecht* 351

Petersen, Niels, 'The International Court of Justice and the Judicial Politics of Identifying Customary International Law' (2017) 28(2) *European Journal of International Law* 357

Punzhin, Sergey M., 'Procedural Normative System of the International Court of Justice' (2017) 30(3) *Leiden Journal of International Law* 661

Reese, Knut, 'The Making of a Case for the International Court of Justice – Icelandic Fishing Rights' (1973) 6(3) *Comparative and International Law Journal of Southern Africa* 394

Reinisch, August and Knahr, Christina, 'From the United Nations Administrative Tribunal to the United Nations Appeal Tribunal – Reform of the Administration of Justice System within the United Nations' (2008) 12(1) *Max Planck Yearbook of United Nations Law* 447

Reisman, Michael, 'Accelerating Advisory Opinions: Critique and Proposal' (1974) 68(4) *The American Journal of International Law* 648

Scheinin, Martin, 'The ICJ and the Individual' (2007) 9(2) *International Community Law Review* 123

Scobbie, Iain, 'Slouching towards the Holy City: Some Weeds for Philip Allott' (2005) 16(2) *European Journal of International Law* 299

Sereni, Angelo Piero, 'Agency in International Law' (1940) 34(4) *The American Journal of International Law* 638

Shany, Yuval, 'Assessing the Effectiveness of International Courts: A Goal-Based Approach' (2012) 106(2) *The American Journal of International Law* 225

Shelton, Dinah, 'The Participation of Nongovernmental Organisations in International Judicial Proceedings' (1994) 88(4) *The American Journal of International Law* 611

Spiegel, Hans W., 'Origin and Development of Denial of Justice' (1938) 32(1) *The American Journal of International Law* 63

Starita, Massimo, 'L'interprétation des traités établissant la frontière' in Société française pour le droit international, *Droit des frontières internationales* (Pedone 2016)

Stone, Julius, 'The Legal Nature of Minorities Petition' (1931) 12 *British Yearbook of International Law* 76

Suedi, Yusra, 'Man, Land and Sea: Local Populations in Territorial and Maritime Disputes before the International Court of Justice' (2021) 20(1) *Law and Practice of International Courts and Tribunals* 30

'Self-Determination in Territorial Disputes before the International Court of Justice: From Rhetoric to Reality?' (2023) 36(1) *Leiden Journal of International Law* 161

Sumner, Brian Taylor, 'Territorial Disputes at the International Court of Justice' (2004) 53(6) *Duke Law Journal* 1779

Talmon, Stefan, 'Determining Customary International Law: The ICJ's Methodology between Induction, Deduction and Assertion' (2015) 26(2) *European Journal of International Law* 417

Tanaka, Yoshifumi, 'Navigational Rights on the San Juan River: A Commentary on the *Costa Rica v. Nicaragua Case*' (2009) 4(3) *Hague Justice Journal* 213

Thirlway, Hugh, 'The International Court of Justice 1989–2009: At the Heart of the Dispute Settlement System?' (2010) 57(3) *Netherlands International Law Review* 347

Tseng, Huan-Sheng and Ou, Ching-Hsiewn, 'The Evolution and Trend of the Traditional Fishing Rights' (2010) 53 *Ocean & Coastal Management* 270

Vázquez, Carlos Manuel, 'Treaty-Based Rights and Remedies of Individuals' (1992) 92 *Columbia Law Review* 1082

Vermeer-Künzli, Annemarieke, 'The Protection of Individuals by Means of Diplomatic Protection: Diplomatic Protection as a Human Rights Instrument' (Leiden University 2007)

Von der Heydte, August, 'L'individu et les tribunaux internationaux' in *Collected Courses of the Hague Academy of International Law*, vol 107 (Brill 1962)

Watts, Sir Arthur, 'Enhancing the Effectiveness of Procedures of International Dispute Settlement' (2001) 5 *Max Planck Yearbook of United Nations Law* 21

Waultrin, René, 'Un conflit de limites maritimes entre la Norvège et la Suède: L'affaire des Grisbådarna' (1910) 17 *Revue générale de droit international public* 77

Woolaver, Hannah and Williams, Sarah, 'The Role of the *Amicus Curiea* before International Criminal Tribunals' (2006) 6(2) *International Criminal Law Review* 151

Yu, Chen, '*Amicus Curiea* Participation in ISDS: A Caution against Political Intervention in Treaty Interpretation' (2020) 35(1–2) *ICSID Review – Foreign Investment Law Journal* 223

Encyclopaedia Entries

Cazala, Julien, 'Good Administration of Justice' in *Max Planck Encyclopedia of Public International Law* (OUP 2019)

Focarelli, Carlo, 'Denial of Justice' in *Max Planck Encyclopedias of Public International Law* (OUP 2015)

Kotzur, Markus, 'Ex aequo et bono' in *Max Planck Encyclopedia of Public International Law* (OUP 2009)

Palombino, Fulvio Maria, 'Judicial Economy' in *Max Planck Encyclopedia of Public International Law* (OUP 2020)

Weiss, Edith Brown, 'Intergenerational Equity' in *Max Planck Encyclopedia of Public International Law* (OUP 2021)

Working Papers and Policy Reports

Bernard, Leonardo, 'The Effect of Historic Fishing Rights in Maritime Boundaries Delimitation' (Presented at the Tenth LOSI Conference, Seoul, May 2012)

Dupuy, Pierre-Marie, 'Le droit à l'eau, un droit international?' (2006) European University Institute Department of Law Working Paper

Dyspriani, Polite, 'Traditional Fishing Rights: Analysis of State Practice' (2011) United Nations Office of Legal Affairs Division for Ocean Affairs and the Law of the Sea

Juratowitch, Ben, 'Individual Rights in Disputes between States' (Dialogues between International and Public Law, a Conference Organised by BIICL and Melbourne Law School, London, June–July 2016)

UK Department of the Environment, *Transport and the Regions, Public Participation in Making Local Environmental Decisions: The Aarhus Convention Newcastle Workshop. Good Practice Handbook* (2000)

Websites

African Court on Human and Peoples' Rights, 'Basic Information', www.african-court.org/wpafc/basic-information

Compliance Advisor Ombudsman, 'About Us', https://www.cao-ombudsman.org/about-us

International Court of Justice, 'Chambers and Committees', www.icj-cij.org/en/chambers-and-committees

'Declarations Recognising the Jurisdiction of the Court as Compulsory', www.icj-cij.org/en/declarations

'Frequently Asked Questions', www.icj-cij.org/en/frequently-asked-questions

'Media Services', www.icj-cij.org/en/media-services

International Labour Organisation, 'Organisations Recognising the Jurisdiction' (*ILO Administrative Tribunal*), www.ilo.org/tribunal/membership/lang–en/index.htm

United Nations, 'UN Web TV', https://webtv.un.org/en

World Trade Organisation, 'Participation in Dispute Settlement Proceedings', www.wto.org/english/tratop_e/dispu_e/disp_settlement_cbt_e/c9s3p1_e.htm#fnt2

Statements

Judge Joan E. Donoghue, 'Speech by H.E. Judge Joan E. Donoghue, President of the International Court of Justice, on the Occasion of the Seventy-Seventh Session of the United Nations General Assembly' (77th Session of the United Nations General Assembly, New York City, 27 October 2022), www.icj-cij.org/sites/default/files/press-releases/0/000-20221027-STA-01-00-EN.pdf

Judge Peter Tomka, 'Speech' (Sixty-Seventh Session of the General Assembly of the United Nations, 1 November 2012) 6, www.icj-cij.org/files/press-releases/0/17150.pdf

Judge Abdulqawi Yusuf, 'Keynote Address' ('70 Years of the International Law Commission: Drawing a Balance for the Future' Conference, Geneva, 5 July 2018) 9 [36], http://legal.un.org/ilc/sessions/70/pdfs/english/key_note_address_5july2018.pdf

Newspapers, Blogs, Videos

Akpan, Anietie, 'Bakassi Returnees' Two-Decade Grueling Sojourn in "New Bakassi"' *The Guardian* (1 May 2022), https://guardian.ng/sunday-magazine/bakassi-returnees-two-decade-grueling-sojourn-in-new-bakassi/

Alves, Danilo B. Garrido, 'The Concept of International Organization in the Practice of the International Court of Justice' (*EJIL Talk!*, 27 July 2023), www.ejiltalk.org/the-concept-of-international-organization-in-the-practice-of-the-international-court-of-justice/

'Cameroon Forces "Kill 97 Nigerian Fishermen" in Bakassi' *BBC News* (14 July 2017), hwww.bbc.co.uk/news/world-africa-40607306

Donoghue, Joan (Judge), 'The Role of International Courts in Global Governance' (Conference at the Graduate Institute of International and Development Studies, 8 October 2018), https://youtu.be/De4unNaIOjs

Milanovic, Marko, 'The ICJ and Evolutionary Treaty Interpretation' (*EJIL Talk!*, 14 July 2009), www.ejiltalk.org/the-icj-and-evolutionary-treaty-interpretation/

Valencia-Ospina, Eduardo, 'Court Clarification: Letters to the Editor' *International Herald Tribune* (Paris, 15 November 1995)

INDEX

CAMBRIDGE STUDIES IN INTERNATIONAL AND COMPARATIVE LAW

Books in the Series

192 *The Individual in the Law and Practice of the International Court of Justice*
Yusra Suedi

191 *Ghosts of International Law: The Figure of the Foreign Fighter in a Cultural Perspective*
Alberto Rinaldi

190 *Merchants of Legalism: A History of State Responsibility (1870–1960)*
Alan Tzvika Nissel

189 *The Functions of International Adjudication and International Environmental Litigation*
Joshua Paine

188 *Demystifying Treaty Interpretation*
Andrea Bianchi and Fuad Zarbiyev

187 *International Law-Making by the International Court of Justice and International Law Commission: Partnership for Purpose in a Decentralized Legal Order*
Omri Sender

186 *The Rebirth of Territory*
Gail Lythgoe

185 *Reimagining Sustainable Development in International Law: Perspectives from African Legal Cosmologies*
Godwin Eli Kwadzo Dzah

184 *Collective Self-Defence in International Law*
James A. Green

183 *Weaponising Evidence: A History of Tobacco Control in International Law*
Margherita Melillo

182 *The Justice Factory: Management Practices at the International Criminal Court*
Richard Clements

181 *A Communitarian Theory of WTO Law*
Chi Carmody

180 *Drones and International Law: A Techno-Legal Machinery*
Rebecca Mignot-Mahdavi

179 *The Necessity of Nature: God, Science and Money in Seventeenth Century English Law of Nature*
Mónica García-Salmones

178 *Making the World Safe for Investment: The Protection of Foreign Property 1922–1959*
Andrea Leiter

177 *National Governance and Investment Treaties*
Josef Ostřanský and Facundo Pérez Aznar

176 *Who Owns Outer Space? International Law, Astrophysics, and the Sustainable Development of Space*
Michael Byers and Aaron Boley

175 *Intervening in International Justice: Third States before Courts and Tribunals*
Brian McGarry

174 *Reciprocity in Public International Law*
Arianna Whelan

173 *When Environmental Protection and Human Rights Collide*
Marie-Catherine Petersmann

172 *The International Law of Sovereign Debt Dispute Settlement*
Kei Nakajima

171 *The Everyday Makers of International Law: From Great Halls to Back Rooms*
Tommaso Soave

170 *Virtue in Global Governance: Judgment and Discretion*
Jan Klabbers

169 *The Effects of Armed Conflict on Investment Treaties*
Tobias Ackermann

168 *Investment Law's Alibis: Colonialism, Imperialism, Debt and Development*
David Schneiderman

167 *Negative Comparative Law: A Strong Programme for Weak Thought*
Pierre Legrand

166 *Detention by Non-State Armed Groups under International Law*
Ezequiel Heffes

165 *Rebellions and Civil Wars: State Responsibility for the Conduct of Insurgents*
Patrick Dumberry

164 *The International Law of Energy*
Jorge Viñuales

163 *The Three Ages of International Commercial Arbitration*
Mikaël Schinazi

162 *Repetition and International Law*
Wouter Werner

161 *State Responsibility and Rebels: The History and Legacy of Protecting Investment Against Revolution*
Kathryn Greenman

160 *Rewriting Histories of the Use of Force: The Narrative of 'Indifference'*
Agatha Verdebout

159 *The League of Nations and the Protection of the Environment*
Omer Aloni

158 *International Investment Law and Legal Theory: Expropriation and the Fragmentation of Sources*
Jörg Kammerhofer

157 *Legal Barbarians: Identity, Modern Comparative Law and the Global South*
Daniel Bonilla Maldonado

156 *International Human Rights Law Beyond State Territorial Control*
Antal Berkes

155 *The Crime of Aggression under the Rome Statute of the International Criminal Court*
Carrie McDougall

154 *Minorities and the Making of Postcolonial States in International Law*
Mohammad Shahabuddin

153 *Preclassical Conflict of Laws*
Nikitas E. Hatzimihail

152 *International Law and History: Modern Interfaces*
Ignacio de la Rasilla

151 *Marketing Global Justice: The Political Economy of International Criminal Law*
Christine Schwöbel-Patel

150 *International Status in the Shadow of Empire*
Cait Storr

149 *Treaties in Motion: The Evolution of Treaties from Formation to Termination*
Edited by Malgosia Fitzmaurice and Panos Merkouris

148 *Humanitarian Disarmament: An Historical Enquiry*
Treasa Dunworth

147 *Complementarity, Catalysts, Compliance: The International Criminal Court in Uganda, Kenya, and the Democratic Republic of Congo*
Christian M. De Vos

146 *Cyber Operations and International Law*
François Delerue

145 *Comparative Reasoning in International Courts and Tribunals*
Daniel Peat

144 *Maritime Delimitation as a Judicial Process*
Massimo Lando

143 *Prosecuting Sexual and Gender-Based Crimes at the International Criminal Court: Practice, Progress and Potential*
Rosemary Grey

142 *Capitalism As Civilisation: A History of International Law*
Ntina Tzouvala

141 *Sovereignty in China: A Genealogy of a Concept Since 1840*
Adele Carrai

140 *Narratives of Hunger in International Law: Feeding the World in Times of Climate Change*
Anne Saab

139 *Victim Reparation under the Ius Post Bellum: An Historical and Normative Perspective*
Shavana Musa

138 *The Analogy between States and International Organizations*
Fernando Lusa Bordin

137 *The Process of International Legal Reproduction: Inequality, Historiography, Resistance*
Rose Parfitt

136 *State Responsibility for Breaches of Investment Contracts*
Jean Ho

135 *Coalitions of the Willing and International Law: The Interplay between Formality and Informality*
Alejandro Rodiles

134 *Self-Determination in Disputed Colonial Territories*
Jamie Trinidad

133 *International Law as a Belief System*
Jean d'Aspremont

132 *Legal Consequences of Peremptory Norms in International Law*
Daniel Costelloe

131 *Third-Party Countermeasures in International Law*
Martin Dawidowicz

130 *Justification and Excuse in International Law: Concept and Theory of General Defences*
Federica Paddeu

129 *Exclusion from Public Space: A Comparative Constitutional Analysis*
Daniel Moeckli

128 *Provisional Measures before International Courts and Tribunals*
Cameron A. Miles

127 *Humanity at Sea: Maritime Migration and the Foundations of International Law*
Itamar Mann

126 *Beyond Human Rights: The Legal Status of the Individual in International Law*
Anne Peters

125 *The Doctrine of Odious Debt in International Law: A Restatement*
Jeff King

124 *Static and Evolutive Treaty Interpretation: A Functional Reconstruction*
Christian Djeffal

123 *Civil Liability in Europe for Terrorism-Related Risk*
Lucas Bergkamp, Michael Faure, Monika Hinteregger and Niels Philipsen

122 *Proportionality and Deference in Investor-State Arbitration: Balancing Investment Protection and Regulatory Autonomy*
Caroline Henckels

121 *International Law and Governance of Natural Resources in Conflict and Post-Conflict Situations*
Daniëlla Dam-de Jong

120 *Proof of Causation in Tort Law*
Sandy Steel

119 *The Formation and Identification of Rules of Customary International Law in International Investment Law*
Patrick Dumberry

118 *Religious Hatred and International Law: The Prohibition of Incitement to Violence or Discrimination*
Jeroen Temperman

117 *Taking Economic, Social and Cultural Rights Seriously in International Criminal Law*
Evelyne Schmid

116 *Climate Change Litigation: Regulatory Pathways to Cleaner Energy*
Jacqueline Peel and Hari M. Osofsky

115 *Mestizo International Law: A Global Intellectual History 1842–1933*
Arnulf Becker Lorca

114 *Sugar and the Making of International Trade Law*
Michael Fakhri

113 *Strategically Created Treaty Conflicts and the Politics of International Law*
Surabhi Ranganathan

112 *Investment Treaty Arbitration As Public International Law: Procedural Aspects and Implications*
Eric De Brabandere

111 *The New Entrants Problem in International Fisheries Law*
Andrew Serdy

110 *Substantive Protection under Investment Treaties: A Legal and Economic Analysis*
Jonathan Bonnitcha

109 *Popular Governance of Post-Conflict Reconstruction: The Role of International Law*
Matthew Saul

108 *Evolution of International Environmental Regimes: The Case of Climate Change*
Simone Schiele

107 *Judges, Law and War: The Judicial Development of International Humanitarian Law*
Shane Darcy

106 *Religious Offence and Human Rights: The Implications of Defamation of Religions*
Lorenz Langer

105 *Forum Shopping in International Adjudication: The Role of Preliminary Objections*
Luiz Eduardo Salles

104 *Domestic Politics and International Human Rights Tribunals: The Problem of Compliance*
Courtney Hillebrecht

103 *International Law and the Arctic*
Michael Byers

102 *Cooperation in the Law of Transboundary Water Resources*
Christina Leb

101 *Underwater Cultural Heritage and International Law*
Sarah Dromgoole

100 *State Responsibility: The General Part*
James Crawford

99 *The Origins of International Investment Law: Empire, Environment and the Safeguarding of Capital*
Kate Miles

98 *The Crime of Aggression under the Rome Statute of the International Criminal Court*
Carrie McDougall

97 *'Crimes against Peace' and International Law*
Kirsten Sellars

96 *Non-Legality in International Law: Unruly Law*
Fleur Johns

95 *Armed Conflict and Displacement: The Protection of Refugees and Displaced Persons under International Humanitarian Law*
Mélanie Jacques

94 *Foreign Investment and the Environment in International Law*
Jorge E. Viñuales

93 *The Human Rights Treaty Obligations of Peacekeepers*
Kjetil Mujezinović Larsen

92 *Cyber Warfare and the Laws of War*
Heather Harrison Dinniss

91 *The Right to Reparation in International Law for Victims of Armed Conflict*
Christine Evans

90 *Global Public Interest in International Investment Law*
Andreas Kulick

89 *State Immunity in International Law*
Xiaodong Yang

88 *Reparations and Victim Support in the International Criminal Court*
Conor McCarthy

87 *Reducing Genocide to Law: Definition, Meaning, and the Ultimate Crime*
Payam Akhavan

86 *Decolonising International Law: Development, Economic Growth and the Politics of Universality*
Sundhya Pahuja

85 *Complicity and the Law of State Responsibility*
Helmut Philipp Aust

84 *State Control over Private Military and Security Companies in Armed Conflict*
Hannah Tonkin

83 *'Fair and Equitable Treatment' in International Investment Law*
Roland Kläger

82 *The UN and Human Rights: Who Guards the Guardians?*
Guglielmo Verdirame

81 *Sovereign Defaults before International Courts and Tribunals*
Michael Waibel

80 *Making the Law of the Sea: A Study in the Development of International Law*
James Harrison

79 *Science and the Precautionary Principle in International Courts and Tribunals: Expert Evidence, Burden of Proof and Finality*
Caroline E. Foster

78 *Transition from Illegal Regimes under International Law*
Yaël Ronen

77 *Access to Asylum: International Refugee Law and the Globalisation of Migration Control*
Thomas Gammeltoft-Hansen

76 *Trading Fish, Saving Fish: The Interaction between Regimes in International Law*
Margaret A. Young

75 *The Individual in the International Legal System: Continuity and Change in International Law*
Kate Parlett

74 *'Armed Attack' and Article 51 of the UN Charter: Evolutions in Customary Law and Practice*
Tom Ruys

73 *Theatre of the Rule of Law: Transnational Legal Intervention in Theory and Practice*
Stephen Humphreys

72 *Science and Risk Regulation in International Law*
Jacqueline Peel

71 *The Participation of States in International Organisations: The Role of Human Rights and Democracy*
Alison Duxbury

70 *Legal Personality in International Law*
Roland Portmann

69 *Vicarious Liability in Tort: A Comparative Perspective*
Paula Giliker

68 *The Public International Law Theory of Hans Kelsen: Believing in Universal Law*
Jochen von Bernstorff

67 *Legitimacy and Legality in International Law: An Interactional Account*
Jutta Brunnée and Stephen J. Toope

66 *The Concept of Non-International Armed Conflict in International Humanitarian Law*
Anthony Cullen

65 *The Principle of Legality in International and Comparative Criminal Law*
Kenneth S. Gallant

64 *The Challenge of Child Labour in International Law*
Franziska Humbert

63 *Shipping Interdiction and the Law of the Sea*
Douglas Guilfoyle

62 *International Courts and Environmental Protection*
Tim Stephens

61 *Legal Principles in WTO Disputes*
Andrew D. Mitchell

60 *War Crimes in Internal Armed Conflicts*
Eve La Haye

59 *Humanitarian Occupation*
Gregory H. Fox

58 *The International Law of Environmental Impact Assessment: Process, Substance and Integration*
Neil Craik

57 *The Law and Practice of International Territorial Administration: Versailles to Iraq and Beyond*
Carsten Stahn

56 *United Nations Sanctions and the Rule of Law*
Jeremy Matam Farrall

55 *National Law in WTO Law: Effectiveness and Good Governance in the World Trading System*
Sharif Bhuiyan

54 *Cultural Products and the World Trade Organization*
Tania Voon

53 *The Threat of Force in International Law*
Nikolas Stürchler

52 *Indigenous Rights and United Nations Standards: Self-Determination, Culture and Land*
Alexandra Xanthaki

51 *International Refugee Law and Socio-Economic Rights: Refuge from Deprivation*
Michelle Foster

50 *The Protection of Cultural Property in Armed Conflict*
Roger O'Keefe

49 *Interpretation and Revision of International Boundary Decisions*
Kaiyan Homi Kaikobad

48 *Multinationals and Corporate Social Responsibility: Limitations and Opportunities in International Law*
Jennifer A. Zerk

47 *Judiciaries within Europe: A Comparative Review*
John Bell

46 *Law in Times of Crisis: Emergency Powers in Theory and Practice*
Oren Gross and Fionnuala Ní Aoláin

45 *Vessel-Source Marine Pollution: The Law and Politics of International Regulation*
Alan Khee-Jin Tan

44 *Enforcing Obligations Erga Omnes in International Law*
Christian J. Tams

43 *Non-Governmental Organisations in International Law*
Anna-Karin Lindblom

42 *Democracy, Minorities and International Law*
Steven Wheatley

41 *Prosecuting International Crimes: Selectivity and the International Criminal Law Regime*
Robert Cryer

40 *Compensation for Personal Injury in English, German and Italian Law: A Comparative Outline*
Basil Markesinis, Michael Coester, Guido Alpa and Augustus Ullstein

39 *Dispute Settlement in the UN Convention on the Law of the Sea*
Natalie Klein

38 *The International Protection of Internally Displaced Persons*
Catherine Phuong

37 *Imperialism, Sovereignty and the Making of International Law*
Antony Anghie

36 *Principles of the Institutional Law of International Organizations*
C. F. Amerasinghe

35 *Necessity, Proportionality and the Use of Force by States*
Judith Gardam

34 *International Legal Argument in the Permanent Court of International Justice: The Rise of the International Judiciary*
Ole Spiermann

33 -

32 *Great Powers and Outlaw States: Unequal Sovereigns in the International Legal Order*
Gerry Simpson

31 *Local Remedies in International Law (second edition)*
Chittharanjan Felix Amerasinghe

30 *Reading Humanitarian Intervention: Human Rights and the Use of Force in International Law*
Anne Orford

29 *Conflict of Norms in Public International Law: How WTO Law Relates to Other Rules of International Law*
Joost Pauwelyn

28 -

27 *Transboundary Damage in International Law*
Hanqin Xue

26 -

25 *European Criminal Procedures*
Edited by Mireille Delmas-MartyJ. R. and Spencer

24 *Accountability of Armed Opposition Groups in International Law*
Liesbeth Zegveld

23 *Sharing Transboundary Resources: International Law and Optimal Resource Use*
Eyal Benvenisti

22 *International Human Rights and Humanitarian Law*
René Provost

21 *Remedies against International Organisations*
Karel Wellens

20 *Diversity and Self-Determination in International Law*
Karen Knop

19 *The Law of Internal Armed Conflict*
Lindsay Moir

18 *International Commercial Arbitration and African States: Practice, Participation and Institutional Development*
Amazu A. Asouzu

17 *The Enforceability of Promises in European Contract Law*
James Gordley

16 *International Law in Antiquity*
David J. Bederman

15 *Money Laundering: A New International Law Enforcement Model*
Guy Stessens

14 *Good Faith in European Contract Law*
Reinhard Zimmermann and Simon Whittaker

13 *On Civil Procedure*
J. A. Jolowicz

12 *Trusts: A Comparative Study*
Maurizio Lupoi and Simon Dix

11 *The Right to Property in Commonwealth Constitutions*
Tom Allen

10 *International Organizations before National Courts*
August Reinisch

9 *The Changing International Law of High Seas Fisheries*
Francisco Orrego Vicuña

8 *Trade and the Environment: A Comparative Study of EC and US Law*
Damien Geradin

7 *Unjust Enrichment: A Study of Private Law and Public Values*
Hanoch Dagan

6 *Religious Liberty and International Law in Europe*
Malcolm D. Evans

5 *Ethics and Authority in International Law*
Alfred P. Rubin

4 *Sovereignty over Natural Resources: Balancing Rights and Duties*
Nico Schrijver

3 *The Polar Regions and the Development of International Law*
Donald R. Rothwell

2 *Fragmentation and the International Relations of Micro-States: Self-Determination and Statehood*
Jorri C. Duursma

1 *Principles of the Institutional Law of International Organizations*
C. F. Amerasinghe

For EU product safety concerns, contact us at Calle de José Abascal, 56–1°,
28003 Madrid, Spain or eugpsr@cambridge.org.

www.ingramcontent.com/pod-product-compliance
Lightning Source LLC
Chambersburg PA
CBHW070634071025
33682CB00004B/121
9781009394499